Family Counseling and Therapy

Major Issues and Topics

Robert L. Smith, Ph.D.
Patricia Stevens-Smith, Ph.D.

With an Introduction by Samuel T. Gladding, Ph.D.

ERIC Counseling and Personnel Services Clearinghouse
2108 School of Education
The University of Michigan
Ann Arbor, Michigan 48109-1259

ERIC Counseling and Personnel Services Clearinghouse
2108 School of Education
The University of Michigan
Ann Arbor, Michigan 48109-1259

Editorial by Penny Schreiber

Cover design and publication layout by Patricia Wisner

ISBN 1-56109-045-X

This publication was prepared with partial funding from the Office of Educational Research and Improvement, U.S. Department of Education under contract no. RI88062011. The opinions expressed in this report do not necessarily reflect the positions or policies of OERI, the Department of Education, or ERIC/CAPS.

ERIC®

Contents

Preface

Few topics have received as much attention and discussion as the contemporary American family. Researchers and helping professionals have mutually identified the family as a mainspring of human development. It is becoming increasingly clear that the family system sculptures the broad outlines of the development of the young and plays a significant role in the attitudes and behaviors of all family members whatever their ages. Changes in family composition and function pose exciting challenges and opportunities for counselors and therapists. A prime challenge to all those engaged in helping families is to assimilate the new ideas and research on marriage and the family. Drs. Robert L. Smith and Patricia Stevens-Smith have done an outstanding job of identifying the major themes in marriage and family counseling and they have assembled an impressive array of incisive articles for this volume. Their own thoughtful transitions and syntheses highlight key ideas and facilitate use of the provocative concepts that abound in this compelling book. It is hard to imagine an educator, experienced therapist/counselor, or aspiring student who once having read this book will not keep it available for ready reference as this is a collection to be read and returned to again and again. I recommend this as a book you will be most pleased to own and use.

Garry R. Walz, Ph.D.
Director, ERIC Counseling and
Personnel Services Clearinghouse

Introduction

The field of family counseling and therapy has mushroomed since the 1970s—it has grown in the number of professionals who practice this specialty and the quality of services delivered. Family counseling and therapy has also become a title that helpers increasingly identify with and that national health boards and accreditation associations now address in regard to recognition and accreditation. The pace of development in the field has truly been phenomenal.

The positive side of this trend is that families, and individuals within them, now receive better treatment than before. Likewise, there has been increased sensitivity to national issues and pressures regarding traditional and nontraditional families. There is even enlivened debate on the topic of values and families. Indeed, events related to families have taken front stage in the media and the minds of the American people.

The drawback to the growth of family counseling and therapy is the sometimes intense debate among the many societal publics regarding who should provide treatment to family units—when, how, and under what circumstances. This discussion sometimes breaks down as champions and crusaders for one point of view lead myopic charges. A lack of understanding and conceptualization of family counseling and therapy also comes to the forefront at such times.

This is why *Family Counseling and Therapy* is such an important text. To my knowledge it is one of the few readable and comprehensive collections in the profession. It fills a void in the area of family counseling and therapy by providing students and professional practitioners a thorough examination of the theories, practices, and issues that are currently part and parcel of this discipline. It does so by offering the reader original sources that explain matters much better than a summary of them alone could do.

Yet, this book is far more than a timely collection of relevant articles. Rather, what Robert L. Smith and Patricia Stevens-Smith have done is to weave words and ideas in such a way that the relevance of what is contained in this volume will remain timely and essential for years. The authors as practitioners, researchers, teachers, and writers have drawn from their comprehensive knowledge of family counseling and therapy to present substantive material that is deep, well-balanced, and broad. Topics and issues presented here transcend periods and problems in family counseling and therapy.

Furthermore, Smith and Stevens-Smith have written the introductory openers to the six chapters of this volume in a personalized and professional manner. These chapters are well crafted and contain clear and thought-provoking content. They provide novice and veteran readers in the field with a bridge to understanding the topics and issues examined. The result is an edited work that reads smoothly and proves interesting.

Family Counseling and Therapy initially focuses on healthy family functioning. The rationale for this beginning is quite sound. In order to understand and treat dysfunctional families, practitioners should first recognize healthy interactions. The basis for treatment is knowing what interactional patterns to observe and what not to change. Growth can come in many forms and it is crucial that family counselors and therapists nourish possibilities as well as help make needed alterations in maladaptive behaviors.

The second chapter of the book, focusing on theories, is notable, too. It does not get bogged down in confusing details. Instead, it contains information that emphasizes how couples and families work together as systems on various levels. I especially like here the emphasis placed on the importance of one's family of origin. Comparisons and contrasts offered in this chapter in regard to differences in therapeutic approaches make it stimulating to read and discuss.

Chapter 3 is noteworthy because it is probably the most practical section of any family counseling and therapy book yet published. The authors/editors show readers how to implement on a pragmatic level such critical concepts as sculpting, circular questioning, and genograms. The material here stands out in its ability to delineate family counseling and therapy practices from those that are more linear. It is a broad coverage of the most crucial aspects of helping families: from knowing the instruments that are available to realizing what mistakes are most likely to be made.

Chapter 4 contains articles that deal with gender issues, the personhood of the counselor/therapist, and the practical matter of establishing a family counseling and therapy curriculum within academic departments. The matter of gender is especially critical since many new practitioners are female and since as a group women have been overtly and covertly discriminated against in American society. Likewise, the ability to integrate and get family counseling and therapy courses accepted within a traditional learning environment is a skill that requires a knowledge of how systems work on various levels. This is informative reading for individuals who are both inside and outside academe.

In Chapter 5, five vital, yet often neglected, ethical issues are addressed theoretically and pragmatically. The treatment of ethnic families and nontraditional families is also covered. From working with AIDS families to a discussion of marital violence, the articles assembled here, like their predecessors, are filled with reader-friendly and practice-relevant information.

The same statement can be made in regard to the final two articles on future trends and projections that comprise Chapter 6. The Smith/Stevens-Smith piece especially shows how scholarship and insight can be combined in a thoughtful and powerful way. These authors have a way of touching the probable by knowing the past. I am impressed with their foresight and insight. This material contains more than projections. Like the opening chapter, it is encompassing and captivating.

Overall, *Family Counseling and Therapy* sets a new standard for compilation books. It is comprehensive, readable, even-handed, and thoughtful. On one level this is a text about the change that goes on in family life when interventions are implemented to resolve dysfunctional patterns. On a second level, this is a work that challenges readers to examine the health of systems in which they reside and initiate the beginning of alterations when necessary. Thus, the material in this book operates on both a personal and professional level.

If I could select just one book of readings in a course on family counseling and therapy, this is definitely the text I would choose. It packages the best material in the field in a professional and personalized way. The writing style of Smith and Stevens-Smith and their contributors is inviting and the direction of their chapters is logical and smooth. In a field of helping that is exciting, demanding, and filled with an array of choices, *Family Counseling and Therapy* is a cut above other collections in its clarity, comprehensiveness, and impact.

Samuel T. Gladding
Professor of Counseling
Wake Forest University
Winston Salem, North Carolina

About the Major Authors

Robert L. Smith, Ph.D., is Professor and Chair of the Division of Counseling Psychology and Counselor Education at the University of Colorado at Denver. He is also Executive Director of the International Association of Marriage and Family Counselors.

Patricia Stevens-Smith, Ph.D., is Assistant Professor of Counseling Psychology and Counselor Education and Program Director of Marriage and Family Therapy Training at the University of Colorado at Denver.

Contributors

Robert L. Beck, Chief Clinical Social Worker, Baylor Psychiatry Clinic; Assistant Professor, Department of Psychiatry, Baylor College of Medicine; Adjunct Associate Professor, University of Houston Graduate School of Social Work; Houston, Texas.

Loretta J. Bradley, Associate Professor, Department of Educational Psychology, Texas Tech University, Lubbock.

Margaret Burggraf, Associate Professor, Counselor Education, University of South Carolina—Columbia.

Brian S. Canfield, Associate Professor and Clinical Director, Marriage and Family Therapy Program, Northeast Louisiana University, Monroe.

Jon Carlson, Professor, Counseling and Psychology, Governors State University, University Park, Illinois; Psychologist, Private Practice, Lake Geneva, Wisconsin.

Marilyn Coleman, Professor and Chair, Department of Human Development and Family Studies, University of Missouri—Columbia.

Luann Costa, Assistant Professor and Clinical Director, Marriage and Family Therapy Training Program, University of Colorado at Denver.

Wynetta Devore, Professor, School of Social Work, Syracuse University, Syracuse, New York.

Don Dinkmeyer, President, Communication and Motivation Training Institute, Coral Springs, Florida.

Don Dinkmeyer, Jr., Editor, Communication and Motivation Training Institute Press, Coral Springs, Florida.

MaryAnna Domokos-Cheng Ham, Associate Professor, Counseling Psychology, Graduate College of Education, University of Massachusetts at Boston.

Carolyn Zerbe Enns, Assistant Professor, Psychology, Cornell College, Mt. Vernon, Iowa.

David L. Fenell, Associate Professor and Chair, Counseling and Human Services, University of Colorado—Colorado Springs.

James L. Framo, Distinguished Professor, United States International University, San Diego, California.

Daniel Fullmer, Professor, Counselor Education, University of Hawaii, Honolulu.

Lawrence H. Ganong, Professor, School of Nursing and Department of Human Development and Family Studies, University of Missouri—Columbia.

Samuel T. Gladding, Professor, Counselor Education, Wake Forest University, Winston Salem, North Carolina.

Jean A. Griffin, Assistant Professor, California State University at Hayward.

Debra Holliday, Graduate Student, University of Colorado at Denver.

Don W. Locke, Associate Dean, Coordinator of Graduate Programs and Director of Marriage and Family Therapy Program, Northeast Louisiana University, Monroe.

Harlan London, Associate Professor, Family Studies, College for Human Development, Syracuse University, Syracuse, New York.

Susan H. McDaniel, Associate Professor, Psychiatry (Psychology) and Family Medicine, and Director, Family Therapy Clinic, University of Rochester School of Medicine and Dentistry, Rochester, New York.

James E. McKeever, Child and Adolescent Psychologist, Virginia Mason Clinic, Seattle, Washington.

Mary A. Ostrovsky, Group Facilitator, West Texas AIDS Foundation, Lubbock.

Barbara Peeks, Family Therapist, private practice, North Platte, Nebraska.

Robert O. Rich, Professor, School of Social Work and Human Services, Eastern Washington University, Cheney.

Elaine Ryan, Counselor, Community College of Denver, Colorado.

Dick T. Sampson, Professor, Department of Applied Psychology, Eastern Washington University, Cheney.

Thomas L. Sexton, Assistant Professor, Department of Counseling and Educational Psychology, University of Nevada—Las Vegas.

Robert L. Sheverbush, Professor, Department of Psychology and Counseling, Pittsburg State University, Pittsburg, Kansas.

Robert L. Smith, Professor and Chair, Division of Counseling Psychology and Counselor Education, University of Colorado at Denver; Executive Director, International Association of Marriage and Family Counselors.

Len Sperry, Associate Professor, Psychiatry, Medical College of Wisconsin, Milwaukee.

Patricia Stevens-Smith, Assistant Professor, Counseling Psychology and Counselor Education, and Program Director, Marriage and Family Therapy Training, University of Colorado at Denver.

Marian Stoltz-Loike, Corporate Consultant, family and career issues, Flushing, New York.

George Stone, Social Work Consultant and Family Therapist, private practice, Albuquerque, New Mexico.

Karen Thys, Therapist, private practice, Denver, Colorado.

Tracy Todd, Director, Brief Family Therapy Institute, Denver, Colorado.

Donald E. Ward, Professor and Chair, Counseling Committee, Department of Psychology and Counseling, Pittsburg State University, Pittsburg, Kansas.

Candace Ward Howell, Graduate Student, University of Wisconsin—Whitewater.

Timothy Weber, Licensed Clinical Psychologist and Senior Faculty, Leadership Institute of Seattle, Washington.

Barry K. Weinhold, Professor of Counseling and Human Services, University of Colorado—Colorado Springs.

Donald J. Wendorf, Clinical Psychologist, Family Therapy Associates, Birmingham, Alabama.

Robert J. Wendorf, Clinical Psychologist, Family Therapy Associates, Birmingham, Alabama.

John D. West, Professor, Counselor Education Program, Kent State University, Kent, Ohio.

S. Allen Wilcoxon, Professor, Counselor Education, University of Alabama, University.

Chapter 1

Healthy Family Functioning

For those working with couples and families, it is crucial to understand one's perceptions, ideas, and ideals of what constitutes "family," as well as what is "healthy." The notions of family and health held by counselors/therapists significantly influence the practitioner's direction in therapy, whether or not such expectations are ever shared with the family itself. The authors believe that often researchers and therapists view the family according to the way it existed in past decades. Many individuals in today's society, including therapists, think of the "traditional family system" when referring to family. Such traditional systems include a working father, a mother, either working or not working, and one to three children. This "idealized" fantasy of the family is inaccurate for today's families. Such myths about family arrangements discredit the richness provided by today's diverse family systems.

In the authors' review of healthy family functioning research it was found that "traditional family systems" were mostly described. Few investigators included adequate representation from: single parent families, step or blended families, mixed marriage families, gay families, etc. Today, single parent families and blended families actually seem to be the norm and fit what was the "typical family arrangement" in our society. Despite these changes in family arrangements, the authors question society's view of this change. For example, are single parent families and blended families viewed differently than "traditional family systems"? Despite changes in today's family systems, are new systems viewed as positive, or "normal"?

The authors critique the literature focusing on healthy family functioning in the first part of Chapter 1. A fair amount of literature was found discussing characteristics of "healthy" families. These discussions are theoretical and ideal. The literature reflects what one would expect when describing healthy families: families that communicate, families that talk about issues equally, that are flexible, that respect one another, and whose members are not enmeshed. Such concepts provide a theoretical focus as to what is healthy. There exists a need for identifying ways that families meet these theoretical standards in their *own* unique way. There is a need as well to view the characteristics describing healthy families as unequal entities. Finally, there is a need to acknowledge change within the family itself and view health on a continuum basis.

In his article, Alan Wilcoxon states that it is about time we viewed families from a healthy perspective. The authors agree with this statement. Wilcoxon states that we have too often examined families from a "dysfunctional" perspective.

In the closing presentation, Carlson takes us a step further by discussing ways to strengthen today's families. The cumulative effect of the three articles selected for this chapter provide the reader with valuable information on the family itself and present current ideas related to health and family functioning.

A Critique of Healthy Family Functioning

Robert L. Smith
Patricia Stevens-Smith

A limited body of research defines healthy family functioning, yet there are a number of hypotheses concerning this phenomenon. Beavers (1982); Fisher, Giblin, and Hoopes (1982); Fisher and Sprenkle (1978); Kantor and Lehr (1975); Olson, Russell, and Sprenkle (1989); Olson, Sprenkle, and Russell (1979); and Reiss (1981) have provided hunches as to its characteristics. This article examines the literature describing healthy families, provides a critique of how healthy family functioning is presented, and emphasizes the problems of defining healthy family functioning and today's family.

Healthy Family Functioning Literature

Family types, characteristics, models, and paradigms discussed in the literature attempt to differentiate healthy from dysfunctional families. Several authors have identified healthy families according to similar characteristics. The early writings of Kantor and Lehr (1975) identified three family types. Within this paradigm reference was made to healthy versus dysfunctional family systems. The first, or "open" type family system, was characterized by flexible rules and boundary arrangements. This family operated democratically and used honest exchanges with outside individuals and groups. The second, or "closed" type family system, was seen as "traditional" as it emphasized family loyalty and allowed a minimum amount of contact with outside systems. According to Kantor and Lehr, rigidity existed in this closed family system and created a dysfunctional system. A third type, the "random" family system, was seen as a fragmented operational family. This system was considered more likely to become chaotic and dysfunctional since few rules and family policies were evident. According to the Kantor and Lehr model, a "healthy functioning family" has *clear rules, set boundaries, operates with flexibility*, and *freely interacts with outside systems*.

Cohesion and *adaptability* were viewed as major factors in healthy family functioning according to Olson et al. (1979). *Cohesion*, the emotional bonding family members have with each other, is complemented by individual autonomy experienced in the family system. *Adaptability* refers to the ability of a family system to change its power structure, family rules, and role relationships in response to situational and developmental stressors. According to this model, healthy families exhibit a balance between cohesion and adaptability. Healthy families are not enmeshed in each other's lives. They are *not overly cohesive*. Healthy families have the right amount of adaptability but are neither overly adaptable nor too rigid. Olson et al. viewed growth and change as possible in healthy families. The healthy family demonstrates *balanced flexibility*, *shared leadership*, *appropriate assertiveness*, *negotiation among members*, *appropriate rules*, *open feedback systems*, and *clear roles*. More specifically, Olson et al (1989) stated that healthy families are balanced in relationship to the following eight aspects of cohesion:

1. Emotional attraction,
2. Differentiation,
3. Supportiveness,
4. Loyalty,
5. Psychological safety,
6. Family identification,
7. Physical caretaking, and
8. Pleasurable interaction.

Reiss (1981) described healthy families as "environment-sensitive." Healthy families view the world as *knowable* and *orderly*. According to his model, healthy families expect each member to contribute to the understanding and mastery of the environment. Healthy family members were seen as having the ability to accept help and advice from others. Healthy functioning families were seen as *flexible* and *cooperative* as they work to overcome adversity. Healthy functioning families examine alternative solutions.

In more recent work, healthy families, as viewed by Beavers (1982), can be identified in relation to *negotiation* and *transaction* patterns. The writings of Beavers and others state that healthy families have an existing parental coalition that sets a level of functioning. Healthy family members communicate their thoughts and feelings. In addition, healthy family members welcome contact with each other and expect transactions to be caring, open, and trusting. Healthy family members respect personal autonomy. Family members express humor, tenderness, warmth, and hopefulness. Beavers sees healthy families as both possessing the capacity for intimacy and seeking intimacy.

In opposition to healthy families, dysfunctional families seek control, concern themselves with power struggles, and tend to use intimidation. In this regard, Lewis, Beavers, Gossett, and Phillips (1976) characterized healthy versus dysfunctional families as demonstrating (1) a caring affiliative attitude versus an oppositional approach to human encounters, (2) high levels of initiative versus passivity, (3) high levels of reciprocity, cooperation, and negotiation versus the opposite, (4) high levels of personal autonomy versus control, (5) openness in the expression of affect, a prevailing mood of warmth, affection, and caring versus the opposite, and (6) high degrees of spontaneity and humor versus constriction (Fisher et al., 1982). In addition, communication is valued in healthy families. Members of a healthy functioning family have communication skills characterized by *spontaneity*, *feedback*, *metacommunication*, and *encouragement*.

Becvar and Becvar (1988) identify health as the family's success in functioning to achieve its goals. They claim healthy families are characterized by the following dimensions:

1. A legitimate source of authority that is established and supported over time.
2. A stable rule system established and consistently acted upon.
3. Stable and consistent nurturing behaviors.
4. Effective and stable childrearing and marriage-maintenance practices.
5. A set of goals toward which the family and each individual works.
6. Sufficient flexibility and adaptability to accommodate normal developmental challenges as well as unexpected crises.

Despite identifying several problems inherent in describing healthy family functioning, Textor (1989) proceeded to describe how a "healthy" family appears according to an "idealistic" approach. Textor addressed concepts and hypotheses from major family therapy theories in relation to identified elements. The elements used to identify healthy families include personality, cognition, relationships, behavior, communication, role, family system, and network (see Table 1). Textor also focused on two additional elements: experience and society/culture.

The characteristics identified as healthy in the context of family according to the Textor model are those one would expect to be in evidence when describing the healthy individual. For example, the healthy personality is open, warm, genuine, authentic, autonomous, responsible, creative, respects self and others, and has ego boundaries and a good self-concept. The individual is seen from a systemic perspective in the same manner as families are viewed systematically. Within healthy family systems, the communication network is clear, has few contradictions, has feeling, is spontaneous, humorous, and so on. Roles of healthy families are distinct, focused, flexible, accepted,

Table 1
Healthy Family Functioning: An "Idealistic" Approach

Elements	Idealistic Characteristics
Personality	Open, unique, warm, empathic, creative, productive, authentic, responsible, autonomous (self), aware of ego boundary, respectful, possessing positive self-esteem
Cognition	Considers events from different views, realistic, flexible, creative, rational
Relationships	Accepting of others, does not try to change others; demonstrates mutual love, devotion, intimate passion, warmth, consideration for others
Behavior	Flexible, reinforces meaning
Communication	Gives clear messages, clear coding, no contradictions; expresses feelings, is spontaneous, has emotional capability and sense of humor
Roles	Distinct, clear, flexible, secure, protected, accepted, consistent, corresponds to age
Family system	Open, constantly changing, distinct but permeable boundaries
Network	Spouses separated from parents, intergenerational relations respected and supported, boundaries respected

consistent, and correspond to age. The healthy family system is open and constantly changing, with distinct but permeable boundaries. Textor advocates the idealistic approach in describing healthy families since only positive characteristics are utilized. According to this model, comparisons between strengths and weaknesses are not useful when discussing healthy family functioning.

Barnhill (1979) described healthy families differently than Textor. Barnhill examined dimensions of health in relation to pathology (see Table 2). Supported by several writers, Barnhill distinguished between individuation and enmeshment. Whereas the former term represents autonomy, ego identity, and independence within the family, the term "enmeshment" limits these positive characteristics and reinforces dependency. Mutuality as used by Barnhill provides family members with a sense of individuation along with emotional intimacy, whereas isolation reflects separation, aloneness, and alienation in the family. Flexibility, a healthy dimension in this model, provides the family with the ability to change and adjust, whereas rigidity prevents any forward movement. Stability is present in healthy families according to this model. Family arrangements are predictable as opposed to disorganized or chaotic.

Lewis et al. (1976) provided empirical data relating to healthy family functioning by conducting a series of investigations over several years. Through the use of trained raters, rating scales, and video tapes, Lewis et al. proposed to identify healthy family functioning by discriminating between patient families and nonpatient families. The researchers claimed to have accomplished their goal. As a result of their findings, Lewis et al. described members of healthy families as characterized by family interactions that:

Table 2
Major Dimensions of Family Functioning

Healthy	Pathological
Individuation	Enmeshment
Mutuality	Isolation
Flexibility	Rigidity
Stability	Disorganization

- demonstrate warmth and trust;
- are open and mutually respectful;
- avoid power games and use negotiation;
- demonstrate high levels of initiative and individual responsibility;
- demonstrate flexibility;
- indicate autonomy and emotional maturity;
- are congruent with society and community expectations;
- encourage positive and negative affect; and
- demonstrate spontaneity, humor, and recognition of others.

Critique of Healthy Family Functioning Literature

Criticism has been directed at the conceptual literature concerning healthy family functioning (Gladding, 1984; Textor, 1989; Wilcoxon, 1985). Gladding stated that most families may never be characterized by the litany of traits seen in the literature describing healthy functioning families. Comprehensive lists describing healthy functioning families often emphasize extremes or polarities. A family frequently is seen as either healthy or dysfunctional. Wilcoxon (1985) raised the issue of value judgment. Researchers, who have their own values, can provide prescriptive ideas as to what is healthy, often using the traditional family as the model. Thus, nontraditional families such as single-parent families and stepfamilies are consistently ignored despite their strong presence in today's society.

To compound these problems, authors who discuss healthy family functioning fail to address cultural differences. What might be considered "normal" in one culture may be seen as enmeshed in another. Concepts such as "normal" and "traditional" need to be considered within a cultural context when discussing the family.

The dramatically changing gender roles in our society also impact the definition of healthy families. Most of the theories reviewed tend to use traditional views of family systems as representative of health. They allow little leeway for nontraditional gender roles within the dual-career, single-parent, or blended families, which constitute the majority of family systems.

A major flaw within existing literature describing healthy family functioning is failure to define the family. Carter (1986) called for psychologists and family therapists to think through and define what is meant by family because the definition influences perceptions of healthy family functioning. Unfortunately, practitioners often define family as it existed decades ago. When this is done, prescriptive notions about healthy family functioning become attached to these definitions. Today, however, the definition of the family must keep in mind the following (Carter, 1986):

- The current divorce rate is almost 50%.
- Seventy-five to 80% of divorced people remarry.
- The rate of divorce in remarried families was projected at 60% in the 1980s.
- Single-parent families headed by women increased 51% between 1970 and 1980; those headed by men also are increasing yearly.
- The number of one-person households has increased almost 200% since 1969, mostly reflecting women over age 45 living alone.
- The number of unmarried couple households increased 331% in the past decade.
- Same-sex couple households currently account for approximately 6% of unmarried men and 5% of unmarried women.

The above data need to be considered when discussing healthy family functioning. Do the characteristics found in the literature describing healthy family functioning apply to diverse family systems? Do healthy functioning single-parent families resemble the healthy functioning traditional nuclear family? The failure to recognize the need to define the family undermines the credibility about hypotheses describing healthy family functioning characteristics.

The issue of practitioners' values has been widely discussed in counseling and psychotherapy. When addressing questions about healthy family functioning, the issue of values as related to what family is and what health is begins to emerge. With family psychology and family therapy at a relatively embryonic stage, greater attention should be directed to values concerning family systems and healthy family functioning.

The above-mentioned criticisms raise the question as to the generalizability of research and writings describing healthy family functioning. This problem is further illustrated by two cases. According to existing literature, the family described in Case 1 might be seen as dysfunctional as it is characterized by high levels of disengagement. This family exhibits few rules, no family policies, and few boundaries. Case 2 represents a family that is functioning but is enmeshed, according to healthy family functioning literature. The high level of enmeshment in Case 2 in part relates to existing cultural values that support what is described as a closed family system. When viewed internally, both families are functioning in a "healthy" manner. When examined externally by using healthy family functioning concepts cited within the literature, both families could be seen as "dysfunctional."

Case 1: The "Disengaged Family"

Single-parent mother Jane is raising Mark with the help of her boyfriend, Will. Jane works irregular hours and sees Mark mainly on weekends. Boundaries are loose and some might even say nonexistent. The unusual timetables of family members appear to make for a chaotic environment with disengaged family members. Jane's boyfriend frequently visits and occasionally spends the night at her home. Will provides little discipline for Mark. He supports both Jane and Mark equally. A parental coalition has not been established.

Yet in sports and school activities, Mark has functioned extremely well. He has several close friends, performs well in school, and has made plans for the future. Jane is up for promotion, feels happy, is highly involved in her work, and has a good feeling about both Mark and Will.

Case 2: The "Enmeshed Family"

Maria and John, a Hispanic couple, have been married for 32 years. They have two daughters, ages 28 and 30. Both daughters spend weekends at home; neither is married. Maria, who is well educated, has no friends of her own. The majority of her time is spent with her husband and daughters. The family takes yearly vacations together, and rarely are "outsiders" allowed to go along. Most holidays are spent in the family home. In the family, only John is allowed to express his opinions and feelings. His authority is rarely questioned. These characteristics result in a closed family system with rigid boundaries, low adaptability, and high enmeshment, according to an external viewpoint.

Yet both daughters are well educated and gainfully employed. They schedule their social life around the family but also have many friends. They are caring and fun-loving women. Maria also schedules her charity work around the family but is content and fulfilled in her endeavors. John is a well-respected and successful businessman in the community.

A cursory review of the two families reveals noticeably few healthy family functioning characteristics as identified in the literature. Yet internally one can see how individuals within the family and the family system itself are functioning in a relatively healthy manner (see Table 3).

After reviewing cases like those discussed above and critiquing the literature on healthy family functioning, we advise psychologists and therapists to be cautious as they interpret both what constitutes "family" and what is considered "healthy" within family systems. Wilcoxon (1985) indicated that the shift toward focusing on health that he observed in the literature could be seen as generally positive in the therapeutic environment. Yet any operational shift toward a health concept should be viewed as positive only when more is known about what is "healthy." Until then, psychologists and therapists need to be careful not to indiscriminately apply what are believed to be healthy family functioning characteristics to all family systems.

The literature examining healthy family functioning is interesting and even convincing. Yet most statements or ideas that have identified healthy families are not supported by scientific rigor or empirical investigation. Ideas presented by family therapists and writers concerning healthy families are in large part hypothetical and abstract. For example, words such as "right amount," "balance," "overly," "high level," and "sufficient" are used throughout the literature. However, few, if any of these words are empirically defined. Since few objective definitions of these words exist, they are often subjectively defined by psychologists and family therapists within the context of their own value system. We concur with Textor (1989) that empirical studies by psychologists, sociologists, social workers, and others about "healthy families" are lacking. An explanation often cited for this is that family therapists rarely work with "healthy" families and therefore place less emphasis on health and more on pathology.

Until a greater understanding is obtained concerning what is "healthy," we recommend that psychologists and therapists proceed with caution when setting goals for families. Furthermore, we recommend that writings that discuss healthy family functioning include a definition of family. The literature on healthy family functioning and the resulting hypotheses characterizing healthy families will be more significant and useful when the problems discussed above are more fully addressed.

References

Barnhill, L. R. (1979). Healthy family systems. *Family Coordinator, 28,* 94–100.

Table 3
Healthy and Dysfunctional Family Characteristics: A Review of the Literature

Healthy Families are Characterized as	Dysfunctional Families are Characterized as
Having flexibility	Rigid (Kantor & Lehr, 1975)
Possessing clear rules, family policies, clear boundaries	Chaotic and unruly (Kantor & Lehr, 1975)
Possessing a balanced cohesion	Enmeshed (Olson et al., 1979)
Possessing a balanced adaptability	In flux (Olson et al., 1979)
Having individual autonomy	Overly bonded (Olson et al., 1979)
Having appropriate assertiveness	Rigid or dogmatic (Olson et al., 1979)
Using negotiation	Experiencing power struggles (Olson et al., 1979)
Having appropriate rules	Chaotic or dogmatic (Olson et al., 1979)
Working together	Disengaged (Reiss, 1981)
Environment-sensitive	Rigid-closed (Reiss, 1981)
Possessing a parental coalition	Dysfunctional at the top (Beavers, 1977)
Communicating thoughts and feelings	Lacking in communication (Beavers, 1977)
Having an expectancy of caring, trusting, with open contact by members and the family system	Distrusting, expecting the worst, oppositional (Beavers, 1977)
Possessing humor, tenderness, warmth	Humorless, cold, lacking in feeling (Beavers, 1977)
Having the capacity for and seeking intimacy	Lacking intimacy and not seeking caring; controlling and power seeking (Beavers, 1977)
Expressing spontaneity and encouragement	Lacking in spontaneity, using intimidation (Beavers, 1977; Fisher et al., 1983)
Having a legitimate source of authority	Chaotic (Becvar & Becvar, 1988)
Having a stable rule system	Random/chaotic (Becvar & Becvar, 1988)
Nurturing	Cold (Becvar & Becvar, 1988)
Using consistency in childrearing	Inconsistent (Becvar & Becvar, 1988)
Having family and individual goals	Random/chaotic (Becvar & Becvar, 1988)
Having flexibility and adaptability	Rigid/dogmatic (Becvar & Becvar, 1988)

Beavers, W. R. (1982). Healthy, mid-range, and severely dysfunctional families. In F. Walsh (Ed.), *Normal family processes.* New York: Guilford Press.

Becvar, D., & Becvar, R. (1988). *Family therapy.* Newton, MA: Allyn & Bacon.

Carter, B. (1986). Success in family therapy. *The Family Therapy Networker, 10*(4), 17–22.

Fisher, B. L., Giblin, P. R., & Hoopes, M. H. (1982). Healthy family functioning: What therapists say and what families want. *Journal of Marital and Family Therapy, 8,* 273–284.

Fisher, B. L., & Sprenkle, D. (1978). Therapist's perceptions of healthy family functioning. *International Journal of Family Counseling, 6,* 1–10.

Gladding, S. (1984). *Healthy families: Counseling issues.* Paper presented at the annual meeting of the American Association for Counseling and Development, Houston, TX.

Kantor, D., & Lehr, W. (1975). *Inside the family: Toward a theory of family process.* San Francisco: Jossey-Bass.

Lewis, J., Beavers, W., Gossett, J., & Phillips, V. (1976). *No single thread: Psychological health in family systems.* New York: Brunner/Mazel.

Olson, D. H., Russell, L., & Sprenkle, D. (1989). *Circumplex model: Systemic treatment of families.* New York: Haworth Press.

Olson, D., Sprenkle, D., & Russell, C. (1979). Circumplex model of marital and family systems I: Cohesion and adaptability dimensions, family types, and clinical applications. *Family Process, 18,* 3–28.

Reiss, D. (1981). *The family's construction of reality.* Cambridge, MA: Harvard University Press.

Textor, M. R. (1989). The "healthy" family. *Journal of Family Therapy, 11,* 59–75.

Wilcoxon, S. A. (1985). Healthy family functioning: The other side of family pathology. *Journal of Counseling and Development, 63,* 495–499.

This article was originally published in *Topics in Family Psychology and Counseling,* Vol. 1, No. 1, 1992, pp. 6–14. Reprint permission granted by the Editor.

Healthy Family Functioning: The Other Side of Family Pathology

S. Allen Wilcoxon

More than ever before, counselors are focusing their attention on the family environment because of its influence on the individuals that they serve. This trend has led to changes in both the format and context of counseling services by involving the client and other family members in the counseling process. Altering the intervention in this way, however, represents more than simply a change in the number of participants in counseling sessions (Zingaro, 1983).

In addition to creating changes in the counseling format, family-based services have led to the introduction of new concepts and terminologies such as the "family system," "systemic intervention," and "systematic therapy" (Searight & Openlander, 1984). This perspective represents the application of the general systems theory (von Bertalanffy, 1968) as a framework for describing the complex nature of interactions between individual members of a family unit. The systemic perspective is based upon the notion that family members develop preferred, predictable patterns for interacting and defining their relationships to one another. As with any system, attempts to alter one component (or member) in a family system will typically elicit resistance from other members until a new pattern is established by mutual adjustment. Noting the comprehensive nature of this model, Framo (1981) observed, "Of all the forces that impinge on people (culture, society, work, neighborhood, friends, etc.), the family by far has the greatest imprinting influence" (p. 133).

Current professional literature provides ample evidence for increased use of family-based, systemic intervention in cases involving vocational choice and career planning (Bratcher, 1982; Zingaro, 1983), single-parent families (Cashion, 1982), work with blended families (Prosen & Farmer, 1982), assaultive adolescents (Madden & Harbin, 1983), school-related difficulties (McDaniel, 1981), and a variety of other needs. This trend is further reflected in the special issues that the *Elementary School Guidance and Counseling* journal (February 1981) and *The School*

Counselor (January 1981) devoted to models and techniques of family-based intervention. Academic departments also have responded to this trend with changes in program emphases, orientation, and coursework (Caulfield & Perosa, 1983; Meadows & Hetrick, 1982; Piercy & Hovestadt, 1980; Wantz, Scherman, & Hollis, 1982).

In light of the increased interest in systematic intervention, it seems noteworthy that the most prevalent perspective both in conceptual and applied literature and in academic training and supervision is based on models that emphasize pathological or dysfunctional characteristics of the family unit. Lewis, Beavers, Gossett, and Phillips (1976) stated that:

> Historic preference for research in the pathological as well as the relative ignorance of the functional is, of course, common in research processes in all health fields...[the] focus is invariably on the dysfunctional. (pp. 3–4)

Similarly, Barnhill (1979) asked, "With so much agreement that the family can be a unit of psychopathology, the question occurs, can it not also be a unit of mental health?" (p. 94). I will present in this article a discussion of the nonpathological patterns of family life, hereafter noted as "healthy family functioning." The purpose is to provide a comprehensive summary of relevant literature, to examine the relationship between conceptual notions and empirical research, and to discuss the implications of healthy family literature for practicing counseling and human development practitioners.

Conceptual Background

Attention to the healthy family developed as an outgrowth of the focus on prevention services in the 1960s and 1970s. At that time speculation grew concerning the features of family life that might promote individual satisfaction and family harmony (Ackerman, 1961; Otto, 1962). Early attempts to describe characteristics of such families, however, often became mired in semantic disagreements. According to Fisher and Sprenkle (1978):

> Given the idiosyncrasies of individual scholars, their varied theoretical persuasions, and the plethora of concepts used in the field, it is not surprising that there is an enormous diversity of opinion on these matters. (pp. 10–11)

Olson, Sprenkle, and Russell (1979) sought to integrate many of the diverse concepts from the healthy family literature through the development of their circumplex model. These authors identified two dimensions of family interaction as a basis for identifying healthy or pathological family functioning. The first dimension, family cohesion, represents the emotional bond between family members and the second dimension, family adaptability, represents familial reactions to situational or developmental stress. The circumplex model features these two dimensions as intersecting continua. Extremes of either continuum represent pathology in family life, whereas moderation (near the point of intersection) represents healthy family functioning along that particular dimension of the family system (see Figure 1).

Families demonstrating an extremely low level of family cohesion would be emotionally alienated from one another, while families

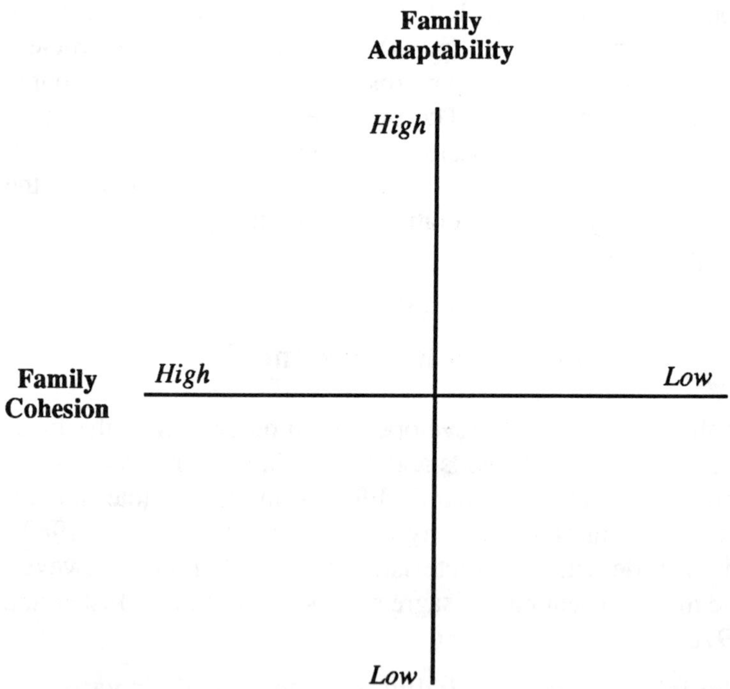

Figure 1
The Circumplex Model of Healthy Family Functioning

demonstrating an extremely high level of family cohesion would have pronounced dependency upon one another for emotional well-being. Families demonstrating an extremely low level of family adaptability would be rigid and would encounter great difficulty adjusting to family transitions, whereas families demonstrating an extremely high level of family adaptability would be chaotic, unpredictable, and unstable (Olson et al., 1979). One might criticize the circumplex model for its limited scope in describing dimensions of family life and its simplistic format for representing complex systemic processes. Modifications have been featured in the more recent literature, particularly for purposes of conducting comparative research (Fisher, Giblin, & Hoopes, 1982; Fisher & Sprenkle, 1978).

The most elaborate conceptual framework for integrating various theoretical perspectives can be found in Barnhill's (1979) "healthy family cycle." This model features a framework for examining eight interrelated dimensions of family life, focusing on healthy versus pathological patterns of family functioning within each dimension (Table 1).

Table 1
Dimensions of the Healthy Family Cycle

Family Process Themes	Family Dimensions	
	Healthy	**Pathological**
Identity Processes	Individuation	Enmeshment
	Mutuality	Isolation
Capacity for Change	Flexibility	Rigidity
	Stability	Disorganization
Information Processing	Clear Communications	Unclear/Distorted Communication
	Clear Perceptions	Unclear/Distorted Perceptions
Role Structuring	Role Reciprocity	Role Confusion/ Conflict
	Distinct Generational Boundaries	Blended Generational Boundaries

Barnhill (1979) arranged his conceptual model by grouping the eight dimensions into four pairs of family process themes. The first two dimensions represent the identity processes affecting family members. *Individuation* denotes one's sense of independence within the family, particularly in terms of ego autonomy, personal responsibility, and self-adequacy. By contrast, *enmeshment* denotes a type of symbiosis in family relations that promotes both exaggerated dependence between members and limited self-adequacy and low self-esteem. The latter characteristic is similar to a high level of family cohesion in the circumplex model. The second identity process dimension is *mutuality* versus *isolation*. Mutuality refers to the emotional intimacy among individuated family members, whereas isolation reflects emotional alienation and separation among family members. The latter characteristic is similar to a low level of family cohesion in the circumplex model.

The third and fourth dimensions reflect a family's capacity for changing and coping with new situations. Barnhill (1979) contrasted *flexibility* (capacity to adjust and adapt customary patterns of behavior in novel situations) with *rigidity* (insistence on repetitive, stereotypic responses in novel situations) and *stability* (consistency and predictability in family organization) with *disorganization* (chaotic and confused family organization). Again, one can clearly note similarities between the concepts of rigidity and disorganization from the healthy family cycle and high and low points, respectively, along the family adaptability continuum of the circumplex model.

The third family theme, reflecting information processing in family life, is composed of the fifth and sixth dimensions of the healthy family cycle. Familial interactions based upon clear perceptions (undistorted and realistic view of self and others) have vastly different consequences when compared with interactions based upon unclear/distorted perceptions (distorted and unrealistic view of self and others). Barnhill (1979) suggested that the former implies agreement between family members concerning events that affect family life, while the latter implies confusion and disagreement about events affecting family life. In a similar fashion, clear communication (successful and accurate exchange of information) versus unclear/distorted communication (unsuccessful and inaccurate exchange of information) in family interactions can affect every aspect of family life (Barnhill, 1979). Families demonstrating clarity in communications foster mutual interchange by clarifying meanings and intentions of verbal (and nonverbal) messages. In contrast, lack of clarity in family communications tends to discourage interactions between family members, thereby promoting confusion and misunderstandings (Satir, 1972).

The seventh and eighth dimensions reflect role structuring processes in a family. *Role reciprocity* denotes complementary behavior patterns (based upon mutual agreement) between individual family members, whereas *role confusion/conflict* denotes a lack of agreement regarding acceptable behaviors for family members and conflict resulting from noncomplementary family roles. A similar dimension of family life concerns the notion of generational boundaries. Families with *distinct generational boundaries* can have intimate and meaningful interactions across generational boundaries (i.e., parent-child relations) but have their primary alliances within their peer generation (e.g., the marital dyad). Families with *blended generational boundaries* have primary alliances across generational boundaries, leading to confusion and dissatisfaction in peer-generation relationships or even to the forming of cross-generational alliances (e.g., parent and child vs. another child).

Barnhill (1979) stressed the interdependent nature of these eight dimensions of family life, noting that no single dimension operates in isolation. For example, rigidity and disorganization in one's family life may lead to distorted perceptions and communications, which may lead to emotional isolation or poor peer-generation relationships, which may lead to cross-generational alliances, and so on. Barnhill (1979) further stated that no family is entirely pathological or entirely healthy along all dimensions of family life. Thus, intervention strategies should primarily focus upon the less healthy dimensions of family functioning.

A noteworthy criticism has been levied against the unrealistic perspective featured in much of the conceptual literature concerning healthy family functioning. Gladding (1984) noted that many of the healthy family concepts lead one to conclude that most families may never demonstrate all of the characteristics at the same time. Essentially, models such as those noted by Barnhill (1979) and Olson et al. (1979) seem to describe the "ideal" family system, which is beyond the resources of many families .

Similarly, whereas the circumplex model addresses the issue of degrees of healthiness demonstrated in a family, much of the conceptual literature seems to denote healthy family functioning as an all-or-nothing proposition. Some suggest, however, that to reach such a conclusion is to miss the intended purpose of these authors (Ebert, 1978; Kleiman, 1981; Walsh, 1982). Research efforts have focused upon these and other issues concerning empirical investigation of healthy family characteristics.

Convergence of Conceptualization and Research

The process of translating conceptual models into a format for research has posed a variety of problems to those investigating healthy family functioning. Barnhill (1975) stated that:

> While problem families can often be identified by meaningful criteria...establishing controls for comparative study is often more difficult. To what types of families should problem families be compared? "Normal" families? "Healthy" families? "Non-problem" families? (p. 7)

Speer (1970) suggested that the complete absence of observable family problems might be an indication of underlying discord, reflecting rigid family beliefs and limited capacity for adapting to transitions in family life. Similarly, Halleck (1974) indicated that a normal family in a given locale or social strata might very well be a family with pronounced pathology. Other criteria such as "strong families" (Otto, 1962), "average families" (Mudd, Mitchell, & Taubin, 1965), and "typical families" (Offer & Sabshin, 1966) were judged unacceptable for comparative study.

Despite methodological difficulties, Lewis et al. (1976) conducted the most comprehensive empirically based research project of its kind in an attempt to investigate the systemic nature of healthy family functioning. Using 12 expert raters to evaluate videotape segments of interactions of 22 families (representing patient and nonpatient populations), the authors developed the Family Health-Pathology Rating Scale (FHPRS) for quantitative measurement of the degree of healthiness demonstrated in familial interactions. With this instrument, raters were able to discriminate patient from nonpatient families with great accuracy and generate high, positive correlations (ranging from .65 to .90) in rating the relative healthiness of families in the sample population. The authors (1976) then collected videotape samples of 44 families (over 7 years) performing standardized "Family Interactional Tasks." Using the FHPRS ratings of 16 experts, Lewis et al. (1976) concluded that members of healthy families:

1. Demonstrate a warm and trusting attitude in familial interactions;
2. Are characteristically open and mutually respectful in their interactions and speak honestly and disagree without fear of retribution;

3. Use negotiation rather than power in problem solving;
4. Demonstrate a high level of personal initiative and assume personal responsibility for their individual choices and interests;
5. Promote a definite yet flexible family structure with appropriate distribution of responsibilities and privileges between parents and children;
6. Demonstrate emotional maturity and autonomy;
7. Share common perceptions of reality that are congruent with the social framework of their community;
8. Encourage affective expression for positive and negative emotions; and
9. Demonstrate other signs of well-being such as spontaneity, humor, and recognition of other members' talents.

Research efforts have also been directed toward investigating healthy family characteristics based upon the constructs from the circumplex model (Olson et al., 1979). Using a sample of 31 family triads composed of a mother, father, and adolescent daughter (14 to 17 years old), Russell (1979) investigated familial interactions using a structured family interaction game (SIMFAM). The study revealed that families demonstrating moderate levels of family adaptability and family cohesion functioned at a significantly higher level on the SIMFAM measure than did those families representing high or low extremes on either of the two dimensions of the circumplex model.

Fisher and Sprenkle (1978) used indicators of family adaptability, family cohesion, and family communication (a variable included to expand upon the circumplex model) to investigate the perceptions of professional therapists ($N=310$) regarding characteristics of healthy family functioning. Using a Likert-type format for subject ratings, these authors noted that therapists identified characteristics such as familial warmth and support, openness for expressing ideas, and problem solving through negotiation as the most valued features of healthy family functioning. In a follow-up study, Fisher et al. (1982) compared the ratings of professionals from the Fisher and Sprenkle (1978) study with those of selected family members ($N=208$). The results of this investigation indicated great similarity in the ratings of these sample populations, suggesting that both professionals and laypersons agree that certain components of familial interaction have a positive effect on family life.

An important and potentially fatal criticism of these and other studies has been the lack of precision in delineating external criteria for identifying healthy family characteristics (Gantman, 1980). Fisher et al. (1982) noted the need for additional data from both an "outsider-objective" (i.e., nonfamily members) and an "insider-objective" (i.e., family members) frame of reference. They contend that the Lewis et al. (1976) study represents the former, whereas no investigations to this point have attempted to investigate healthy family functioning from the latter frame of reference. In fact, it seems rather difficult to conceive of one being both "objective" and an "insider" regarding one's family.

An additional criticism lies in the inherent problems with value judgments concerning healthy families. Do the aforementioned characteristics apply to only a certain segment of the total population, or do they generalize across populations? What about cultural differences? What about nontraditional families (e.g., single-parent families, stepfamilies, etc.)? In this regard, Lewis et al. (1976) observed that "psychological health cannot have a value-free, universal applicability. Any system for distinguishing the functional from the dysfunctional must involve a consideration of culture-based values" (p. 14). These and related topics seem to be coming to the forefront in contemporary healthy family literature (David, 1978; Lewis & Looney, 1983).

Despite methodological criticisms, a noteworthy trend in the collective research literature is the remarkable similarity between conclusions noted in empirical studies and ideas featured in the conceptual literature. This seems to represent a convergence of conceptualization and research in healthy family functioning. As Ebert (1978) stated, "these are exciting times in family therapy as the focus is moved towards the positive" (p. 231).

Implications for Counselors

The first, and possibly most salient, implication of the healthy family literature is its affirmation of the systemic properties of family interactions, regardless of the level of healthiness promoted by those interactions. In this regard, Lewis et al. (1976) noted the necessity for perceiving family relationships as interrelated, pluralistic, and multidimensional in nature. Thus, assessment and intervention strategies reflecting a systemic perspective in counseling seem to be confirmed by models based on family pathology as well as family healthiness.

Second, knowledge of healthy family characteristics should be helpful in assessment and intervention in the counseling process. As Barnhill (1979) noted, no family is entirely dysfunctional; therefore, interventions along "healthy" dimensions of family life could be, at best, time-consuming and, at worst, counterproductive or symptom-aggravating. Thus, knowledge of healthy family characteristics might expedite intervention in "less healthy" processes of family life.

A third implication pertains to the developmental nature of family life. Many professional counselors would agree that a large number of their requests for service stem from developmental crises, often described as "transitional crises" in the family life cycle (Carter & McGoldrick, 1980; Duval, 1971). In such cases, an effective mode of intervention is that of supportive affirmation, which focuses upon linking previously successful coping strategies to the current crisis (Killilea, 1982). It is not unusual for even the healthiest of families to experience stress during such transitions. A counselor's awareness of healthy family characteristics could be quite valuable in providing assurance that healthy family processes are not completely eroded, but rather are undergoing adjustment and change. In fact, it is quite possible that these very characteristics have brought the family to its current stage of readiness for entry into a new phase of growth and development.

Fourth, an awareness and appreciation of healthy family characteristics seems highly appropriate at the preparatory level for counselors in training. Barnhill (1979) observed that this is essential in light of the tendency of novice counselors to "overpathologize" with clients. Similarly, Lewis et al. (1976) stated that:

> It may be that exposure to the pathological in training and practice would be balanced better by a broader view, that experience with "health" is valuable in the development of a perspective for those who are committed to the helping professions. (p. 21)

Additionally, in light of new research in the field, it seems appropriate that the well-prepared student be readied for critical review of contemporary investigations in healthy family literature.

A final implication may be somewhat, though not entirely, philosophical in nature. For some professionals, there seems to be a propensity for interpreting client data in terms of deficits, weaknesses, and other indicators of pathology. The impetus behind the healthy family movement was an attempt to alter this epistemological preference for definition based upon deficit by focusing on assets, strengths, and healthiness demonstrated in family interactions. Lee (1983) noted that one's epistemological position affects one's opinion regarding human nature and, consequently, the process of counseling. Thus, a "healthiness shift" in one's philosophical base could influence one's counseling practice in areas such as assessment, intervention strategies, and the identification of indices of change. Such a shift could be a vital link in the support of developmental and preventive programming in agency and school settings.

Although conceptual and applied information pertaining to healthy family functioning can be noted throughout the professional literature, the purpose of this article has been to consolidate the collective literature in a concise, systematic fashion. An awareness of these conceptual and applied notions represents an avenue through which both we and our clients may benefit from knowledge regarding "the other side of family pathology."

References

Ackerman, N. (1961). Preventive implications of family research. In G. Caplan (Ed.), *Prevention of mental disorders in children* (pp. 142–167). New York: Basic Books.

Barnhill, L. R. (1975). *Dimensions of healthy family interaction.* Unpublished doctoral dissertation, Southern Illinois University.

Barnhill, L. R. (1979). Healthy family systems. *Family Coordinator, 28,* 94–100.

Bratcher, W. E. (1982). The influence of the family on career selection: A family systems perspective. *Personnel and Guidance Journal, 61,* 87–91.

Carter, E., & McGoldrick, M. (Eds.). (1980). *The family life cycle: A framework for family therapy.* New York: Gardner Press.

Cashion, B. G. (1982). Female-headed families: Effects on children and clinical implications. *Journal of Marital and Family Therapy, 8,* 77–85.

Caulfield, T., & Perosa, L. (1983). Counselor education—Quo vadis? *Counselor Education and Supervision, 22,* 178–184.

David, H. P. (1978). Healthy family functioning: A cross-cultural appraisal. *Bulletin of the World Health Organization, 56,* 327–342.

Duval, E. (1971). *Family development.* New York: J. B. Lippincott.

Ebert, B. (1978). The healthy family. *Family Therapy, 5,* 227–232.

Fisher, B., Giblin, P., & Hoopes, M. (1982). Healthy family functioning: What therapists say and what families want. *Journal of Marital and Family Therapy, 8,* 273-284.

Fisher, B., & Sprenkle, D. (1978). Therapists' perceptions of healthy family functioning. *International Journal of Family Counseling, 6,* 9–18.

Framo, J. L. (1981). The integration of marital therapy with sessions with family of origin. In A. Gurman & D. Kniskern (Eds.), *Handbook of family therapy* (pp. 133–158). New York: Brunner/Mazel.

Gantman, C. A. (1980). A closer look at families that work well. *International Journal of Family Therapy, 2,* 107–119.

Gladding, S. (1984). *Healthy families: Counseling issues.* Paper presented at the annual meeting of the American Association for Counseling and Development, Houston, Texas.

Halleck, S. (1974). *Politics of therapy.* New York: Jason Aronson.

Killilea, M. (1982). Interaction of crisis theory, coping strategies and social support systems. In H. Schulberg & M. Killilea (Eds.), *The modern practice of community mental health* (pp. 163–214). San Francisco: Jossey-Bass.

Kleiman, J. (1981). Optimal and normal family functioning. *American Journal of Family Therapy, 9,* 37–44.

Lee, D. (1983). Philosophy and counseling: A metatheoretical analysis. *Personnel and Guidance Journal, 61,* 522–526.

Lewis, J. M., Beavers, W. R., Gossett, J. T., & Phillips, V. A. (1976). *No single thread: Psychological health in family systems.* New York: Brunner/Mazel.

Lewis, J. M., & Looney, J. M. (1983). *The long struggle: Well-functioning working class black families.* New York: Brunner/Mazel.

Madden, D., & Harbin, H. (1983). Family structures of assaultive adolescents. *Journal of Marital and Family Therapy, 9,* 311–316.

McDaniel, S. (1981). Treating school problems in family therapy. *Elementary School Guidance and Counseling, 15,* 214–222.

Meadows, M., & Hetrick, H. (1982). Roles for counselor education departments in marriage and family counseling: Current status and projections. *Counselor Education and Supervision, 22,* 47–54.

Mudd, E., Mitchell, H., & Taubin, S. (1965). *Success in family living.* New York: Association Press.

Offer, D., & Sabshin, M. (1966). *Normality.* New York: Basic Books.

Olson, D., Sprenkle, D., & Russell, C. (1979). Circumplex model of marital and family systems: I. *Family Process, 18,* 3–28.

Otto, H. A. (1962). What is a strong family? *Marriage and Family Living, 24,* 77–80.

Piercy, F. P., & Hovestadt, A. J. (1980). Marriage and family therapy within counselor education. *Counselor Education and Supervision, 20,* 68–74.

Prosen, S., & Farmer, J. (1982). Understanding stepfamilies: Issues and implications for counselors. *Personnel and Guidance Journal, 60,* 393–397.

Russell, C. S. (1979). Circumplex model of marital and family systems: III. *Family Process, 18,* 29–45.

Satir, V. (1972). *Peoplemaking.* Palo Alto, CA: Science and Behavior Books.

Searight, H. R., & Openlander, P. (1984). Systemic therapy: A new brief intervention model. *Personnel and Guidance Journal, 62,* 387–391.

Speer, D. C. (1970). Family systems: Morphostasis or morphogenesis or "is homeostasis enough?" *Family Process, 9,* 259–278.

von Bertalanffy, L. (1968). *General systems theory.* New York: George Braziller.

Walsh, F. (1982). *Normal family processes.* New York: Guilford Press.

Wantz, R., Scherman, A., & Hollis, J. (1982). Trends in counselor preparation: Courses, program emphases, philosophical orientation and experiential components. *Counselor Education and Supervision, 21,* 258–268.

Zingaro, J. (1983). A family systems approach for the career counselor. *Personnel and Guidance Journal, 62,* 24–27.

Family Counseling: Principles for Growth

Jon Carlson
Dan Fullmer

Sticks in a bundle are unbreakable.
—Kenyan proverb

The national barometer of mental health seems to be dropping at an ever-accelerating rate as more and more people become symptom-ridden victims of stress. Psychoses, neuroses, high blood pressure, ulcers, backaches, headaches, nervous tics, and bodily discomforts are all commonplace. In today's world of emphasis on technology and change, the situation seems to be changing—for the worse. Preventive interventions are not occurring, and remedial efforts are still producing a 50% chance of recovery—the same percentage as no treatment at all. This is a time when people must decide to live a healthy life or to have a new car, to have a body or to be a body, to continue to just exist or to begin to live and grow.

Typical mental health treatment (counseling, therapy, analysis) involves reducing, or *shrinking*, the symptoms of the injured, sick, or identified patient. Research, however, indicates that this procedure is, for the most part, inefficient (in terms of use of money, resources, and time) and largely ineffective (especially in terms of permanent rather than short-term changes). This situation need not be. Approaches to mental health that are anchored in *expanding* our educational and growth-centered perspectives produce effective, efficient, and permanent mental health. These approaches practice equality and collaboration, center upon complete systems rather than elemental analysis, and flow or work with the natural flow of living.

Research indicates that the family is the prime source for establishment of healthy and "growthful living" as well as the breeding ground for our pathology. "Growthful living," or wellness, is more than just being alive. Human development is a lifelong process, and growth can be facilitated or arrested at any stage. The family plays a major role in personality formation and development, and we are just now realizing its lifelong importance. Our nuclear families are the first and most important educational delivery system for children, and yet, for many understandable reasons, we as a nation continue to fail to equip families to do the necessary job (White, 1976).

The counseling profession has not been effective in helping people. Research does not seem to support our traditional or current paradigms. The purpose here is to acquaint the reader with the rationale, essential principles, and constructs of family counseling, provide a description of the healthy family, present a set of directions on how to use a strength-oriented educational approach with families, and discuss how counselors can used these ideas in a school setting.

Rationale for Family Work

Although family counseling has existed for some time, it has come into prominence in both professional and public eyes over the last 25 years. The AACD (American Association for Counseling and Development) and the APA (American Psychological Association) have both added divisions for the study of family. This recognition and acceptance have resulted from a growing awareness that the individual cannot be responsible for all the problems that he or she encounters, many of which come from outside pressures and influences including the family and social environment. Often, the problems of children are the result of family interaction, and family counseling has become the treatment of choice.

No one model or pattern can be used for conducting family counseling. The approach depends upon the problems, the conditions surrounding them, and the counselor's theoretical orientation (Sperry & Carlson, 1991). Nevertheless, several basic, universal principles are important for all family work.

General systems theory (Bertalanffy, 1968) applies the principle of *synergy*. Synergy is defined as: "The whole is more than the sum of its parts." Extending the principle to family practice, it is claimed that if one family member changes behavior, all other family members need to change enough to cope with the new conditions, especially the emotional climate in the family network. Fullmer's (1971) relationships theory of behavior focuses on the relationship definition between family members (i.e., mother-father, father-daughter, sibling peer group, symbiotic parent-child, friendship). The basic principle is that behavior is the expression of each individual's personal experience of meaning acted out of the relationship definition perceived by each significant other in the dyad. Adlerian or individual psychology has a well-developed system for family work (Sherman & Dinkmeyer, 1987). The primary focus for application has been on childrearing practices. The central principle treats the individual's behavior as goal-directed. The child's goal is to achieve a place of importance in his or her environment. The motivation principle is a will to belong or find a meaningful place in society.

The variety of approaches continues to grow, as does the number of counselors using family systems approaches. The "Related Readings" at the end of this article are sources for exploring the various approaches and can serve as a starting place for readers who desire further background in family counseling.

Principles Used in Family Work

The foundation on which behavior is based can be expressed in principles that represent the key components in the family counseling model described here. The principles incorporate motivation, needs, communication, identity, and power. Through an understanding of the following principles, counselors can learn to understand, communicate, and facilitate effectively within a family context.

Principle 1: Context is Fundamental to Meaning

The concept of "context" is simply the setting one is in. Given your behavior in an elevator, look quickly at your behavior in your bedroom. How are the two alike? How are they different? Notice your emotional response when you imagine yourself making love in the elevator. What you feel is what we refer to as "meaning." This principle can be seen within a family setting where a child is encouraged to fight at home but not at school; where the wife is sensuous when the lights are out and frigid when the lights are on; using loose and colorful language when eating at home and being sent to the car when using these words in a public restaurant. The behaviors are the same, but the meanings or feelings are different.

Meaning has feelings because it is tied to the emotional system, the basis of the relationship system. What you feel is the way communication takes place within your family context. Processing one's own feelings is what leads to meaning. Feelings of anger, joy, sadness, elation, sorrow, and so on determine the meaning of the event. Feelings are the connection between the emotional system (myself) and the relationship system (others) (Papero, 1990). *Your perception determines what you are going to do.*

Principle 2: Relationships are Substance and Behavior is Form

The concept of relationship is illustrated by the complex feelings one gets when faced with an enemy as contrasted with a friend. The enemy relationship feels like flight or fright, but the friendship feels warm and free. Our behavior in each instance serves to express the meaning we are experiencing. The form may vary from each instance, but undoubtedly we will each display a consistent pattern of behavior with latitude for unique variation. *How you feel is how you act.* The "why" of your feeling is relationship definition.

When someone does things for someone else, the message may be, "I love you and care for you" or "I'll dominate and trap you," depending upon the relationship. Relationship is substance and behavior is form. A mate may agree to participate in family counseling (behavior) one week to placate or "butter you up" to *control,* and may not agree to participate the next week to show you who is boss and to *control.* Although the relationship remains unchanged, the behavior is different.

Principle 3: Patterns of Behavior Repeat Themselves in Cycles

Patterns of behavior are derived from the redundance in communication as people repeat themselves again and again and receive acceptable results. The redundant behavior can be either verbal or nonverbal, both verbal and nonverbal, and contextual-verbal/nonverbal.

Take a quick imaginary trip through your past 48 hours. What do you find? A counselor typically does the same thing at a given moment of time each day. Nobel Prize winners Konrad Lorenz (1965) and Nikko Tinbergen (1951) have observed that much of the motor behavior of any species can be described by specifying only a few dozen fixed action patterns. Your schedule is a concrete example of redundant patterns of behavior. *What is stable is predictable. What is unstable is unpredictable. Redundance in pattern is the predictable way of life.*

One specific example of our consistent patterns can be found in the "buzz phrases" (Sperry & Hess, 1974) we frequently and automatically use in conversation. Buzz phrases are simply words, explanations, exclamations, or questions that a person uses consistently. In fact, some people actually can be identified with one or more of their buzz phrases. Researchers have found that from one-half to two-thirds of a person's verbalizations may be reduced to 15 to 30 buzz phrases. The buzz phrases, of course, relate to the person's dominant goal. Some possible buzz phrases associated with certain goals are (Sperry, 1975, p. 24):

Buzz	**Goal**
"How do you like my…?" "Have you ever gone to…?" "I'll bet you didn't know…."	Attention or Elevation
"If this job's too hard for you…." "I want it done *this* (my) way..." "Who does he think he is?"	Power or Control
"Just you wait and see!" "It's impossible to get anything through his thick skull."	Revenge
"Well, I didn't volunteer for this job anyway." "I'll try, but I know I can't do it."	Inadequacy
"Remember how things used to be..." "Say, what did you do over the weekend?"	Time-wasting
"Don't get so excited. It's nothing." "There must be *something* we can do about it."	Peacemaking
"Wow, that's really something!" "I might as well try it. I've done everything else."	Excitement

When we take this concept into a family and quickly map the individual patterns, it frequently is immediately apparent where the conflicts are likely to happen. The myriad of familial problems recur in a predictable fashion as the same action chains or patterns are triggered. Each family is like an individual in that it has a characteristic way or pattern of generating conflict. Your action chain is another way to see how your relationships are defined.

Principle 4: Action Chains Express Definition and Relationships

The concept of an action chain (Hall, 1976) comes from observing what you do following a given cue or stimulus. All behaviors actually consist of sequences, or chains of behaviors. The links in the chains are each composed of simpler behavioral components.

For example, the behavior "going to bed" can be broken down into a set of component behaviors: proceeding to the bedroom; taking off clothes; putting on sleeping attire; using bathroom and toilet facilities; saying goodnight to spouse; turning out light; getting into bed. Each of these component behaviors could be broken down into even smaller components. Taking off clothes, for instance, may be composed of: untying right shoe; reaching down and removing shoe with hands; untying left shoe; reaching down and removing left shoe; removing right sock; removing left sock; removing pants; removing sweater; removing shirt; removing underwear; removing jewelry. *You are chained to your routine of actions.*

Chains are learned by taking simple behaviors already in the individual's repertoire and combining them into more complex behaviors. Each behavior in a chain has a dual function—serving as a reinforcer for the previous response and as a stimulus for the next one. The action chain utilized depends on what a situation means to the individual.

For example, if someone compliments you, you probably will activate an action chain and pass it on to someone else at the first opportunity. If someone gives you a put-down, you probably will activate an action chain and pass it on to someone else. The action chain expresses the meaning each experience has for you, completing the communication of your definition of relationship with the sender.

Principle 5: Families From a Given Culture Will Display Similar Behavior in a Given Context

Context is the manifestation of culture parameters or rules for the way it is supposed to be. *What I do is natural because it is culturally correct. What you do is unnatural because it is culturally incorrect.* A family teaches children the culture of which it is a part. The family is an entire culture on a small scale (microcosm). Rarely does a given family master a culture's entire rule system; therefore, each family represents a unique pattern in a given culture.

Because each family emphasizes unique patterns and symbols, the range of microcosm equals the number of families in the culture. Yet, each family resembles each other family within a given culture in the global dimensions such as language, values, attitudes, and basic patterns of behavior. This phenomenon provides the basic rationale for working with multiple families in groups. The healthy family is able to accommodate the wide range of differences encountered in other families without losing its own uniqueness.

Context as a concept defines meaning to an individual in any given situation. The culture's rules for "the way it is supposed to be" form the person's emotional system, complete with physiological and biochemical consequences. The way you feel in a given situation is the manifestation of the principle. The human potential movement claimed that feelings could be the basis of behavior. The fallacy is in omission of the fact that individuals can create a new context and, therefore, new feelings by their own initiative.

Principle 6: People Learn Social Behaviors all at Once, in Gestalts, not in Pieces

The context in social behavior may be more important than the specifics of what is learned. The conditions under which you come into your learning (knowledge and behavior) may be more important than the context of the learning (Loukes, 1964). *It is not what you do; it is the way you do it.*

For example, think of what is learned about sex if you are raped as your initial experience. Or think of the child who learns toilet behavior from a mother who always rewards successful execution with candy. The context may teach many values in addition to the central content in the learning experience. The counselor's attitude toward the family sets the tone for what will occur. The first few minutes of contact between people, according to Zunin and Zunin (1972), usually determine whether a successful relationship will develop. The counselor's prejudgments in regard to prejudices, values, and attitudes influence the depth of subsequent interactions.

Principle 7: The Healthy Family Solves Problems Through Support and Trust From Within the Group

The power of the family bond endures because no matter when you go to your family, it will take you in. No other human group has approached that characteristic functioning in the families of the world. After more than 50 years in the kibbutz, for example, the grandparents relate to the children in much the same way as in most extended families—with a strong emotional bond.

The strong emotional bond is the base for a healthy family. The family bond helps to solve problems because it is the source of support and the essence of trust. With this emotional base a healthy family can use the most effective means of problem solution and conflict resolution. The most effective means for solving problems is to redefine the family's relationship to the source of the problem. This can be done by stepping outside the context containing the problem. Communications experts call it *meta-communicating*. Essentially, the process requires each participant in any encounter to step outside the frame or context and look at the larger stage or picture. *The view from out here is different from the view from within.* The counseling process centers on helping families learn this method in order to become self-healing.

Principle 8: Encouragement is Fundamental to Creative Behavior

Individuals must gain the courage to violate their own rules for behaving if they are to achieve new behavior (Bateson, 1972). Learning is fun if the risk is manageable. If the risk is too great, the result is traumatic. Pathology in behavior frequently is generated by the anxiety or fear of failure. Failure is the deterrent to foolishness. To risk, to go beyond what you know and can predict the consequences of, requires you to violate your rule of safety. Whenever you violate your rules and survive the pathology generated, you stand to learn in significant terms or degrees. Bateson calls this "trans-contextual learning." You begin in context A and end up in context B.

Transpersonal experience is similar in social learning terms. You are as usual in context A; then a transformation happens (you learn something new) and find yourself changed and living in context B. I left home at age 20. Five years later I returned home to visit. Home was different, though the same people were there. My experience of home was from the perceptions in context B. I cannot go home again in terms of the old context A perceptions. Experience is altered by the new perception achieved in context B.

This process has to be anchored in a stable and secure setting. Individuals and their families gain security through understanding and accepting their assets and where they are in life. *Tell me what is right with me—not what is wrong*. Security does not result from a diagnosis of liabilities or a concentration on one's problems or weaknesses. This results in insecurity, discouragement, depression, and failure.

Counselors should model encouraging behavior, identify existing strengths in the family, and facilitate activities that increase the possibilities of future encouraging behaviors (Dinkmeyer & Losoncy, 1980). Counselors should make frequent use of confrontation—not confronting individuals with their mistakes, but rather, with their strengths. Research has not shown much support for negative confrontation (Berenson & Mitchell, 1974) but strongly supports positive changes resulting from positive confrontation (Jacobs & Spradlin, 1974; Lieberman, Yalom, & Miles, 1972).

Principle 9: Overemphasis on Individual Achievement Leads to Erosion of Basic Support Within Families

A social system that has produced Howard Hughes, Albert Einstein, Henry Ford, B.F. Skinner, William Douglas, Tom Dooley, and Mohammed Ali has had a powerful emphasis upon individual achievement. *The price society pays for outstanding individual achievement is ultimate destruction of the basic social support system, the family group.* In *Earthwalk*, Slater (1974) hypothesizes that this will lead to ultimate destruction of the world. You can decide for yourself if the price is right.

Counselors have to be constantly aware of keeping a balance between individual and family achievement. This same balance is necessary for our survival in larger or world affairs (Slater, 1974).

Principle 10: People do not Change: They Become More and More Like Themselves.

In a healthy environment this principle is true. In a traditional environment the principle is modified to read: People change; they become more and more like themselves. The shrinking, correcting, evaluation paradigm leads to reductionism, almost to zero or nothingness. The person, for example, may feel a void or nothingness and powerlessness. Contrast this unhealthy condition to the growth paradigm that encourages people to become more and more like themselves. *Happiness is finding more and more where there used to be less and less.*

Necessary Competencies for Healthy and Growthful Family Life

Family competencies are defined as those vital elements responsible for maintaining the growth and health of the family unit. To help teach people to become healthy and growthful, we need to know what we want to teach. Imagine math teachers teaching a unit on algebra if they aren't too sure what equations are, or mechanics instructing on carburetion when they are unfamiliar with fuel systems. This is, however, the situation in mental health. We previously have had little agreement on standards of growthful living for an individual, let alone a family.

The following are among the essential competencies for healthy and growthful family life. These are not isolate variables, but rather, form clusters, constellations, and chains that are dynamic, fluid, interrelated, and variable at different stages in a family's life cycle (Otto, 1975, p. 11):

- *Uniqueness* of each member is allowed to develop.
- The constructive use of *power* is facilitated, and each member learns to achieve intellectually, socially, and emotionally.
- *Flexibility,* and creative coping with the ever-changing environment, is a must. The ability to adapt to each other's needs creates a collaborative environment.
- Accurate *communication* among all members of the family is fostered.
- An atmosphere of *belonging* is essential. The family should represent a stronghold where changing needs can be met, a system in which individual problems can be resolved conjointly.
- A supportive climate that provides enough *security* for family members to attempt various endeavors is healthy for the family and its members.
- *Democratic principles* of family management are needed.
- Frequent use of *feedback* and *feedforward* helps members assess themselves and grow.
- *Problem solving* and *decision making* are needed for healthy living.
- The use of *consequences* and *consistency* in everyday family interactions is also regarded as a competency.

Otto (1975) sets forth "primary strength clusters" that should be nourished, developed, and expanded throughout the life span of a family. He believes that these clusters have a great deal to do with a family's adaptability, resiliency, and optimum functioning. A partial list includes:

- The capacity to give love, affection, and support to each other.
- Open communication and listening.
- The ability to give encouragement.
- Each family member helping the other to develop his or her unique potential.
- The capacity for understanding.
- Sensitivity to each other.
- Empathy.
- Fostering curiosity, creativity, and the spirit of adventure.

The family counselor can learn to encourage primary strength clusters or positive action chains and facilitate their continued development through teaching family members this process. By encouraging appropriate segments of these chains, the entire chain is affected and "strength syndromes" are created. Table 4.1 demonstrates how to encourage specific behaviors and how these behaviors are linked to bigger action chains or clusters.

The Strengths-Oriented Education Model

Using a strengths-oriented model in education and in family living has many ramifications. The single element most significant to behavior change for any individual is a *new life situation.* The introduction of family and group counseling has created situational changes that have led to more opportunity for new expectations and, consequently, new behavior.

The second element significant to a strengths-oriented education model is *encouragement.* New life situations create anxiety. Anxiety must be counter-balanced by hope. Hope comes from the encouragement to risk oneself in a new situation.

In contrast to the prevailing weaknesses model, the strengths model does not require retooling. You are OK as you are—just give it a try. The task is to get the other person to try to act in a new situation. If he or she does, the reinforcement helps maintain the new relationship definition and the new self-definition acquired. Going back to the previous

Table 4.1
Encouragement of Action Chains

Positive Behavior	Positive Mental Health Principle or Larger Action Chain	Facilitative Response
Doing a job that is yours	Having social interest or concern for others	"I like the way you see a job that needs to be done and do it!"
Waking up with a smile and making a nice remark (e.g., "good morning")	Encouraging others and demonstrating ability and willingness to live cooperatively	"You sure seem to know how to make me smile."
Asking for other family members' opinions	Democratic decision making	"It feels good to be a part of the family and to know that what I have to say matters to you."

behavior even becomes difficult. As long as a situation in life does not change, the tendency will be to maintain the familiar behavior. The same is true for changed behavior, but the new situation must become stable.

Weaknesses make us losers. Strengths make us winners. In the strengths-oriented model, relationships are made (tamed) and maintained over time. The rules we live by create the situation or define the relationships in which we behave. Strengths make us OK. Weaknesses make us not OK. If I am OK, I can try to imitate new behavior demonstrated in an old situation. I am free to create new behavior in a new situation. If I am not OK, none of the above is likely to happen.

To be a winner, a person has to have rules by which to live that permit exercise or expansion and, consequently, growth. To be a loser, a person has to have rules by which to live that require "exorcise" or shrinkage by casting out or reducing the "not OK" part of yourself. Win or lose, the myth of unchangeability in people persists. Evidence is legion that the situation in which people find themselves influences behavior more than do inner traits of personality (Bakker, 1975; Weisstein, 1970). Cohen (1953), Milgram (1965), and Zimbardo (1971) have each concluded that the situation influences behavior beyond the individual's personal expectations. Thus, the unpredictability of human behavior has persisted.

Counseling and education have given lip service to the idea that we should begin with individuals wherever they are when we find them. To start where the person is constitutes the cardinal rule for a strengths-oriented education model. This does not allow a chance to bring individuals up to the grade level or put them back into their mythical group. They must be treated as unique, and new situations must be created for them to learn and grow. When this was done in our Peer Counselor-Consultant Training Program (Fullmer, 1976b), the new behavior the students were able to create made the significant difference in the way they saw themselves. Low self-esteem became aspiration to post-high school training in the spirit of a winner, whereas, prior to training, the despair of losing prevailed. Peer counseling training is one way to actualize a strengths-oriented education model in a school.

Two systems are suggested for counselors working with families. The first is aimed at *skill development for parents* (Carlson & Faiber, 1976; Dinkmeyer & McKay, 1989). Parent education has been gaining acceptance as a necessary role of the counselor. It is important for helping people help themselves. A second system or model, however, has gained prominence. Counselors can use *family counseling as a form of group counseling*. Two family counseling cases illustrate how the 10 stated principles were applied from the perspective of counseling in a school context. To change behavior, the life situation has to be changed, encouraged, and stabilized. The aim is to change the life situation or family system. Thus, individuals will behave in new ways.

Case 1

The school counselor was experienced in family counseling. The case involved the family of a seventh-grade girl in a suburban setting. The presenting complaint was disruptive behavior and deterioration in the girl's behavior generally, especially in school achievement. Because her teachers found no obvious reasons, the counselor invited the parents to come in for an information session.

During the initial session with the family, several items of information were disclosed. The most significant change in the family's life situation was that the father, 41, had just lost his job, which had provided the family with a very comfortable living. A check of dates between his daughter's change in behavior at school and the father's job situation confirmed the guess that her behavior change came a short time after her father lost his job.

Several of the 10 principles are apparent in this case. The relationship between father and daughter was robust (Principle 2). Principle 4 claims that action chains express definitions of behavior. The heavy emphasis on individual achievement in the family (Principle 9) seemed to have intensified the daughter's reaction.

The case was handled successfully by encouraging (Principle 8) them each to assess their individual and family strengths and to develop ways of communicating to each other what pleases them. The family came for three additional sessions. During the family counseling, the daughter learned of resources in her family (both financial and psychological) of which she had been unaware. A new pattern of behavior was proposed to meet and stabilize the new situation. The girl's schoolwork improved, and her behavior modified in a new and more acceptable fashion.

Case 2

The counselor decided to try family counseling with a case of a first-grade boy referred by a teacher. The counselor had used parent conferences before, but this was the first time she tried to convene the entire family to help.

The referral stated that the boy was unable to handle social interaction without becoming panicky. Sometimes he would withdraw, and other times he would become hyperactive. In either mood it was difficult to reach him and to help him restore the balance of normal affect. During each event he was unable to participate with the group in the room or on the playground. He had been removed from a private school a week earlier for similar behavior. The public school he attends is not in his neighborhood because of the existing busing policy in his district. Consequently, the boy, in his second month of school, has to attempt to make it under adverse conditions. The child has the additional drawbacks of being from a disadvantaged community and being ethnically different from the majority of children in his class. His new school is in an affluent neighborhood.

The counselor began by using the family counseling method of asking for help from outside resource persons. She started with the mother of the boy. The boy is from a single-parent family; he has three older siblings and one younger brother. None of the other school-age children were experiencing any reported difficulties in school. The counselor visited the mother at home because the mother does not have private transportation. The counselor was welcomed into the home and experienced the impact of being out of her familiar context because of the cultural "differentness" (Principle 5). She had to learn from the mother what behavior was appropriate, and the mother displayed strengths and a depth of understanding that initially proved disarming to the counselor until she realized that her first impression of the case came out of her own culture and was inappropriate.

The happy ending did not come easily. Time was required to bridge the cultural gap. The new learning for each participant, including counselor, teacher, and student peers, came with application of Principle 1, that new context(s) supplied new meaning(s). Principle 2 was applied when the counselor came to the mother for help to gain understanding of the new situation. The action chain forged by the counselor defined the relationship with the mother as one of mutual trust, and the reciprocity of the helping relationship flourished. For the counselor, Principle 6 fits the learning she needed for new social behavior.

Application to School Counseling

Few school counselors have skills to work with families, because few school counselors have permission to enter this domain. Role statements separate home and school. Professional counselors have debated the legitimacy of whether school counselors have the right to go into the home. The real issue, however, is whether we have an obligation to help in the most effective manner available. Most school counselors deal on the periphery of family work, however, through parent conferencing and involvement with students who have home problems. These marginal approaches bring about marginal results, as the real issues are being overlooked.

By switching the focus to direct family work, permanent change can take place. Individuals learn to become more creative and more understanding, to communicate better with the world in general, and to live and work with other people. School counselors traditionally have been noneffective because they have searched for inner traits when they should have been looking for the social context.

> Man's behavior is not primarily determined by unchangeable personality traits or other essential characteristics; on the contrary, his behavior is extremely changeable as a function of the situation in which he finds himself. Change the situation and the person's behavior will change. If one wants to predict his behavior, it is more important to know the situation than the person. (Weisstein, 1970)

In dealing with the entire family, permanent direct change can occur. The community and school feel secondary gains as their social context is changed when the "new" family ripples out.

Through family counseling, some individuals are helped that could not be reached with other methods. Individuals experience dissonance as previous behaviors no longer work when contexts are modified. Many ineffectual responses are reinforced and, even though somewhat troublesome, accepted.

Methods

The counselor may choose from any or all of the following suggested interventions:

Family Education

A family education program is a formal learning experience that teaches families in a didactic setting how to live in a healthy fashion. Topics might include communication, family planning and decision making, conflict resolution, family activities and recreation, vacations, stages of family development, encouragement, sexual issues, and birth order.

Family Demonstration Model

Each week a different family volunteers to receive counseling on normal problems in front of an audience. The counselor uses this format to teach or educate all present. From any given group, an estimated 80% to 90% of the parents can make direct use of the information that the family in focus receives (Christensen, 1972; Christensen & Schramski, 1983).

Family Involvement Communication System (FICS)

The FICS model provides a human relations "umbrella" approach for parent and teacher input and participation in a school's guidance program. This system offers a variety of strategies to enhance the educational growth of children by providing information and assistance to families who are experiencing normal and problematic growth (Shelton & Dobson, 1973).

Multiple Family Group Counseling (MFGC)

MFGC is a short-term treatment in which several families are brought together in weekly group sessions. MFGC combines the advantage of group therapy and family counseling and increases the counselors' effectiveness and the size of the population they reach (Sauber, 1971).

Family Counseling

Assisting families with normal or abnormal problems is an important counselor function. Treatment involving the family unit directly affects the situation in which an individual lives rather than dealing with the "identified patient." Treating the living unit rather than the "symptom bearer" has proven effective for problems of different types and magnitudes.

Other strategies available to counselors include:

- Referral to other sources: psychologists, mental health centers, clergy.
- A community-wide family clinic where several professionals volunteer their services on a minimal or no-fee basis. Lay people, paraprofessionals, graduate students, and so on may intern under a professional's supervision.
- Family life education courses for junior and senior high school students (Dinkmeyer, McKay, Dinkmeyer, Dinkmeyer, & Carlson, 1985).
- Newsletters and other printed materials that provide information and activities to help families with normal issues such as caring, sharing, thinking positively, communicating, recreation, finances.

Checklist of Healthy Family Chains or Strengths

	Never				*Repeatedly*
1. Regular periods of relaxation, recreation, and rest are scheduled.	1	2	3	4	5
2. Positive feedback and encouragement are noted frequently.	1	2	3	4	5
3. In daily conversation, assets are mentioned more than liabilities.	1	2	3	4	5
4. Family activities are scheduled frequently and family has a lot of fun together (many common interests).	1	2	3	4	5
5. Decision making is done in a democratic fashion.	1	2	3	4	5
6. Communication among family members is accurate (including facts and feelings).	1	2	3	4	5
7. Family problems are dealt with as they come up—never staying at odds long (willing to forgive) or burying problems.	1	2	3	4	5
8. Family work responsibilities are divided fairly and equitably.	1	2	3	4	5
9. Sharing daily experience is done on a regular basis and with respect.	1	2	3	4	5
10. Rules are made cooperatively.	1	2	3	4	5
11. Personal goals and family goals are interfaced in an agreeable fashion (a sense of mission).	1	2	3	4	5
12. The family's physical needs are provided for.	1	2	3	4	5
13. The family's spiritual needs are provided for.	1	2	3	4	5
14. The family's emotional needs are provided for.	1	2	3	4	5
15. Support of family members and security are ever present—liking/loving, caring for each other, freedom of expression.	1	2	3	4	5
16. Growth-producing relationships and experiences are initiated and maintained both within and outside of the family.	1	2	3	4	5

Checklist of Healthy Family Chains or Strengths (Continued)

	Never				*Repeatedly*
17. Constructive and responsible community involvement is created and maintained.	1	2	3	4	5
18. Growth is evidenced through and with children.	1	2	3	4	5
19. The family has the ability for self-help, as well as to accept outside help when appropriate.	1	2	3	4	5
20. The family uses "injuries" and "crises" as experiences from which to grow.	1	2	3	4	5
21. Time is spent together and alone.	1	2	3	4	5
22. A good circle of friends is available.	1	2	3	4	5
23. Good humor is valued.	1	2	3	4	5
24. Family finances are understood and agreed upon.	1	2	3	4	5
25. Good food and nutrition are present.	1	2	3	4	5
26. Family traditions and celebrations are practiced.	1	2	3	4	5
27. Family members share respect for self and each other and are sensitive to each other's needs.	1	2	3	4	5
28. Family has ability to plan ahead rather than to react.	1	2	3	4	5

- Parent education to develop strong relationship and management skills (Dinkmeyer & McKay, 1989).
- Marriage enrichment (Dinkmeyer & Carlson, 1984, 1989).

Family counseling is an efficient and effective process that counselors need to utilize. A wide variety of theoretical approaches and techniques is available. Procedures focusing on strengths and encouragement are the most successful.

References

Bakker, C. B. (1975). Why people don't change. *Psychotherapy*, *12*(2), 164–172.

Bateson, G. (1972). *Steps to an ecology of mind.* New York: Ballantine.

Berenson, B. G., & Mitchell, K. M. (1974). *Confrontation for better or worse.* Amherst, MA: HRD Press.

Bertalanffy, von, L. (1968). *General system theory: Foundations, development, application.* New York: Braziller.

Carlson, J., & Faiber, B. R. (1976). Necessary skills for parenting. *Focus on Guidance, 8*(7), 1–12.

Christensen, O. C. (1972). Family education: A model for consultation. *Elementary School Guidance & Counseling, 7*(2), 121–129.

Christensen, O. C., & Schramski, T. (1983). *Adlerian family counseling.* Minneapolis: Educational Media.

Cohen, E. A. (1953). *Human behavior in the concentration camp.* New York: Grosset & Dunlap.

Dinkmeyer, D., & Carlson, J. (1984). *Training in marriage enrichment.* Circle Pines, MN: American Guidance Service.

Dinkmeyer, D., & Carlson, J. (1989). *Taking time for love: How to stay happily married.* New York: Prentice Hall.

Dinkmeyer, D., & Losoncy, L. E. (1980). *The encouragement book.* New York: Prentice Hall.

Dinkmeyer, D., & McKay, G. (1989). *Systematic training for effective parenting.* Circle Pines, MN: American Guidance Service.

Dinkmeyer, D., McKay, G., Dinkmeyer, D., Dinkmeyer, J., & Carlson, J. (1985). *PREP for effective family living.* Circle Pines, MN: American Guidance Service.

Fullmer, D. W. (1971). *Counseling: Group theory and system.* Scranton, PA: Intext.

Fullmer, D. W. (1976). *Peer counselor-consultant training manual.* Honolulu: Hawaii Department of Education.

Hall, E. T. (1976). *Beyond culture.* Garden City, NY: Anchor Press/Doubleday.

Jacobs, A., & Spradlin, W. (1974). *The group as agent of change.* New York: Behavioral Publications.

Lieberman, M. A., Yalom, I. D., & Miles, M. B. (1972). *Encounter groups: First facts.* New York: Basic Books.

Lorenz, K. (1965). *Evaluation and modification of behavior.* Chicago: University of Chicago Press.

Loukes, H. (1964). Passport to maturity. *Phi Delta Kappan, 46,* 54–57.

Milgram, S. (1965). Liberating effects of group pressure. *Journal of Personality & Social Psychology, 1,* 127–134.

Otto, H. A. (1975). *The use of family strengths concepts and methods in family life education.* Beverly Hills, CA: Holistic Press.

Papero, D. V. (1990). *Bowen family systems theory.* Boston: Allyn & Bacon.

Sauber, S. R. (1971). Multiple family group counseling. *Personnel & Guidance Journal, 49*(6), 459–465.

Shelton, J. E., & Dobson, R. L. (1973). FICS: An expanded view of counselor-consultation. *Elementary School Guidance & Counseling, 7*(3), 210–215.

Sherman, R., & Dinkmeyer, D. (1987). *Systems of family therapy: An Adlerian integration.* New York: Brunner/Mazel.

Slater, P. (1974). *Earthwalk.* New York: Bantam.

Sperry, L. (1975). *Developing skills in contact counseling: A workbook.* Reading, MA: Addison-Wesley.

Sperry, L, & Carlson, J. (1991). *Marital therapy.* Denver, CO: Love Publishing Co.

Sperry, L., Hess, L. R. (1974). *Contact counseling: A workbook.* Reading, MA: Addison-Wesley.

Tinbergen, N. (1951). *The study of instinct.* Fairlawn, NJ: Oxford University Press.

Weisstein, N. (1970). Kinder, Kuche, Kirche as scientific law: Psychology constructs in the female. In R. Morgan (Ed.), *Sisterhood is powerful.* New York: Vintage Books.

White, B. (1976). Exploring the origins of human competence. *APA Monitor, 7*(4), 4–5.

Zimbardo, P. G. (1971). *The psychological power and pathology of imprisonment.* Statement prepared for the U.S. House of Representatives Committee on the Judiciary (Subcommittee No. 3, R. Kastenmeier, Chm: Hearings on Prison Reform), October 25.

Zunin, L., & Zunin, N. (1972). *Contact: The first four minutes.* Los Angeles: Nash.

Related Readings

Ackerman, N. W. (1958). *The psychodynamics of family life: Diagnosis and treatment of family relationships.* New York: Basic Books.

Ackerman, N. W. (1966). *Treating the troubled family.* New York: Basic Books.

Ackerman, N. W. (1984). *A theory for family systems*. New York: Gardner Press.

Allred, G. H. (1974). *On the level: With self, family, and society*. Provo, UT: Brigham Young University Press.

Andreozzi, L. L. (1985). *Integrating research and clinical practice*. Rockville, MD: Aspen Systems Corp.

Andrews, E. E. (1974). *The emotionally disturbed family*. New York: Jason Aronson.

Ault-Riché, M. (1986). *Women and family therapy*. Rockville, MD: Aspen Systems Corp.

Bagarozzi, D., Jurich, A., & Jackson, R. W. (1983). *Marital and family therapy: New perspectives in theory, research, and practice*. New York: Human Sciences Press.

Baruth, L. G., & Huber, C. H. (1984). *An introduction to marital theory and therapy*. Monterey, CA: Brooks/Cole Publishing Co.

Bentovin, A., Barnes, G. G., & Cooklin, A. (1982). *Family therapy: Complementary frameworks of theory and practice* (Vols. 1 & 2). New York: Grune & Stratton.

Bjorksten, O. J. W. (1985). *New clinical concepts in marital therapy*. Washington, DC: American Psychiatric Association Press.

Block, D. A. (1973). *Techniques of family therapy: A primer*. New York: Grune & Stratton.

Bowen, M. (1971). The use of family theory in clinical practice. In J. Haley (Ed.), *Changing families*. New York: Grune & Stratton.

Breunlin, D. C. (1985). *Stages: Patterns of change over time*. Rockville, MD: Aspen Systems Corp.

Campbell, D., & Draper, R. (1985). *Application of systemic family therapy: The Milan approach*. Orlando, FL: Grune & Stratton.

Coleman, S. B. (1985). *Failures in family therapy*. New York: Guilford Press.

Curran, D. (1985). *Stress and the healthy family*. Minneapolis: Winston Press.

Dreikurs, R., Gould, S., & Corsini, R. J. (1974). *Family council*. Chicago: Henry Regenery.

Einstein, E. (1985). *The step-family: Living, loving, and learning*. Boulder, CO: Shambhala Publications.

Feldman, H., & Feldman, M. (1985). *Current controversy in marriage and family*. Beverly Hills, CA: Sage Publications.

Fishman, H. C., & Rosman, B. L. (1985). *Evolving models for family change*. New York: Guilford Press.

Foley, V. D. (1986). *An introduction to family therapy* (2nd ed.). Orlando, FL: Grune & Stratton.

Framo, J. L. (Ed.). (1972). *Family interaction: A dialogue between family researchers and family therapists*. New York: Springer.

Friesen, J. D. (1985). *Structural-strategic marital and family therapy*. New York: Gardner Press.

Fullmer, D. W., & Bernard, H. E. (1968). *Family consultation.* Boston: Houghton Mifflin.

Galvin, K. M., & Brommel, B. J. (1986). *Family communication: Cohesion and change* (2nd ed.). Glenview, Il: Scott Foresman & Co.

Geismar, L. L., & Wood, K. (1986). *Family and delinquency: Resocializing the young offender.* New York: Human Sciences Press.

Gelles, R. J., & Cornell, C. P. (1985). *Intimate violence in families*. Beverly Hills, CA: Sage Publications.

Glick, I. D., & Kessler, D. R. (1974). *Marital and family therapy*. New York: Grune & Stratton.

Goldenberg, I., & Goldenberg, H. (1985). *Family therapy: An overview* (2nd ed.). Monterey, CA: Brooks/Cole Publishing Co.

Grebe, S. C. (1985). *Divorce and family mediation*. Rockville, MD: Aspen Systems Corp.

Grunwald, B. B., & McAbee, H. V. (1985). *Guiding the family: Practical counseling techniques*. Muncie, IN: Accelerated Development.

Gullotta, T. P., Adams, G. R., & Alexander, S. J. (1986). *Today's marriages and families: A wellness approach*. Monterey, CA: Brooks/ Cole Publishing Co.

Gurman, A. S. (1985). *Casebook of marital therapy*. New York: Guilford Press.

Haley, J. (1969). *The power tactics of Jesus Christ and other essays*. New York: Avon.

Haley, J. (1971). *Changing families*. New York: Grune & Stratton.

Haley, J. (1973). *Uncommon therapy*. New York: Ballantine.

Haley, J., & Hoffman, L. (Eds.) (1967). *Techniques of family therapy*. New York: Basic Books.

Handel, G. (1985). *The psychosocial interior of the family* (3rd ed.). Hawthorne, NY: Aldine Publishing Co.

Horne, A. M., & Ohlsen, M. M. (1982). *Family counseling and therapy*. Itasca, IL: F. E. Peacock Publishers.

Howells, J. G., & Guirguis, W. R. (1985). *The family and schizophrenia*. Madison, CT: International Universities Press.

Howells, J. G., & Lickorish, J. R. (1984). *Family relations indicator.* Madison, CT: International Universities Press.

Jackson, D. D. (Ed.). (1968). *Communication, family, and marriage.* Palo Alto, CA: Science and Behavior Books.

Kantor, D., & Lehr, W. (1975). *Inside the family.* San Francisco: Jossey-Bass.

Kaufman, E. (1985). *Substance abuse and family therapy.* Orlando, FL: Grune & Stratton.

Koledzon, M. S., & Green, R. G. (1985). *Family therapy models convergence and divergence.* New York: Springer Publishing Co.

L'Abate, L., (1985). *The handbook of family psychology and therapy* (Vols. 1 & 2). Homewood, IL: Dorsey Press.

L'Abate, L., Ganahl, G., & Hansen, J. C. (1986). *Methods of family therapy.* Englewood Cliffs, NJ: Prentice Hall.

L'Abate, L., & McHenry, S. (1983). *Handbook of marital interventions.* New York: Grune & Stratton.

Laing, R. D., (1969). *The politics of the family and other essays.* New York: Pantheon.

Laing, R., & Esterson, A. (1964). *Sanity, madness, and the family.* Baltimore: Penguin.

Lansky, M. R. (1981). *Family therapy and major psychopathology.* New York: Grune & Stratton.

Lansky, M. R. (1985). *Family approaches to major psychiatric disorders.* Washington, DC: American Psychiatric Press.

Levant, R. F. (1936). *Psychoeducational approaches to family therapy and counseling.* New York: Springer Publishing Co.

Luthman, S. G., & Kirschenbaum, M. (1974). *The dynamic family.* Palo Alto, CA: Science & Behavior Books.

McGoldrick, M., Pearce, J. K., & Giordano, J. (1982). *Ethnicity and family therapy.* New York: Guilford Press.

Miller, S., Nunnally, E. W., & Wackman, D. B. (1975). *Alive and aware: Improving communications in relationships.* Minneapolis: Interpersonal Communication Programs.

Minuchin, S. (1974). *Families and family therapy.* Cambridge, MA: Harvard University Press.

Moynihan, D. P. (1986). *Family and nation: The Godkin lectures, Harvard University.* Orlando, FL: Harcourt Brace Jovanovich.

Nerin, W. F. (1986). *Family reconstruction: A long day's journey into light.* New York: W.W. Norton & Co.

Newberger, E. H., & Bourne, R. (1985). *Unhappy families*. Littleton, MA: PSG Publishing Co.

Otto, H. A. (1975). *The use of family strengths concepts and methods in family life education*. Beverly Hills, CA: Holistic Press.

Papp, P. (1983). *The process of change*. New York: Guilford Press.

Patterson, G. R. (1975). *Families: Applications of social learning to family life*. Champaign, IL: Research Press.

Patterson, G. R., Reid, J. B., Jones, R. R., & Conger, R. E. (1975). *A social learning approach to family intervention*. Eugene, OR: Castalia.

Peseschkian, N. (1986). *Positive family therapy: The family as therapy*. New York: Springer-Verlag New York, Inc.

Richman, J. (1985). *Family therapy with suicidal people*. New York: Springer Publishing Co.

Roy, R. (1985). *The family and chronic pain*. New York: Human Sciences Press.

Sager, C. J., & Kaplan, H. S. (Eds.). (1972). *Progress in group and family therapy*. New York: Brunner/Mazel.

Satir, V. (1967). *Conjoint family therapy* (rev. ed.). Palo Alto, CA: Science & Behavior Books.

Satir, V. (1972). *Peoplemaking*. Palo Alto, CA: Science & Behavior Books.

Sauber, S. R., L'Abate, L., & Weeks, G. R. (1985). *Family therapy: Basic concepts and terms*. Rockville, MD: Aspen Systems Corp.

Sherman, R., & Fredman, N. (1986). *Handbook of structured techniques in family therapy*. New York: Brunner/Mazel.

Speck, R., & Atteneave, C. (1973). *Family networks*. New York: Pantheon.

Springer, J. R., & Woody, R. H. (1985). *Healthy promotion in family therapy*. Rockville, MD: Aspen Systems Corp.

Turk, D. C., & Kerns, R. D. (1985). *Health, illness, and family: A life span perspective*. New York: Wiley-Interscience.

Umbarber, C. C. (1983). *Structural family therapy*. New York: Grune & Stratton.

Wahllroos, S. (1974). *Family communication*. New York: Macmillan.

Will, D., & Wrate, R. M. (1986). *Integrated family therapy*. New York: Methuen.

Ziffer, R. L. (1985). *Adjunctive techniques in family therapy*. Orlando, FL: Grune & Stratton.

This article was originally published in *Family Counseling*, 1991, pp. 57–78. Reprint permission granted by Love Publishing.

Chapter 2

Marriage and Family Counseling Theories

Theory becomes relevant after addressing the notion of direction in family counseling, i.e., healthy family functioning. In its most basic form, theory is a set of interrelated ideas that describe and explain a phenomenon. Theory in most disciplines is viewed as providing a set of guidelines and serving as the basis for hunches and hypotheses. Within the behavioral sciences, theory is often developed through inductive methods. Under such procedures, data are gathered from observations. When adequate samples are obtained, hypotheses are developed which lead to theory. A number of family therapists representing a variety of disciplines have relied upon their experiences with families as the basis of theory. After trying a number of methods, often linear in approach, professionals began to work with couples and families using more systemic methods. As techniques evolved and new interventions were tried, theories were developed and subsequently shared with others in marriage and family counseling/therapy.

The authors provide a synopsis of the traditional theories in marriage and family therapy. It is our belief that basic theories in this field have much in common. Fundamentally, they all focus on the family system with differences resulting from what the therapist punctuates during therapy. Five of the "established" theories in marriage and family therapy are reviewed. Structural, strategic, transgenerational, experiential, and behavioral approaches are examined. Each theory is reviewed in relation to its view of healthy family systems, basic beliefs or concepts held, and theoretical goals. The authors stress the importance of integrating theory with one's own belief system and personality. Emphasis is placed on avoiding a haphazard selection of one particular theoretical model or attempting to mirror a master therapist associated with a set theory.

Marian Stoltz-Loike reviews approaches used in working with couples and families by beginning with an overview of family systems theory. Included within this section is a discussion of feminist family therapy followed by a review of psychotherapeutic techniques a la Ackerman, Minuchin, Papp, Haley, Satir, and Rice. The author provides an interesting focus on working with couples, particularly dual career couples.

In one of his classic writings, *The Integration of Marital Therapy with Sessions with Family of Origin*, James Framo discusses a number of issues germane to family therapy and the training of family therapists. As related to theory, Framo summarizes the main tenets of transgenerational family therapy. Further in-depth analysis by Framo involves: examining healthy or well-functioning marriages or families, conceptualizing pathology or dysfunctional systems, assessment in therapy, goal setting, structure, treatment, and techniques. In this landmark article, Framo closes with his views on training marriage and family therapists.

As his title indicates, Dinkmeyer presents key concepts associated with Adlerian family therapy. The basic tenets are well presented in a clear, succinct manner. A review of brief family therapy closes out this section. The brief model described by Todd as "the therapy of the 90s" presents challenges and opportunities for the field. The basics of the brief model are thoroughly presented while addressing some of the myths related to brief family therapy.

Marital and Family Therapy: Direction, Theory, and Practice

Robert L. Smith

Life is not a matter of holding good cards, but of playing a poor hand well.

—Robert Louis Stevenson

A comprehensive critique of the marital and family therapy (MFT) profession could fill volumes and still be considered incomplete. Sourcebooks, manuals, casebooks, and texts that are widely available cover many of the topics included here. Some of these have been authored by Becvar and Becvar (1988), Brown and Christensen (1986), Carter and McGoldrick (1989), Fenell and Weinhold (1989), Goldenberg and Goldenberg (1985), Gurman (1985), Nichols (1984), Piercy and Sprenkle (1986), and Sperry and Carlson (1991). Because marriage and family therapy is a dynamic field, harnessing all MFT vicissitudes in a single piece of writing is not possible. Therefore, I omit certain MFT topics, exclude some theories, and fail to address many of the issues. This overview, however, does address:

- The direction of marital and family therapy—a review of healthy family functioning.
- Major theories in marital and family therapy.
- Techniques most often applied during the practice of marital and family therapy.

If marital and family therapy is directed toward understanding, creating, and developing "healthy" or "healthier" marriages and families, clearer and more comprehensive road maps are needed. A limited body of research leads to speculation about healthy family functioning.

Currently, a number of well-developed hypotheses have been proposed concerning family functioning. Many theories in marital and family therapy are not truly scientific if they are critiqued according to inductive or deductive methods of theory development. Yet, existing theories are acknowledged as quite useful, both in the training of therapists and for practitioners. Theoretical approaches discussed here are: structural, strategic, transgenerational, experiential, and behavioral.

An exaggeration of the presenting problem or family system often surfaces when attempting to describe how theoretical hypotheses relate to practice. This occurs when emphasizing the application of key theoretical constructs to day-to-day work with families. Several texts have used this approach (Becvar & Becvar, 1988; Brown & Christensen, 1986; Goldenberg & Goldenberg, 1985). Rather than following the case approach, I have chosen to identify those techniques often used during the practice of marital and family therapy. This allows the reader to adapt techniques according to presenting family cases.

Direction: Healthy Family Functioning

Carter (1986) states that it is essential for each of us to wrestle with several questions related to family therapy. At the top of her list is: "What is the purpose of family therapy?" Assume that the purpose of the marital and family therapy profession is to understand and strive toward healthy family functioning. This assumption, then, recognizes the existence of "dysfunctional" families. Societal problems support our second assumption. Dysfunctional behavior, divorce rates, murder, drug abuse, incest, and crime support the notion of dysfunction. The family literature discusses pathogenic family systems generationally trapped in a status quo. Enmeshment, scapegoating, disengagement, and violence exemplify dysfunctional family systems. Families are seen as maintaining themselves in an "unhealthy" manner, perpetuating problems from generation to generation.

For change in the family system to take place, the therapist and the family alike need direction, as well as examples and models from which to work. This sort of empirical evidence can help direct one as to what eventual change would be like or what would be a "healthy functioning family." This information provides family therapists with notions, hypotheses, and direction.

I contend that the above fundamental question as to what is healthy family functioning has not been adequately addressed. Furthermore, identification of healthy family functioning possibly is so fugitive in nature that health can be described only from the point of view of cultural consensus without reference to the logic or cohesion of the family. Yet, Beavers (1982), Fisher, Giblin, and Hoopes (1982), Fisher and Sprenkle (1978), Kantor and Lehr (1975), Olson, Sprenkle, and Russell (1979), and Reiss (1981) have provided hunches as to characteristics of "healthy" family functioning.

Kantor and Lehr (1975) make reference to healthy versus dysfunctional family systems. They identified three family types. The first, "open" type, is viewed as healthy and is characterized by flexible rules and boundary arrangements. The family is democratic and makes honest exchanges with outside individuals and groups. The second type of family, a "closed" system, is "traditional," emphasizing family loyalty with minimum contact with outside systems. Rigidity exists in this family and creates dysfunctional systems. The third type, a "random" system, is a fragmented operational family. This system often becomes chaotic and dysfunctional because it has few rules and family policies. According to the Kantor and Lehr model, healthy family functioning exists in families that have clear rules, set boundaries, are flexible, and interact freely with outside systems.

Olson, Sprenkle, and Russell (1979) and others see cohesion and adaptability as major factors governing healthy family functioning. *Cohesion* is viewed as the emotional bonding of family members with one another and the degree of individual autonomy they experience in the family system. *Adaptability* refers to the capability of a family system to change its power structure, rules, and role relationships in response to situational and developmental stressors. Healthy families, according to this model, exhibit a balance between these two dimensions. Healthy families are not enmeshed in each other's lives—not overly cohesive. Healthy families have the proper amount of adaptability—not overly adaptable and in flux or too rigid to prevent growth and change. More specifically, the healthy family has a *balance* as related to the following 10 specific aspects of cohesion (Olson et al., 1979):

1. Emotional attraction.
2. Differentiation.
3. Mature dependency.
4. Supportiveness.
5. Loyalty.
6. Psychological safety.
7. Reliability.
8. Family identification.
9. Physical caretaking.
10. Pleasurable interaction.

The healthy family is adaptable. It demonstrates a balanced flexibility, shared leadership, appropriate assertiveness, negotiation among members, appropriate rules, open feedback systems, and clear but interacting roles.

Healthy families (Reiss, 1981) are "environment-sensitive," because they believe the world is knowable and orderly. Healthy families expect each member to contribute to its understanding and mastery. Healthy family members are able to accept help and advice from others, are flexible, work together to overcome adversity, and examine alternative solutions.

Through extensive study, Beavers (1982) identified healthy families in relation to negotiation and transaction patterns. Research by Beavers identified healthy families as having a parental coalition that sets a level of functioning for the family. Healthy family members communicate their thoughts and feelings. In healthy families, members welcome contact with each other and expect transactions to be caring, open, and trusting. In healthy families, members respect personal autonomy. Families express humor, tenderness, warmth, and hopefulness. Beavers sees healthy families as having the capacity for seeking intimacy.

Less healthy families seek control, concern themselves with power struggles, and tend to use intimidation. In fact, the following dimensions (Lewis, Beavers, Gossett, & Phillips, 1976) characterize healthy versus dysfunctional families: (1) a caring affiliative attitude versus an oppositional approach to human encounters, (2) high levels of initiative versus passivity, (3) high levels of reciprocity, cooperation, and negotiation, (4) high levels of personal autonomy, (5) openness in the expression of affect, a prevailing mood of warmth affection, and caring, and (6) high degrees of spontaneity and humor (Fisher, Giblin, & Hoopes, 1982). In addition, communication is valued in healthy families. General skills of healthy family functioning as related to communication include: *spontaneity, feedback, metacommunication,* and *encouragement.*

When discussing healthy families, Becvar and Becvar (1988) define health as the family's success in functioning to achieve its own goals. They have observed the following dimensions as characteristic of healthy families:

1. A legitimate source of authority, established and supported over time.
2. A stable rule system established and consistently acted upon.
3. Stable and consistent nurturing behavior.

4. Effective and stable child-rearing and marriage-maintenance practices.
5. A set of goals toward which the family and each individual works.
6. Sufficient flexibility and adaptability to accommodate normal developmental challenges as well as unexpected crises.

The literature discussing healthy family functioning is interesting and even convincing. Yet, the statements and ideas about healthy family functioning are not supported by scientific rigor or empirical investigation. A concise summary of ideas regarding healthy versus unhealthy family functioning characteristics, as provided in the literature, is presented in Table 2.1.

Statements by family therapists and writers about healthy families are mostly hypothetical and abstract. I believe, in concurrence with Textor (1989), that empirical studies by psychologists, sociologists, social workers, and others about "healthy" families are sorely lacking. One explanation is that because family therapists rarely work with "healthy" families, the emphasis is less on a "health" concept and more on pathology. This phenomenon is somewhat akin to individual psychotherapy's utilization of the DSM-III-R and other schemes identifying mental health disorders. Yet, despite the lack of an empirically supported direction pertaining to family therapy when viewed from the "healthy family functioning perspective," a fairly comprehensive set of theories has been advocated in an effort to change family systems. The current major theoretical approaches are described next.

Major Theoretical Approaches of Family Therapy

Family therapists view the family in terms of interactions and relationships. Theories about family therapy have much in common, with the most fundamental being the *focus on the system*. Differences, in large part, are determined by what the therapist punctuates when working with the family. Most of today's theories of family therapy can be viewed as speculations or unsubstantiated hypotheses providing information about family functioning (Goldenberg & Goldenberg, 1985). Yet, these theoretical constructs often generate additional hypotheses leading to the implementation of intervention strategies.

Table 2.1
Healthy and Dysfunctional Family Characteristics: A Review of the Literature

Healthy Families are Characterized as:	Dysfunctional Families are Characterized as:	Literature Source
Flexible	Rigid	Kantor & Lehr, 1975
Possessing clear rules, family policies, clear boundaries	Chaotic and unruly	Kantor & Lehr, 1975
Having a balanced cohesion	Enmeshed	Olson, Sprenkle, & Russell, 1979
Possessing a balanced adaptability	In flux	Olson et al., 1979
Having individual autonomy	Overly bonded	Olson et al., 1979
Having appropriate assertiveness	Rigid or dogmatic	Olson et al., 1979
Using negotiation	Experiencing power struggles	Olson et al., 1979
Having appropriate rules	Chaotic or dogmatic	Olson et al., 1979
Working together	Disengaged	Reiss, 1981
Environment-sensitive	Rigid/closed	Reiss, 1981
Possessing a parental coalition	Dysfunctional at the top	Beavers, 1977
Communicating thoughts and feelings	Lacking in communication	Beavers, 1977
An expectancy of caring and trusting, with open contact by members and the family system	Distrusting, expecting the worst, oppositional	Beavers, 1977
Possessing humor, tenderness, warmth	Humorless, cold, lacking in feeling	Beavers, 1977
Having the capacity for intimacy	Lacking intimacy and seeking caring; controlling and power seeking	Beavers, 1977
Expressing spontaneity and encouragement	Lacking in spontaneity; using intimidation	Beavers, 1977 Fisher et al., 1982
Having a legitimate source of authority	Chaotic	Becvar & Becvar, 1988
Having a stable rule system	Random/chaotic	Becvar & Becvar, 1988
Nurturing	Cold	Becvar & Becvar, 1988
Using consistency in child rearing	Inconsistent	Becvar & Becvar, 1988
Having family and individual goals	Random/chaotic	Becvar & Becvar, 1988
Flexible and adaptable	Rigid/dogmatic	Becvar & Becvar, 1988

Each theory has its own master or identified masters demonstrating their work. What works or does not work seldom if ever differentiates the theory from the therapist's personality, relationship-building skills, or professional status. Although much can be learned from the master demonstrations, I agree with Corsini (1984) in that the best theory and methodology have to be of one's own making.

The five major theories summarized here are believed to exemplify the "established" state of theory in family therapy. Additional theoretical principles, hypotheses, and hunches for working with families are evident in the literature, but to a lesser extent than structural, strategic, transgenerational, experiential, and behavioral approaches. The focus on "what is considered healthy" by each theory precedes key constructs and goals.

Structural Family Therapy

Healthy family systems. In structural family therapy the family's health is directly related to the configuration and operational structure of the family system (Becvar & Becvar, 1988). The healthy family builds on the spouse subsystem. Through this arrangement partners accommodate and support each other's uniqueness. A measure of autonomy is maintained while complementary roles are negotiated. The traditional family of two parents living together with children is not necessarily viewed as the ideal family or today's norm. In the healthy family the parental system provides the grounding, security, and support for the sibling subsystems. Healthy families have executive systems that are differentiated from their families of origin. Subsystems operate in the family system with adaptability, reciprocity, and accommodation.

In healthy families a mother-daughter or father-son subsystem does not interfere with, or disrupt, other family relationships and subsystems. Harmony with the family is stressed, producing a natural evolvement of a multitude of structural arrangements.

Basic concepts. Several basic concepts underlie the structural approach to family therapy. One of the most important of these involves subsystems. The family system can contain several subsystems. The *marital subsystem* is the first to form, and it provides the basis of the family system (Becvar & Becvar, 1988; Brown & Christensen, 1986). Mutual satisfaction of the couple's needs, autonomy, and accommodation are important. Often referred to as the "spouse subsystem," this subsystem is formed at marriage. Autonomy is more readily established in this subsystem when enmeshment with respective families of origin is absent and when roles and rules are negotiated. Complementarity is emphasized. Accommodation—allowing each partner to develop his or her talents and skills while keeping one's own individuality—is considered important.

The *parental subsystem,* often (but not necessarily) consists of the same two people that comprise the marital subsystem. The parental or executive subsystem, the second subsystem described in structural family therapy, could include a single parent and a friend, extended family members, or members of the community. The parental subsystem centers on child-rearing issues.

The parental subsystem's method of interacting with siblings is expected to change based upon the age and developmental stage of children. Although accommodation and negotiation are factors that play out during childrearing, the children in the family need to understand and see that parents are not peers. Parents are in charge. The family is not a democracy.

Structural Family Therapy

- Systems
- Subsystems
    - Marital
    - Parental
    - Sibling
- Boundaries
    - Permeability
    - Disengaged Families
    - Enmeshment
- Coalitions
- Accommodations
- Tracking
- Mimesis

In structural family therapy the *sibling subsystem* provides children with their first experiences in relating with peers. Negotiation, accommodation, working out differences, and learning about mutual respect is looked for within the sibling subsystem. An important part of the sibling subsystem is its relationships with the parental subsystem. This negotiation process of working out problems becomes a focal point in structural family therapy. The relationships within and between subsystems define the structure of the family.

Boundaries—their presence, absence, use of, and changeability—are significant in structural family therapy. Boundaries are the interactional rules of who participates. They guide, tell, and determine what is said, when, by whom, and under what conditions. Each subsystem has its own rules and identity. The rules of the total family system, spoken or unspoken, combine to form the family system's boundary. Boundary difficulties can create barriers to healthy family functioning and can produce several dysfunctional patterns leading to the impediment of individual growth, allowing family members to take inappropriate roles in the family system, creating enmeshment, disengagement, or triangulation (triangulation is discussed under basic concepts of transgenerational family therapy).

The boundaries can be clear, rigid, or diffuse. *Clear boundaries* in a system are considered ideal. They are characterized as firm, flexible, nurturing, and supportive. Access across subsystems is present, including systems outside of the family that may, over time, change the roles and rules within the family system itself.

Rigid boundaries are impermeable, creating extremely autonomous individuals with little interaction. Minuchin (1974a) describes this as a "disengaged family" system. Families with rigid boundaries experience less communication across family subsystems, are less nurturing, and are least likely to change. With little access or permeability across family subsystems, adjustment and change are difficult. According to Minuchin, members of families with rigid boundaries rely on outside systems for support and nurturance.

Diffuse boundaries characterize *enmeshed* relationships. As contrasted with a family having rigid boundaries, members of this type of family are involved in everyone else's business. For example, an enmeshed family may allow children to consistently permeate and interfere with the spouse, or marital subsystem.

Goals of structural family therapy. The goals of structural family therapy relate to the status and characteristics of the family system. General goals include:

1. Movement toward and eventual presence of a parental subsystem with parental/executive authority. This is a coalition of support and accommodation.

2. A sibling subsystem characterized by a system of peers.
3. Independent activity fostering differentiation, if enmeshment is present.
4. Flexible and clear boundaries, if disengagement is present.
5. Establishment of the spouse subsystem as a distinct entity.

In structural family therapy the therapist works to change transactional patterns and realign the family structure. The process structural family therapists use to create change involves *joining* with the family (often called *accommodation*), *mimesis* (adopting the family's style and pace), and *tracking* the family's communication pattern.

In summary, the structural family therapist: (a) focuses on the family structure and subsystems, (b) identifies patterns, rules, and boundaries operating in the system, (c) hypothesizes structural changes desirable within the family system, (d) joins with the family by respecting the current family structure, (e) intervenes in the family in a direct manner, and (f) works with the family successes through praise and support (Becvar & Becvar, 1988).

Strategic Family Therapy

Healthy family systems. The concepts of *health, normal, abnormal,* and *dysfunction* are terms that strategic family therapists do not deal with lightly. They see families as operating logically or functionally rather than as "normal or abnormal." Yet, several of the cited masters of strategic family therapy indicate a direction toward health. For example, Haley (1976) sees the importance of a family hierarchical system and Selvini-Palazzoli, Boscolo, Cecehin, and Prata (1978) view healthy families as having fewer alliances. Other strategic family therapists see the importance of clear family rules and flexibility within the family.

Basic concepts. Jay Haley (1973) defines strategic family therapy as being initiated by the clinician and designed according to the presenting problem. Goal setting takes place in accordance with the presenting problem. Assessment of the family system occurs by listening and looking for sequential patterns of behavior. Therapists ask themselves, for example, "What behaviors trigger a sequence of events?" The therapist often asks directly, "What is it that has to be worked on?" Emphasis is placed on measurable goals. The strategic therapist takes the final responsibility for selecting the goals.

The strategic approaches evolved from communication theory and general system theory. Strategic therapy also is known by other descriptions. Major constructs of focus for the strategic family therapist are symptoms, metaphors, hierarchy, and power.

Strategic therapists focus less on insight and more on *symptoms* that are seen as a way of maintaining a homeostatic balance in the family system. Symptoms provide a means by which family members communicate. The family uses symptoms when members are stuck. The symptom is seen as providing the family member with a way out or a means of functioning in the system. Strategic family therapists often view symptoms as *metaphors* (Haley, 1976; Madanes, 1981). The symptom might be used to avoid conflict, redirect attention from other issues, keep people away, manipulate, and so on.

In strategic family therapy the family system hierarchical structure is examined. Questions as to the existing hierarchy, maintenance of the system, and how symptoms, coalitions, communication patterns and generational interfaces can affect the hierarchy are reviewed.

Strategic therapists (e.g., Haley, 1976) see the importance of *power* in all relationships. In the family system the strategic therapist attempts to reestablish a hierarchy, with the parents being restored to a position superior to the children. Rules and consequences are stressed in the restoration of power.

Strategic Family Therapy

Symptoms
Metaphors
Hierarchy
Power
Intervention
Paradoxical Directives
Positive Labeling
Mental Research Institute
Brief Family Center
Milan Center for Family Studies

Goals of strategic family therapy. Strategic family therapists emphasize clear goal statements. They consider observed behavior important. They often use intermediate goals. They apply strategies based upon goal statements. They give tasks or directives to the family to solve presenting issues and reach goal statements. The tasks can be straightforward or paradoxical. A number of adaptations of the strategic approach to family therapy have evolved, including work from the Mental Research Institute Brief Therapy Center (Palo Alto, California) and the Milan Center for Family Studies (Milan, Italy).

Transgenerational Family Therapy

Transgenerational family has its roots in psychodynamic and systems theory. Transgenerational therapies, or extended family therapies, see the past as being active in the present.

Healthy family systems. According to Bowen (1978), the partners in healthy marriages are capable of emotional intimacy without loss of autonomy. Family members experience differentiation as related to their families of origin. Healthy family and individual functioning is seen on a continuous scale. High levels of differentiation are generally tied to healthy functioning. Yet, based upon circumstances and stress conditions, symptoms of "abnormality" may exist from time to time. Bowen focuses on optimal functioning levels. Optimal-functioning individuals are inner-directed, establish personal goals, are rational and objective, and operate as their own persons.

Boszormenyi-Nagy and Ulrich (1981) describe healthy families as those that transmit a legacy of fairness and responsibility. In the healthy family, members are not deprived, nor are they overindulged. In healthy families, open and honest communication serves as a method of what Boszormenyi-Nagy calls "balancing a ledger."

Basic concepts. The major construct of transgenerational family therapy is that *the past is active in the present*. Understanding the past is therefore basic to transgenerational family therapy. Object relations theory provide some clues to the past. Fairbairn (1954) and Dicks (1967) both saw how object relations theory and past internalized functioning affects present behavior. Fairbairn saw individuals unconsciously attempting to influence or change intimate relationships according to internalized ideals. Dicks focused on marital complementarity and saw each partner seeking from the other what was missing in past relationships. Framo (1981) further saw people attempting to use current relationships to heal conflicts in one's own family of origin.

Family loyalty is another major construct of transgenerational family therapy. Family loyalty is examined in terms of unhealed wounds, generational legacies, and expectations. Transgenerational family therapists look at how family loyalties play a role in one's current functioning.

Bowen has made major contributions to transgenerational family therapy. His view of the nuclear family living within a family emotional system affected by extended family—living and dead—has provided tremendous insight into family functioning.

A key concept related to this theoretical foundational construct is that of *differentiation of self*. This includes differentiation of self from others in the family's emotional web, as well as the ability to differentiate one's feeling process from the intellectual process. According to Bowen, the differentiated person feels but is able to maintain objectivity.

Triangulation takes place, according to Bowen, when stress is introduced to the dyadic system. Under extreme stress, one of the marital partners, often the one most undifferentiated, seeks a third-party ally. This could be a friend, family member, work, and so forth. Bowen sees this effort to create a solution as being more likely a method of preventing a resolution.

Bowen further refers to the term *family projection process* when discussing how a child's level of differentiation approximates that of the parents. A key element in the family projection process is the extent to which parents project their own emotional conflicts onto children and thus create triangles within the family system.

Transgenerational Family Therapy

- Object Relations
- Family Loyalty
- Differentiation
- Triangulation
- Family Projection Process
- Family of Origin
- Genograms

Goals of transgenerational family therapy. According to transgenerational family therapy, intergenerational issues create problems for the nuclear family. The major goal is to change intergenerational interference operating with the current family. Detriangulation is often a necessary intermediate goal.

Experiential Family Therapy

Healthy family systems. According to experiential family therapy, healthy family systems are open and flexible. Healthy family systems have the capacity for individual growth and change, as well as change in the system itself. Even under stress (Whitaker & Keith, 1981) healthy families tend to grow. Family members in these systems are free to play and experience different roles (Kempler, 1973; Satir, 1972). Healthy family systems, according to experiential family therapy, are "open systems," allowing individuals the freedom to move in and out of the family system.

Basic concepts. The focus of experiential family therapy is on the here and now. Borrowing from a number of schools of thought including Perls (1969) (Gestalt), and Rogers (1961) (client-centered), experiential family therapists emphasize the construct of individuality, personal freedom, and self-fulfillment. Experiential family therapy does not rely on therapy but, rather, on the therapist's capacity to be involved with the family. Theory is seen as getting in the way of therapy.

Experiential family therapists promote self-expression and negotiation. They encourage family members to find self-fulfilling roles (Kempler, 1981). Because experiential family therapy is largely atheoretical, specific approaches tend to rely on the therapist's spontaneity (Whitaker, 1976).

Experiential Family Therapy

- Atheoretical
- Individuality
- Freedom of Choice
- Personal Growth
- Co-Therapists
- Paradoxical Intention
- Family Sculpting

Whitaker views therapy as having three phases: *engagement, involvement,* and *disentanglement.* During this process the therapist becomes a part of and then separates from the family. Experiential family therapists challenge the family by redefining the symptom, using paradox, and suggesting fantasy. In addition, they frequently utilize psychodrama and sculpting.

Goals of experiential family therapy. *Growth* is the goal of experiential family therapy. This does not necessarily mean the reduction of symptoms. Whitaker and Keith (1981) add *creativity* as a major goal of experiential family therapy. Under the general goal of growth, experiential family therapists strive for individuality, personal freedom, independence, and self-fulfillment.

Behavioral Family Therapy

Healthy family functioning. From a behavioral approach viewpoint, effective communication and problem-solving skills can be taught within the family structure (Patterson, 1971). A good, healthy relationship has a greater frequency of pleasant behavior than unpleasant behavior. Viewed from another perspective, good relationships involve a positive reward system. A healthy family system rewards positive, functional behavior and extinguishes or changes dysfunctional behavior.

Basic concepts. The basic concepts of behavioral family therapy were founded upon the principles of behavior modification. *Reinforcement,* positive and negative, is a key construct. Positive reinforcement within the family structure is examined, and often taught and encouraged. Negative reinforcement also is observed with the intention of identifying those reinforcers and modifying or eliminating them when necessary.

Shaping or the process of *successive approximation* is used to change behavior. Through this process, parts of a total behavior pattern are separated out to eventually reach a more complex set of behaviors (Bandura, 1974). Before making systematic interventions, *baselines* are recorded to determine the use of inappropriate behavior.

Social learning theory principles and constructs, such as modeling, time-out, and extinction are implemented. Behavior family therapists often work with family subsystems. For example, they may work with the marital subsystem to make the marriage better or with the parental subsystem to increase effective parenting skills.

Behavioral Family Therapy
Reinforcement
Shaping
Successive Approximation
Baselines
Social Learning Theory

Goals of behavioral family therapy. The goals of behavioral therapy are decided by the client. The therapist, in turn, decides on the appropriate interventions. General goals of behavioral family therapy are to eliminate undesirable behavior and substitute desirable behavior. Assisting family members in clarifying goals is an intermediate goal of behavioral therapy. Specific outcome behaviors are identified to determine when goals are met.

The Practice of Family Therapy: Techniques

What takes place during the practice of marital and family therapy is often different from what one might expect as related to theory. Structural, strategic, and transgenerational family therapists at times may seem to be operating alike, using similar interventions with a family. Differences might become clear when the therapist explains a certain technique or intervention. Most of today's practicing family therapists go far beyond the limited number of techniques usually associated with a single theory. The following techniques are those that practicing clinicians most often use. The when, where, and how of each intervention always rests with the therapist's professional judgment and personal skills.

The Genogram

The genogram, a technique often used early in family therapy, provides a graphic picture of the family history. The genogram reveals the family's basic structure, demographics, functioning, and relationships (McGoldrick & Gerson, 1985). Through symbols, it offers a picture of three generations. Names, dates of marriage, divorce, death, and other relevant facts are included in the genogram. It provides an enormous amount of data and insight for the therapist and family members early in therapy. As an informational and diagnostic tool, the genogram is developed by the therapist in conjunction with the family.

The Family Floor Plan

The family floor plan technique has several variations. Parents might be asked to draw the family floor plan for their family of origin. Information across generations is therefore gathered in a nonthreatening manner. Points of discussion bring out meaningful issues related to one's past.

Another adaptation of this technique is to have members draw the floor plan for their nuclear family. The importance of space and territory is often inferred as a result of the family floor plan. Levels of comfort between family members, space accommodations, and rules are often revealed. Indications of differentiation, operating family triangles, and subsystems often become evident. Used early in therapy, this technique can serve as an excellent diagnostic tool (Coppersmith, 1980).

Reframing

Most family therapists use reframing as a method to both join with the family and offer a different perspective on presenting problems. Specifically, reframing involves taking something out of its logical class and placing it in another category (Sherman & Fredman, 1986). For example, a mother's repeated questioning of her daughter's behavior after a date can be seen as genuine caring and concern rather than that of a nontrusting parent. Through reframing, a negative often can be reframed into a positive.

Tracking

Most family therapists use tracking. Structural family therapists (Minuchin & Fishman, 1981) see tracking as an essential part of the therapist's joining process with the family. During the tracking process the therapist listens intently to family stories and carefully records events and their sequence. Through tracking, the family therapist is able to identify the sequence of events operating in a system to keep it the way it is. What happens between point A and point B or C to create D can be helpful when designing interventions.

Communication Skill-Building Techniques

Communication patterns and processes are often major factors in preventing healthy family functioning. Faulty communication methods and systems are readily observed within one or two family sessions. A variety of techniques can be implemented to focus directly on communication skill building between a couple or between family members. Listening techniques including restatement of content, reflection of feelings, taking turns expressing feelings, and nonjudgmental brainstorming are some of the methods utilized in communication skill building.

In some instances the therapist may attempt to teach a couple how to fight fair, to listen, or may instruct other family members in how to express themselves with adults. The family therapist constantly looks for faulty communication patterns that can disrupt the system.

Family Sculpting

Developed by Duhl, Kantor, and Duhl (1973), family sculpting provides for re-creation of the family system, representing relationships to one another at a specific period of time. The family therapist can use sculpting at any time in therapy by asking family members to physically arrange the family. Adolescents often make good family sculptors as they are provided with a chance to nonverbally communicate thoughts and feelings about the family. Family sculpting is a sound diagnostic tool and provides the opportunity for future therapeutic interventions.

Family Photos

The family photos technique has the potential to provide a wealth of information about past and present functioning. One use of family photos is to go though the family album together. Verbal and nonverbal responses to pictures and events are often quite revealing. Adaptations of this method include asking members to bring in significant family photos and discuss reasons for bringing them, and locating pictures that represent past generations. Through discussion of photos, the therapist often more clearly sees family relationships, rituals, structure, roles, and communication patterns.

Individual and Team Feedback via Telephone

Strategic family therapists often are credited for their creative use of teams and the telephone as an intervention method. From behind a one-way mirror, an individual supervisor or supervision team can call the therapist regarding notions about therapy. The team can help the therapist join with the family in cases in which the therapist does not agree with a team member's assessment. Individual supervisors or team members also can use the telephone to call a specific family member during therapy.

Special Days, Mini-Vacations, Special Outings

Couples and families that are stuck frequently exhibit predictable behavior cycles. Boredom is present, and family members take little time with each other. In such cases, family members feel unappreciated and taken for granted. Caring days can be set aside when couples are asked to show caring for each other, or at least act in a caring manner. Specific times for caring can be arranged with certain actions in mind (Stuart, 1980). Adaptations of this technique include fantasizing a mini-vacation together or planning a special outing. Interesting insights can be obtained during the planning process.

Gift Giving

Similar to the previously described techniques, gift giving can serve as a method of recognizing a spouse or a family member. The gift might be a verbal statement to a family member or a tangible gift of some nature. True feelings of a helping nature are allowed to be expressed. How the gift is presented (e.g., verbal context, caring, supportive) as well as how it is received (e.g., positive, defensive) can provide valuable insights.

Contracting

Traditionally considered a technique of behavioral therapy, therapists from a variety of theoretical backgrounds now frequently use contracting. Contracting with a couple requires specificity in regard to time and place. Contracts can be verbal or written. The contract should be measurable, detailed, and of recognized importance to family members involved.

The Empty Chair

The empty chair technique, most often utilized by Gestalt therapists (see Perls, Hefferline, & Goodman, 1951), has been adapted to family therapy. In one scenario, a partner may express his or her feelings to a spouse (empty chair), then play the role of the spouse and carry on a dialogue. Expressions to absent family members, parents, and children can be arranged through utilizing this technique.

Family Choreography

In family choreography, arrangements go beyond initial sculpting; family members are asked to position themselves as to how they see the family and then to show how they would like the family situation to be. Family members may be asked to reenact a certain family scene and possibly resculpt it to a preferred scenario. This technique can help a stuck family and create a more lively situation.

Family Council Meetings

Family council meetings are organized to provide specific times for the family to meet and share with one another. The therapist might prescribe council meetings as homework, in which case a time is set and rules are outlined. The council should encompass the entire family, and any absent members would have to abide by decisions. The agenda may include any concerns of the family. Attacking others during this time is not acceptable. Family council meetings help provide structure for the family, encourage full family participation, and facilitate communication.

Strategic Alliances

This technique, often used by strategic family therapists, involves meeting with one member of the family as a supportive means of helping that person change. Individual change is expected to affect the entire family system. The individual often is asked to behave or respond in a different manner. This technique attempts to disrupt a circular system or behavior pattern.

Family Sociogram

The sociogram charts relationships among people. By devising a series of questions relevant to a given family, the therapist can gain information about special alliances and relationship power sources. This technique promotes identification of family roles and new insights by family members.

Family Rituals

The family therapist can prescribe rituals as a method of change. Often, rituals are directed to the family to add needed structure. Examples are dinner times, house clean-up time together, and a family homework time. Specific rules during these ritual times often are prescribed. These rules might include discussing positive items only, not criticizing others, and allowing everyone to talk.

Prescribing Indecision

The stress level of couples and families often is exacerbated by a faulty decision-making process. Decisions not made in these cases become problematic in themselves. When straightforward interventions fail, paradoxical interventions often can produce change or relieve symptoms of stress. Such is the case with prescribing indecision. The indecisive behavior is reframed as an example of caring or taking appropriate time on important matters affecting the family. A directive is given to not rush into anything or make hasty decisions. The couple is to follow this directive to the letter.

Putting the Client in Control of the Symptom

This technique, widely used by strategic family therapists, attempts to place control in the hands of the individual or system. The therapist may recommend, for example, the continuation of a symptom such as anxiety or worry. Specific directives are given as to when, where, with whom, and for what amount of time one should do these things. As the client follows this paradoxical directive, a sense of control over the symptom often develops, resulting in subsequent change.

Conclusion

The techniques suggested here are examples from those that family therapists practice. They are customized according to presenting problems and are basically atheoretical in nature. With the focus on healthy family functioning, therapists cannot allow themselves to be stuck according to a prescribed operational procedure, a rigid set of techniques or set of hypotheses. Therefore, creative judgment and personalization of application are encouraged.

Healthy family functioning, theoretical constructs concerning the family, and interventions to change the system are focal points of marital and family therapy. Although additional scientific inquiry is needed in each of these areas, we have seen progress.

References

Bandura, A. (1974). *Social learning theory.* Englewood Cliffs, NJ: Prentice Hall.

Beavers, W. R. (1977). *Psychotherapy and growth: Family systems perspective.* New York: Brunner/Mazel.

Beavers, W. R. (1982). Healthy, midrange, and severely dysfunctional families. In F. Walsh (Ed.), *Normal family processes.* New York: Guilford Press.

Becvar, D., & Becvar, R. (1988). *Family therapy.* Boston: Allyn & Bacon.

Boszormenyi-Nagy, I., & Ulrich, D. (1981). Contextual family therapy. In A. S. Gurman & D. P. Kniskern (Eds.), *Handbook of family therapy* (pp. 159–186). New York: Brunner/Mazel.

Bowen, M. (1978). *Family therapy in clinical practice.* New York: Aronson.

Brown, J. H., & Christensen, D. N. (1986). *Family therapy: Theory and practice.* Monterey: Brooks/Cole.

Carter, B. (1986). Success in family therapy. *Family Therapy Networker, 10*, 16–22.

Carter, B., & McGoldrick, M. (1989). *The changing family life cycle.* Boston: Allyn & Bacon.

Coppersmith, E. (1980). The family floor plan: A tool of training, assessment, and intervention in family therapy. *Journal of Marital & Family Therapy, 6,* 141–145.

Corsini, R. (1984). *Current psychotherapies.* Itasca, IL: F. E. Peacock.

Dicks, H. (1967). *Marital tensions.* New York: Basic Books.

Duhl, F. S., Kantor, D., & Duhl, B. S. (1973). Learning space and action in family therapy: A primer of sculpting. In D. Block (Ed.), *Techniques of family psychotherapy: A primer.* New York: Grune & Stratton.

Fairbairn, W. (1954). *An object-relations theory of the personality.* New York: Basic Books.

Fenell, D., & Weinhold, B. (1989). *Counseling families.* Denver: Love Publishing.

Fisher, B. L., & Sprenkle, D. (1978). Therapists' perceptions of healthy family functioning. *International Journal of Family Counseling, 6,* 1–10.

Fisher, B. L., Giblin, P. R., & Hoopes, M. H. (1982). Healthy family functioning: What therapists say and what families want. *Journal of Marital & Family Therapy, 8,* 273–284.

Framo, J. (1981). The integration of marital therapy with sessions with family of origin. In A. S. Gurman & D. P. Kniskern (Eds.), *Handbook of family therapy.* New York: Brunner/Mazel.

Goldenberg, I., & Goldenberg, H. (1985). *Family therapy: An overview* (2nd ed.). Monterey: Brooks/Cole.

Gurman, A. S. (Ed.). (1985). *Casebook of marital therapy.* New York: Guilford Press.

Haley, J. (1973). *Uncommon therapy: The psychiatric technique of Milton H. Erickson.* New York: Norton.

Haley, J. (1976). *Problem-solving therapy.* New York: Harper/Colophon Books.

Kantor, D., & Lehr, W. (1975). *Inside the family: Toward a theory of family process.* San Francisco: Jossey-Bass.

Kempler, W. (1973). *Principles of gestalt family therapy.* Costa Mesa: Kempler Institute.

Kempler, W. (1981). *Experiential psychotherapy with families.* New York: Brunner/Mazel.

Lewis, J., Beavers, W., Gossett, J., & Phillips, V. (1976). *No single thread: Psychological health in family systems.* New York: Brunner/Mazel.

Madanes, C. (1981). *Strategic family therapy.* San Francisco: Jossey-Bass.

McGoldrick, M., & Gerson, R. (1985). *Genograms in family assessment.* New York: Norton.

Minuchin, S. (1974a). *Families and family therapy.* Cambridge, MA: Harvard University Press.

Minuchin, S. (1974b). Structural family therapy. In G. Caplan (Ed.), *Child and adolescent psychiatry, sociocultural and community psychiatry* (2nd ed., pp. 178–192). New York: Basic Books.

Minuchin, S., & Fishman, H. (1981). *Techniques of family therapy.* Cambridge, MA: Harvard University Press.

Nichols, M. P. (1984). *Family therapy—Concepts and methods.* New York: Gardner Press.

Olson, D., Sprenkle, D., & Russell, C. (1979). Circumplex model of marital and family systems: I. Cohesion and adaptability dimensions, family types, and clinical applications. *Family Process, 18,* 3–28.

Patterson, G. (1971). *Families.* Champaign, IL: Research Press.

Perls, F. S. (1969). *Gestalt therapy verbatim.* Lafayette, CA: Real People Press.

Perls, F. S., Hefferline, R. F., & Goodman, P. (1951). *Gestalt therapy.* New York: Julian Press.

Piercy, F. P., Sprenkle, D. H., & Associates. (1986). *Family therapy sourcebook.* New York: Guilford Press.

Reiss, D. (1981). *The family's construction of reality.* Cambridge, MA: Harvard University Press.

Rogers, C. (1961). *On becoming a person.* Boston: Houghton Mifflin.

Satir, V. (1972). *Peoplemaking.* Palo Alto, CA: Science & Behavior Books.

Selvini-Palazzoli, M., Boscolo, L., Cecehin, G., & Prata, G. (1978). *Paradox and counterparadox.* New York: Jason Aronson.

Sherman, R., & Fredman, N. (1986). *Handbook of structural techniques in marriage and family therapy.* New York: Brunner/Mazel.

Sperry, L., & Carlson, J. (1991). *Marital therapy: Integrating theory and technique.* Denver: Love Publishing.

Stuart, R. (1980). *Helping couples change.* New York: Guilford Press.

Textor, M. R. (1989). The "healthy" family. *Journal of Family Therapy, 11,* 59–75.

Whitaker, C. A. (1976). The hindrance of theory in clinical work. In J. Guerin (Ed.), *Family therapy: Theory and practice* (pp. 154–164). New York: Gardner Press.

Whitaker, C. A., & Keith, D. V. (1981). Symbolic-experiential family therapy. In A. S. Gurman & D. P. Kniskern (Eds.), *Handbook of family therapy* (pp. 187–225). New York: Brunner/Mazel.

This article was originally published in *Counseling and Human Development,* Vol. 23, 1991, pp. 13–34. Reprint permission granted by Love Publishing.

Couple and Family Counseling

Marian Stoltz-Loike

Unresolved questions relating to family and career balance can lead to marital tension or dissolution in dual career couples. Two general areas can create particular problems for the couple. First, marital tension may be expressed in overt ways, such as anger or resentment, and in more covert ways, like unavailability to the partner both psychologically and physically. These reactions diminish the couple's satisfaction with home life and may lead to dissatisfaction with their work lives as well. Second, dual career couples need to communicate effectively to reach a balance among their many competing career- and family-related demands. For example, both partners may be offered different relocation packages during their careers, or be expected to work late or on weekends on a regular basis. Unless couples can plan their work schedules together, there will be repeated conflicts between his needs, her needs, and family needs. This may require mastery of communication, negotiation, and empathic listening skills through counselor modeling and training. Even in well-functioning and well-meaning couples, the balance of responsibilities may be nonequitable because couples feel unable to discuss family and work issues directly. Negotiation and compromise may be critical to resolving differences between the distinct styles and standards of each partner.

This chapter reviews a variety of approaches to couple therapy and marriage and family counseling. Both the underlying theory and the methods of counseling are reviewed and analyzed. Examples of how methods from this literature can be used with dual career couples are presented.[1]

Family Systems Theory—Overview

Underlying family systems theory is the assumption that the family functions under the same laws as other systems. Systems try to maintain homeostasis or balance and attempt to reestablish this balance when disturbed. Similarly, families function as balanced systems that operate to maintain equilibrium. When the balance is disturbed, the family changes its way of functioning to reestablish homeostasis.

Families differ in the way they cope with environmental stresses and social strains, and how they maintain equilibrium between career and family. If the family's method of dealing with stress is effective, the family functions well. However, in dysfunctional families the inability to deal with stress becomes apparent as the family adopts counterproductive methods to cope with crisis situations and reestablish equilibrium. Because family and individual functioning are linked, when the family does not function effectively, one or more family members will exhibit psychosocial difficulties. Family-related problems that are addressed within the family context are solved more effectively. When these problems are addressed instead in individual therapy, outside the family context, the family "problem" cannot be resolved and the dysfunctionality will continue in the individual client or appear in another family member.

The goal of the family is to support both individual expression and membership in a functional family unit. Families support growth and development of their members, evolve rules concerning family interactions, and require flexibility in dealing with "normal" stresses throughout family life cycles, such as children's growing up and leaving home, or parents' aging. Each new demand may lead to familial stress, imbalance, and disequilibrium which, when properly addressed, will lead to positive growth in family functioning.

The family systems approach to family functioning is particularly relevant for dual career couples who may experience pronounced stress as they balance multiple roles and require flexibility to function effectively. If family equilibrium is based on equity and fairness, then when one partner changes his or her family or career roles, creating a systemic disequilibrium, family rules will reestablish couple/family homeostasis. This will result in a new, equitable way of functioning for all participants. If the balance is not based on equity and if one partner changes his or her roles, the couple may lack effective coping mechanisms and be unable to reestablish equilibrium, or may establish a new equilibrium again characterized by nonequity.

Family Stresses

The stresses families experience throughout their life spans may be differentiated into three crisis situations (Goldenberg & Goldenberg,

1980): *Acute situational stresses* are crises that all families experience during the family life cycle. These stresses include the death of family members, the birth of a baby, and relocation, and require immediate changes in family functioning. *Interpersonal stresses* involve the lack of harmony within the family and may be due to competition between career-minded partners, disagreements over money, or problems with children. *Intrapersonal stresses* are the conflicts that occur within an individual. These may be due to a variety of external concerns, including factors related to family of origin and current familial situations, and also include decisions about balancing family and career demands. Although no two families have identical ways of functioning, patterns of effective and ineffective interactions among family members are evident to the experienced family therapist.

Well-functioning families respect the individuality and autonomy of each family member. For example, Lewis, Beavers, Gossett, and Phillips (1976) assessed the functioning of "healthy" families and found that "no single thread" defined their interactions. Rather within the functional family, members were able to express thoughts and feelings and parents were able to function effectively as a subsystem. In other words, personal autonomy was respected and individuality and separateness among family members were tolerated (Goldenberg & Goldenberg, 1980). Moreover, family members expressed their own opinions comfortably even when this led to disagreements with other family members. Thus, negotiation and discussion rather than authoritarian control were the effective means of resolving family conflicts.

To counsel a family effectively, the "rules" of family behavior must be ascertained. Couples operate within a set of rules (also referred to as expectations or contracts) that define what they are willing to bring to the relationship and what they expect from their partners. Family rules are learned within the context of family interaction and are viewed as determining individual patterns of behavior, so that each person's behavior is associated with, and depends upon, the functioning of the rest of the family. These rules may be overt, clearly admitted and discussed, or covert, not admitted or known and not openly discussed.

Dual career couples can benefit by overt, agreed-upon family rules regarding employment and family responsibilities. Without rules, family responsibilities are performed haphazardly and families become overwhelmed by normal dual career couple responsibilities. Therefore, rules are necessary to determine who cooks and cleans, who takes care of unexpected household demands or a sick child, or who makes the kinds of preparations necessary for partners working late or traveling. When family rules are covert and when dual career couples have demanding lives both at home and at work, each partner operates with a different set of expectations about the family, leading to stress, disappointment, and dissatisfaction with the family. Thus, without articulating their assumptions about interdependent family roles, individuals may be disappointed when their significant others do not fulfill their expectations. An important goal of family therapy is for couples to verbalize these covert expectations as a first step in resolving their conflicts (e.g., Rice, 1979; Sager, 1976; Satir, 1972).

Families consist of subsystems that may be formed by age, sex, or interest (Minuchin, 1974), and fulfill many roles related to socialization and education. Family members may simultaneously belong to a variety of different subsystems within the family and learn different skills and possess different levels of power within each subsystem. Parental, spouse, and sibling subsystems are the most significant within the family (Minuchin & Fishman, 1981). Mother and daughter can also simultaneously form another subsystem within the family. Problems within the spouse or parental subsystem are associated with dysfunctionality that reverberates throughout the rest of the family system. Lack of respect for boundaries or distinctions between different subsystems can lead to stress that can result in intrafamilial dysfunctionality. For example, when the boundary between the spouse and parent-child subsystems is not distinct, each relationship suffers and the family does not function effectively, leading to opportunities for children to manipulate and control parents, rather than parents functioning in their powerful parental roles (Minuchin & Fishman, 1981).

Relationship difficulties between partners in dual career couples can arise from resentment over rules for balancing family and career roles, or dissatisfaction with rules about the priorities given to each partner's role. These difficulties can lead to problems in other interactions within the family system. If the couple lacks opportunities for nurturing the continual growth and development of their relationship, there may be a breakdown in the couple/parent subsystem that can greatly affect the partners and their family. When boundaries are clearly defined and rules are overt and supported by family members, both the family and its subsystems function effectively and interactions are healthy and provide support for individual growth and development.

The "how well" of family functioning is more important than the "how," underscoring the importance of the therapist's responding to family needs and not his or her own standards. The goal of therapy is to help families become better able to function within the possibilities that exist for them. For dual career couples this means that the goal is not to avoid conflict but to address conflict in productive ways that can lead to individual growth and development. Thus, counselors should work together with couples to set standards of family and career balance that feel fair to the couple and can be achieved.

Dysfunctional Patterns

A variety of communication and family subsystem difficulties characterize dysfunctional families. Families may communicate but may not accept responsibility for feelings or actions. Shaky parental coalitions are common, making it unclear where family power resides and permitting stereotyping of family members. In severely dysfunctional families, members tend to be chaotic and rigid and exhibit little interaction with the external world, demonstrating that change represents a difficult challenge for these families. When counselors who work with dual career couples encounter dysfunctional families, then couple issues must be addressed with a trained family therapist. The need for change may be extremely threatening for some families because standard patterns of behavior may preserve covert dysfunctionality within the family, and any attempts at change may threaten to expose hidden problems. Furthermore, lack of family flexibility can by itself cause stresses for family members trying to achieve change.

Family members communicate their support and emotions as well as dysfunctional patterns both verbally and nonverbally. Nonverbal messages may include facial expressions, body rigidity, tone of voice, and eye contact. Verbal communication may involve negative or impossible messages, such as double-bind messages, which contain two messages that are inherently contradictory but must both be addressed. It is impossible to respond to both messages because the truth of one message is dependent on the falseness of the other. As an example, a woman may return home from work looking extremely angry. When her husband asks her what is wrong, she claims to be quite happy. He believes both his perception and what his wife says. However, if she is not angry, his perception is wrong. If his perception is accurate, she is lying. Accepting one message means that the other message is not true, which results in a problematic, double-bind contradiction.

Communication in dysfunctional families can be constricted by family rules concerning the expression of family information. Only certain members may be permitted to offer opinions, and these opinions may be valid only when expressed in specific ways. Moreover, children can play special roles in dysfunctional families, articulating messages that parents cannot express, or having problems that deter parents from confronting aspects of their own problematic relations. One child carries the pathology of the dysfunctional family, and he or she along with other family members perpetuate that role to ensure that the real family problem is not expressed.

Feminist Family Therapy

A major goal of feminist psychology is to engender social change regarding how men and women are viewed. The family plays a critical role in this reformulation because family has traditionally been "women's domain" and because families are responsible for transmitting social norms. It is the goal of feminist family therapy to restructure contradictions between gender, power, family, and society (Goodrich et al., 1988).

Within this framework, feminist writing has cautioned that counselors who work with families must reexamine some of the basic assumptions of systems theory relating to how families are organized (Walters, Carter, Papp, & Silverstein, 1988). First, feminist therapists distinguished between role complementarity and role symmetry. Complementarity suggests that men and women have different domains, but power in the relationship resides with the man. In contrast, role symmetry indicates that both sexes are involved in instrumental and expressive roles, representing an egalitarian power model. Second, the traditional view of mature adults was that they would become autonomous (see also Gilligan, 1988). In fact, within a context of egalitarian power for men and women, the adult goal for development would be interdependence or "autonomy with connectedness." Third, systems theory assumes that family members play reciprocal roles within the family in maintaining family dysfunctionality. This, however, is true only when the family members have equal power. When family power is not egalitarian, it cannot be assumed that there is a reciprocal balance.

Within this context, feminist therapists like Walters et al. (1988) cautioned that therapy can be genderless only if the rules of the family system are genderless. For example, therapists may focus on balance of power in the family; however, this assumes that all members have equal access to family roles. When the woman chooses a role in response to one already chosen by or assigned by society to a man, the family balance cannot be egalitarian. These writers also encourage therapists to avoid blaming the mother for any child dysfunctionality.

Although many clinical case studies reflect deep respect for individual goals of men and women, therapists may not actively advocate gender-sensitive approaches in their counseling, which can undermine the effectiveness of treatment for both members of the couple. Walters et al. (1988) outlined a number of guidelines relevant to practicing more effective feminist family therapy:

1. Consider the impact that gender may have on the couple/family.
2. Recognize the limits of women's access to social and economic resources.
3. Understand the social constructs that constrain women's ability to direct their lives.
4. Address the implications of women's socialization to take the central role in family responsibility.
5. Evaluate the challenge for women who have children because children create a conflict between women's role as mother and other roles.
6. Consider the meaning of the fact that women typically derive power through their relationships with men.
7. Validate women's values of connectedness, nurturing, and emotionality.
8. Respect women's roles outside of marital and family roles.
9. Assume that interventions are not gender-free and will have different meaning for members of each sex.

For the dual career couple, a feminist perspective would mean valuing both home and career roles of both partners. Moreover, it could provide a framework for traditional couples to adopt more gender-fair methods of functioning. Although achieving egalitarian gender roles can require a great deal of work on the part of the therapist, the benefits to the partners with respect to increased opportunities for functioning would be well worth the time and effort.

Psychotherapeutic Techniques

Basic to family therapy is the belief in the institution of marriage and the commitment to the positive value of a good family life.[2] Related to the positive value placed on marriage is the assumption that partners had a reason for choosing one another, that the strength of the couple is greater than either individual's strength, that both partners have overt and covert expectations of benefits and contributions to their relationship, that partnership survives only through the conscious decision of each member to remain together, and that because of individual resistance to change, couples who divorce and remarry often choose a reasonable facsimile of the first spouse and eventually have similar problems (Goldenberg & Goldenberg, 1980). The goal of family therapy is to develop a functionally appropriate framework so that these positive relational aspects can be expressed.

A particular difficulty for the dual career couple is the contradiction between this model of couple functioning and the corporate model of the ideal employee, which assumes that institutional needs take priority over couple concerns. In many corporations today, there is a growing concern with the impact of employee mental and physical health on productivity. Therefore, greater attention is being paid to the demands of work and other roles, including family roles. It is still largely assumed, however, that reaching the executive suite requires single-minded devotion to corporate success.

The varied therapeutic approaches of five major couple/marriage and family therapists will be reviewed to benefit those counselors who work with dual career couples. This section presents the therapeutic approaches of Ackerman (1938, 1954, 1956, 1958, 1960, 1965, 1968, 1970a, 1970b), Ackerman & Behrens (1974), Bloch & Simon (1982), Haley (1970, 1976), Minuchin (1974), Minuchin & Fishman (1981), Papp (1983), Satir (1967a, 1967b, 1972), and Satir, Stachowiak, & Taschman (1975). Additionally, Rice's (1979) use of family therapy techniques in his work with dual career couples will be discussed. Although all these theories share some common ideas, they reflect differences in outlook, technique, and the role of the therapist. In Table 3.1 many differences and similarities among these theories are outlined.

Table 3.1
Summary of Differences Among Couple/Marriage and Family Therapeutic Approaches

Therapist	Role of Therapist	Role of Family	Dysfunctionality	Therapeutic Intervention
Ackerman	1. Reorganize, reeducate, and resolve couple conflicts 2. Induce change via diagnostic plan 3. Act as participant/ observer	1. Security, child raising, couple development, socialization of children	1. Family conflicts 2. Failure of complementarity	1. Use psychoanalytic techniques 2. Assess family history 3. Clearly delineate roles
Minuchin	1. Join the family 2. Understand reality they experience 3. Develop with family way of functioning	1. Define interaction between family and outside world 2. Define boundaries and space between family subgroups 3. Adults model appropriate behaviors for children	1. Lack of adherence to family structure 2. Crossing of boundaries between subsystems	1. Realign family organization to produce change and ultimately achieve appropriate structural alignment within family
Papp	1. Define meaning of change for family 2. Regulate rate of change 3. Connect symptom with dysfunctional behavior	1. Create significant inter-relationships among family members 2. Develop functional system where the whole is greater than the individual parts	1. Ineffective responses to stress 2. Identified patient presents symptoms	1. Identify family themes 2. Use cotherapeutic group 3. Direct intervention using logic and advice

Table 3.1 (Continued)

Therapist	Role of Therapist	Role of Family	Dysfunctionality	Therapeutic Intervention
Haley	1. Solve the problem client presents 2. Increase problem-solving possibilities for approaching family 3. Therapist does not reveal hypotheses about family dysfunctionality to client	1. Develop effective system of communication 2. Develop functional hierarchies of power within family	1. Symptom protects other family members 2. Inappropriate hierarchies within family	1. Give directions for change 2. Reassert family rules 3. Reestablish appropriate family hierarchy
Satir	1. Model and foster effective communication 2. Evaluate receptiveness of family to change 3. Assess congruence between verbal and nonverbal communication	1. Model effective means of communication 2. Provide positive support to family members	1. Poor communication 2. Lack of accurate perception of self and others	1. Model good communication 2. Reinterpret negative in positive terms
Rice	1. Help partners verbalize and achieve goals 2. Make marriage contract and expectations overt 3. Point out positive benefits of change	1. Establish equity 2. Manage time and organize family function	1. Competition between partners 2. Power struggle 3. Lack of support structures	1. Use psychodynamic methods involving historical perspective 2. Discuss marital contract 3. Model communication, negotiation, and empathic listening

Ackerman

Nathan Ackerman (1938, 1954, 1956, 1958, 1960, 1965, 1968, 1970a, 1970b) was one of the founders of the contemporary family therapy movement. He explored the inclusion of the family in therapy because he found that it was not unusual in individual therapy for a person to improve and then for others in the family to get worse. Individual therapy had not solved the family pathology. Therefore, he developed new techniques for therapy that were problem-oriented, not technique-oriented, and that were directed to assist the individual within the context of the family.

The basic function of the family is related to security, child raising, socialization, and the development of the partners as a couple and as individuals. Family functions are sexual, reproductive, social, economic, and educational. Stability of the family is a function of the emotional interaction between members. Because family members are interdependent, problems in one family member result in the dysfunctionality of other members.

To understand family behavior, several issues need to be considered and assessed, including the integration of members into the family, the interrelationship and interdependence of family members, and the impact of adaptation in one family role to functioning in another family role. Family roles are interdependent and reciprocal, and each family member can take on multiple roles simultaneously. Moreover, each family member affects family functioning, and overall family functioning affects the well-being of each family member.

Family therapy is designed to affect family relationships directly rather than to change family interactions indirectly, as in classical psychotherapy. By developing rapport with the couple, the therapist "catalyzes" conflicts, stimulates new methods of coping within the family, and exposes the "real context of the conflict" within the family, which leads to the dissolution of barriers and obstacles to conflict resolution. This enlightens marital partners about their problems, and stimulates the partners' ability to empathize and communicate with one another and develop essential problem-solving skills. Another aspect of the reciprocal interplay of the family and the individual is the fact that individuals derive support from the family for growth and development while the family relies on individual members for continuity and functioning. The nature of this relationship between the family and the individual varies both as the family group progresses through developmental stages and as the individual matures. Family therapy is therefore oriented to the different needs of the family and its individual members at different stages of the life cycle. A primary goal of the family is to deal effectively with conflict within a context of shared family experiences and normal family functioning. When the family's ability to deal with conflict is impaired, the family's ability to grow and develop is also affected.

In the course of therapy, the family's emotional life is expanded and the perceptions of family relationships are altered. These changes lead to new levels of family intimacy, sharing, support, and identity, which enhance the possibility of growth in family interrelations. The job of the therapist is to simulate closeness and sharing by challenging and questioning conflicts and disassociation within the family. Moreover, the therapist makes the family aware of new ways to share identity and form alignments, and assesses the family's resources for developing effective solutions to conflicts.

Understanding both the history of the couple and their individual past within their families of origin is necessary to comprehend current marital crisis. Therapeutic processes involve verbal and nonverbal methods to challenge unrealistic family and individual beliefs. Because symptoms within the family are functions of unresolved family conflicts, the therapist moves the symptom from the individual to the family arena, where conflicts may be resolved.

When family members can delineate their roles, relationships become smoother and more meaningful. Re-education, reorganization of communication, and resolution of conflicts are associated with family well-functioning and the opportunity for change and growth within the family. Thus, the therapist helps family members to understand the working dynamics of the family and to develop new skills in conflict resolution and familial functioning.

Many elements of Ackerman's theory are directly related to some dual career couple issues. His perspective on the interdependence of individual, couple, and family functioning is comprehensive. Partners take on many roles, and each role affects all other aspects of family functioning. For dual career couples, this relates to overlapping demands and responsibilities of each partner within family and career domains. Ackerman views creative conflict resolution as a goal of family well-functioning. Both this idea and the notion of recasting conflict as a problem to be solved are essential to growth in the dual career couple.

Minuchin

Transcripts of Minuchin's therapy sessions read like novels, and his technique is colorful, spontaneous, and flexible. Minuchin argued for mastering technique so well that the therapist can transcend technique and function spontaneously in each therapy session. Family therapy requires the ability "...to join a family, experiencing reality as the family members experience it, and becoming involved in the repeated interactions that form the family structure and shape the way people think and behave. The goal of the therapist is to become an agent of change who works within the constraints of the family system intervening in ways that are possible only with this particular family to produce a different, more productive way of living" (Minuchin & Fishman, 1981, p. 2).

Families may initially resist change. When therapists are able to enter into the client's family context, they can agitate for change in a way that is tolerable to the family. Although Minuchin's success within his methods is legendary, it is difficult to imagine all therapists having the capacity to put themselves within a particular family framework. In the therapeutic setting, therapists build common ground with client-families, but leave space to join and distance themselves from the family as necessary. When therapists join the family, they participate in family experiences and emotions along with family members. Joining the family, however, requires that therapists know their own resources and limitations. As therapists accommodate to the family, they also expect the family to accommodate to them. By challenging dysfunctional behaviors, therapists give families confidence that change can occur.

Minuchin's work is distinguished by his deep respect for each client-family and its individual members. Every family has something positive to offer its members and every member possesses unique potential because of his or her specialness. Therapists assist families and individual members in expressing that potential.

A "holon" refers to the unit of intervention in family therapy. The holon may be an individual, the family, or the community, and is simultaneously a whole and also a part of some nonconflicting larger entity. Each holon strives for independence as a unit and affiliation with the larger system of which it is a subunit. At the time of couple formation, the spouse holon, whether it consists of legally bound individuals or two mutually committed partners, requires that each partner give up some of his or her individuality to belong to the new system. Within the new couple transactional patterns develop, and, eventually, any deviation from these accustomed transactions will lead to a sense of disappointment or betrayal. The spouse holon also develops boundaries while establishing psychological and physical space for the partners and warding off intrusion by friends and other family members. Minuchin views these boundaries as "...one of the most important aspects of the viability of the family structure."

Ideally the spouse subsystem offers a basis for dealing with the external world and perhaps a way of personal protection from external stressors. Individuals must also develop independent identities. When spouses cannot incorporate independent external experiences into their subsystem or cannot achieve diversified self-expression when alone, the spouse holon becomes impoverished and dysfunctional and cannot provide a source of growth to the couple. Dysfunctions within the spouse holon are evident in family problems.

The parental holon involves socializing children, educating them about authority, informing them about how their needs are met, and training them in effective communication, negotiation, and rules concerning appropriate and inappropriate family interactions. Parents model interactions and affective behavior for their children, and wide variations in parental holons are typical. The parental holon must be flexible so that it can change as children develop and their abilities for mastery and self-control evolve. In the parental holon, parents have rights and duties to make decisions to protect the total family system and to guard the privacy of the spouse holon.

Problems in the parental holon are often solved by trial and error, and the dynamics of effective solutions change throughout family life stages. Difficulties in dealing with common family problems represent a cue for the therapist that family members may be part of a dysfunctional unit, and underscore the need for the family to develop problem-solving techniques. Dysfunctional parental holons are associated with various children's problems. Deviant parental models can affect the child's values and expectations. Moreover, children can be scapegoated or drawn into alliances with one spouse against the other.

Couple formation involves defining the boundaries between couples and the outside world. Questions arise about how partners will relate to members of their families of origin, friends, coworkers, or neighbors. To achieve intimacy, a functional balance between external contacts and couple privacy must be reached. Individual differences in expectations, emotional expression, and relationships with other adults must be negotiated. Also, couples must decide on rules for closeness, responsibilities, and cooperation, and also evolve common values, learn to listen to each other, and decide how to handle their differences and deal with conflict. Minuchin considers couple formation as a complex transition from functioning as an individual to functioning as part of a new couple unit. Therapy may help couples to appreciate the value of this complementarity.

Couples with children. Immediately upon the child's birth, new holons of parental, mother-child, and father-child subsystems are formed. Reorganization and redefinition of the spouse holon is required so that parents can care for the dependent newborn with his or her own personality. Couples must establish new definitions to preserve their relationship but expand their family boundaries to include their child. Parents must negotiate new relationships with neighbors, friends, and extended family. Moreover, as the child grows, rules must be established that give parents space together, yet maintain safety and parental authority. As additional children are born, family patterns and subsystems are renegotiated.

Minuchin's approach to family therapy has significant implications for dual career couples. First, Minuchin underscores the close connection between the individual and the family. Positive family relations are viewed as integral to individual functioning. Within dual career couples, partners' goals should not be viewed as antagonistic but rather should result from couple negotiation so that they are mutually respected and supported. When the family functions well, individual members can express their greatest potential. Second, conflicts between partners should be viewed as problems to be solved that will strengthen the integrity of couple functioning. Third, Minuchin views flexibility as a key to the family's accommodating to change. Dual career couples who can function flexibly are the most successful at supporting partners' various career and family roles. Fourth, Minuchin underscores the importance of the couple's establishing boundaries between themselves and the outside world. For dual career couples, an important boundary may be the couple's ability to separate themselves from the demands of work. Using cellular phones and beepers during nonbusiness hours may compete with couple well-functioning. Instead, couples sometimes need impermeable boundaries to ensure couple intimacy. Fifth, Minuchin also underscores that couples must be able to negotiate for roles and responsibilities within the family and appreciate rules established by the family. Negotiation is an essential skill that dual career couples must master to function effectively.

Papp

According to Peggy Papp (1983), the family functions as a highly interrelated system in which the whole is greater than the sum of its parts and which is regulated by feedback loops. Thus, during therapy, individual functioning can be understood only in the context of the entire family, and change in any part of the family results in changes throughout the family system. Although therapists may advocate change in the family, they must also ensure that change occurs at a pace the family can accept. This means that advocating change is not a solution but rather represents a dilemma for the therapist. If the symptom is eliminated, what will replace it to regulate the family system? Only by ensuring that the family is prepared to change can the therapist support altered patterns of family behavior.

In the course of the family life cycle, families are exposed to many sources of stress. Families may manifest a variety of behaviors in an attempt to balance unacceptable stresses. Some behaviors may have adaptive value; however, families may also adopt dysfunctional patterns in response to stress. It is the job of the therapist to identify problems within the family and change dysfunctional, stress-related patterns of interaction.

Rules governing the family are defined by members' many intersecting beliefs. Dysfunctional rules involve family themes, or a "specifically emotionally-laden issue around which there is recurring conflict" (Papp, 1983, p. 14). When partners become disenchanted with each others' way of enacting a theme, they may turn elsewhere for a solution. A child, for example, may then occupy the position formerly held by the partner, a sign of dysfunctionality in the family. Therapists deduce family themes by listening for metaphorical language, tracking behavioral sequences, and picking up key attitudinal statements, but they cannot assess themes by direct questioning. Once they recognize family themes, therapists form hypotheses about family symptoms and the effect of change in the family system.

With some problems, direct interventions, including logical explanations and rational advice aimed at altering the family's rules and roles, may be effective. Therapists can work with clients to train them in effective, open communication, in controlling children, or in managing family life. In addressing complex cases, Papp employs more complex approaches to therapy. One technique involves a partnership between the therapist and a cotherapeutic group, called the consultation group, that watches the session from behind a one-way mirror. (A single cotherapist in the consultation room may be used instead of the cotherapeutic group.) This group provides commentary to the therapist on the course of therapy. The consultation group is preoccupied with change and comments on how change will occur, what its consequences will be, which family members will be affected, and what the alternatives to change are.

Messages from the consultation group are sent into the therapy room. The therapist then decides how to use the content of the messages to create the strongest impact on individual family members and the course of family therapy. The group can be used "to support, confront, confuse, challenge, or provoke the family," and the therapist can support or oppose the group's message.

An essential way to use the group is as part of a therapeutic triangle where there is a planned conflict between the therapist and the group. The therapist encourages the family to change, whereas the group warns the therapist about the dangers of change for the family system and underscores who or what subsystem is the antagonist of change. The therapist regulates change within the family by agreeing or disagreeing with the group.

Two particular aspects of Papp's therapeutic program are relevant to dual career couples. First, Papp's notion of themes relates to the recurring maladaptive behavior patterns and areas of conflict characteristic of some interactions within couples. Such themes may involve financial issues, career-career balance, household responsibilities, or other concerns. Only when couples master skills related to communication, negotiation, and conflict resolution can they begin to address and resolve these themes. Second, change leads to a behavioral vacuum that may result in a new dysfunctional pattern of behavior. Counselors can assist dual career couples in resolving partner conflict and planning creatively for change. Additionally, follow-up with the couple can ensure that creative approaches that change dysfunctional couple patterns and solve problematic couple themes do not result in new couple or family problems.

Haley

From the perspective of Jay Haley (1970, 1976), families face a variety of adjustment periods throughout life. Early in their marriages husbands and wives must develop ways of separating from their parents. When children are born, partners extend the couple dyad into a family triad. Thus, flexibility is the necessary hallmark in a well-functioning relationship. Families are characterized by hierarchical structures and rules governing who is primary and secondary in status and power. When family subsystems are organized within defined hierarchies and when executive subsystems are in control, the result is autonomy, responsibility, and cooperation. Symptoms, however, result when this hierarchical structure is not clearly defined and family members are not sure about who is their peer and who is their superior. Dysfunctional confusion can also result from coalitions between members at different levels of the hierarchy and may lead to a power struggle within the family. The therapist's job is to reestablish hierarchical family power structures within the family context.

Families typically come to therapy with one member of the family as the identified patient. In fact, the symptom is carried by this one person to protect the other family members and is maintained by ineffective family organization. Haley sees members of the family together because he believes that interviewing individual family members is like functioning in the dark. Only when family members are brought together can they learn how to differentiate themselves from the family successfully. Therapists can solve client problems only within the context of the family because relationship problems are viewed differently when partners are seen individually or conjointly. By seeing an entire family initially, therapists can grasp problems and perpetuating social conditions. Couples often cannot see how they elicit and respond to each other's behaviors; instead, they see behaviors out of context. For example, individuals may report that their partners criticize them for no apparent reason. In fact, the "nonoffending" partner may use a variety of nonverbal signals that elicit the other partner's behavior. Neither partner's behavior is correct, and both sets of behaviors would need to be addressed in therapy.

Therapeutic change occurs in sequential steps. Initially, behaviors that maintain problems are identified. Next, the goal for therapy is specified. Then, change proceeds by a series of steps that transform family dysfunctionality into resolvable problems. The job of the therapist is to help solve clients' problems by initiating, planning, and expediting appropriate changes during the course of effective counseling.

Therapists use spontaneity and flexibility as part of their therapeutic approach. Intervention highlights the family problem and relationships that need to be changed. Problems must be specified precisely before they can be solved. Therefore, psychodynamic language or terms like "low self-esteem" or "unhappiness" are not used. A well-defined problem, like a child who will not go to school or a husband who does not participate at home, is identified, and clear therapeutic goals are specified.

Successful therapy, according to Haley, involves changing the way that families communicate. Change within the family therapy context can result in positive change for all members when it occurs under the supervision of a therapist who sees the family through a period of stabilization and accommodation. In contrast, change in a single family member can lead to disastrous consequences for the family. Therapists help clients develop alternate modes of relational interactions so that symptoms can be abandoned. Therapists are attuned to how family members speak about themselves and other family members and how attentive each individual is to the statements of other family members. In these statements, individuals provide both overt and covert messages concerning family interactions and the presenting problem.

An important therapeutic task is giving directives. The therapist encourages the family to adhere to directives by underscoring the positive gains for each family member. Directives support the relationship between therapist and family by making families think about the therapist between sessions, thereby helping to stimulate change. Client responses to directives provide important information for the therapist. Directives may involve asking a husband to do something special for his wife and asking the wife to be gracious in her reception of it. This encourages the husband to begin something new in the relationship and to think about the wife and her needs and desires as he decides to do something unique for her.

Like Ackerman, Haley focuses on couple dysfunctionality as a problem to be solved. For dual career couples, this is a productive approach to conflict, especially because their problem-solving skills may already be well developed through a variety of work-related experiences. For example, by listening to and observing couple behaviors, a counselor may highlight a variety of aspects of the couple relationship the clients have not yet verbalized. Couples can also reenact particular conflict situations, and counselors can prescribe specific behaviors to encourage alternate patterns of behavior and to further develop positive aspects of the relationship. Effective couple communication is the critical aspect for dual career couple functioning. As Haley indicates, no change can occur without the couple's ability to communicate effectively. Moreover, clear communication is a prerequisite for assessing the impact of change on the couple relationship. Identifying the significance of change for the couple and training couples in negotiation skills are critical to ensuring that these changes will be implemented and will lead to productive couple growth.

Satir

According to Virginia Satir (1967a, 1967b, 1972, 1975a, 1975b, 1975c; Satir, Stachowiak, & Taschman, 1975: Stachowiak, 1975a, 1975b, 1975c; Taschman, 1975), the family is a system that constantly changes, sometimes slowly, sometimes quickly, as it attempts to maintain homeostasis. Because of the balance in the family system, changing one element of the system will affect all constituent parts. Each individual in the couple must learn to process the continually changing environmental input so that he or she can address problems openly. Satir does not subscribe to a democratic model of the family, believing instead that families need leaders to direct decision making. Functional families are more comfortable expressing direct, open conflict and both positive and negative emotions. Moreover, well-functioning families can achieve a significant structural goal by helping family members develop self-esteem and self-worth. Because partners of the couple are the "architects" of the family, any problems they experience have repercussions throughout the entire family. During family therapy, family members are treated "conjointly," or together, using transactional communication techniques rather than discussion of thoughts and feelings.

Satir focused on four critical issues that distinguish functional and dysfunctional families. First, functional families can use their time effectively for family tasks like decision making. There is also a balance between work or task effort and family members' social and emotional needs. Maladaptive families have an imbalance of attention to task and emotional needs. Second, family leadership is important to the functioning of the family. A matriarchal or patriarchal structure is necessary for effective family functioning, so that one parent operates as leader and the other partner and family members can cooperate with that role. In adaptive families, different members take on leadership roles at different times. Maladaptive families are characterized as being autocratic or inept and have no leader. Third, the family must support expression of differences in a way that can be discussed and resolved. The critical issue for the family is not how much conflict is expressed but how the family supports and reacts to conflict. Fourth, clarity of communication also distinguishes functional and dysfunctional families. In functional families clear communication is encouraged and supported. Members of dysfunctional families often communicate with no one, making speeches instead of speaking to one another.

Because the way people communicate is a reliable indicator of their interpersonal functioning, the goal of the therapist is to foster communication between partners as a prerequisite for individual growth and development. *Clear* communication is necessary for effective interactions. When words become abstract, communication becomes obscure. Even nonverbal information can be used to bolster clear messages.

Family growth is related to individuals' ability to alter ineffective ways of communicating. When family members can communicate congruently, they recognize that all feelings are valid and may be expressed. Thus, a further goal of effective communication involves learning to get in touch with how people look and sound when they speak to one another. Effective functioning means that the individual recognizes the vast repertoire of behavioral options available and is not constricted by a single way of doing things. Each family member learns to recognize differences among individuals as the therapist encourages each person to speak for him- or herself, accept differences in opinions and perceptions of the same situation, and say what he or she feels, thinks, and sees. Individual capacity for change is related to the skill of the therapist. Therefore, the job of the therapist is to train clients in new ways of feeling and thinking. Partners must learn how to assert their own thoughts and feelings while paying attention to each other's thoughts and feelings. The result is clear communication—characterized by direct requests and supportive communication. Poor communication is associated with covert requests, failed expectations, accusations, and recriminations. Partners in dysfunctional couples suffer from low self-esteem, which derives from relationship difficulties in their families of origin. Couple problems develop when individuals focus on what they get (which leads to failed expectations) rather than what they can give to the relationship.

Therapists act as resources and models of communication for the family. Their clarity of communication and ability to reveal themselves may be the first experience the family has had in clear communication. By using congruent verbal and nonverbal communication, therapists can exemplify and teach clients how to behave. Developing such communication skills takes time, so that lessons should be repeated and conclusions explained. Because the goal of couple therapy is to communicate directly, recognize the boundaries between self and others, and ask clear questions and make clear statements, "...treatment is completed when everyone in the therapy setting can use the first person 'I' followed by an active verb and ending with a direct object" (Satir, 1967a, p. 177). In addition, successful therapy, according to Satir, is related to family members' ability to handle "the presence of differentness" in planning for family responses to change. In a functional family there is congruence between what people say and how they look.

Satir used her personal experience to understand client needs more effectively. If the other person backed away, she reflected on whether she was sending a double-level message, where what she said and what she was projecting were different, in order to explain what made the other person draw back. Recognizing the significance of self-reflection, Satir advocated the use of videotape as an essential therapeutic tool for helping people see themselves as others do.

Therapists create a setting where people feel secure in taking the risk of looking at themselves and their actions objectively. Because the therapist requests and responds to information in a straight, nonjudgmental way and offers statements that reflect the positive values of family, clients develop self-esteem. Family members are encouraged to do things that bring pleasure to one another and set effective rules for family interactions to foster healthy functioning and self-esteem at home.

Satir's focus on communication parallels the focus of this article on the need for good communication skills within dual career couples. Clear expression of individual needs is prerequisite to the couples' effective functioning. Counselors can assist clients in reaching a high level of mutual trust, which stimulates comfortable discussion about goals and values. Satir's focus on verbal and nonverbal aspects of communication is critical for achieving meaningful couple communication. Just as therapists can encourage positive self-esteem through communication skills, dual career couples can foster their own healthy functioning by using direct, supportive statements about positive regard for a partner to foster that individual's self-esteem. Satir's techniques for developing listening and speaking skills and using videotapes to develop congruence between verbal and nonverbal messages can be helpful for counselors.

Rice

David Rice (1979) views the establishment of equity as the guiding principle for marriage and believes that "the achievement of a perceived equitable relationship is enhanced if the individuals manifest flexibility and relative freedom from the constraints of gender-role prescribed behaviors" (p. 103). Most theories about couple and family therapies focus on relationships between family members, but do not evaluate the impact of career roles on family functioning. Recently, family counselors have begun to advocate the recognition of the interdependence of work and family life (e.g., Ulrich & Dunne, 1986). Rice's approach is unique because he applies psychodynamic techniques directly to the conflicts and stresses of dual career couples and includes discussion of the interdependence of family and career roles in the application of his therapeutic techniques.

The dimension of couple equity changes over the family life cycle as family and individual parameters evolve. Effective functioning among dual career couples is characterized by couple equity, or the expectation that responsibilities balance over time. According to Rice, if couples perceive that there is nonequity, they will attempt to re-achieve equity through changes in one partner's behavior, or try to achieve psychological equity through distorting reality and perceiving a nonequitable task distribution as fair.

Dual career couples have different marital structures than more traditional families. Rather than their roles being complementary, dual career couples have overlapping roles. Responsibilities within each of these roles must be negotiated and addressed so that couples can establish rules about caring for children, managing family and personal time, and handling relationships with other people. Dual career couples may experience particular conflicts when they have children because they have few role models for fulfilling parent and career roles simultaneously. Planning, discussion, and negotiation are fundamental for establishing appropriate role expectations of dual career couples who become parents.

A particular problem Rice highlighted involves the relationship between members of dual career couples and other individuals. Dual career couples may experience less need for one another and for outside social contacts because of a high degree of association at their place of employment with like-minded people. Although this can be personally satisfying, couples may feel threatened by their partners' close relationships with coworkers. High involvement in work may indicate individual satisfaction or may mask specific problems. Open discussion about relationships, employment, and boundary issues within a counseling setting increases the couple's ability to balance family and career demands.

Benefits of the dual career couple lifestyle include enhanced intellectual partnership, increased income and resources, and a greater intellectual fulfillment and contentment of each partner. Roles and expectations are flexible within a healthy relationship. Partners in dual career couples may also experience stress associated with their lifestyles, and particular developmental events in the family life cycle may lead to relationship stresses or problems. For example, partners may experience significant personal growth at different points in their relationships. Berman, Sacks, and Lief (1975) found that wives experienced significant growth in self-esteem a few years following professional training. Husbands at that point were focusing on the positive sense of establishing stability within the marriage. These distinct developmental patterns can result in couple conflict and strain as the partners address different priorities. Rigid adherence to socially approved gender role norms also constrains well-functioning in dual career couples.

Therapists form a therapeutic alignment with the couple. The initial agenda of therapy is related to helping couples address their past experiences so that they can learn to function effectively. Issues like money management, decision making, relationship to family of origin, and permeability of couple boundaries are relevant because the couple's current attitudes to each of these issues are associated with the way they addressed these concerns in their families of origin. Because the couple constructs boundaries to outsiders, partners may exhibit pronounced resistance to change, so that the therapist should be more active in counseling dual career couples than clients in individual therapy. Partners learn through therapy how to relate to one another with regard to negotiation, communication, empathic listening, and offering emotional support. The goal of therapy involves dissolving a family's defensive behaviors, which may make clients anxious until they learn new cognitive skills. Dual career couples may offer particular challenges to the therapist because of their unique demands and because behaviors for which they have been rewarded in the past may be counterproductive to the success of current therapy. To progress in counseling, dual career couples need to address cognitive issues, like working out a schedule, and affective issues, like not sidetracking the therapist by using verbal repartee, because dual career couples may use verbal means and intellectualization to resist therapy. Expressing affect and achieving change may be difficult for some dual career couples because tuning out affect and adhering to their own beliefs may have been highly rewarded in the past. Therapists can help couples develop ways for expressing personal needs and offer supportive verbal feedback.

Many family members behave as if they derive positive gains from family dysfunctionality. When therapists underscore the apparent positive benefits as well as the more realistic drawbacks of dysfunctional behavior, the family can be restructured in a more positive fashion. Later in therapy, partners might address issues of competition and power struggles and the difficulties of arranging a support structure. By discussing these issues, couples gain additional channels of communication as well as opportunities to redefine their relationship. In this way, therapists help partners develop trust and respect for each other. By focusing on earlier positive experiences within the couple, partners regain positive perspectives on their relationship.

Marital contract. A marital contract, as viewed by Rice, represents both the verbalized and nonverbalized expectations about the relationship and is revised throughout the life cycle as partners mature. Within dual career couples, partners are motivated by goals of career success and personal and marital fulfillment. Clear communication about these expectations increases the satisfaction individuals can offer to partners and derive from their relationship. When the marital contract is not discussed, both partners may be dealing with different sets of unstated, but conflicting expectations and be frustrated by their inability to achieve important family and career goals within their relationship.

Dual career couples may benefit by developing an effective marital contract. The counselor can help partners elaborate the evolution of their expectations from the time of relationship formation to the present. A counseling goal involves developing a single, agreed-upon contract characterized by reciprocal equity and appropriateness to the couple's current demands and lifestyle. Issues relevant to the development of a marital contract include the husband's and wife's anticipation of support and reinforcement for occupational efforts and successes, expectations that partners will buffer external stresses and provide support, or the assumption that parenting roles will be shared. Because of the often stressful and highly demanding nature of their work, dual career couples may at times be unable to fulfill these expectations effectively, a condition that may also need to be addressed within the contract.

Conclusions

Several underlying themes emerge from the various theories of marriage/couple and family counseling that are directly related to relationship success. First, couples must establish boundaries between themselves and others in the outside world. Second, partners must be able to express emotional and physical supportiveness for each other. Third, good couple relationships depend on direct and sophisticated communication skills. Fourth, couple functioning depends not on the absence of conflict, but on the couple's mastery of effective conflict resolution techniques. Fifth, couple dysfunctionality can be viewed as a problem to be solved. Sixth, couple development depends on the process of change, which couples often resist and fear. Counselor-guided change can enhance the couple relationship.

Each of these aspects of couple functioning is of special relevance to dual career couples. Because of the pressures and demands of their lives, dual career couples are more vulnerable to stress and must master sophisticated communication and negotiation skills. These various skills enhance the couple relationship and lead to opportunities for individual and couple growth. Counselors play critical roles in training couples and encouraging them to incorporate these skills into their behavioral repertoire. By recognizing the interdependence of individual choices within the family system, counselors can assist couples in individual decision making and in anticipating the impact of independent decisions on the partner and on other parameters of family life.

Notes

[1]The couple and marriage and family literature typically addresses couple issues in terms of marital relationships. Nonetheless, these concerns are equally applicable to long-term nonmarital couple commitments.

[2]These various therapists refer to the couple relationship of marriage. Therefore, I have used terms like husband, wife, and spouse in reviewing these diverse approaches. Again, the theories would be equally applicable to partners in a long-term nonmarital commitment.

References

Ackerman, N. W. (1938). The unity of the family. *Archives of Pediatrics, 55,* 51–61.

Ackerman, N. W. (1954). Interpersonal disturbances in the family: Some unresolved problems in psychotherapy. *Psychiatry: Journal for the Study of Interpersonal Processes, 17,* 359–368.

Ackerman, N. W. (1956). Interlocking pathology in family relationships. In S. Redo & G. Daniels (Eds.), *Changing concepts of psychoanalytic medicine*. New York: Grune & Stratton.

Ackerman, N. W. (1958). *The psychodynamics of family life*. New York: Basic Books.

Ackerman, N. W. (1960). Theory of family dynamics. *Psychoanalysis and the Psychoanalytic Review, 46,* 33–49.

Ackerman, N. W. (1965). The family approach to marital disorders. In B. Greene (Ed.), *The psychotherapies of marital disharmony.* New York: The Free Press.

Ackerman, N. W. (1968). The family approach and levels of intervention. *American Journal of Psychotherapy, 1,* 5–14.

Ackerman, N. W. (1970a). Family psychotherapy and psychoanalysis: The implications of difference. In N. W. Ackerman (Ed.), *Family process.* New York: Basic Books.

Ackerman, N. W. (Ed.). (1970b). *Family therapy in transition.* Boston: Little, Brown.

Ackerman, N. W., & Behrens, M. L. (1974). Family diagnosis and clinical process. In S. Arieti & G. Caplan (Eds.), *American handbook of psychiatry II. Child and adolescent psychiatry, sociocultural and community psychiatry* (2nd ed.). New York: Basic Books.

Berman, E., Sacks, S., & Lief, H. (1975). The two-professional marriage: A new conflict syndrome. *Journal of Sex and Marital Therapy, 1,* 242–253.

Bloch, D., & Simon, R. (Eds.). (1982). *The strength of family therapy: Selected papers of Nathan W. Ackerman.* New York: Brunner/Mazel.

Gilligan, C. (1988). Remapping the moral domain: New images of self in relationship. In C. Gilligan, J. V. Ward, & J. M. Taylor (Eds.), *Mapping the moral domain: A contribution of women's thinking to psychological theory and education.* Cambridge, MA: Harvard University Press.

Goldenberg, I., & Goldenberg, H. (1980). *Family therapy: An overview.* Belmont, CA: Wadsworth.

Goodrich, T. J., Rampage, C., Ellman, B., & Halstead, K. (1988). *Feminist family therapy: A case book.* New York: Norton.

Haley, J. (1970). Family therapy. *International Journal of Psychiatry, 9,* 233–242.

Haley, J. (1976). *Problem-solving therapy.* San Francisco: Jossey-Bass.

Lewis, J. M., Beavers, W. R., Gossett, J. T., & Phillips. V. A. (1976). *No single thread: Psychological health in family systems.* New York: Brunner/Mazel.

Minuchin, S. (1974). *Families and family therapy.* Cambridge, MA: Harvard University Press.

Minuchin, S., & Fishman, H. C. (1981). *Family therapy techniques.* Cambridge, MA: Harvard University Press.

Papp, P. (1983). *The process of change.* New York: Guilford Press.

Rice, D. (1979). *Dual-career marriage: Conflict and treatment.* New York: Free Press.

Sager, C. J. (1976). *Marriage contracts and couple therapy: Hidden forces in intimate relationship.* New York: Brunner/Mazel.

Satir, V. (1967a). *Conjoint family therapy: A guide to theory and techniques.* Palo Alto, CA: Science and Behavior Books.

Satir, V. (1967b). A family of angels. In J. Haley & L. Hoffman (Eds.), *Techniques of family therapy.* New York: Basic Books.

Satir, V. (1972). *Peoplemaking.* Palo Alto, CA: Science and Behavior Books.

Satir, V. (1975a). Intervention for congruence. In V. Satir, J. Stachowiak, & H. A. Taschman, (Eds.), *Helping families to change.* New York: Aronson.

Satir, V. (1975b). Problems and pitfalls in working with families. In V. Satir, J. Stachowiak, & H. A. Taschman, (Eds.), *Helping families to change.* New York: Aronson.

Satir, V. (1975c). You as a change agent. In V. Satir, J. Stachowiak, & H. A. Taschman, (Eds.), *Helping families to change.* New York: Aronson.

Satir, V., Stachowiak, J., & Taschman, H. A. (1975). *Helping families to change*. New York: Aronson.

Stachowiak, J. (1975a). Family structure and intervention techniques. In V. Satir, J. Stachowiak, & H. A. Taschman (Eds.), *Helping families to change*. New York: Aronson.

Stachowiak, J. (1975b). Family therapy in action. In V. Satir, J. Stachowiak, & H. A. Taschman (Eds.), *Helping families to change*. New York: Aronson.

Stachowiak, J. (1975c). Functional and dysfunctional families. In V. Satir, J. Stachowiak, & H. A. Taschman (Eds.), *Helping families to change*. New York: Aronson.

Taschman, H. A. (1975). Developing in family therapy. In V. Satir, J. Stachowiak, & H. A. Taschman (Eds.), *Helping families to change*. New York: Aronson.

Ulrich, D., & Dunne, H. (1986). *To love and work: A systemic interlocking of family, workplace and career.* New York: Brunner/Mazel.

Walters, M., Carter, B., Papp, P., & Silverstein, O. (1988). *The invisible web: Gender patterns in family relationships*. New York: Guilford Press.

The Integration of Marital Therapy With Sessions With Family of Origin

James L. Framo

Anyone who treats families and couples knows of the deep satisfactions and measureless sacrifices of family life, and also of the hurts and emotional injuries that closely related people can inflict on one another. In most families children are treasured and cared for, yet in some families children are neglected, overindulged, discriminated against, exploited, seduced, persecuted, and occasionally killed. Some marriages are growthful and enrich peoples' lives, yet husbands and wives are also capable of creating a whole range of miseries for each other, ranging from loneliness in marriage, bitter frustration, cruelty, degrading conflicts, to spouse murder or waiting for each other to die. Whitaker has said, "...marriages end up driving some people mad, pushing others into homicidal and suicidal acts, producing hateful demons out of perfectly nice people, and inducing alcoholism in others" (Whitaker & Keith, 1977, p. 69). Professional therapists have developed many theories and techniques for understanding and treating such problems, most of which are quite resistant to change. When one considers the billions of pieces of input that have gone into individuals over many years, and the fact that therapy effects can occur only during a relatively fleeting moment of time, inducing change is a formidable task indeed. I believe it is very difficult to alter attitudes and behavior in individuals, much less change systems. Of all the forces that impinge on people (culture, society, work, neighborhood, friends, and others) the family by far has the greatest imprinting influence. And as every family therapist knows, a family or marital system is a well-oiled machine that often musters all its resources to neutralize and impede change while yearning for something better.

I started seeing families and couples in 1958, and since the publication of *Intensive Family Therapy* (Boszormenyi-Nagy & Framo, 1965), my work has undergone various changes as I refined and modified my conceptual thinking and techniques in order to get the most favorable results. The treatment methods to be described therein represent the culmination and direction toward which those 21 years of experience have led me. I have streamlined my approach from the early days of long-term family therapy to a more efficient short-term treatment progression.

This article will describe a treatment sequence (starting with conventional family or marital therapy, utilizing the couples group format, and aiming toward the adults having sessions with their parents and siblings) which can have powerful effects on the original problems for which the families or couples entered treatment. Although these methods do not always work and are not easy to use, I have found them, through trial and error, to be the most effective in producing lasting change. These procedures are the clinical application of my depth theoretical orientation, which postulates that current family and marital difficulties largely stem from attempts to master earlier conflicts from the original family; these conflicts and transference distortions from the past are being lived anachronistically through the spouse and children (Framo, 1965a, 1970). When these adults are able to go back to deal directly with their parents and brothers and sisters about the previously avoided hard issues that have existed between them, an opportunity exists for reconstructive changes to come about in their marital relationship and in the relationship between these adults and *their* children. The great resistances of adult clients toward bringing in family of origin testifies to the great power of this approach. Because of my conviction that even one session with original family can accomplish more than many regular individual, family, or marital therapy sessions, I have developed techniques for dealing with client resistances and for preparing clients in special kinds of ways for these sessions. This procedure has general applicability and serves diagnostic as well as therapeutic purposes. Not only can clients discover what from the original family is being worked out through the spouse and children, but these adults are being given the chance to come to terms with parents before the parents die.

The methods to be described in this chapter will be largely oriented toward marital theory and conjoint marital therapy rather than the two-generational situation of family therapy. Although I still do see whole families, including the children, from the beginning of therapy to the end, most of the family therapy I do these days is converted to conjoint marital therapy when the originally symptomatic children have been defocused. Those couples who enter therapy specifically for marital problems either do not have children or do not present their children as the primary focus of concern. The major reason for this strategy is that, in my judgment, most children's problems are metaphors about the quality of the relationship between the parents. In a previous publication I wrote, "Whenever there are disturbed children there is a disturbed marriage, although all disturbed marriages do not create disturbed children" (Framo, 1965a, p. 154). Consequently, it is suggested that the best way to help children is to help their parents. The greatest gift parents can give their children is a viable marriage relationship based on each parent's having a strong sense of self. My treatment sequence does not consist only of orienting clients toward working things out with the previous generation. Much of the therapy that goes on with the couple alone or in the couples group consists of dealing with the current marital issues. Consequently, I will be describing my marital assessment methods as well as marital treatment techniques, in both the early as well as later phases of therapy.

Background of the Approach

Those who write textbooks on family therapy have had difficulty classifying my work as a readily identifiable "Framo" theory, in the way that there is Bowen Theory or Minuchin's Structural Family Therapy. Every family therapy student knows that there are a number of family therapy "schools," classified variously as communication, systems, brief/strategic, structural, psychodynamic, experiential, gestalt, behavioral, intergenerational, problem solving, and so forth. The history of various movements reveals a repetitive pattern of initial unity and then separation into various factions, sometimes resulting in denunciations between the "true believers" and the revisionists. The bitterness between Freud, Jung, Adler, and other factions within the psychoanalytic movement is well known. The family therapy movement is no exception to this historical sequence of events, except that the rivalries are more or less friendly ones. The early workers in the family therapy field are like a family; they are sometimes jealous of each other and they compete for preeminence, but they also care for each other. It is always difficult to separate ideological, theoretical differences from issues of territoriality, however. The family therapy pioneers were highly creative, charismatic individuals who, being mavericks within their own profession, needed to establish their unique professional identity and stake out their domain. One unfortunate consequence has been the politicization of the field, which sometimes resulted in one or other of the family therapy schools using pejorative labels about the other schools. I wince, for example, when I see myself categorized in the textbooks as a "psychoanalytic family therapist," not only because the word "psychoanalytic" has fallen into disrepute, but also because that characterization is largely inaccurate. I would like to take this opportunity, as a family therapist, to briefly state my views on psychoanalytic theory.

In recent years it has become fashionable to attack psychoanalysis, both as a theory and as a method of treatment. It is difficult today to take a long perspective and appreciate the truly profound nature of Freud's discoveries. For the first time in human history, explanatory concepts were applied to disorders of behavior, experience, and feeling. He brought the *person* into the study of emotional disorder by tying in mental phenomena with the substance of human existence. With Freud, mental processes began to make sense and become lawful; an emotional disorder was not just something that happened, or the result of satanic influence or a diseased body organ, but came to be understood as part and parcel of being biological and human, of being aggressive, of needing, hoping, fearing, loving, and hating in a world which required socialization in order to survive. Freud's concept of the unconscious and the principle of psychological determinism aroused intense fear and hostility, however. Even today there are mental health professionals who disavow or give lip service to the unconscious and cannot emotionally accept the idea, partially because the unconscious, by definition, is not acceptable. The phenomenon of ready aversion to the unconscious is similar, I have found, to the automatic repulsion and denial to which the family-system approach is subject, by professionals as well as families. (In one family I evaluated, referred by the court, in which consummated incest had occurred between father and daughter, the fear of family exploration was so intense—especially mother's role in the incest—that the father and his wife preferred for the father to accept the possibility of a 30-year prison sentence rather than to continue with the family sessions.)

Psychoanalytic theory in its comprehensiveness deals with a staggering range of phenomena. If we wiped out all knowledge which psychoanalysis has given us, how much would be left to explain human motivation and why people feel and behave as they do? Although some psychoanalytic constructs have not stood the test of time, and others are so mystical that they are untestable, few seriously question the validity of such concepts as defense mechanisms, narcissism, the repetition compulsion, mourning, and the like. Insofar as therapy is concerned, it must be kept in mind that psychoanalysis was never intended as a treatment for the masses; its real value lies in the insights that its depth, long-term, clinical-laboratory work can give to basic knowledge of human psychology. Psychoanalysis is not suitable for reality problems; it is not a good idea, for example, to be in analysis when one's marriage is falling apart.

I have my own criticisms of psychoanalysis. One gets the curious feeling in reading the psychoanalytic literature that the patient lives in a vacuum, that the intrapsychic world is almost a closed system, that life stops when one is in analysis, and that the environment is largely treated as a constant. With characteristic perceptive genius Freud identified the fundamental extrinsic determinants of human distress when he classified the external dangers as loss of the object, loss of the penis (castration), loss of the object's love, and loss of the superego's love. There are also occasional references to such exogenous factors as the primal scene, or the effects of poor mothering upon ego development, or some unusual circumstance in the patient's life, and there is even recognition that neurotic parents bring up neurotic children. Most psychoanalysts, however, operationally function from the assumption that it is not the environment that makes people sick (even though Freud in his philosophical writings on applied psychoanalysis does discuss the deleterious effects of society on human adjustment), but that *people do it to themselves* via fantasy and intrapsychic work and elaboration of what goes on outside.

Experience in family therapy has indicated that symptoms or disordered behavior can be viewed as adaptive, nay, necessary responses to the intimate social contexts of a person's life. The most powerful social influence is, perforce, the family, yet psychoanalytic theory has been ambiguous and contradictory about the role of the family in the etiology and maintenance of emotional disturbance. Freud, admittedly, was the first person to recognize in a systematic way the part that love, hate, jealousy, rivalry, ambivalence, and generational differences which arise from the inherent nature of family relationships, play in the development of psychopathology. He was certainly not oblivious to the actual reality of the family environment. In his case histories, he described his involvement with the families of his patients, such as in the cases of Dora and Little Hans.[1] Despite all this understanding, however, Freud set the model that psychotherapy should consist of a one-to-one confidential relationship between patient and therapist, and that the family should be kept out because the transference field would be contaminated. Psychoanalytic theory, which utilizes a family dynamic in its nuclear concept of the Oedipus complex, deals either with the intrapsychic struggle over the Oedipal wishes, or leaps to its wider social aspects in the culture at large. In *Totem and Taboo, Civilization and its Discontents,* and *Group Psychology* Freud proposed that the function of the Oedipus complex was to protect the family from disruption—for only if incest and patricide are outlawed can the family and thus society survive. Yet though in one sense psychoanalytic thought sees the survival of man as dependent on the preservation of the family, the lack of focus on the transactional dynamics of the family itself represents a real gap in the theory.

Over the years since the heyday of psychoanalysis a series of developments in many different fields (ego psychology, group dynamics, child development, sociology of the family, communication theory, general systems theory, and others) have blended into a family transactional approach. Jackson (1967) gave explicit recognition to this movement when he stated, "We are on the edge of a new era in psychiatry, and the related disciplines of psychology, social work, anthropology and sociology. In this new era we will come to look at human nature in a much more complex way than ever before. From this threshold the view is not of the individual *in vitro* but of the small or larger group within which any particular individual's behavior is adaptive. We will move from individual assessment to analysis of contexts, or more precisely, the *system* from which individual conduct is inseparable" (p. 139). To be sure, as Zilboorg and Henry (1941) have pointed out, for each stage of history emotional disturbances have been defined in a manner which is congruent with the spirit and ethos of the age. It may well be that the family movement reflects, in part, an American emphasis on environmental reform, as Spiegel and Bell (1959) have noted.

There is a major theoretical controversy within the family field. There are the so-called family-systems "purists" like Haley (1975), who polarize the intrapsychic and the interactional, claiming that family theory and therapy should only concern itself with what goes on *between* people. For these family therapists, intrapsychic phenomena and the past are irrelevant for producing change. My own point of view is that while I believe that psychoanalytic theory cannot explain family-system phenomena, I do not agree that in understanding and treating family relationships we should discard everything we have known about dynamic psychology. My position is that what goes on inside people's heads is just as important as what goes on between them, in their interpersonal relationships. *Neither level can be reduced to the other; one does not have to make a choice as to which is more important.*

More technically, the core of my theoretical approach is the *relationship* between the intrapsychic and the transactional. That is to say, I see insoluble intrapsychic conflicts, derived from the original family, being acted out, replicated, mastered, or defended against with the current intimates, via some very complicated processes that are poorly understood. Not only do spouses have transference distortions of each other, giving rise sometimes to outlandish expectations of marriage and of their partners, but the children can also be caught up in bizarre "transference fixes" that are impervious to reality considerations (such as that the small child should mother the parent, or that the child is inherently a "bad seed" that needs to be repaired or exterminated). Indeed, the interpersonal resolution of inner conflict is what creates the kind of profound human distress that we see clinically in troubled families and couples. Whenever a group of people are closely related to each other, as in a family, they reciprocally carry part of each other's psychology and form a feedback system which in turn patterns and regulates their individual behaviors. The creative leap of this family-system theory was recognition of this interlocking, multi-person motivational system whereby family members collusively carry psychic functions for each other. Exploration of this phenomenon, in which dynamic and systems concepts are amalgamated, can provide a conceptual bridge from the personal to the social. The foregoing perhaps explains why Foley (1974), in his classification of family theorists, refers to me as an "integrationist."

A summary of the main tenets of the theory of intergenerational transmission of beliefs, attitudes, and symptoms, expanded from Fairbairn's (1954) object-relations theory, and elaborated by Framo (1970, 1976a), follows:

1. Fairbairn (1954) has postulated that Man's need for a satisfactory object relationship constitutes the fundamental motive of life. His object-relationship approach is contrasted with Freud's theory of instinctual gratification as being primary in Man.
2. Since they are unable to give up the maternal object or change it in outer reality, infants incorporate the frustrating aspects of their relational world. These internalized objects are retained as introjects, psychological representatives of the external objects.
3. These introjects form part of the structure of the personality and undergo various splits. During the course of development of the

individual, external real figures may be assimilated in successive strata or by fusion into the existing bad-object situations.

4. Intrapsychic conflicts arise from experiences in the original family, and reparative efforts to deal with these conflicts impel the individual to force close relations into fitting the internal role models.
5. One's mate or children are perceived largely in terms of the individual's own needs, or as carrying for him his own denied, split-off traits. Mates select each other on the basis of rediscovering lost aspects of their primary object relations which they had split off and which, in their involvement with the spouse, they reexperience by projective identification (Dicks, 1967). A main source of marital disharmony is that spouses project disowned aspects of themselves onto the mate and then fight them in the mate.
6. Children are especially prone to these projections; some children cannot get their parents to love them even if they sacrificed their life. One's current intimates, one's spouse and children, are shadowy stand-ins for old ghosts, the embodiments of old introjects.
7. The adult, by having sessions with his or her family of origin, takes the problems back to their original sources, thereby making available a direct route to etiological factors. These sessions serve diagnostic as well as therapeutic purposes in that both the old and new families can be cross-referenced for similar patterns.
8. Dealing with the real, external figures loosens the grip of the internalized representatives of these figures and exposes them to current realities. The parents and siblings of today are not the parents and siblings of the past; indeed, they never were. The original transference figures can also be the objects of transference today; few adults ever get to see their parents as real people.
9. Having gone backward in time, the individual can then move forward in behaving toward the spouse and children in more appropriate fashion, as persons in their own right, since their transference meaning has changed.
10. Family-of-origin sessions not only can help resolve problems in the current family, but coming to terms with parents and siblings before they die can be a profoundly liberating experience.

In addition to my work being based on the intrapsychic object-relations theory of Fairbairn and the marital interaction theory of Dicks, I have been influenced by theories of family therapists as well. A theoretical debt is owed to Bowen (1978), who was the first to relate present family difficulties to multigenerational processes. The professional world is still reverberating to the account of his study of his own family, reported at a family conference under the title of "Toward the Differentiation of a Self in One's Own Family" (Anonymous, 1972). Boszormenyi-Nagy and Spark (1973), Whitaker (1976), Haas (1968), Paul and Paul (1975), and Headley (1977) have dealt with related concepts in work with the family of origin. My approach to marital therapy, based originally on my family therapy experiences (Framo 1965a), has been more recently described (Framo, 1980).

I would like to clarify one other misconception about my approach. As I stated previously (Framo, 1975b), changing a family system is for me the ultimate professional challenge, and my therapeutic philosophy is to learn as many kinds of treatment approaches as possible in order to have a full repertoire of techniques available to shift a system. Consequently, I have attended workshops on Transactional Analysis, gestalt, encounter groups, behavior therapy, rational-emotive, EST, existential therapy, and other methods. I have used methods of working with families from a number of different schools (communicational, paradoxical, strategic, sculpting, and so forth), and believe it is necessary to be eclectic in dealing with the tremendous variety and kinds of difficulties presented by families and couples. It takes years of experience to be appropriately and selectively eclectic in the sense of choosing a specific method for a particular problem.[2] One cannot apply one's theory to all problems. I do not use object-relations theory and family-of-origin sessions with all my couples. There are aspects of marriages and families that are unrelated to problems hanging over from the families of origin, such as those reflecting social and cultural changes. Furthermore, some uncomplicated marital problems can be treated by "conventional" marital therapy techniques, focusing on the marital interaction in the here and now. These couples' marital difficulties are temporary, not deep-seated, largely situational, a function of the stage of marriage they are in, and for the most part based on misunderstandings which can be untangled in a few sessions. (In a later section of this article, when I specify different types of marital problems, this point will be further elaborated upon.) It is the more serious marital problems which require depth exploration of the conflict paradigms from original family and how they get played out in the marriage. Having said that, however, I believe that everyone can profit from meeting with their parents and brothers and sisters; the family members get to know each other better and can work toward more differentiated intimacy.

The Healthy or Well-Functioning Marriage or Family

There are a number of considerations to be taken into account in determining what is a healthy or well-functioning marriage or family. First, most clinicians have been trained to recognize or deal with abnormality and therefore have a tendency to miss the adaptive features of individual's personalities or family/marital relationships. Little is known about the self-corrective mechanisms that all families have. Since family therapists usually see families and couples when they are under stress and behaving at their worst, therapists often get distorted views of the positive sides of the relationships. Besides, most people think of therapy as the place where one talks about what goes wrong rather than what goes right. (I have observed couples being intensely hostile to each other during treatment sessions, and then as soon as they leave the office, walking away arm in arm.) Finally, under the intensive scrutiny of the therapy microscope almost every individual, family, or couple can look sick. I believe that nearly every person, family, and marriage, over the course of their lives, goes through periods of turmoil and disorganization that at the time appear pathological.

Little systematic work has been done on the so-called normal family (Lewis et al., 1976); I am not aware of any family theoretician or family therapist who has developed a comprehensive theory of healthy marital or family functioning. Most family researchers have used minimal operational criteria for defining normal families—such as that a normal family is one that has not come to community attention for a problem (been arrested, in therapy, school problem, and so forth). Most family therapists, myself included, however, have indirectly alluded to aspects of healthy functioning, largely in contrast to descriptions of pathological families and couples. Accordingly, I have gleaned out of my various writings some ideal principles of healthy or normal family and marital functioning:

1. That partners each be well-differentiated, having developed a sense of self before separating from their families of origin.

2. Clear separation of generational boundaries within the family. The children should be free of the role of saving a parent or the parental marriage.
3. Realistic perceptions and expectations by parents of each other and of their children.
4. The loyalty to the family of procreation is greater than to the family of origin.
5. The spouses put themselves and each other before anyone else, including the children; the marriage, however, is not a symbiotic one which excludes the children. The children do not feel that to be close to one parent means they are alienating the other.
6. Encouragement of identity development and autonomy for all family members. Successful development in the children will mean that they will leave home at some point to start families of their own.
7. Nonpossessive warmth and affection be expressed between parents, between parents and children, and among the siblings.
8. The capacity to have open, honest, and clear communication, and to deal with issues with each other.
9. A realistic, adult-to-adult, caring relationship between each parent and his or her parents and siblings.
10. An open family in the sense of involvement with others outside the family, including extended family and friends; allowing outsiders inside the family.

Insofar as the marital relationship is concerned, in a recent publication (Framo, 1980), I specified criteria for improvement in marital therapy; these criteria have implications for a healthy marriage. They are:

1. The partners are more personally differentiated, and dependency on each other is voluntary.
2. They have come to terms with the roots of their irrational expectations of marriage and of the spouse derived from the family of origin.
3. They have developed a more empathetic understanding of their mate.
4. They can meet each other's realistic needs in the face of their differentness.
5. They can communicate more clearly and openly.
6. They like each other more and they enjoy sex with each other.

7. They have learned to deal with the issues between them.
8. They can enjoy life more, and get pleasure from work and from their children.
9. They have developed flexibility in dealing with situational stresses and crises.
10. They have adjusted to the disenchantment of romantic love and have more realistic appraisals of the vicissitudes of mature, de-idealized love.

As I said, the foregoing criteria are ideal ones; I am sure no family or marriage meets all of them. In addition, in light of the fact that 40% of new marriages are likely to end in divorce, I should make a statement about families that break up. In my judgment some divorces are steps of growth, whereas others I perceive as manifestations of unresolved problems from original family. In a paper on divorce therapy (Framo, 1978a), I specified its goals as helping the couple to disengage from their relationship with a minimum of destructiveness to self, the partner, and the children, and with the freedom to form new relationships. I do believe that, although difficult, it is possible for divorce and remarriage to occur without enduring cost to the children or parents. In other words, a stepfamily can be a healthy, well-functioning family (Visher & Visher, 1979).

The Pathological or Dysfunctional Marriage or Family

My main conceptualizations and ideas about dysfunctional families and couples are contained in previous publications (Framo, 1965a, 1970). I postulated that symptoms are formed, selected, faked, exchanged, maintained, and reduced or extinguished as a function of the relationship context in which they are naturally embedded. Children's symptoms are frequently the outcome of irrational role assignments which one or both parents ascribe to the child; these designations usually have nothing to do with the inherent nature of the child. Children who are assigned the role of "the troublemaker," "the crazy one," "mother's protector," or "the stupid one" may incorporate and *become* their assigned role, may spend a lifetime disputing the role, may play-act at the role, or the child may learn to become his own person, independent of the role.

Examples of other factors which create or affect symptoms are: blurring of generational boundaries (as when the mother goes to her son to complain about her husband); family traumas (the death or absence of a parent, divorce, or the unemployment of a parent); maintenance of symptoms for system purposes (the child is being sick so mother will have someone to take care of); scapegoating ("Our marriage would be fine if it weren't for that kid."); emotional overburdening of the child (the child being expected to be marriage counselor for his parents); and over/covert rejection or infantilization of the child. The particular type of symptom developed depends, in general, on what the system requires. Some dangerous symptoms of children are ignored by parents, although the school or others may recognize their seriousness. On the other hand, a child's "symptom" may be trivial as seen by outsiders, yet the parents may exaggerate its importance and may want to use drastic measures for handling it (such as wanting to institutionalize a child because "he lies.")

Among the factors that enable some children to survive and be relatively untouched by the family pathology are the following:

1. These children, for reasons having to do with the parents' backgrounds, did not become the focus of concern. Even their physical appearance could play a role in not being selected as special.
2. These siblings used the identified patient as a model of what to avoid.
3. These children may have had resources outside the family (such as an aunt, friend, or teacher), and therefore established wider emotional investments.
4. These children were more successful at utilizing defenses of isolation, but paid a price by having constricted personalities.

I have not developed any system for typing or classifying families, although I have recently (Framo, 1980) devised an informal scheme for classifying marriages. This very crude classification system is based on responsiveness to therapy; that is, those in the early part of the list I find, in general, less difficult to treat than those toward the latter part. The scheme is not precise enough to call it "marital diagnosis." Diagnosis suggests that specific treatment strategies have been devised for each discrete category, which is certainly not the case.

1. Couples whose marriage relationships are basically sound and whose problems largely stem from communicational misunderstandings. These couples essentially rehabilitate their own marriage, needing only a couple of therapy sessions.
2. Marriages where the partners love each other, are committed to the marriage, but "can't get along." Some of these couples are

responding to the impact of parenthood, others have in-law complications, some argue a lot, and others avoid conflict.

3. Brother-sister marriages where the spouses care a great deal for each other, but there is little excitement in the relationship. Sex is routine and marital life is comfortable but dull.
4. Conflictual marriages where the spouses feel markedly ambivalent about each other. The partners are engaged in a power struggle and are in conflict over a variety of issues, ranging from feminist issues to sex, disciplining of the children, dual-career conflicts, in-laws, money, and all the other "cover" issues.
5. Marriages in which one partner is symptomatic. Involving both partners in conjoint treatment can move this kind of marriage into the "conflict" category. The symptoms (such as depression) may become unnecessary as the couple begins to deal with their issues.
6. Marriages whose problems are a consequence of incomplete marital maturation. These partners have never really left home and are overinvolved with one or both families of origin.
7. Marriages of mental health professionals or of "professional patients" are not easy to change. For some of these couples, being in therapy is a way of life. The professional therapist-spouses have been doing bad therapy on each other, sometimes for years; each is an expert on the partner's dynamics.
8. Second or third marriages are usually complicated by ghosts of the previous marriages, children, and obligations to the former spouses. Loyalty rearrangements, problems of step-parenting, financial stresses, and grandparents all present difficulties.
9. Older couples whose relationship problems have calcified and whose options are limited. These couples came to therapy too late.
10. "Pseudo-mutual" couples who deny all problems in the marriage and present a child as the problem. These couples cannot admit to the ordinary difficulties all couples can acknowledge. The therapist may reach these couples indirectly by accepting the child as the problem (Montalvo & Haley, 1973). An alternative method of working with child-focused families is offered by Bradt and Moynihan (1971).
11. The marriage that is in extremis, where the couple come to therapy as a last resort before seeing lawyers. One partner may be finished with the marriage and the other is trying to hold on. Some of these couples can be engaged in divorce therapy.

12. Finally, there is the kind of chronically unhappy marriage where the partners "can't live with and can't live without." These couples may have had many unsuccessful individual or marital therapy experiences; they should have divorced and could not because permanent separation means psychic death.

The Assessment of System Dysfunction

My unit of treatment is the whole family when there are problems involving the children. As I stated earlier, sometimes I do family therapy (parents and children together) from beginning to end. Other times, when the problems in the children have been alleviated, I dismiss the children and work with the parents' marriage. Still other couples enter therapy explicitly for marital problems and either do not have children or state that their marital relationship is the problem.

I no longer do individual therapy. When I treat a couple I insist on seeing them together, usually with a female cotherapist. If one spouse wants to be seen alone first or wants the partner to be seen alone, and either one refuses to come in for a conjoint interview, I will refer them elsewhere. During therapy I refuse interviews with a single individual, although during ongoing couples group therapy I will see a couple unit for emergencies. I am aware that there are therapists who find it diagnostically valuable to have separate interviews with a single spouse, but in my experience the advantages of single sessions (such as learning about secrets, affairs, and so forth) are not worth the suspicions of the absent partner, the temporary relief of the confiding spouse, or the conflicts of loyalty and confidentiality in the therapist that such sessions promulgate. Furthermore, each spouse lives in the context of an intimate relationship, and separating the partners for private sessions negates the context, obscures the interactional collusiveness, and violates the integrity of the marital unit. The only exception made to my own rule is when I may separate divorcing spouses in the later stages of divorce therapy, although even under this circumstance I consider that the person who cannot tolerate the presence of the partner has not emotionally divorced that partner.

The only method of assessment I use is the clinical interview, which I find far superior to any formal questionnaire, guided interview schedule, situational test, or experimental procedure. Questionnaires and formal tasks do not give an observer the opportunity to follow up on leads or observe reactions. It is much easier to deceive a questionnaire than it is to fool an experienced clinician. Besides, questionnaires tell you nothing about how partners typically behave with each other, because people do not know how they interact with their intimates. Previously, I have stated my objections to the use of questionnaires in family research (Framo, 1965b).

Initial interviews, on the other hand, can also be misleading; it takes several interviews to get a fairly clear picture of what is going on.[3] Generally speaking, I do not make interventions in the first few sessions, as my cotherapist and I assess the couple, and while they, to be sure, assess us. The reason for early nonintervention is that I want to get maximum information without deliberately affecting the process. To be sure, assessment and treatment are inseparable, even when the therapist does not make a purposeful intervention. Among the factors that have therapeutic or antitherapeutic effects in the initial interviews are: history of previous therapies, therapy expectations, reputation of the therapist, the basis of the decision to come to therapy, the physical setting of the office, the therapist(s) physical appearance, the kinds of questions asked, how they are asked, amount of the fee, degree of "connectedness" between clients and therapist(s), a sense of hope or despair stimulated by the first interview, and so forth. When I see a couple I consider there are three main areas of inquiry: the husband and wife as individuals, and their relationship—how their intrapsychic spheres intermesh. More specifically, I attempt to cover such topics as the following in the early interviews: referral source, brief statement of problems from each spouse, age, occupation, length of marriage, ages and gender of children, previous therapies, prior marriages, basis of mate selection, family's reactions to choice of partner, the partners' fight styles, whether the spouses basically love each other, whether they ever had a good relationship, commitment to the marriage, the quality and quantity of their sexual relationship, a brief history of each family of origin, current relationship with parents and siblings, how they relate to each other in the interview, motivation for therapy, and so forth.

Goal-Setting

One of the ways that family and marital therapy differ from all other psychotherapies is that there are varied and sometimes competing vested interests at play during treatment sessions. In individual therapy the therapist is dealing with warring elements within one person, but when there are issues between people, their goals of therapy will vary. For instance, a wife's goal might be to get out of the marriage without guilt, whereas the husband's goal might be to make the marriage relationship better; if the marriage ends in divorce the wife may consider the therapy a great success, and the husband may consider it to be a failure and may refuse to pay for the treatment. In family therapy a divorced woman who feels she has a second chance for happiness with a man who does not want her child, may have the goal of institutionalizing the child with the blessing of a mental health professional; the child, of course, has the goal of staying with the mother.

In the first interview I routinely ask each person what his or her goals of therapy are: What would they like to accomplish in therapy? One complication surrounding treatment goals is that the husband and wife may openly state goals that are at variance with their secret agendas for therapy outcome. For example, the husband may profess interest in saving his marriage, yet all the while be hoping the therapist will pronounce that the marriage is over. Some of the secret agendas are unconscious: a wife may unwittingly be attempting to prove to the therapist how cruel and heartless her husband really is, while praising his generosity. A husband may punish his wife for each step she takes toward autonomy (such as by not speaking to her for several days when she goes back to school), yet may state that he wants a wife who is independent. Finally, clients' goals almost always change as therapy progresses. They shift goals to accommodate to their widening awareness and changing perception of their problems. For instance, in the early part of therapy a couple may state as their problem the cliché, "We do not communicate," and later they may realize that their problems are not only more complicated than communication ones, but that they have entirely different values about the meaning of marriage. Goals of therapy, moreover, may clash not only among the family members, but with the goals of the therapist as well. Perhaps part of the skill of a therapist resides in finding the appropriate balance between the conflict of goals and expectations of all the family members as well as those of the therapist. (Not under discussion is the subject of differences between cotherapists about treatment goals.) I have often wondered whether, in some situations, it is not necessary for someone in the family to lose if someone is to gain. For instance, if a 40-year-old man finally gets to the point where he can leave his suffocating, widowed mother and get married, from his and the therapist's view, he is better, but from his mother's point of view he is worse.

Since my treatment model involves different settings and interventions at different stages as the typical couple progress through single couple therapy, couples group therapy, and family-of-origin sessions, my own goals of therapy change from one sequence to the next. My long-range goals of marital therapy were stated earlier in this chapter. In the early phases the first goal is the establishment of a working relationship between the couple and cotherapists; without trust therapy will never get off the ground.

The great majority of couples that I see enter a couples group following several diagnostic interviews (Framo, 1973). My goal during the couples group sessions consists primarily of utilizing the group process to further the therapy of the couple. The feedback the members get from each other is quite therapeutic; feedback from group members often has more impact than the statements of the therapists. Some other benefits of the group format are: the partners come to recognize the universality of certain marital problems and do not feel so different from other couples; the couples usually develop trust of each other and consequently become more open; in a "good" group even deep secrets will be revealed; problems across couples are contrasted or are found to be similar, so couples use each other as models of what to imitate or avoid; observations of each other become sharper as treatment progresses; the couples usually come to care for each other, and caring is always therapeutic; the goals of the spouses usually undergo modification in response to therapists' activity and feedback from the group, and other benefits. Consequently, during the couples group sessions, the spouses become much more aware of their unrealistic expectations of marriage and of their spouse. These realizations bring about curiosity as to the genesis of their irrational expectations—which provides the opening for me to suggest anew that working things out with original family is one way of getting beyond the marital impasse. The group process helps individuals to become less resistant to bringing in their family, especially since this goal of mine becomes the group goal; family-of-origin sessions come to be perceived by the group as a sort of final examination or graduation ceremony. The two major goals for the family-of-origin sessions are discovering what, from the old family, is being projected onto the spouse, and having a corrective experience with parents and siblings. The ultimate payoff or goal is a more differentiated self, with consequent improvement in the marital or family relationships.

Treatment Applicability

Most of the couples I have treated were seen in my private practice and therefore were, economically at least, upper middle class. However, I have used these methods in a community mental health center where the social classes of the clients spanned the entire spectrum. I have seen couples conjointly, done couples group therapy, and had family-of-origin sessions with clients who were severely disadvantaged, poor, and nearly illiterate.

There are certain universals of family and marital life that exist with all human beings, in all classes and cultures. One family problem has been mentioned as being universal among those seeking treatment—that the loyalty of a spouse to the family of origin was greater than to the spouse and children. Almost everybody has a peer intimate relationship and has a parent, brother, or sister, and whenever there are intimates there are going to be relationship difficulties. Interestingly, those people who are not psychologically minded and who want something concrete, like a pill, when they are in distress often do not resist meeting with a spouse or with parents or siblings—although they have no concept of psychotherapy. Their very nonsophistication makes them more open to conjoint family or marital therapy since they do not know enough about therapy to know that that is not what is usually done.

In one sense I think everyone, people in treatment or not, can profit from family-of-origin sessions. Few people ever get to know their parents as real people, few families ever share, all together as a family, the really meaningful thoughts and feelings, and few people get to that last stage with parents, that of forgiving them and telling them that they are loved. So I see family-of-origin sessions as not being just a therapy method but as a kind of pandemic experience for people in general. As a matter of fact, in recent years I have been meeting the requests of family therapists to have one-time sessions with their original families. These sessions have been most productive.

Clinically, however, there are some marital situations where the family-of-origin sessions are more necessary, and still others where, although they are needed, there are certain unique circumstances which preclude their being held. Everyone transfers irrational attitudes and projects onto their spouse, including prominent people and professional marriage therapists; this phenomenon is part of being human and is a byproduct of the nature of intimate relationships. However, some people, who are more differentiated in Bowen's (1978) sense, have less need of fusion and can more accurately perceive the spouse as a person in his or her own right. These are the couples seen in marital therapy for relatively superficial problems, and for whom family-of-origin sessions are not necessarily indicated. At the other extreme are those people who view their spouses as plasticine objects to be molded to their own needs, who do not really know where they end and the spouse begins, who are overdependent (for example, one spouse cannot go to the bathroom without the other asking, "Where are you going?"), and who may exhibit intense transference rage toward the mate (culminating sometimes in spouse murder). These people are unable to commit themselves to anyone, because the deeper involvement is with the parents (thus, the only time they may come alive during treatment sessions is when they discuss their parents). Their marital relationship is unreal, shadowy, and dream like because where they "live" is in the old family. For these kinds of couples family-of-origin sessions are a must; but, as might be expected, they are also the most difficult to set up, to conduct, and to handle from the standpoint of subsequent emotional fallout.

From time to time when I have given workshops, I have been asked whether there are couples who should *not* be seen in a couples group. I have never had the experience of having a couple in a group and thinking they would have done better as a single couple. There are couples who are reluctant to enter a group, but once in the group their apprehensions vanish. I am usually able to get them to come into a group by telling them that in the group they will accomplish their goals quicker—which is true. The only couples I see as a single couple are those who need only a few sessions or those who are unable to arrange for the times that the groups meet. Although I have not yet met such a marital situation, it is possible that there may be some unique combination of circumstances and dynamics that would make couples group therapy contraindicated for a given couple. For instance, it is possible that a couple where incest with their children had occurred might not be able to deal with that even in the group. On the other hand, I have seen some pretty heavy secrets revealed in that setting, such as a man whose father was in jail for child molesting.

Contraindications for family-of-origin sessions is a topic that we know little about, largely because there have only been a few years' experience with the method. I consider family-of-origin therapy as the major surgery of family therapy, and, like major surgery, there are risks and there can be complications, especially short-term emotional upsets.

I have referred various family members for specific therapies, such as sex therapy, vocational guidance, behavior therapy, remediation of learning disabilities, group therapy, marathons, and even for individual psychotherapy. I prefer that an individual in marital therapy with me not be in individual therapy with someone else while the marital therapy is going on. The main reason for this stance is that these clients will frequently reserve important material for their individual sessions; besides, the outside therapist and I could be working at cross-purposes, especially if that other therapist is an adherent of the illness model. I do not feel that I have a right to tell clients to terminate their individual therapy or analysis before starting marital therapy, but I do inform them of the handicaps that their separate therapy could impose on the marital therapy. When the desire for more extensive work on self is expressed, or when I think it advisable, however, I do refer clients for individual therapy when the marital therapy has terminated.

The final point on treatment applicability concerns the question as to whether no treatment of any sort is ever recommended. There are couples, especially those who have had too much therapy, to whom I make the recommendation that the best thing they can do for themselves is not be be in treatment. I have also dismissed some couples from ongoing therapy who have been using therapy as a substitute for living. I tell them, "Go out and live your lives and stop examining yourselves."

The Structure of the Therapy Process

As stated earlier, couples are seen only conjointly, and almost all couples are seen in a couples group format after a few diagnostic sessions with the couple alone. There are no sessions with individuals. One major goal of the couples group setting is to prepare clients for the family-of-origin (intergenerational) sessions, which usually occur toward the end of therapy. The reasons for having the family-of-origin sessions late in therapy is that these sessions are more productive when the clients have changed in therapy, and are ready to deal with the difficult issues with their parents and siblings.

Occasionally I have family sessions with couples and their children, particularly if a couple in marital therapy expresses some concern about their children. These sessions are, of course, held outside the group. These family sessions have been valuable on several counts: the children are given the message that they are no longer responsible for handling their parents' problems, because that job has been taken over by the therapists; the children give the kind of ingenuous, truthful accounts of what is going on at home that only children can give; and if the session occurs toward the end of therapy the children can give a reading on how they perceive changes in their parents' relationship. Many couples at the end of successful marital therapy report "improvement" in their children even when I have never seen the children.

Insofar as combined therapies are concerned, the one form of treatment that I find does not interfere with family therapy is for adolescents to be in peer group therapy concurrent with the family therapy. The separate adolescent group and family settings have seemed to enhance each other. (I do not conduct the group therapy; that is done by someone to whom I refer the adolescent.)

Although I have had to work as a solo therapist at times, I prefer to work with a cotherapist, particularly a female. Through the years I have worked with many cotherapists and I have come to see the value of having someone there to share responsibility, to notice things I do not see, to fight with me about what's going on, to provide more therapeutic leverage, to protect my flank, to make observations I do not think of, to allow me to remove myself psychologically, and to provide a reassuring presence during the kinds of chaotic or frightening events which can occur during family or marital therapy. Families and couples always respond more favorably to being seen by cotherapists rather than a single therapist, especially male-female teams. Women especially are pleased that another woman is present to understand a woman's point of view. Over the past 7 years, in addition to working with other cotherapists, I have worked with my wife (Mary Framo, MSS, family therapist), in our evening private practice. The subject of husband-wife cotherapy is a large, rather complicated one that must await a separate publication. The only disadvantages I have seen with cotherapy is when there is a poor match between the personalities of the therapists. A cotherapy team can become like a marriage, and differences will inevitably arise—about strategy, interruptions, status, and who is chief honcho. If the cotherapists do not have the mechanisms for working out their differences, then they should divorce, because couples and families will exploit their alienation, try to cure the cotherapy rift, or terminate prematurely.

The physical arrangement of sessions is as follows: swivel chairs are used (so partners can turn and face each other) and the chairs are arranged in a circle. I cannot imagine conducting family or marital therapy sessions from behind a desk. All my sessions are audiotaped, and clients are free at any time to borrow the tapes to listen to at home. Many people take advantage of this offer, or bring their own cassette recorders to sessions. Sessions listened to at home can add an important dimension to the treatment in that, with anxiety being less, the observing ego is more operative at that time. Many clients report that while listening to sessions at home they noticed aspects of themselves (anger, sulking, conning, phoniness, obsequiousness, contempt, and so forth) that their defensiveness during sessions blocked them from seeing. I make no apologies about taping, the microphone is clearly present, and I communicate, in effect, "This is the way I work." Almost never does anyone object to being taped. (In those early days, when we used to ask permission and apologize for taping, there were many objections). After every session a summary of the session is written up; if you do not do this you will never remember what is on the tape, and the tape will be useless.

Marital or family therapy, as I conduct it, is not time-limited; it does not seem appropriate to me to specify arbitrarily how many sessions are needed for a given problem. However, when I calculated the average number of sessions that couples come for marital therapy, the average turned out to be 15 sessions. This figure is an average one; the range was from one session to about 50 sessions. Sessions are generally held once a week; with interruptions for holidays and vacations; the average length of treatment is about 5 months. Occasionally some families and couples are seen on an irregular basis; some people seem to profit more when there is more than one week between sessions, whereas others come irregularly because they cannot afford to come more frequently. Decisions about therapy structure are made explicitly by the cotherapists, subject to occasional negotiation with the clients.

The Role of the Therapist

Like practically all family therapists, I am rather active in therapy sessions; I cannot conceive of doing marital or family therapy in a passive, nondirective way. Because of the multiplicity of events on numerous levels, some degree of control of sessions by the therapist is necessary. For instance, since there is such deep and abiding resistance to bringing in family of origin, and because of my convictions about its value, I tend to come down rather hard on that subject; that is the one area where I am most directive.

Following the initial diagnostic sessions, where I abstain from making interventions, my conversational style usually consists of a fluid blend of questioning, empathizing, challenging, stage directing, avoiding snares, confronting, balancing, supporting, reflecting, disagreeing, and, when relevant, judicious sharing of some of my own life experiences. On the subject of self-disclosure, I think it important that the therapist convey in some form that he has experienced pain and loss, shame, guilt, and disappointment, as well as the exhilaration and joys of living. I even think it is helpful at times to communicate the reality of one's own parenting difficulties as well as of one's own marriage as going through up-and-down phases. It is just as unwise to support the fantasy of the therapist's life as ideal as it is to overburden clients with one's own problems.

In our efforts to read the punctuation of the couple and raise concealed intrapsychic and interpersonal conflicts into open interactional expression, I and my cotherapist will move in and out of their orbit and emotional field. While one therapist is "inside" it is better for the other to be "outside," and be in a position to rescue the one who got caught up in the couple's or the group's irrationality. When partners will not talk to each other and only want to talk to the therapist(s), I insist they talk to each other; when they only will talk to each other, I insist that they talk to me. Any behavior can be used as a defense.

My role as a therapist is fairly consistent throughout the course of treatment, although there may be times when the cotherapists will flexibly alternate roles. That is, the one who has usually been the rescuer may become the confronter, and vice versa. By the time the end of therapy has approached, I have noticed there is a tendency for me to become more personal and social with clients. Some couples groups after termination have had parties in one of the couple's homes, and although there was a time when I would never mix socially with some clients, I have found no problems arising from social contact of this sort with the great majority of couples following termination. Family therapists have tended to break down a number of traditional professional taboos without the sky falling in.

Techniques of Marital—Family Therapy

In my earlier writings on therapy techniques in *Intensive Family Therapy,* (Framo, 1965a), I dealt with the phases of family therapy as well as such technical problems as resistance, marriage problems, the "well sibling," transference/countertransference, and cotherapy. At that time most of my experience was with families with a schizophrenic member. Although some of those observations and techniques have held up over time, others have been modified; an update on my techniques can be found in an informal paper written in 1975 (Framo, 1975b).

My techniques vary according to whether I am seeing a couple, a couples group, or family of origin, not only because of the number and kind of people in the room, but because of the variation in goals, the nature of the therapy contract, and the psychological set of the clients. When couples first enter therapy they are intensely preoccupied with the fate of their relationship. Standard marital therapy techniques are used to deal with the relationship itself, such as accepting the couple, both as individuals and as a relationship, no matter how strange or unusual they seem at first; helping them develop congruent communications; the feedback technique (partners repeating back to each other what they think they heard); quid pro quo negotiations; work on differentiation; changing the rules of the relationship; teaching the couple how to "fight" or deal with issues with each other (Bach & Wyden, 1969); audiotape playback; as well as such conventional techniques as reflection, confrontation, interpretations, eliciting of affect, and so forth. On occasion, paradoxical tasks are assigned, but this sort of "homework," as well as some Masters and Johnson sex-therapy exercises, are used sparingly.[4] Techniques will differ according to the kind of marital problem being presented. The greatest mistake made by beginning marital therapists, in my judgment, is that they are often misled by spouses' rage or apparent indifference toward each other, and they conclude that the marriage is unworkable. I have learned to respect the integrity and the tenaciousness of bonds in marital relationships, even in the most alienated of couples or unlikeliest matches.

I originally put couples together in a group in order to free myself from the transference/countertransference logjam that occurs with certain kinds of couples (Framo, 1973). While some couples are a pleasure to work with, there are others who "triangle in" the therapist as judge or prosecutor, those incapable of hearing anyone but themselves, those who become overdependent and helpless, and still others who try to solve their marital problems by joining in an attack on the therapist. In order to handle my own reactions of frustration, impotence, or exasperation, I began putting my difficult couples together. It was only later, after experience with the couples group format, that I recognized the power of this form of treatment. I now believe that couples group therapy is the treatment of choice for premarital, living-together, marital, and separation or divorce relationship problems. Indeed, all the couples I see come into a couples' group unless there are scheduling difficulties or unless the relationship problem does not require more than a couple of sessions.

The group contains three couples, and the method, in brief, consists of focusing on one couple at a time while the other two couples observe, and then eliciting feedback from everyone in the group; then the next couple is attended to, and then the next, all of the individuals getting and giving feedback. Sessions last for 2 hours and are conducted with a female cotherapist.[5] The couples groups are open-ended, in that as couples terminate, new ones are added. The focus is on the marital pair within the group context; it is recognized that other therapists conduct couples groups more like conventional peer group therapy where anyone can talk at any time. My primary focus is on the couple rather than the group because that pair had a history before the group started, and are likely to have a future together long after the group has disbanded. I am particularly interested in the transference distortions which occur between partners, not so much in the transference reactions across couples. Although I place the group as secondary to the couple, a group process is inevitable and must be managed and utilized to therapeutic advantage.

I find that couples do better when they are with couples who are not too far removed from them by age or stage of the life cycle. That is, I tend to put together couples recently married or with young children, and have other groups with older couples whose children are grown. It has not worked too well when I have put, say, a young couple with two older couples; the latter would often lecture the young couple about the troubles that lay ahead. The couples are usually seen alone for several sessions before coming into a group. Some people are fearful of entering the group, and I am usually able to get them in by saying, truthfully in my experience, that whatever goals of therapy they have they will accomplish faster in the group.

The rules of the couples group are stated in the first session: Violence is not permitted; partners are not to discuss the other couples where they can be overheard by others; when one partner cannot attend, the other should come to sessions; terminations should never occur on the telephone, and should be announced a week in advance; and individuals should try to give feedback in a constructive way. Unlike most therapists, I do not discourage the couples from having social contact with each other outside the sessions; during the 10 years I have conducted couples groups I have seen only benefits arising from the couples becoming friends with each other. Indeed, one of the curative factors in couples groups is the caring that the participants come to have for each other. I once had in a class a psychiatric resident from Ghana who said that in his country, when a couple had a serious marital problem, the two extended families would gather together in a circle and help the couple work it out. It is unfortunate that in our country people have to pay for supportive networks. One resource rarely used by therapists in treating marital problems is the extended family of each partner; my work with family of origin is designed, in part, for this purpose.

When the couple is seen in the context of the couples group, the presence of other couples and the group process add another dimension to the therapy. Now there is a wider audience for the interactional behavior; in this atmosphere there is less blaming of each other and more focus on self. At a certain stage in the course of a couples group, each individual usually hits a plateau and starts questioning his or her own behavior or attitude toward the spouse; some even start wondering about the source of their irrational perceptions and beliefs. There is considerable variation in the readiness of people to get to this point, depending not only on the differentiating capacity of the individual for insight, but on what is happening in the marital relationship as well. Some people, of course, never get beyond blaming the spouse; some couples become stalemated this way, and treatment can only progress by avoiding their interaction and focusing on the individuals. In any event, the person starting to examine self provides my entry into trying to get the client to bring in family of origin as a way of dealing with his or her unrealistic expectations of the partner or the marriage.

Early in the work with a couple, I indicate that I make it a practice of having each individual meet with his or her own family of origin, without the spouse being present. Anticipating the anxiety that this statement precipitates, I state that the sessions are usually held toward the end of therapy, after the clients have been prepared for the family conference and can see its value. During the couples group sessions, while working directly on the marital problems, I will occasionally ask direct questions about what is happening between a spouse and his or her parents and siblings. I have noticed that although all sorts of important things may be going on in the family of origin, if you do not directly ask, clients do not tell you; they consider such events to be extrinsic to their marital problems. (I recall one fellow who said, "I don't see why you ask about my stopping at my mother's house everyday. What does that have to do with my relationship to my wife?") In addition to asking about current relationships to family-of-origin members or about the in-law relationships, from time to time I remind group members that everyone is expected to bring in original family. There are usually members of the group who, although frightened at the prospect, plan to follow though and bring in their family. Some of them report that they have even mentioned the session to selected family members who might be receptive to the idea. There are other members of the group who firmly rule out ever bringing in their family of origin. The therapists' expectations along these lines, and the varying degrees of readiness to meet that expectation on the part of the couples group members, becomes part of the culture of each group. Usually the more willing members ally themselves with the therapists, and attempt to persuade the reluctant ones to consider doing it. Some individuals become strongly motivated to work things out with a parent or sibling. After some clients have had their family-of-origin sessions they can present more convincing evidence of their value; some of the most intransigent clients have reconsidered their negative positions upon hearing these accounts.

Over the years I have developed certain techniques for dealing with the aversive response of most people to the prospect of sitting with their parents and brothers and sisters and discussing openly the heretofore avoided hard issues. The resistances assume manifold forms. An early one is when clients state that they get along fine with their family and there are no issues to be dealt with. When I get a detailed family-of-origin history, however, which disassembles the global characterization, issues become apparent in nearly every sentence. Gradually, most clients begin to see that the family-of-origin sessions not only have the potential of benefiting themselves or the marriage, but other reasons begin to emerge for having the sessions. As the agenda for the session is prepared, the marital problems recede in importance and clients gradually are induced to deal with past and present issues with their family. It is fascinating to observe how the marital conflicts, which totally preoccupied the client several weeks earlier, fade away and are replaced by the dawning realization that maybe something can be done about that longstanding guilty overcloseness or alienation from a mother, father or sibling. Working out a better relationship with family of origin frequently becomes a goal in its own right. Some clients, however, resist the endeavor to the end, either saying that their family situation is hopeless or indicating that meeting with the family could make things much worse by "opening up a Pandora's Box." Especially difficult to deal with is the client who describes his or her family as "close and extremely loving," with the implication that it is not possible for people to love too much. Spouses' reactions to their mates' accounts of family history frequently reveal undisclosed facts. For instance, one client never mentioned the suicide of her father until her spouse brought it up. On the basis of the family histories the client is assisted in developing an agenda of issues to bring up with each and every member of the family. Each concrete issue becomes anxiety-laden. When the adult male says he always longed for affection from his father, and I suggest he tell father that in the session, his apprehensive reaction is predictable. An adult daughter preparing to tell her mother that she can no longer be responsible for mother's happiness approaches that confrontation with great fear.

I do not have spouses present in the session because the focus is on what transpired in a given individual's family as that person was growing up, long before the spouse was met. If the spouse were present, the incoming family would be inhibited from discussing sensitive issues in the presence of an "outsider" or could not resist triangling in the client's marriage instead of dealing with the relationships in *this* family. (There are occasions when I have included the spouse in order to deal with problems in the in-law relationships, but I do not consider these sessions "family-of-origin" work in the sense in which I use it.) Usually one spouse is more ready to deal with his or her family than is the other. Most of the time partners urge each other to do it even if they themselves are unwilling; as a matter of fact, I have seen some partners threaten divorce if the spouses do not attempt to work things out with their family. Only once did I have a spouse oppose the partner meeting with his family.

Most of the resistance to bringing in family of origin resides in the client, because usually when he or she becomes motivated the family follows. The reasons given by clients for not wanting to bring in original family are infinite, each one sounding most convincing and legitimate to the therapist unfamiliar with family-of-origin work ("They live too far away," "I know they would never come," "My mother is in bad health," "My father doesn't believe in psychiatrists or psychologists," and so forth). Occasionally, despite all the efforts of a client to get his or her family in, some families refuse; some of these refusals are based on clients' sabotaging the session by implicitly presenting it to the family as punishment, whereas other times there are circumstances peculiar to a given family situation that preclude such a session. I have the clients themselves take responsibility for writing and phoning and gathering their family members together to come in. Some families are scattered around the country, but in this age of jet travel, geographical distance does not present a serious barrier. Family members come in from all parts of the country, and some have traveled from overseas. The emotional barriers are far more critical, and when these are overcome the reality problems are not difficult to deal with. As the session approaches, anxiety starts building up in the client, and usually starts spreading to the family outside. I begin to get calls from various family members about a parent's poor health and whether the emotional strain of such a session could bring about a medical disaster. One message I attempt to communicate, both to the client and the family members, is that the parents or siblings themselves have issues they might like to bring up with the client or other family members.

Techniques must be modified for the family-of-origin sessions inasmuch as the parents and siblings are usually not coming in with an acknowledged need for help. Similar to when I interview a family at a workshop in front of an audience, I find it necessary to tread a fine line between dealing with meaningful things and yet not explicitly treating the incoming family members like patients. In my experience in working with many families of origin I have found that there are certain tactical and strategic errors which should be avoided. Historically, one of the earliest identified resistances in family therapy was that of the "absent member maneuver," a process whereby the family members collude to keep a significant member out of the session (Sonne, Speck, & Jungreis, 1962). This resistance is especially likely to come into play when planning family-of-origin sessions. For instance, sometimes the client is willing to bring in parents but refuses to bring in a brother or sister. Or the family shows up without an important member despite assurances that everyone would be there. Generally speaking I will not hold the session without a significant family member; the session is postponed until that person can make it. The presence of siblings is especially critical in family-of-origin sessions, and they are the ones most likely to be absent.

I believe that a male-female cotherapy team that is congruent is a potent therapeutic force; especially is this true in working with families of origin. Whenever by necessity I have had to conduct these sessions alone, I have felt undefended and powerless. Part of the reason for this is that family-of-origin sessions are so unpredictable; you never can tell what they are going to be like. Families described by clients as docile and passive sometimes turn out to be hostile and difficult, and families described as impossible sometimes create a "love in." The incoming families find it reassuring that a man and woman are seeing them, not only because both sexes are represented but because that arrangement seems to remove the session from the stereotype of psychiatry, which most people distrust. The cotherapy arrangement allows the initial human contact to take place more easily and then, throughout the session, can bring to bear the kinds of bilateral, complementary, and opposing interventions that only a well functioning cotherapy team can do.

There is considerable variation in these family-of-origin sessions; they differ in intensity, time focus, issues, degree of relatedness, amount of fusion, content, pace, awkwardness, defensiveness, and every other dimension that can occur when family members are brought together for the purpose of getting to know each other better and dealing openly with each other. One error that can be made is to accept the client's anger toward the parents or siblings at face value, and miss the positive feelings and yearnings. The natural feeling toward parents is one of ambivalence, and if the therapists support the client's bitterness toward parents, the session will rapidly go downhill. Indeed, the anger in these sessions sometimes goes in all directions (parents to their children, siblings to each other, parents to their own siblings or parents), but the deeper levels of caring almost always eventually emerge in these sessions.

The sessions are audiotaped and it is suggested that they be listened to later by all the family members, including those who could not be present, as well as the spouse. Although most of these sessions are one-shot ones (lasting now for 4 hours in two separate sessions, with a break in between), some families return for several sessions. A detailed account of a full-length case study of a couple, including couples group and family-of-origin therapy, is contained in Framo (1978b).

Following the family-of-origin sessions of both partners, most marriage relationships improve, since some of the mythologies have been cleared away and the transference distortions diminished. My theoretical formulation of change, based on the object-relation inner and outer interchanges, is in the earliest stage of hypothesis formation. Empirically speaking, however, these sessions usually work; there is something about facing and dealing with old issues with original family that seems to take the charge out of the negative reactions to the spouse. Some partners, however, following the family-of-origin sessions, having more fully discovered who they were really married to, begin to consider seriously whether or not to stay in their marriage. They agonize over such questions as the effect on the children, what a single life would be like, the financial aspects, and all the other difficult reality consequences of divorce. Some of these couples then become engaged in divorce therapy (Framo, 1978a).

The best terminations, to be sure, are those that are mutually agreed upon. Some couples terminate prematurely for various reasons, whereas I have had to terminate others unilaterally when I estimated that the couple were going nowhere in therapy. Terminations are always prepared for, and all clients are always told that my door is always open for needed sessions in the future.

Curative Factors

Despite the thousands of articles written on how and why psychotherapy works, when it does, definitive answers have not been established. Many ideas have been put forth about the root therapeutic factors, depending on the theoretical orientation of the proponent. Among the various curative elements which the more than a hundred kinds of psychotherapies have proposed are the following: the relationship to the therapist; acceptance and sensing that someone cares; emotional insight; modeling; power influences; unconditional positive regard; conditioning; systematic desensitization; corrective emotional experience; awareness of body sensations; analysis of the transference; game-free training; restructuring; paradoxical or "illogical" problem resolution; and so forth. I can only speculate about what is curative in my methods of treatment; independent observers might arrive at quite different hypotheses. In the second section of this article I stated some criteria for marital improvement, and in the first section I suggested some ideas as to why family-of-origin sessions are usually helpful. I will now elaborate on a few of those points.

Insofar as marital therapy is concerned, spouses who report a successful therapy experience seem to have become more separate as persons, have higher self-esteem, are more tolerant of each other's regressive features and idiosyncrasies, can communicate more clearly about formerly anxiety-laden topics, can fight less destructively, can treat formerly loaded issues with humor, have more realistic expectations of marriage and of each other, are more affectionate and sexual with each other, manifest less hostility (in its various forms) to each other, are more accepting of the zig-zag course that intimate relationships take, and are not deeply disappointed that they are not wildly, romantically "in love." (At the end of marital therapy one woman said incredulously about her marriage relationship, "You mean this is *it*?") Just how the couples arrive at this final stage is not clear to me in terms of what I do or do not do. Usually clients perceive therapist(s') interventions differently than they were intended. Greater understanding of what happened in the therapy is not always achieved by asking clients either. Jay Efran, a colleague of mine, is fond of telling the story that when he asked a client at the end of therapy what really helped him the most in all those months, he expected to hear some profound insight, and instead the client replied, "It was that time when I was feeling low and you said something like, 'Behind every cloud there is a silver lining.'" Carl Whitaker says that one of his clients reported his most successful session as being one in which "nobody was up to anything." As someone once put it, the damnedest things help people.

One of the things which seems to help marriages, as I stated previously, is that the partners have a more empathic understanding of each other. Having been given the opportunity to hear each other's life history, and in the light of knowledge of what the spouse had to struggle with, partners find each other's behavior more understandable. One wife said, "I still don't like my husband's rages, but after learning what his father did to him I know where they come from and I don't take them personally any more." Furthermore, I have noticed that most married people do not really listen to each other; they are like amateur actors who wait for their cue to recite memorized lines and do not listen to the meaning of the words of the other actors. In marital therapy the partners have learned to listen and to really hear each other, thereby diminishing their own preoccupations, righteousness, and self-centeredness.

I do not fully understand why an adult meeting with his or her family of origin, in the special way I have described, should frequently produce such profound changes, particularly the way such sessions often affect the problems for which the couple or family originally entered therapy. Most psychotherapies focus on unscrambling the inner life of a client and then leave it up to that person to work things out with the parents or siblings on his or her own. Individual therapy or analysis may help a man gain insight into the unconscious reasons why he cannot get close to his father, yet in actuality he and father may remain distant. Psychoanalysts and other individual therapists will not get involved with healing the real problems in family relationships. Some otherwise very mature adults are currently enslaved in their relationship with their parents (such as the executive who must call his mother every day), or are completely cut off from a hated brother or sister. The family-of-origin method is designed to deal with these kinds of problems—which certainly have their effects on the marital or parental functioning.

In addition to adults hurting from difficulties with their parents and siblings in the present, they are also locked into the fantasy family of the past. As a matter of fact, the real source of marital conflicts of today, in my view, has to do with unconscious attempts to deal with and master that fantasy family, using the current intimates as stand-ins.[6] Something happens to that repressed fantasy family when the adult meets with his or her actual, real original family and confronts them with the heretofore avoided issues which had existed between them. Dealing with the real, external figures seems to loosen the grip of the introjects of those figures and exposes the past to current realities. Following the sessions the old family can never go back to the way they used to be, and the adult client frequently begins to perceive the spouse and children in a more realistic way. Family-of-origin sessions change marital relationships in many different ways. For instance, the wife whose husband complained of her being "bossy, super-independent, and not seeming to need me," in her family-of-origin session told her parents she was giving up her role of taking care of them and instead wanted them to take care of her. When her parents at least tried to meet this need, she could allow herself to be more vulnerable with her husband. See the case history in Framo (1978b) for a more complete account on how working things out with family-of-origin directly can help a marriage.

My interpretations to a couple do take historical factors into account, but in vivo. That is to say, since I have seen the actual parents and siblings I am in a better position to point out how patterns and behaviors from the old family are being inappropriately played out with the spouse and children. Some of these interpretations catch hold on the basis of what is customarily called "insight." Insight is a much abused term, particularly under attack by those who claim that "understanding" never really changed anybody. Insight, as I see it, is an extraordinarily complicated phenomenon combining cognitive, emotional, and motoric elements. From my viewpoint, unless insight leads to behavioral or attitudinal change, it is not insight.

Although ideally it is best if each member of a family or both marital partners change, it is not necessary for each individual, qua individuals, to change if there are to be relational alterations. Small system or interactional changes can have powerful effects, such as an excluded father being more involved in the family, or a couple's fight style not having such deadly intensity, or the children being able to deal with mother directly instead of having to go through grandmother, and so forth.

Transference is a ubiquitous human phenomenon and will develop over time in any significant relationship. Over the years, as my experience accumulated, however, I have come to deemphasize the transference to the therapist(s) and instead I now focus attention on the transference distortions which occur between the intimates. While transference to the therapist(s) will always be present, a therapist can choose not to deal with it explicitly, unless it is seriously getting in the way of therapy. For example, when a couple insist on my telling them how I feel about them, I indicate that my feelings are not as important as their feelings about each other, since they will be dealing with each other long after I have been forgotten. One of the reasons I started doing couples groups was to dilute the transference to me, since some couples had such strong needs to view me as judge, rescuer, or persecutor that they were unable to move in treatment.

Family or marital therapy is much more likely to elicit countertransference feelings than is individual or group therapy because of the ways in which the ghosts of the therapist's own family intrude into the treatment room (Framo, 1968). I agree with Bowen (1978) that the best safeguard against inappropriate reactions to a family or couple is for the therapist to get his or her own house in order and improve his or her own functioning. This goal can best be accomplished by working out problems with one's own original family, as well as family of procreation.

Effectiveness of the Approach

Any theoretician always feels somewhat abashed when he has to admit that concrete, hard data has not been provided as evidence for the effectiveness of his conceptual approach to psychotherapy. The discipline of psychology is more committed to research than any of the other mental health disciplines; as a matter of fact, in some quarters any psychologist who does not do numerical studies with proper experimental design and probability statistics is regarded as not really being a psychologist. Having been originally trained as a clinical psychologist, my mortification should be complete because I have done no systematic research on my treatment methods. In a recent paper, Wells and Dezen (1978) stated,

"...a number of these [family therapy] schools (in some instances led by major figures in the family therapy movement, the very role models for the aspiring practitioner) have never submitted their methods to empirical testing and, indeed, seem oblivious to such a need" (p. 266).

Still, I am not yet deserving of being drummed out of the corps. In demonstration of my not being oblivious to research needs not only did I prepare a lengthy survey of family interaction research in the early days of family therapy (Framo, 1965b), but in 1967 I organized the first national conference on family interaction research with 29 family researchers and family therapists, the proceedings of which were published in a book (Framo, 1972). In the introduction to that book I stated perennial basic conflict between the clinician and the researcher:

> (S)ystematic researchers would argue that, while clinicians can provide vital information and inspiration for the formulation of hypotheses via hunches and impressions, opinions are still opinions, unable to be proved or refuted by any scientific standard ...there is general agreement that observations must be organized into theory, that theories should be operationally stated and put in the form of testable hypotheses, and that variables should be manipulated by certain rules so as to permit the data to confirm or disprove the hypotheses by other than personal means. Only in this way, the researchers state, can laws of broad applicability be abstracted from the individual instance. The clinicians dispute this thesis, saying that problems are defined by researchers in terms that are most convenient to research, and that experimentalists, in their quest for scientific objectivity, end up measuring pallid, trivial variables and distill all humanity from their investigations.

The dilemma between studying "the significant or the exact," as someone put it, keeps many clinician-theoreticians from doing research. As soon as one starts converting theory into operational definitions, much is lost in translation, and one ends up measuring something that bears little resemblance to the original.

There are many other intricate problems associated with doing research in this area, particularly therapy outcome research. There are such technical problems as adequacy of control groups, how to handle no-treatment groups who seek help on their own, the homogeneity of samples, the size of a sample, finding sophisticated measuring instruments, and so forth. It seems to me that the field needs some creative designs for studies that will take into account the unique features of marital and family therapy. From whose vantage point do we evaluate success or failure? Marital and family therapy differ from all other psychotherapies; each person has a different agenda for therapy goals, both stated and secret, and the goal usually is that someone else should change. How can client satisfaction be the sole criterion of change? If a divorced woman feels she has a second chance for happiness with a man, but if the man says he wants to marry her and does not want her child, would the therapy be successful if the clients were pleased that the family therapist went along with institutionalizing the child?

In addition to the enormous complexity of the treatment situation, which can create formidable barriers to systematic investigation, there are also the practical obstacles to doing research in clinical settings, especially the problem of staff cooperation. There are very few clinical settings where the clinical director will allow interference in the routine; psychotherapists generally do not want any researcher examining ("tampering with"?) their treatment. Gurman and Kniskern (1978), in a comprehensive review of over 200 marital and family therapy outcome studies, have performed a valuable service by specifying criteria for evaluating the adequacy of outcome studies. The problem with these criteria is that they would be nearly impossible to meet in a clinical setting (such as random assignment of families and couples, or, more difficult to meet, random assignment of therapists—a criterion which would require a huge clinic).

In the academic setting where I now work, a doctoral program in clinical psychology, the students are rightfully preoccupied with getting their doctorate as quickly as possible. A problem exists in communicating about systems in an academic clinical psychology setting, as in most psychiatric settings (Framo, 1976b), where the study of the individual is paramount. More traditional studies in clinical psychology are favored by students over family interaction research because, frankly, the latter are more difficult to do and take more time. A few motivated students have done their dissertations in this area, but they are exceptional and, besides, they selected the kinds of studies that were feasible within their doctoral time frame.

I am the kind of clinician who needs to step back from his practice and conceptualize about what has been observed. One quandary of a theoretician—clinician is how to treat and conceptualize, teach, write, give workshops, and still have time to do systematic studies. I have had fantasies of having a support staff to handle all the inquiries and requests that I get, and a large group of research assistants who would study and evaluate my treatment methods. There are very few family therapists in the country who work with family of origin as I do, and I think it necessary to confirm with hard data my clinical impressions on how powerful such sessions can be in producing change. Not only treatment results need to be examined, utilizing systematic follow-up, but greater understanding is needed on why and how sessions with family of origin can break up deep-seated attitudes and behavior patterns.

Training of Marital–Family Therapists

I believe that family therapists were "trained" by their original families, and the formal training they get today refines that lifelong process. In my judgment, while there are certain kinds of family problems that can be handled by any reasonably intelligent person or paraprofessional trained in the problem-solving method, there are other, more complex situations, which require the kind of "natural" who has been trained as a general psychotherapist first and later as a family therapist. That is to say, I believe that every family therapist should have had individual and peer group therapy experience as well as experience with the whole range of emotional disturbances in varied clinical settings. Intensive supervision by a supervisor who knows what he or she is doing is also a must in the training of any therapist. Whether or not those individual or group therapy experiences should occur prior to or concurrent with the learning of marital or family therapy is a moot question, open to study. This viewpoint of prior individual and group therapy experience is consistent with my theoretical perspective of exploring the relationship between the intrapsychic and the transactional. There is something about working through people's internal and interpersonal defenses, it seems to me, that helps one know how to deal with the intimate system operations. If, for example, a man has an internalized fear of women which he handles by projection of anticipated attack from his wife, we are in a position not only to understand why he beats up his wife, but to help him deal directly with his mother about his earlier fear of her.

It is interesting that several family therapists have recommended that family therapy trainees have a personal therapy experience (meaning individual therapy), but no one recommends that trainees should have marital or family therapy with his or her spouse, family of origin, or family of procreation. While I do not think it should be a requirement, I personally believe such experiences to be among the best preparations for becoming a family therapist (Framo, 1979). Bowen's method of training includes having trainees conduct genealogical searches in the quest for self, an extremely valuable method of training. In my classes there are no formal examinations; the only requirement is the writing of a family biography. Students have reported that this was the most painful and difficult, yet the most meaningful assignment of their lives. I have become aware, further, of the high rate of divorce among family therapy trainees, a phenomenon insufficiently studied. One could speculate that the trainee and the spouse are living in such different worlds that they lose touch with each other. The foregoing is one of the reasons I encourage trainees to include their spouse or other family member in certain aspects of my training program.

There is insufficient space to go into detail on the didactic and experiential aspects of my training program. I believe that trainees should be exposed to the various theories and methods of working with families so that eventually they will develop a style that is comfortable for them. In addition to becoming familiar with the classical literature in the field, I think trainees can learn a lot about marital and family dynamics from plays, movies, and novels. Another area that is neglected in our family therapy training programs is knowledge about ethnic family cultures. Other aspects of training, such as group supervision, live supervision, simulated families, videotape, program evaluation, and so forth each would require separate treatment, a task beyond the purposes of this paper. Although I stress the value of students working things out with their own family, I do believe they must learn skills. Overall, however, it is the personal development of trainees, rather than *just* their technical skill alone, which will determine their effectiveness as family therapists in dealing with what I have called the "gut" issues of family life—the passions, hates, loves, injustices, sacrifices, comforts, disappointments, frustrations, ambivalences, and gratifications of family life. These are the universals that everyone raised in a family has had to struggle with.

Notes

[1]Even in Freud's case histories there were some notable omissions. For example, he did not mention that during the course of Little Han's treatment Han's parents were in the process of getting a divorce and indeed did divorce when the treatment was over. For a reexamination of the case of Little Hans from the standpoint of family dynamics see Strean (1967).

[2]Every therapist comes up against unique kinds of problem situations for which there are no known techniques; the art of psychotherapy often consists of on-the-spot improvisation.

[3]I have had the experience of thinking in the first interview that a husband was crazy or unreachable, and wondering to myself why this lovely woman ever married a guy like that. By the end of the second interview he would seem reasonable and she would turn out to be impossible to deal with.

[4]Most sexual problems disappear as a function of working on the relationship difficulties of the couple. Those couples who still have a sexual dysfunction after their relationship improves are referred elsewhere for sex therapy.

[5]Cotherapists I have worked with in recent years have been: My wife, Mary D. Framo, MSS, PhD candidate; Cheryl Keats, MSW; Joann Gillis-Donovan, PhD; Ann Gravagno, MFT; Peggy Tietz, MSW; and Gail Hogeboom Wilson, MA, PhD candidate.

[6]It is not surprising that among the anger-provoking insults spouses will hurl at their partner during an argument are such statements as the following: "You're just like your mother," or "You're not going to treat me the way your father treated your mother," or "You keep forgetting I'm your husband, not your father."

References

Anonymous. (1972). Toward the differentiation of a self in one's own family. In J. Framo (Ed.), *Family interaction: A dialogue between family researchers and family therapists*. New York: Springer.

Bach, G., & Wyden, P. (1969). *The intimate enemy: How to fight fair in love and marriage*. New York: Morrow.

Boszormenyi-Nagy, I., & Framo, J. (Eds.). (1965). *Intensive family therapy*. New York: Harper & Row Medical Department.

Boszormenyi-Nagy, I., & Spark, G. (1973). *Invisible loyalties: Reciprocity in intergenerational family therapy*. New York: Harper & Row Medical Department.

Bowen, M. (1978). *Family therapy in clinical practice*. New York: Aronson.

Bradt, J., & Moynihan, C. (1971). A study of child-focused families. In J. Bradt & C. Moynihan (Eds.), *System therapy*. (Available from Groome Child Guidance Clinic, 5225 Loughboro Rd., N.W., Washington, D.C. 20016.)

Dicks, H. (1967). *Marital tensions*. New York: Basic Books.

Fairbairn, W. (1954). *An object-relations theory of the personality*. New York: Basic Books.

Foley, V. (1974). *An introduction to family therapy*. New York: Grune & Stratton.

Framo, J. (1965a). Rationale and techniques of intensive family therapy. In I. Boszormenyi-Nagy & J. Framo (Eds.), *Intensive family therapy*. New York: Harper & Row, Hoeber Medical Division.

Framo, J. (1965b). Systematic research on family dynamics. In. I. Boszormenyi-Nagy & J. Framo (Eds.), *Intensive family therapy*. New York: Harper & Row, Hoeber Medical Division.

Framo, J. (1968). My families, my family. *Voices: Art and Science of Psychotherapy, 4*, 18–27.

Framo, J. (1970). Symptoms from a family transactional viewpoint. In N. Ackerman, J. Lieb, & J. Pearce (Eds.), *Family therapy in transition*. Boston: Little, Brown and Company. [Also reprinted in C. Sager & H. Kaplan (Eds.). (1972). *Progress in group and family therapy*. New York: Brunner/Mazel.]

Framo, J. (1973). Marriage therapy in couples group. In D. Bloch (Ed.), *Techniques of family psychotherapy: A primer*. New York: Grune & Stratton.

Framo, J. (1975). Personal reflections of a family therapist. *Journal of Marriage and Family Counseling, 1*, 15–28.

Framo, J. (1976a). Family of origin as a therapeutic resource for adults in marital and family therapy: You can and should go home again. *Family Process, 15*, 193–210.

Framo, J. (1976b). Chronicle of a struggle to establish a family unit within a community mental health center. In P. Guerin (Ed.), *Family Therapy*. New York: Gardner Press.

Framo, J. (1978a, February). The friendly divorce. *Psychology Today*.

Framo, J. (1978b). In-laws and out-laws: A marital case of kinship confusion. In P. Papp (Ed.), *Family therapy: Full-length case studies*. New York: Gardner Press.

Framo, J. (1979). A personal viewpoint on training in marital and family therapy. *Professional Psychology, 10*, 868–875.

Framo, J. (1980). Marriage and marital therapy: Issues and initial interview techniques. In M. Andolfi & I. Zwerling (Eds.), *Dimensions of family therapy*. New York: Guilford Press.

Gurman, A., & Kniskern, D. (1978). Research on marital and family therapy: Progress, perspective, and prospect. In S. Garfield & A.

Bergin (Eds.), *Handbook of psychotherapy and behavior change: An empirical analysis*. New York: Wiley.
Haas, W. (1968). The intergenerational encounter: A method in treatment. *Social Work, 13*, 91–101.
Haley, J. (1975). Why a mental health clinic should avoid family therapy. *Journal of Marriage and Family Counseling, 1*, 3–13.
Headley, L. (1977). *Adults and their parents in family therapy*. New York: Plenum Press.
Jackson, D. (1967). The individual and the larger contexts. *Family Process, 6*, 139–147.
Lewis, J., Beavers, R., Gossett, J., & Phillips, V. (1976). *No single thread: Psychological health in family systems*. New York: Brunner/Mazel.
Montalvo, B., & Haley, J. (1973). In defense of child therapy. *Family Process, 12*, 227–244.
Paul, N., & Paul, B. (1975). *A marital puzzle*. New York: Norton.
Sonne, J., Speck, R., & Jungreis, J. (1962). The absent-member maneuver as a resistance in family therapy of schizophrenia. *Family Process, 1*, 44–62.
Spiegel, J., & Bell, N. (1959). The family of the psychiatric patient. In S. Arieti (Ed.), *American handbook of psychiatry* (Vol 1). New York: Basic Books.
Strean, H. (1967). A family therapist looks at Little Hans. *Family Process, 6*, 227–234.
Visher, E., & Visher, J. (1979). *Step-families: A guide to working with stepparents and stepchildren*. New York: Brunner/Mazel.
Wells, R., & Dezen, A. (1978). The results of family therapy revisited: The non-behavioral methods. *Family Process, 3*, 251–274.
Whitaker, C. (1976). A family is a four-dimensional relationship. In P. Guerin (Ed.), *Family therapy*. New York: Gardner Press.
Whitaker, C., & Keith, D. (1977). Counseling the dissolving marriage. In R. Stahmann & W. Hiebert (Eds.), *Klemer's counseling in marital and sexual problems*. Baltimore: Williams & Wilkins.
Zilboorg, G., & Henry, G. (1941). *A history of medical psychology*. New York: Norton.

This article originally appeared as a chapter in *Handbook of Family Therapy*, 1980, by A. S. Gurman and D. P. Kniskern, Eds., pp. 191–224. Reprint permission granted by Brunner/Mazel Publishers.

Adlerian Family Therapy

Don Dinkmeyer
Don Dinkmeyer, Jr.

Adlerian psychology has a long history of interest in family therapy. Alfred Adler was the first psychiatrist to do public demonstrations with a family. Adler emphasized the importance of the family constellation upon the emerging lifestyle of each child. He taught that the siblings had a more significant influence on a person's personality than the mother. Dreikurs established the influence of the methods of training on the difference in personality (Dreikurs & Soltz, 1964).

Adlerian family therapy is similar to the systems approach in its use of the patterns of communication and the relationships between members of the family to improve the relationship. However, Adlerians put more emphasis on diagnosing the assets and resources in the family. The focus is on helping the family to establish more active-constructive goals.

One of the major goals of family therapy is to increase the self-esteem and feelings of worth of the members of the family while stimulating their social interest, willingness to participate in the cooperative give and take of family life. The formula to success in family therapy includes SE + SI = NH: To get the family to grow and develop *self-esteem*, *social interest*, and feelings of belonging, the result is a *natural high* or personal growth (O'Connell & Bright, 1979).

In Adlerian family therapy, the members of the family learn to communicate more congruently, to listen attentively, and to resolve conflicts more productively by pinpointing the real issue, reaching new agreements, and by having all members become involved in the decision making. The therapy teaches members of the family mutual respect, conflict resolution techniques, and to reorient negative, counterproductive beliefs and attitudes while establishing new behaviors.

In Adlerian family therapy, all members of the family are seen at once. Family therapy focuses on the psychological movement and transactions between family members. It addresses the purposive nature of the negative transactions and eventually helps the family member to establish more positive and constructive goals.

The Adlerian family therapists recognize that the family exerts the most significant influence on the development of the individual. Parents provide a model, often unconsciously, of what it means to be a human being. Aggressive or passive, cooperative or rebellious, behaviors are observed and influence the individual. Family values and expectations about the meaning of trust, love, adequacy, and acceptance are conveyed.

If the family believes it is important to achieve, cooperate, or fight for one's rights, these values may be either internalized or rejected so that the individual becomes exactly the opposite of what the family advocates. In either instance, the family values have an influence on the emerging personality.

The methods of training—autocratic and oppressive, permissive and lenient, or laissez-faire—influence each future generation. Again, the individual chooses what he or she will do about the methods of training. Each person's position in the family constellation influences his or her perception of the world (Shulman, 1973). When two siblings are very different, this is often a result of competition between them: for example, one is good at school, another athletic, etc. Likewise, when both adhere to a certain trait, it may emerge from family values, i.e., to be musical, religious, or handy around the house.

Adlerian Assumptions

Adlerian psychology understands persons as indivisible, social, decision-making beings whose actions and psychological movement have a purpose (Dinkmeyer, Pew, & Dinkmeyer, 1979).

Purpose of Behavior

In all transactions within the family, the therapist looks at the movement and the intentions to ascertain their purpose. Since all human movement is guided by subjective goals, it is through influencing this movement and any faulty, mistaken perceptions that we can best influence human behavior.

Carl is the oldest of three boys. He has high standards and seldom feels he is "enough." His younger brothers do well in athletics and academics. Carl is less adequate in these areas and, therefore, concludes that he is not as good as his brothers. He fails to recognize and value his interests and abilities in electronics. He believes, "I am not as much as others." As these faulty, mistaken, self-defeating perceptions are changed, he is able to function more effectively in the family.

Social Meaning of Behavior

We live in a world which requires effective interpersonal relationships. Social interaction is not an option but a requirement. Family therapy can teach pragmatic procedures for relating with each other. The family meeting or family council helps us to put democratic procedures into practice. The family meeting is a weekly meeting which provides an opportunity to discuss differences, plan for time together, encourage each other, and deal with any issues in the family. It is an opportunity for each member of the family to have a voice and contribute to decision making (Dreikurs & Soltz, 1964).

In family therapy, it is helpful to have your content heard and paraphrased. However, it is even more insightful to be put in touch with your values and intention. The therapist observes the psychological involvement and offers a tentative hypothesis about the purpose of the transaction. By dealing with the purpose and social meaning of their behavior, the family gains a deeper understanding of their conflict. In the early phases of family therapy, there is an emphasis on reflective listening, paraphrasing, and encouragement. The therapist strives to understand and relate effectively with each member of the family.

Mr. Jones and his oldest son, Bob, have daily fights over Bob's bedtime. Bob is on the soccer team this season, so his father is concerned about his health and whether he gets enough rest. Mr. Jones, however, says to Bob, "Get to bed before I lock you in," or "You'll have to go to bed earlier tomorrow because you were late tonight." Bob hears only messages like, "I'll decide when you sleep," and "I'm going to make you do as I say." The family therapist recognizes the positive intent of Mr. Jones' actions and helps Mr. Jones recognize that he means to communicate, "I am concerned about your doing the best you can in sports." Now there is an opportunity for Bob and his father to recognize how important it is to do well in sports and whose problem bedtime really is. Many problems in the family occur because parents assume ownership of problems that belong to the child.

Mr. and Mrs. Saxon have two boys, nine and five. There is much conflict in the family. Mr. and Mrs. Saxon are having problems in cooperation as evidenced by her desire to move back to their original home area and the almost total lack of a sexual relationship or any other cooperative relationship. The older boy, Rick, who has done well at school, is now on the verge of suspension, and Billy has regressed to bed-wetting.

Much of the communication in the family is nonverbal. Mrs. Saxon is always too tired to relate to Mr. Saxon. Mr. Saxon resents his role as family provider with no respect or love from family members. Rick's communication is in his rebellion at school, while Billy's is with bed-wetting.

The pattern of communication is that they all make their own rules and are most concerned about getting their way. In the early interviews, the therapist listens closely for the strengths or resources. The therapist notes that the members of the family are strong-willed in their commitments to their goals. The challenge is to move them from passive or destructive behavior to active-constructive behavior. It is apparent that the boys and mother are bright and clever in obtaining the power and control they desire.

The members of the family have some of the following mistaken perceptions: Mrs Saxon: "I must be in control"; Mr. Saxon: "There is nothing I can do about my lot in life"; Rick: "I can control others by my behavior"; and Billy: "I will get even if I'm treated unfairly."

The task of the therapist is to help the family go through the four steps of conflict resolution.

1. *Mutual respect.* By working with the family as a unit and through modeling attentive listening and accurate communication, the therapist can increase the family's level of mutual respect. Members of the family are encouraged to improve communication and develop mutual respect in communication exercises at home; thus they learn through encouragement council, family council, and listening exercises (Dinkmeyer & McKay, 1973; 1976).
2. *Pinpointing the issue.* Usually the complaint that is presented—as in Saxon's case, differences about where to live and the sexual relationship—is not the real issue. Instead, the real issue may be concern about being treated as special, getting my way, getting even, or proving no one can make me do it. When one helps the family look at the real issues, more basic and permanent change can be obtained.
3. *Reaching a new agreement.* When families fight, they do it because they have reached an agreement to fight. Fighting is a form of cooperation in that both individuals must agree to stay

and fight. To resolve the conflict the family needs to develop a new agreement. This agreement would indicate what action each person would take to improve the relationship.

4. *Participation in decision making*. All members of the family need to participate in decisions which affect them. Violation of this principle communicates a lack of respect.

Sessions with the Saxons help them to look at issues like where they will live, Rick's rebellion at school, and Billy's bed-wetting, not just in terms of the symptom, but in terms of the purpose of the symptom and the goals of power and getting even.

Mr. and Mrs. Saxon both come to family therapy with the opinion that their spouse is responsible for the difficulties in the marriage. "If only he would not be so demanding sexually." "Her constantly putting the children before me is demeaning." The therapist seeks to stimulate social interest and begins by pointing out how they are already cooperating by fighting, since fighting requires that they agree to fight about a certain issue. Now the therapist encourages them to cooperate in a new way. They are both to look for what they can change in themselves. Once this is identified, they make a plan for change. They are to encourage each other as they notice any effort, attempt, or even minor progress. Thus, the focus is shifted from fault finding to finding positive movements to encourage.

Social interest includes the ability to give and take for the communal good. It is a criterion of one's ability to contribute and cooperate, a measure of mental health (Adler, 1938).

Unity and Patterns of Behavior

The family can be understood in terms of the unity and patterns of its behavior. The therapist works to understand the family as a whole. When apparently isolated events occur, they are understood in relation to the total pattern, purpose of the behavior, and the relationship of the movement to the unity and goal of the pattern.

The Saxon family problems started with the dissonance between the parents. As the quarrels become more frequent, Rick developed problems at school. While he believed that he could not rebel at home, school served the purpose even more adequately in a family which values achievement. Billy, feeling hurt by his parents and rejected by the attention given to Rick, developed his revenge through "water power."

The therapist does not see all of this as a series of isolated events but instead as interrelated. The objective is to get the members of the family to treat each other with mutual respect, to openly discuss their differences, and to become more empathic to each others' feelings. When Mr. and Mrs. Saxon begin to cooperate and change their behavior, the boys' symptoms subside. We believe that in the family everyone is responsible, but no one is to blame.

Adlerian Family Therapy Techniques and Treatment Concepts

The Adlerian therapist uses a variety of techniques which facilitate the therapy process. Since Adlerian therapy has an educational component, the family members are encouraged to learn some of the skills which improve communication in the family.

Understand and Influence the Psychological Movement

Family members pursue individual goals which are influenced by their private logic, faulty beliefs, and mistaken perceptions. This results in psychological movement, the goal-directed transactions between family members, which are purposive. The individual's transactions and behavior reveal the psychological movement and intentions. Behavior never lies, though talk may be misleading and deceptive. The family therapist learns to trust only movement. She or he teaches the family to communicate their intentions early.

Children's mistaken goals sometimes can be more easily identified than adults. Dreikurs described the four goals of misbehavior as attention getting, power, revenge, and the display of inadequacy (Dreikurs & Soltz, 1964). The child's response to correction and the adult's feeling about the misbehavior reveal the purpose of misbehavior. A feeling of annoyance indicates the attention-getting mechanism; a feeling of anger indicates power; feeling hurt indicates revenge; and feeling despair or "I give up" indicates a display of inadequacy.

It is equally important, however, to understand adult intentions and goals. Parents and children frequently are in conflict over the issue of power and control. Bedtime, responsibilities, and curfew are examples of the basic question, "Who's in charge here, you or me?"

Therapists must understand the interaction and resulting conflicts and help the family develop an agreement to facilitate changes in family goals and methods of interaction.

Work with the Family Communications System

Basic ground rules which the therapist sets forth include:

1. *Speak directly to each other.* This is accomplished by intervention and the redirecting of verbal and nonverbal messages.
2. *Each person speaks for himself/herself.* Do not permit members to give feelings or opinions of others. Insist they speak for themselves.
3. *No scapegoating.* The victimizing of family members is blocked and not permitted. When victims are found in the family, the therapist works to extricate the family member from this position. Parents and children are equally susceptible to scapegoating.

In addition to these basic communication ground rules, the family's interaction can be improved by working on the following communication skills:

1. *Paraphrasing and clarification.* When people speak, are they being understood? Either the therapist or another family member can paraphrase important statements. The message becomes clear in this process; and the family member can clarify any inaccuracies in the feedback.
2. *Uncovering negative feelings.* A family or one of its members may have the faulty belief, "No unpleasant feelings are allowed." Denial of unpleasant feelings or an inability to express them may be overcome by therapist intervention. Structuring a dialogue between a parent and child, for example, can facilitate this process by encouraging the members to speak to each other and to speak directly about how they feel, i.e., "I feel...," instead of denying and masking real beliefs and feelings.
3. *Feedback on recommendations.* An essential part of family therapy is the commitment to work on change. While therapists can recommend many ideas, they must check their feasibility. A family's homework assignment, such as a new set of household chores, requires that all family members involved in the change share their feelings and reactions in the form of feedback. Through open communication, the therapist facilitates commitment and subsequent change.

Focus on the Real Issue: Help People Identify Their Goals

In a conflict, people frequently focus on the thing which on the surface appears to cause the conflict, such as clearing the table, hanging up clothes, or being in on time. The argument centers on a particular task. We help the family most as they resolve the *real* issue, which is for both parent and child more often winning, power, getting even, or displaying inadequacy in order to be excused. The therapist helps the family members deal with the real issue by focusing on the purpose of the conflict.

Of the many themes which families share, only a few can be usefully utilized in the therapy process. The real issue may not be, for example, mother's new job, but the resulting new demands on family members to be more responsible.

Resolve Resistance Problems

Resistance is a lack of alignment between the family and therapist. An example is found when the family fails to work on the task assigned for the week. For example, family members may agree to let a child experience the consequences of being late to school. However, in the next session it is clear that the parents are still reminding and protecting the child from being tardy. Resistance occurs when the family is not in agreement with the suggested procedure. They may feel the recommendations were imposed and not chosen by them. When there is resistance, the therapist becomes aware that the goals of the family and the therapist are not aligned. The immediate task is to clarify what the family hopes to get from the sessions. The therapist begins by asking the family if they'd like to explore why the recommendations were not followed. This is the first step in realigning goals. Then the therapist alludes to the purpose of not cooperating by offering a tentative hypothesis: "Could it be this is a way to show no one can make you change?" Resistance impedes the change process and must be dealt with for progress to occur.

Stimulate Social Interest

A basic Adlerian concept in therapy is the utilization of social interest. Social interest includes the willingness to participate in the give and take of life and cooperate rather than compete (Adler, 1938). In this case, it is cooperation for the common benefit of the family. Social interest may be found in a father who gives up his recreation to read to the child at bedtime, or in a child who participates in the family chores. A person who possesses social interest is capable of cooperating with others. Social interest does not ask, "What is in it for me?" It is in juxtaposition to selfish interest.

Therapists can stimulate the process by recognizing strengths and utilizing assets of each family member. If an older brother or sister is capable of certain responsibilities, are they being allowed to do them? One effective way to stimulate communication and develop social interest is through the regular family meeting (Dreikurs, Gould, & Corsini, 1974).

Encourage to Create Confidence

Encouragement is the process of increasing the individual's feelings of worth and self-esteem. Encouragement cannot be overemphasized as a powerful force in change. It must be differentiated from praise. Praise is often inappropriate, because in conflict there may be nothing "praiseworthy." Encouragement recognizes assets and contributions, and stimulates positive movement. A step in the right direction can be encouraged.

Examine the Private Logic, Faulty Beliefs, and Mistaken Perceptions

Each family member has their own unique set of beliefs and perceptions. Private logic is the process in which a person holds certain faulty beliefs, the result of mistaken perceptions. It is the opposite of common logic or common sense. Behavioral changes occur when the underlying beliefs, etc., are changed. It is important to recognize that each behavior and misbehavior has an accompanying belief. Therapists struggling to facilitate desired behavior changes often do not understand the beliefs, perceptions, and goals which direct the behavior. Behavior changes when beliefs and expectations change.

Intervene by Sharing Tentative Hypotheses

Tentative hypotheses are statements by the therapist which focus on underlying intentions and beliefs. The therapist does not assert that he or she is correct; in fact, he or she may not be correct. The tentative hypotheses may help clarify the intentions and beliefs being expressed. As the family members reject the tentative hypotheses, they are helped to clarify their understanding of the situation. The tentative hypothesis allows them to respond, not defend. Common methods of sharing tentative hypotheses allude to the goal or purpose of the behavior: "I have an idea why you are behaving that way. Would you like to hear it?" "Could it be...?" "Is it possible...?"

Antisuggestion and Role Reversal

Antisuggestion is the process whereby the family is encouraged to do the very thing they fear or the habits they claim they want to stop. A family involved in regular verbal arguments may be told to argue continuously for one hour each day. The family is asked to set aside a specific time for the argument. While the family may be initially confused as they schedule arguments, they will soon see the *purpose* of this procedure. The initially paradoxical intention becomes a way for the family to see the ineffectiveness of arguments. It allows them to become aware of their preoccupation with negative interaction.

Role reversal is useful in parent/child conflicts. Children are often eager to "become" father and show him how he comes across. Father has the chance to show the children how he experiences their behavior. As father attempts to deal with an authoritarian approach, or as the children are confronted with attention getting or a display of inadequacy role-played by a parent, both parent and child develop empathy for each other.

Summary of the Change Process

The change process is facilitated through the following cycle:

1. Intervene with faulty perceptions and beliefs.
2. Develop a support system so people feel they belong and have the courage to try on new behavior. Encourage, value, and emphasize assets and progress.
3. See that, as individuals communicate and risk, they are rewarded for their spontaneity and courage by acceptance.
4. As family members have the courage to be imperfect, anxiety and discouragement are decreased and self-esteem and feelings of worth are increased.

The family members are helped to feel more competent and worthwhile by increasing their social interest (care and concern for each other) and their self-esteem (by learning to value their assets and encourage others).

The family therapist, as leader of the group, helps people to stay with the purpose, see common problems, and deal with all here and now events by understanding the purpose of the communication and behavior. Family members are then led to process feedback and speak directly, openly, and honestly with each other. Resistance in the family is understood as the failure to have the goals mutually aligned. Although people may have come to therapy with an implicit agreement to fight and fuss, they are helped to make a new decision to cooperate, care, and encourage.

References

Adler, A. (1938). *Social interest: A challenge to mankind.* London: Faber and Faber, Ltd.

Dinkmeyer, D., & McKay, G. (1973). *Raising a respectable child.* New York: Simon & Schuster.

Dinkmeyer, D., & McKay, G. (1976). *Systematic training for effective parenting.* Circle Pines, MN: American Guidance Service.

Dinkmeyer, D., Pew, W., & Dinkmeyer, D., Jr. (1979). *Adlerian counseling and psychotherapy.* Monterey, CA: Brooks/Cole.

Dreikurs, R., Gould, S., & Corsini, R. (1974). *Family council.* Chicago: Henry Regnery.

Dreikurs, R., & Soltz, V. (1964). *Children: The challenge.* New York: Duell, Sloan & Pearce.

O'Connell, W., & Bright, M. (1979). *Natural high primer.* Chicago: Alfred Adler Institute.

Shulman, B. (1973). *Contributions to individual psychology.* Chicago: Alfred Adler Institute.

This article was originally published in *The American Journal of Family Therapy*, Vol. 9, No. 1, 1981, pp. 45–52. Reprint permission granted by Brunner/Mazel Publishers.

Brief Family Therapy

Tracy Todd

Touring in the Land of Brief Therapy

A psychotherapy evolution has been occurring in recent years. It appears that a shift from long-term, insight oriented therapy to focused, problem resolution therapy is taking place. How come? There seems to be two factors playing influential roles in the evolution of this shift. First, there has been a proliferation of publications and presentations by individuals who espouse more efficient and effective forms of psychotherapy. Individuals such as Steve de Shazer, Michele Weiner-Davis, William O'Hanlon, and Paul Watzlawick have made significant contributions in the areas of efficient and effective therapy. Second, insurance companies, mental health centers, managed care organizations, and employee assistance programs are requesting that clinicians be educated and trained in briefer forms of psychotherapy so that the objectives of the organization can be met.

For the purpose of this writing brief therapy models, "brief therapy" will not be defined by number of sessions, but rather as a form of therapy that utilizes time and client resources in the best change producing manner. Frequently, the resulting side effect is decreased number of sessions. Brief therapy models can range from short-term dynamic therapy (Sifneos, 1987) to solution based therapy (de Shazer, 1985). We will journey into the brief therapy models of Paul Watzlawick (Mental Research Institute), Steve de Shazer (solution based), and Michael White and Don Epston (narrative).

Mental Research Institute of Palo Alto (MRI)

There are certain stops that families make when taking a family trip: in New York, the Empire State Building; in Florida, Disney World; in Wyoming, Yellowstone National Park. The MRI model is such a stop, no journey of brief therapy would be complete unless a tour was taken of the MRI. The MRI is probably one of the most recognized originators in the principles and techniques of brief family therapy. The clinicians and philosophers that originated the MRI seemed to have one thing in mind, NOT to accept traditional psychotherapy ideas and to challenge the status quo in psychotherapy.

A prominent figure in the evolution of brief therapy is Gregory Bateson. During the 1940s several events took place involving Gregory Bateson that became catalytic in the emergence of brief therapy. Becvar and Becvar (1988) reported that he was exposed to the works of Milton Erickson, studied the cybernetic works of Norbert Weiner and Warren McCulloch, worked with Juergen Ruesch and learned about *Principia Mathematica* (1910), and participated in the Macy Conferences. These events resulted in Gregory Bateson, an anthropologist, receiving a grant from the Rockefeller Foundation in 1952 to study the communication patterns in families with a schizophrenic member (Becvar & Becvar, 1988). This study put him in the company of Jay Haley, John Weakland, William Fry, and Don Jackson, and the landmark double bind hypothesis was proposed (Bateson, Jackson, Haley, & Weakland, 1956). In 1958 Don Jackson opened the Mental Research Institute of Palo Alto, California. He initially invited Jules Riskin and Virginia Satir to join him, but shortly thereafter increased the staff to include Jay Haley, Paul Watzlawick, Richard Fisch, and John Weakland (Becvar & Becvar, 1988). Bateson's anthropological (naturalistic) influence on various members of the MRI team (Haley, Weakland, and Jackson) in conjunction with Watzlawick's constructivism philosophy radically influenced the assumptions of the clinicians at the MRI, and created a group of therapists and philosophers that soon began to challenge the traditional assumptions and practices of psychotherapy.

Two major characteristics of this approach are constructivism and naturalistic inquiry.

Constructivism

Glaserfeld (1984) described constructivism as a philosophy that maintains that the observer can never mirror a reality, but that a reality is constructed that fits with the observer's experiences. Simon, Stierlin, and Wynne (1985) explained that constructivism is a reflection of the observer who is describing the reality, and not the reality itself. The importance of constructivism in brief family therapy is that as therapists we must consider how the family "sees" the problem, and how we "see" the problem. When we have a better understanding about the family's definition of the problem we can begin to reformulate the problem. Haley (1977) stated, "If therapy is to end properly, it must begin properly, by negotiating a solvable problem" (p. 9). Unlike the more traditional, long-term approaches, brief therapists will co-create the problem with the family so that it can be solved. For example, a family may come to therapy with the presented problem that their four-year-old child continuously cries when left with the baby sitter. Some theoretical speculations that can be made on this limited information is that there is separation anxiety present, or the family is enmeshed, or the parents are being split, and/or the child is the scapegoat for the parents conflictual relationship. From this simple example we can create many different problems, all of which may depend on the theoretical perspective of the therapist and the family. The significance of constructivism is that it demonstrates that "problems" are elastic, and can be negotiated with the family (Haley, 1977). This negotiation process helps the family and the therapist to define a solvable problem; in turn, usually helping the family to gain positive momentum, hope, and independence from the therapy process. This co-creation of a reality between the therapist and families is crucial in the understanding and the executing of the MRI approach. Without understanding constructivism, therapists may begin to work on problems that have not been defined as solvable.

Naturalistic Paradigm

Lincoln and Guba (1985) outlined the paradigmatic differences between positivism and naturalism. One area of difference between the two paradigms involves values. Positivism holds that research/observation is value free, and that if the researcher is to utilize solid empirical methods, the values would be eliminated from the study. Whereas the naturalist would maintain that observation and research are value bound. These values are quickly exhibited simply by the research questions being asked. The study being conducted is determined by someone's research interest (values).

A second area of contention involves the relationship of "knower to known" (Lincoln & Guba, 1985). The positivistic paradigm would argue that these two entities are independent, while the naturalistic paradigm maintains that they mutually influence one another and are inseparable. For example, a naturalist would believe that someone studying couples that survived an extramarital affair would shape what is known via the research questions asked. Reciprocally, the experience of studying these couples would shape the researcher, possibly through how the research is reported (conclusions and discussions).

The third area the two paradigms differ on involves generalizations. The positivistic paradigm holds that given enough data, generalizations can be made about the reality. The naturalistic paradigm contends that generalizations cannot be made and that hypotheses are context determined.

Causation is another area of difference between the two paradigms. Positivists would argue that given enough study of social interactions, causal claims can be discovered. However, naturalists would believe that "effects" are interactive in nature, and it is impossible to differentiate between cause and effect.

The belief about reality itself is a final area of debate between the paradigms. A positivist would maintain that reality is something "out there" (Lincoln & Guba, 1985, p. 37), and can be "touched" and studied independently of the observer. However, the naturalist would argue that reality is actually made of multiple realities, is studied holistically, and reflects the observer.

The combination of constructivism and the naturalistic paradigm creates an unique way of examining families. With this combination the therapist becomes less interested in causation, identified patient, and the intrapsyche, and more interested in examining interactional communication and behavioral patterns, and the family's own theories and culture.

In discussing brief family therapy we need to focus on second order change. Watzlawick, Weakland, and Fisch (1974) described the concept of second order change as involving a qualitative change in the family's organization and structure which is created by interventions that are well placed and not based on causality/linearity. O'Hanlon (1987) listed a number of areas to assess for intervention points: frequency/rate, duration, time of symptom, location of symptom, intensity, quality, order of events. As a therapist if you can create an intervention that changes, for instance, the location of the problem, the typical pattern will most likely be altered. For example, a couple who has not had frequent and satisfying sexual intercourse and reports that sexual activity always takes place in the bedroom, may be instructed to sleep on the hideaway in the living room for three weeks. Possibly, the change in location of sleeping will also change their sexual behavior.

Solution-Based Psychotherapy

While all other psychotherapy models are concerned with the problem, the solution-based model is primarily concerned with non-problem time (de Shazer, 1982, 1985). Although the solution-based model has evolved from the influences of Milton Erickson and the MRI, it detours in practice by keeping the therapeutic focus on the exception to the problem rather than on the problem itself (de Shazer, 1985). According to de Shazer, while the MRI therapist identified interactional and communication patterns concerning the presented problem and then tried to interrupt the patterns, the solution-based model was more interested in working with the identified solution sequences.

This detour in practice has landed us in unknown territory, and our first task will be to learn the cultural beliefs of this approach. O'Hanlon and Weiner-Davis (1989) outlined these beliefs with exceptional clarity.

Clients Have Ability to Resolve Problems

Often times clients present problems that they have already solved numerous times, but they do not remember doing so. One task of the solution-based therapist is to identify the tools and resources clients possess to resolve their complaints. Additionally, therapists need to learn the family's culture regarding previous successes so that interventions can be created that will fit with the family's abilities (O'Hanlon & Weiner-Davis, 1989).

Change is Constant

Keeney (1983) maintained that a dualism exists between stability and change, that is, the more stability is sought after the more change must occur. For example, a person who wants to remain stable while riding a mountain bicycle down a steep and rough decline, must make continuous changes while riding to account for the rocks, sticks, bumps, holes, loose dirt, and gravity. Similarly, clients are continuously changing, if just to maintain stability. Clients do not live in a vacuum and even the complaint that brings them to therapy must change. O'Hanlon and Weiner-Davis (1989) stated that a therapist who embraces the notion that families are always changing will conduct sessions in which solutions and change are constantly examined.

Therapist's Job? Produce Change

O'Hanlon and Wilk (1987) use the analogy that the therapy process should have natural lighting. That is, an environment should be created during sessions that is conducive to carrying out therapeutic tasks. The therapist should not create an environment that is always "heavy" or mysterious, but rather "light" and productive. The purpose of therapy is to find solutions that will produce change, and can be used between sessions and after therapy has been completed.

Minimal History is Needed About the Problem

Characteristic of solution-based therapy is the investigation of what is working for families rather than a detailed history of the problem (O'Hanlon & Weiner-Davis, 1989). As they stated, "If the camera is focused mainly on the problems and pathology, both therapists and clients perceive problems and pathology" (p. 39). I often wonder when I read a ten-page psychosocial history of a referred client, that might include a paragraph of the client's coping skills, just how different the therapy would have been if the same psychosocial history would have been done emphasizing the client's adaptation skills, resources, supports, and there was only a summation paragraph of the presented problem.

Causal Understanding is Unnecessary

O'Hanlon and Wilk (1987) described how they believe that every psychotherapy office should have a couch in it. They reason that the need for the couch is not for the client, but for the therapist because "...every now and then, in the course of a session, a hypothesis might accidentally enter the therapist's head, and the best remedy for it is to lie down until it goes away" (p. 98). They further add that an attempt to find the cause will only limit the therapy process and create a set of deductions, assumptions, imperatives and prerequisites for the therapy process.

Only a Small Change is Needed

De Shazer (1985) used the analogy that if a pilot flying from New York to San Francisco were to make a one degree error in calculating a flight pattern, the result will be a plane that is considerably off course when it is supposed to be in San Francisco. O'Hanlon and Weiner-Davis (1989) stated that a small positive change can have an effect on clients by creating confidence and optimism about trying to solve other problems (ripple effect).

Clients Define Goals

An oft-quoted Milton Erickson saying applies here:

> Each person is a unique individual. Hence, psychotherapy should be formulated to meet the uniqueness of the individual's needs, rather than tailoring the person to fit the Procrustean bed of hypothetical theory of human behavior. (Zeig, 1982, p. vii)

O'Hanlon and Weiner-Davis (1989) maintained that solution-based therapists do not believe that "real problems" exist and that therapists are best suited to define therapeutic goals. Rather, a solution-based therapist will let the client define the therapeutic goals. O'Hanlon and Wilk (1987) sum up this cultural belief this way, "Therapy is over when the agreed outcome has been reached, not when certain 'hypothetical therapeutic' issues have been dealt with" (p. 109).

Rapid Change is Possible

Simply because a problem has persisted for a long period of time does not mean it will need a long period of treatment (de Shazer, 1985; O'Hanlon & Wilk, 1987; O'Hanlon & Weiner-Davis, 1989). Solution-based therapists would argue that the reason a chronic problem has not been solved is because no one has yet found the solution (O'Hanlon & Wilk, 1987). Too often cases are staffed in which therapists essentially give up on the client due to the long-standing nature of the presented problem, rendering the treatment less effective. Weiner-Davis (1992) stated, "...Solution based therapists make no distinction between recent and long-standing problems in regard to their solveability" (p. 92). She uses the analogy of the Butterfly Effect: small changes can quickly lead to big changes.

Multiple Views are Valid

When working with families multiple views of the problem or complaint are examined. Family therapists have long been amused, and frustrated, by hearing the many versions of the problem, and often wondering, "Are these people talking about the same thing?" Solution-based therapists will not attribute labels such as correct or incorrect regarding each description of the problem. However, they will tend to focus on those descriptions that will assist in generating solutions (O'Hanlon & Weiner-Davis, 1989).

Focus is on What is Changeable

Solution-based therapists will emphasize what is changeable (behaviors) instead of developing treatment based on a category or label (O'Hanlon & Weiner-Davis, 1989). When comparing a treatment plan of a solution-based therapist with that of a more traditional, long-term therapist one major difference will be noticed. This difference is what is being treated. The more traditional, long-term therapist will focus on changing the personality constructs and characteristics of the clients, and such a process, if it can ever be completed, will take a long time (O'Hanlon & Weiner-Davis, 1989). A solution-based therapist will focus on specific, obtainable behaviors. For example, an indicator of someone who is depressed may be poor work attendance. The solution-based therapist will focus on getting the depressive to work more often. O'Hanlon and Wilk (1987) argued that a therapist's office should have large windows and the curtains should be wide open. They feel such conditions are necessary as the work in therapy occurs outside the office and we should be able to see the change.

Michael White and David Epston

White and Epston (1990) proposed that a differentiation be made between the logico scientific and narrative forms of psychotherapy. They reported on their clinical strategy of externalizing the problem.

Logico Scientific Versus Narrative Reasoning

Logico scientific reasoning. White and Epston (1990) described the logico scientific mode of thought as being characterized by empiricism, logic, analysis, and the exploration of "truth." They discussed how logico scientific reasoning is an epistemology that categorizes and diagnoses; transcends the temporal dimension; uses technical language; maintains that forces act on and within individuals; the observer is excluded from the observed; and the practice of psychotherapy resembles an empirical study. This reasoning is essentially the same as the naturalistic paradigm we explored while touring the MRI.

Narrative reasoning. In contrast to logico scientific reasoning, White and Epston (1990) argued that a narrative form of thought is concerned with stories and lifelikeness. This shift in emphasis allows narrative reasoning to develop options and varying perspectives rather than absolute truths. The characteristics of narrative reasoning include lived experiences that have a beginning, middle, and end; language that is the user's and allows a rich, non-technical conversation; people interact with the "forces"; the observer and observed are inseparable; and the practice of psychotherapy resembles a story, script, and/or authorship.

Narrative reasoning could be considered a model within the paradigm of naturalism previously discussed. The importance of narrative reasoning is that therapy can be viewed as a process individuals and families seek out when their "story" does not represent what they are living (White & Epston, 1990). For example, if the parents of a 14-year-old male have a "story" that their son should be holding at least a 2.5 grade point average and not have a police record, then when their son brings home a report card with Fs and Ds and is on probation they may seek out therapy.

How is narrative reasoning important to therapy? Its importance comes in that therapy becomes a process of generating alternate stories for families that will help them exercise new options and strategies (White & Epston, 1990). As with any story, a therapeutic task is helping families identify that the story is not complete, and they have the ability to write their own successful, more satisfying script. By maintaining a narrative reasoning process during therapy, the therapist can begin to perform the second component of White and Epston's process, externalizing the problem.

Externalizing the Problem

Depending upon one's training, externalizing the problem could be viewed as a fresh or contradictory idea. White and Epston (1990) defined externalizing the problem as,

> ...an approach to therapy that encourages persons to objectify and, at times, to personify the problems that they experience as oppressive. In this process, the problem becomes a separate entity and thus external to the person or relationship that was ascribed as the problem. (p. 38)

Some of the benefits of externalizing the problem include a decrease in arguing who owns the problem; it does not allow the sense of failure to continue regarding the presence of the problem; it allows teams to form against the problem; it helps options to become evident in reclaiming one's life from the problem; more effective and less heavy sessions can be conducted; and dialogue rather than monologue is used in discussing the problem (White & Epston, 1990). When a problem has been externalized, it allows therapists and clients to examine the relationship between the problem and person. White (1986) utilized what he calls "relative influence questioning" to begin to externalize the problem, and he proposed that two maps can be created. One map explores the problem's influence on the person, and the other explores the influence of the person on the problem.

Influence of the problem. During the therapy process questions are asked and homework is given that assists families in mapping the influence of the problem on their lives (White & Epston, 1990). They discussed that by mapping the influence of the problem, the description of the problem becomes more broad and not unique to one person. That is, the problem's influence becomes storied with everyone involved; in turn, a search can better be conducted for where to intervene, and the intervention does not need to be centered on the "owner" of the problem.

Influence of the persons. A second set of questions and homework that White and Epston (1990) reported involves the influence individuals make on the problem. This identification process assists clients in developing maps that demonstrate when they have dealt successfully with the problem (unique outcomes). These unique outcome maps can then be developed so they are utilized more frequently, and assist clients in creating a futuristic story that does not include the problem (White & Epston, 1990).

An example is appropriate at this time. Clients who are involved in a "committed" relationship, but have difficulty setting limits with previous significant others often place their current relationship in jeopardy. Questions can be asked how this desire to remain connected impacts the current relationship (influence on person). Some common answers are that the current relationship would be over if the rendezvous was discovered, and that there is almost an obsession in contemplating how to set limits and/or not be discovered. Subsequently, questions can be asked about how these individuals promote the problem (influence on problem). Typical responses include, "I call or get called by my past lovers," and "I, when I am alone, doing nothing, I think of the others." This combination of questions allows the problem to become externalized and clients feel less pathological when they can see the relationship they have developed with their problem. Interventions can be built based on what clients report as successful management of the problem. Some examples include calling the current significant other when feeling lonely, developing a routine when alone, changing the phone number.

As can be expected from this description of the work of Michael White and David Epston, their interventions focus on written text to assist in producing change. They utilize letters, certificates, and other documents to script interventions that will assist families (White & Epston, 1990). An example they give is a misery certificate. Such a certificate congratulates clients when they "turn their back on misery," and have "deprived misery of her company" (p. 198).

The work of Michael White and David Epston promises to be exciting and challenging. They do not identify themselves as "brief therapists," but they were included in our journey because their theoretical beliefs and clinical practices seemed to fit the territory we were touring. They appear to maintain the highest respect for the strengths, resources, and solutions of their clients.

Some Brief Therapy Misunderstandings

There are many misunderstandings regarding the brief therapy culture. One misunderstanding is that brief therapy is a "band aid" approach to mental health issues. Those who embrace this misunderstanding frequently state that the "real problem" is not dealt with. However, the "real problem" is usually defined by their theoretical position, not by the client. Above all, brief therapists respect their client's definition of what constitutes a problem and resolution. When asked this question I frequently respond with my own question, "When do therapists know that the surgery is complete, and how do they know it was successful or not?"

A second misunderstanding is that brief therapy is only used with minor, superficial problems, and that it cannot be used with chronic, "deep" problems. This misunderstanding reflects that the believer does not grasp how brief therapists define problems. Brief therapists avoid treating categories of problems (e.g., borderline personality). O'Hanlon and Weiner-Davis (1989) stated, "Those of us who are more solution oriented like to work with fairly well-defined goals that are realizable within a reasonable amount of time" (p. 49). It seems somewhat ironic to consider that someone who is being "treated" for depression and the treatment includes working through some historic issue, and after nine months that person is still unable to sleep, is withdrawn, frequently suicidal, etc. These symptoms remained at the expense of having to treat the "deep" problem.

Another misunderstanding about brief therapists is that they are mostly concerned with number of sessions. All therapists should be concerned if the treatment they are providing is not being effective with the presented problem. However, brief therapists do not try to solve problems in a predetermined period of time. Rather they develop a style that is solution and change oriented, and the result is typically a decrease in number of sessions. Even brief therapists have long-term clients (O'Hanlon, 1990).

A final misunderstanding about brief therapy to be discussed is that it is a "tricky" form of therapy. At first glance, brief therapy may appear "tricky," but when a close examination is conducted about how interventions are constructed, the mystique is quick to disappear. The reason the mystique dissipates is that brief therapists utilize the clients' resources and strategies that work, and often times clients present solutions that appear illogical, but work. Brief therapists will then help clients expand on their own solutions; in turn, the style of therapy is contingent upon the clients repertoire of solution-oriented patterns.

Reflections

This article explored three models of brief therapy: MRI, solution based, and narrative form. Our investigation found that these models have their own cultural beliefs and customs that frequently depart from the more traditional methods of psychotherapy. Although the models differed in their clinical practice, ranging from intervening in communication/behavioral patterns to externalizing the problems, these models share a common theme. The theme is that the psychotherapy process should be directed by the client's theory (story) and the defined problem should be achievable. Additionally, sessions should be conducted in such a manner as to assist families in leading more satisfied and fulfilling lifestyles, not to meet the therapist's theoretical and clinical needs.

References

Bateson, G., Jackson, D., Haley, J., & Weakland, J. (1956). Toward a theory of schizophrenia. *Behavioral Science*, 251–264.

Becvar, D. S., & Becvar, R. J. (1988). *Family therapy: A systematic integration*. Boston: Allyn & Bacon.

de Shazer, S. (1982). *Patterns of brief family therapy*. New York: Guilford Press.

de Shazer, S. (1985). *Keys to solution in brief therapy*. New York: Norton.

Haley, J. (1977). *Problem solving therapy*. San Francisco: Jossey-Bass.

Keeney, B. (1983). *Aesthetics of change*. New York: Guilford Press.

Lincoln, Y., & Guba, E. (1985). *Naturalistic inquiry*. Beverly Hills: SAGE Publications.

O'Hanlon, W. H. (1987). *Taproots: Underlying principles of Milton Erickson's therapy and hypnosis*. New York: W. W. Norton.

O'Hanlon, W. H. (1990). Debriefing myself: When a brief therapist does long-term work. *The Family Therapy Networker, 14*, 48–49, 68–69.

O'Hanlon, W. H., & Weiner-Davis, M. (1989). *In search of solutions: A new direction in psychotherapy*. New York: W. W. Norton.

O'Hanlon, W. H., & Wilk, J. (1987). *Shifting contexts: The generation of effective psychotherapy*. New York: Guilford Press.

Sifneos, P. (1987). *Short-term dynamic psychotherapy evaluation and techniques* (2nd ed.). New York: Plenum Press.

Simon, F., Stierlin, H., & Wynne, L. (1985). *The language of family therapy*. New York: Family Process Press.

von Glaserfeld, E. (1984). An introduction to radical constructivism. In P. Watzlawick (Ed.), *The invented reality: How do we know what we believe we know?* (pp. 17–40). New York: W. W. Norton.

Watzlawick, P., Weakland, J., & Fisch, R. (1974). *Change: Principles of problem formation and problem resolution*. New York: W. W. Norton.

Weiner-Davis, M. (1992). *Divorcebusting*. New York: Summit Books.

White, M., & Epston, D. (1990). *Narrative means to therapeutic ends.* New York: W. W. Norton.

Whitehead, A. N., & Russell, B. (1910). *Principia mathematica* (3 vols.). Cambridge, England: Cambridge University Press.

Zeig, J. (1982). *Ericksonian approaches to hypnosis and psychotherapy.* New York: Brunner/Mazel.

Chapter 3

The Practice of Marriage and Family Counseling

The day-to-day activities of the professional working with couples and families is too often lost in conversations involving theory or family history. Yet there are a wide range of effective techniques and practices that have been introduced to the profession by individuals engaged in marriage and family counseling/therapy. The writings within this chapter focus on counselor/therapist activities as they work with couples and families.

In the practice of family counseling the authors review five of the basic interventions employed by family therapists. Major interventions examined include: reframing, tracking, the use of family rituals, prescribing indecision, and the use of metaphors. Emphasis is placed on the appropriateness of each technique, spontaneity, and avoiding prescriptive methods of dealing with family issues.

West, in a well-written article, provides an overview of assessment inventories used in marriage and family therapy. Viewing assessment as related to a systemic perspective provides the major theme of this presentation. Weber, McKeever, and McDaniel help beginning therapists with a model of what to look for in the first family interview. A structured practical guide is presented to assist both the therapist and the supervisor.

Several articles in this chapter provide specific interventions used within a variety of settings. Stone and Peeks provide an overview of strategic family therapy in the school setting. They illustrate how changes in the student's family can take place through this approach. Circular questioning is defined, illustrated, and explored in the article by Smith, Griffin, Thys, and Ryan. As a tool, circular questioning is advocated as a method of obtaining significant information about the family. In the final article, Beck discusses genogram construction and how it can be used beyond simply gathering facts about the family system.

The purpose of this chapter is to provide the reader with a glimpse of practices and techniques used in marriage and family counseling/therapy. Specific texts such as Sherman and Fredman (1986) provide more extensive reviews of techniques often used in the field. However, the authors believe that this chapter provides valuable information to beginning as well as seasoned practitioners.

The Practice of Marriage and Family Counseling

Robert L. Smith
Patricia Stevens-Smith

The practice of marriage and family counseling/therapy[1] has grown at an unprecedented rate over the past two decades. Private practitioners, agency counselors, school counselors, pastoral counselors, counselors in business and industry, and other professionals working in a variety of settings regularly see couples and families as a part of their practice. Such professionals work on a day-to-day basis with issues and problems presented by the family unit.

When asked to define the practice of marriage and family counseling/therapy, the most frequent response comes in the form of a statement or comment that includes systems or systems theory language. More scholarly constructed responses to this question cite systems (1981) á la von Bertalanffy, and include several schools of thought or theorists such as Jackson (1959), Ackerman (1982), Bateson (1972), Bowen (1978), Minuchin (1974), and more. In such discussions most frequently lacking is a clear picture of what family counselors/therapists do and how they actually work with couples and families. This article does not claim to fully clarify all vicissitudes related to one's work with couples and families, but rather attempts to provide the reader with some of the more basic practices used in marriage and family counseling.

Techniques

Overview

Techniques are what the counselor or therapist introduces or uses when working with couples or families. Described as tools (Sherman & Fredman, 1986), the efficacy of techniques is determined by their appropriate fit with a presenting problem or dilemma, and by the therapist's personal skills. Techniques have little meaning outside of the therapist's relationship/communication skill level. When core dimensions of counselor functioning are present (Carkhuff, 1969, 1971; Egan, 1986; Ivey, 1988; Brammer, 1973, 1979), techniques can help couples more fully understand presenting problems, develop new relationships between children and parents, reveal true caring among family members, help family systems become aware of patterns and the sequencing of events, and generally create movement and at least a greater understanding during a time when couples and families are stuck or immobilized.

The following techniques are often used by practicing marriage and family counselors and therapists. The techniques are not inclusive, nor are they presented as a "bag of tricks" to be implemented in a cookbook fashion. While a number of techniques could have been selected, the authors chose the following five: reframing, tracking, family rituals, prescribing indecision, and use of metaphors. The rationale for the selection of these techniques is that the authors believe they most clearly represent the activities of marriage and family counselors that work systemically with families. Additional practices that could have been included such as communication skill building, role playing, and the empty chair have been described elsewhere when referring to the counselor's work with individual clients rather than couples or families. The overall intent is to clarify the practice of marriage and family counseling/therapy and stimulate readers to explore such practices in their work with couples and families.

Reframing

Reframing, based on the constructivist perception of reality (Coyne, 1985), emphasizes the idea that people create their own reality. A reframe in working with a couple or family is a statement made by the counselor that attempts to change the meaning of a behavior or situation, without changing the actual facts or events. In therapy, the counselor will often attempt to reframe something that seems quite hopeless or pessimistic to something more hopeful or optimistic. A reframe provides the opportunity for family members to see a presented phenomenon in a new context. Through reframing a new set of rules may be established.

Satir (1983) has viewed the purpose of the reframe as a means to create a shift in the perceptions of family members with respect to the behavior so that it may be handled more constructively. As an example, Satir provides the following reframe:

Son: "My dad often yells and has a temper."
Satir: "Your father gets over angry and brings out his thoughts." (p. 34)

Another example of a reframe relates to a therapist working with a couple who have tried endless responses to stop the constant fighting between their two sons. Typical solutions tried by parents are usually of a first order variety using punishment, etc. In such a case the therapist may interject a reframe by describing the fighting as "normal sibling behavior" and further see it as "more loving behavior expressed in the only way that the children known how to express such towards each other."

For reframing to be successful it must be plausible and acceptable to the clients. It is the counselor's job to present the reframe in a manner that makes sense to the clients. Therefore the counselor needs to clearly understand the problem along with each individual's perception and role as related to the problem.

Tracking

Tracking is a technique used by family therapists despite one's theoretical orientation or background. The purpose of tracking is to gain a clear understanding of patterns of behavior, thought process, and feelings, as related to the family system. Members of the family are asked in detail to provide the sequence of an event or phenomenon. Minuchin and Fishman (1981) see tracking as a method used by therapists to join with the family system. Tracking involves careful listening to the family story. The therapist does not judge or evaluate during this process. The therapist learns about the family, how it functions, rules it follows, and cycles of family practice. The therapist observes the roles played by various family members, who is involved, to what degree, when, how, and under what circumstances.

The behaviors used by the therapist involve listening, clarifying questions, supporting discussion, and encouraging sharing. The therapist does not question or challenge family members. In a systemic manner the therapist might ask questions in the following order: Who is the first to act or do something in a particular situation? Then what happens? Who acts next? Then what does the first person do? What are other family members doing? This process continues with the therapist obtaining a full picture of sequences of events and how self-reinforcing feedback loops are established.

Some additional practices may be utilized in tracking including having family members enact a sequence of events, or asking each member to tell their story about a sequence of events to check each member's perception. The tracking technique encourages specificity as to what happens within the family system, creates a concrete discussion, avoids vague generalizations, and allows for greater insight by family members leading to changing a stuck sequence that has been habitually utilized.

Family Rituals

Family rituals are used after the therapist has an idea about the rules of the family. The prescription of a family ritual is used to change the system and break up the old rules of the family. Sequences of behavior are often interrupted through family ritual prescriptions. Typically the ritual is created by the counselor without explanation. Yet, emphasis is placed on details involving specific actions by family members, time, sequence, membership participation, environment, etc. The prescription is often written out in detail for family members. The actual ritual, based upon the therapist's knowledge of the family, its interactional system, etc., can range from the very simple to an elaborate level of complexity involving more than one generation.

An example of a fairly simple prescribed ritual centers around parenting. In such cases the therapist might arrange days where each parent is responsible for the discipline and where the other parent is not to interfere. Monday, Wednesday, and Friday might be days directed where the husband is in charge, while, Tuesday, Thursday, and Saturday would be left to the wife. Such a ritual (Selvini-Palazzoli, Boscolo, Cecchin, & Prata, 1978) can block the usual patterns of interaction in the family. Other examples of prescribed straightforward rituals include: (1) the arrangement of a fixed time for dinner with the rules being that arguing, complaining, and criticizing are not allowed; (2) directing the parents to go out on dates without going into detail as to where they are going, thus adding mystery to the behavior; (3) prescribing a fixed time to discuss a family issue with each individual given 15 minutes of uninterrupted time, or setting the prescription around how to celebrate family members' birthdays or special events in their lives. Often rituals are directed to the family to add needed structure. Examples might center upon homework, housecleaning, or dinner. Yet in all cases the prescription of the ritual would be preceded by an understanding of current family functioning and existing patterns.

Prescribing Indecision

Prescribing indecision is a paradoxical technique often used after working with a couple over a period of time. The couple or family may be stuck in indecision. The status of the presenting problem has stayed the same and it doesn't seem as though much activity is about to take place. In such a case the therapist cannot move the clients in a direction of action.

In prescribing indecision the counselor discusses with the client that she/he has been wrong in trying to push them to move ahead. Instead the thought is expressed that it is too early to make any decisions and they should wait and not rush. To follow this up the counselor specifically details the terms of staying undecided, therefore creating a therapeutic double bind of either resisting the prescription, or acquiescing.

An example of prescribing indecision in marital counseling (Todd, 1984) involves working with a couple unable to decide on whether to stay with one another or get a divorce. After seeing the couple for a lengthy period of time and unsuccessfully trying nonparadoxical strategies, a prescription of indecision was presented. The couple was asked to delay on any decision relating to divorce, and to spell out clearly how they wanted to interact. Thus the couple was placed in a bind where they either lived together and settled their affairs, or rejected the prescription and decided to divorce.

The positive feature of a paradoxical technique is that the counselor does not have to directly confront the family and create conflict. Very often stress levels of couples and families are exacerbated by faulty decision making. With the prescription of indecision, indecisive behavior is actually reframed as a positive way to look at an issue, to take one's time, and to be sure.

Use of Metaphors

Marriage and family counselors/therapists often use metaphors in their work with couples and families. Metaphors are used to stimulate new ways for client systems to communicate and interact. The metaphoric intervention can be helpful in defining or clarifying a presenting issue by providing symbolic ways of dealing with the problem itself.

Prior to the use of metaphors the therapist should clearly understand the presenting problem. Utilized extensively in strategic therapy (Haley, 1976; Zeig, 1980), metaphors attempt to challenge relationships in a nonthreatening manner. The analogy created by the therapist is not explained to the family as it relates to the original problem.

In the most basic form a metaphor can be a word that is used to represent an idea followed by an analogy. Satir, for example (Thomas, 1992), would use the word "pot" as a metaphor to represent a family member's self-esteem. A follow-up would be, "how full is your pot?", "how does it fill up?", or "how is it emptied?" Bunny Duhl (1983) has used the metaphor of a "toy." As a follow-up she asks family members to visualize themselves as toys and asks questions about their shape, size, function, noises made. She then proceeds by asking the "toys" to find other "toys" in the family with which to interact.

Metaphoric tasks have been effectively used with couples. In such cases, the therapist speaks in a metaphor that symbolizes the problem presented by the family. Erickson would see this as planting seeds for potential change. An example (Becvar, 1988) is to discuss with a chaotic family how an orchestra might be successfully conducted with two conductors. The added caveat would be discussing how they might work together if they have differences of opinion as to how the orchestra should perform.

Conclusions

An article of this nature is far from complete when considering the list of therapeutic tools available to marriage and family counselors. The reader is encouraged to use the references provided in this article to gain familiarity with a variety of other widely practiced techniques such as: the genogram, sculpting, the family sociogram, role playing, the family council meeting, the empty chair, communication skill building, the use of letters, etc. All such techniques are recommended with a cautionary note of accurately diagnosing the family system and judiciously applying each intervention. By reviewing techniques frequently used in marriage and family counseling/therapy, it is hoped that individuals will not only more accurately relate to that which occurs in practice, but also further appreciate its richness and excitement.

Notes

[1]The terms "counseling" and "therapy" are considered interchangeable in discussions of working with couples and families.

References

Ackerman, N. W. (1982). The psychoanalytic approach to the family. In D. Block & R. Simon (Eds.), *The strength of family therapy: Selected papers of Nathan W. Ackerman* (pp. 250–259). New York: Brunner/Mazel.

Bateson, G. (1972). *Steps to an ecology of mind.* New York: Ballantine Books.

Becvar, D., & Becvar, R. (1988). *Family therapy.* Boston: Allyn & Bacon.

Bertalanffy, von L. (1981). *A systems view of man* (P. A. Laviolette, Ed.). Boulder, CO: Westview Press.

Bowen, M. (1978). *Family therapy in clinical practice.* New York: Jason Aronson.

Brammer, L. M. (1973). *The helping relationship.* Englewood Cliffs, NJ: Prentice-Hall.

Brammer, L. M. (1979). *The helping relationship: Process and skills* (2nd ed.). Englewood Cliffs, NJ: Prentice-Hall.

Carkhuff, R. R. (1969). *Helping and human relations.* New York: Holt, Rinehart & Winston.

Carkhuff, R. R. (1971). *The development of human resources.* New York: Holt, Rinehart & Winston.

Coyne, J. C. (1985). Toward a theory of frames and reframing: The social nature of frames. *Journal of Marital and Family Therapy, 11*, 337–344.

Duhl, B. S. (1983). *From the inside out and other metaphors: Creative and integrative approaches to training in systems therapy.* New York: Brunner/Mazel.

Egan, G. (1986). *The skilled helper: A systematic approach to effective helping* (3rd ed.). Monterey, CA: Brooks/Cole.

Haley, J. (1976). *Problem-solving therapy.* New York: Harper/Colophon Books.

Ivey, A. E. (1988). *Intentional interviewing and counseling: Facilitating client development* (2nd ed.). Pacific Grove, CA: Brooks/Cole.

Jackson, D. D. (1959). Family interaction, family homeostasis, and some implications for conjoint family therapy. In J. Masserman (Ed.), *Individual and family dynamics*. New York: Grune & Stratton.

Minuchin, G. (1974). *Families and family therapy*. Cambridge, MA: Harvard University Press.

Minuchin, S., & Fishman, H. (1981). *Techniques of family therapy*. Cambridge, MA: Harvard University Press.

Satir, V. (1983). *Conjoint family therapy* (3rd ed.). Palo Alto, CA: Science and Behavior Books. (Original work published in 1967)

Selvini-Palazzoli, M., Boscolo, L., Cecchin, G., & Prata, G. (1978). *Paradox and counterparadox*. New York: Jason Aronson.

Sherman, R., & Fredman, N. (1986). *Handbook of structural techniques in marriage and family therapy*. New York: Brunner/Mazel.

Thomas, M. B. (1992). *An introduction to marital and family therapy*. New York: Macmillan Publishing Company.

Todd, T. C. (1984). Strategic approaches to marital stuckness. *Journal of Marital and Family Therapy*, *10*(4), 373–374.

Zeig, J. K. (Ed.). (1980). *A teaching seminar with Milton H. Erickson*. New York: Brunner/Mazel.

This article was originally published in *Awareness: The Journal of the Colorado Association for Counseling and Development*, Vol. 20, 1992, pp. 1–11. Reprint permission granted by the Editor.

Marriage and Family Therapy Assessment

John D. West

The literature suggests a high level of involvement in marriage and family therapy training among counselor education departments (Gladding, Burggraf, & Fenell, 1987; Meadows & Hetrick, 1982; Peltier & Vale, 1986). Moreover, an increasing level of involvement may be anticipated in the last part of this decade (Gladding, Burggraf, & Fenell, 1987). Similar to counselors using other modalities (individual and group therapy), marriage and family therapy practitioners recognize the need for client assessment. Brock and Barnard (1988), for example, mentioned several advantages of using self-report instruments with couples and families:

> (1) they can help to objectify and organize the treatment effort while establishing an atmosphere of purposeful direction to replace family chaos; (2) they provide family members an opportunity to systematically understand what the other members' concerns are (perhaps for the first time, the confusing cloud of emotionality is somewhat dispelled); and (3) individuals are provided with the opportunity to self-disclose through paper and pencil rather than their usual method, which has failed. (p. 41)

Cromwell, Olson, and Fournier (1976b) noted that in addition to serving as a diagnostic aid, data from formal assessments can provide feedback to the couple or family: "This not only makes clients more aware of how they are functioning but can serve to motivate them to become more seriously involved in the treatment process" (p. 30).

Marriage and family therapy assessment is distinguishable from assessments that traditionally occur as part of individual and group therapy. Hansen noted that a differentiating factor is the counselor's epistemological perspective (cited in Ritter, West, & Trotzer, 1984). He indicated that individual and group modalities often rely on linear thought processes whereas marriage and family therapy is frequently grounded in systemic theory. Systemic theory is holistic in character, and emphasizes patterns of interaction among family members, with each member influencing and, in turn, being influenced by every other member (Goldenberg & Goldenberg, 1985). Linear thinking explains behavior through "less complex cause-and-effect patterns, by analyzing...how A causes B, B causes C, C causes D, and so on" (p. 96). The systemic perspective captures the interactive aspect of family relationships by indicating that "A may cause B, but B also affects A, which affects B, and so on in circular causality" (p. 96).

The epistemological difference between the systemic and linear models influences assessments that occur before therapy, during therapy, and upon terminating therapy. Systemic assessment in marriage and family therapy focuses on patterns of interaction among family members, whereas techniques designed to measure characteristics of individual family members reflect the linear mode. The latter cannot fully capture a marriage and family systems perspective (Keeney, 1983). This article reviews a number of procedures designed to measure dimensions from family systems theory and then provides a discussion of family systems assessment.

Family Inventories

Couple's Inventories

The *Inventory of Marital Conflicts* (IMC) (Olson & Ryder, 1970) can be used to evaluate power or influence in a couple's relationship, and systems theory suggests that patterns of interaction in the couple's relationship reflects a covertly agreed upon balance of power (Haley, 1963). The IMC consists of 18 vignettes that describe typical marital conflicts. At first, the couple is asked to individually evaluate each vignette, indicating which vignette partner is primarily responsible for each problem and which of two problem-solving procedures is most acceptable. The couple is then brought together to jointly decide which vignette partner is primarily responsible for each problem and which of the two problem-solving procedures is preferred. Each individual's level of influence is evaluated according to a win score. The win score is based on vignettes in which the couple's individual evaluations differ and is determined by noting whose decision is accepted during the conjoint session. Of the 18 vignettes, 12 are designed to stimulate conflict between the couple. Validity data for 200 couples indicates that, on the average, at least one spouse perceived each item as similar to problems they had encountered or similar to problems of other couples they had known. On the average, couples disagreed on 10 of 12 conflict items (86%) and agreed on 5 of 6 identical items (86%). Additional data, based on 100 couples, indicates that 81% of the participants became somewhat or very involved in the inventory, 77% of the spouses reacted as usual when resolving IMC conflicts, and 90% found the procedure either somewhat or very enjoyable. Reliability estimates are found in Table 1.

The *Relationship Style Inventory* (RSI) (Christensen & Scoresby, 1975; Harper, Scoresby, & Boyce, 1977; Scoresby & Christensen, 1976) measures an individual's perceptions of interaction styles in family relationships. It can be used to assess the couple's relationship according to dimensions of complementarity, symmetry, and parallelness. Each of these dimensions is maintained by the couple's pattern of interaction. The RSI is composed of 63 true-false items, and construct validity has been strengthened by a factor analysis (Scoresby, 1975). Table 1 provides reliability estimates from research completed by Christensen and Scoresby (1975).

Family systems theory focuses on covertly agreed to patterns of interaction in the spousal subsystem, and some theorists have been especially interested in the balance of power (Haley, 1976; Madanes, 1981). Bowen (1978) suggested, for example, that the continuously submissive spouse becomes more vulnerable to psychological decompensation. The IMC acts as a stimulus for helping couples experience and discuss how levels of influence or power are demonstrated in their relationship. The three dimensions evaluated on the RSI have been discussed at length by members of the Mental Research Institute in Palo Alto, California (Lederer & Jackson, 1968; Watzlawick, Beavin, & Jackson, 1967). The dimensions have been absorbed into family systems theory (Nichols, 1984), and Scoresby and Christensen (1976) described these patterns of interaction.

Complementary interaction can be viewed as an exchange of opposite behavior; for example, one partner is dominant while the other is submissive. With symmetrical patterns, there is an exchange of identical behavior in juxtaposition; for example, each partner attempts to be right or attacks the other. Parallel patterns are different from the complementary or symmetrical styles. Here, the couple does not simply hold to exchanging opposite behavior (complementary style) or identical behavior (symmetrical style) but can call forth a greater variety of exchanges that are sensitive and responsive to situation demands

Table 1
Reliability Estimates

Couples Inventories	
IMC:	Internal consistency (.41)
RSI:	Test-retest (complementarity .76, symmetry .95, parallelness, .93)
	Interrater reliability (ranges from .41 to .88)
Nuclear Family Inventories	
FACES:	Internal consistency for FACES III (adaptability .62 and cohesion .77)
KFST:	Test-retest (wive's perceptions of spousal relationship .82 and father-child relationship .86)
	Test-retest (children's perceptions of mother-child relationship .70)
	Test-retest (consensus-distance scores for spousal relationship .80 and father-child relationship .57)
FAD:	Internal consistency (ranges from .72 to .92)
	Test-retest (ranges from .66 to .76)
FAM:	Internal consistency (ranges from .66 to .77 with children and .64 to .82 with adults)
FES:	Internal consistency (ranges from .61 to .78)
	Test-retest (ranges from .68 to .86)
SFI:	Internal consistency (ranges from .84 to .88)
	Test-retest (ranges from .39 to .85)
BT:	Internal consistency (.94)
	Interrater reliability (ranges from .72 to .89)
CP/CF:	Internal consistency (.84)
	Interrater reliability (ranges from .61 to .83)
Family-of-Origin Inventories	
FOS:	Internal consistency (.75)
	Test-retest (.97)
PAFS:	Internal consistency (ranges from .80 to .95)
	Test-retest (ranges from .55 to .95)

(Harper, Scoresby, & Boyce, 1977). As a result, by focusing on patterns of interaction in a couple's relationship, data from the IMC and RSI are interpreted from a family systems perspective.

Nuclear Family Inventories

The *Family Adaptability and Cohesion Evaluation Scale III* (FACES III) (Olson, McCubbin, Barnes, Larsen, Muxen, & Wilson, 1985) is the third version in a series of FACES scales and assesses two dimensions of the Olson et al. circumplex model of family functioning (i.e., family adaptability and cohesion). The adaptability and cohesion scales contain 10 items each. The FACES III can be taken twice to attain perceived and ideal descriptions of the family. Calculating the perceived-ideal discrepancy provides a measure of family satisfaction with current levels of adaptability and cohesion. The correlation between the adaptability and cohesion scales on the FACES III is .03, thus suggesting the independence of each dimension. Correlations between adaptability items and the total adaptability score range from .42 to .56, while correlations between cohesion items and the total cohesion score range from .51 to .74. The correlation between adaptability and social desirability is zero, but Olson and associates (1985) mentioned that high levels of cohesion are culturally embedded in the ideal family and, as a result, the correlation between cohesion and social desirability could only be reduced to .35. Reliability estimates are noted in Table 1. Finally, Pratt and Hansen (1987) recently suggested that a more precise measure of adaptability and cohesion might be obtained by changing the FACES III response options from a unipolar Likert format to a bipolar response format.

The *Kvebaek Family Sculpting Technique* (KFST) (Cromwell, Fournier, & Kvebaek, 1980) is a self-report instrument that integrates aspects of "family sculpting" (Duhl, Kantor, & Duhl, 1974; Papp, Silverstein, & Carter, 1973; Simon, 1972) by highlighting closeness and distance among members, triangulation within the family, and the degree of influence held by each family member. The KFST requires that figurines representing family members be placed on what resembles a chess board (i.e., a 100 square grid). The KFST is scored by calculating the distance between figurines. Although not all members need to be present to complete the assessment, all members are represented on the game board. Initially, each individual completes a "real" and "ideal" sculpting of closeness and distance among all family members. Then, the entire family is asked to reach a consensus on what a "real" and "ideal" sculpting would look like. One investigation found that data from KFST supported the notion that families of hospitalized substance abusers demonstrate or desire maladaptive patterns of interaction (West, Hosie, & Zarski, 1987). Reliability estimates from research by Russell (1980) are reported in Table 1. In addition, Russell presented some evidence for convergent and discriminant validity of the KFST. Although the instrument's validity and reliability remain under study, Cromwell, Olson, and Fournier (1976a, 1976b) identified the KFST as a promising diagnostic tool.

The *Family Assessment Device* (FAD) (Epstein, Baldwin, & Bishop, 1983; Miller, Epstein, Bishop, & Keitner, 1985) is a self-report instrument of 60 items that measures six dimensions of family functioning: problem solving, communication, roles, affective responsiveness, affective involvement, and behavior control. The FAD provides scores on each of the dimensions, with a seventh scale included to describe general functioning. The scales are described as relatively independent, and the FAD is reported to distinguish between clinical and nonclinical families (Epstein et al, 1983). Miller and associates (1985) also noted that correlations between FAD scales and the Marlowe-Crowne Social Desirability Scale (Crowne & Marlowe, 1964) range between -.06 and -.19, and that scores correspond to clinician's ratings of healthy and unhealthy families. Evidence for concurrent validity of the FAD was found by studying its relationship with the Family Unit Inventory (Van der Veen & Olson, 1981; Van der Veen, Howard, & Austria, 1970; Miller, Epstein, Bishop, & Keitner, 1985), and Table 1 provides evidence for internal consistency (Epstein et al., 1983) and test-retest reliability (Miller et al., 1985).

The *Family Assessment Measure* (FAM) (Skinner, Steinhauer, & Santa-Barbara, 1983) is another self-report instrument measuring family dimensions similar to those evaluated by the FAD: task accomplishment, role performance, communication, affective expression, involvement, control, and values and norms. In addition, the FAM also evaluates the family's dyadic relationships according to these seven dimensions. The dyadic relationship scale contains 42 statements about relationships with another family member. Each statement is rated on a continuum from strongly agree to strongly disagree. Reliability estimates for the FAM are noted in Table 1.

The *Family Environment Scale* (FES) (Moos & Moos, 1981) is a self-report instrument designed to assess three dimensions of family functioning: the relationship dimensions, the personal growth dimensions, and the systemic maintenance dimensions. Relationship dimensions are assessed across three subscales measuring the cohesion in the family, the expressiveness in the family, and the amount of conflict in the family. Personal growth dimensions are assessed across five subscales measuring independence of family members, achievement orientation in the family, interest in intellectual and cultural pursuits, participation in social and cultural activities, and emphasis on values and ethical and religious issues. System maintenance dimensions are assessed across two subscales measuring the importance of organizing family activities and responsibilities, and the extent to which rules and procedures are used for running the family. As a result, the FES is composed of 90 items and consists of three parallel forms: a "real" form measuring perceptions of the actual family environment, an "ideal" form measuring perceptions of the ideal family, and an "expectations" form measuring expectations for new family settings. Because there may be variation in the perceptions of family members, a family incongruence score can be calculated to measure the degree of disagreement among members. Intercorrelations among the 10 subscales average approximately .20, which indicates that they measure rather distinct aspects of a family environment (Moos & Moos, 1983). Moos and Moos (1981) also noted that several studies have found the FES to be sensitive to changes in the family during treatment. Reliability estimates from the FES manual are recorded in Table 1.

The *Self-Report Family Instrument* (SFI) (Hulgus, Hampson, Beavers, & Beavers, 1985) is one of three assessment measures in the Beavers systems model. The other two instruments are the Beavers-Timberlawn Family Evaluation Scale (BT) and the Centripetal/Centrifugal Family Style Scale (CP/CF). A theoretical foundation for these instruments can be found in part in earlier work completed by Beavers and associates (Lewis, Beavers, Gossett, & Phillips, 1976). The SFI is a 36-item self-report instrument designed to assess each member's perceptions of family functioning. The SFI evaluates six areas: family health, conflict, communication, cohesion, directive leadership, and expressiveness. The SFI is not significantly related to the Marlowe-Crowne Social Desirability Scale (Crowne & Marlowe, 1964), and it is described as significantly correlated with other measures of family functioning: the Locke-Wallace Marital Satisfaction Scale (Locke & Wallace, 1959); the Family Adaptability and Cohesion Scales (Olson et al, 1985); the Bloom Family Evaluation Scale (Bloom, 1985); the Family Environment Scale

(Moos & Moos, 1981); and the Family Assessment Device (Epstein, Baldwin, & Bishop, 1983). Reliability estimates are noted in Table 1.

The BT and CP/CF (Hulgus, Hampson, Beavers, & Beavers, 1985) are used by observers to rate family competence in resolving specific tasks; for example, "Discuss together what you would like to change about your family." Observers use the BT to rate family functioning on 13 dimensions (e.g., the type of power demonstrated in the family, the type of coalition in the family, and the level of closeness in the family). The CP/CF is used to evaluate the family's style of togetherness. Two styles are highlighted: the centripetal style views the outside world as threatening and the family is seen as the main hope for gratifying needs; the centrifugal style perceives the outside world as less threatening and a place where needs may be gratified. These styles imply two different perspectives on relating to systems beyond the family. The CP/CF consists of nine subscales such as the family's tendency to discourage or encourage dependency, the tendency to develop different degrees of physical distance between members, and the global centripetal/centrifugal scale. The BT is reported to differentiate nonclinical from clinical families. Reliability estimates for the BT and the CP/CF are noted in Table 1.

Each of these nuclear family inventories collects information on process dimensions of the family system. The FACES III defines adaptability as the ability of the "family system to change its power structure, role relationships, and rules in response to situational and developmental stress," while cohesion is described as "the emotional bonding that family members have toward one another" (Olson et al., 1985, p. 4). The central theoretical position states that too little or too much of either dimension is dysfunctional to the family system. The KFST highlights closeness and distance among family members, triangulation within the family, and the degree of influence held by each family member. As a consequence, Cromwell and associates (1980) mentioned that the KFST has theoretical ties with family systems theory. The FAD is theoretically based on the McMaster Model of Family Functioning (Epstein & Bishop, 1981), and the FAM is based on the Process Model of Family Functioning (Steinhauer, Santa-Barbara, & Skinner, 1984). Finally, family environments assessed with the FES reflect patterns of interaction among family members, as do instruments from the Beavers systems model.

Family of Origin Inventories

The *Family-of-Origin Scale* (FOS) (Hovestadt, Anderson, Piercy, Cochran, & Fine, 1985) is a self-report instrument designed to measure perceptions of health in the family of origin. The FOS contains 40 items and uses a 5-point Likert format. The FOS yields a total score indicating the degree of perceived health in the family of origin as well as subscale scores indicating the degree of autonomy and intimacy in the family of origin. Autonomy is based on an investigation into family health (Lewis, Beavers, Gossett, & Phillips, 1976) and consists of five subscales: the clarity of expression among family members, the personal responsibility taken for one's actions, the respect shown for other family members, the openness or receptiveness to one another, and the acceptance of separation and loss in the family. Intimacy is also based on an investigation into family health (Lewis et al., 1976) and consists of five subscales: the expression of a wide range of feelings, the existence of a warm and positive atmosphere in the family, the resolution of conflict without undue stress, the empathic sensitivity in the family, and the extent to which the family trusts in the goodness of human nature. Moreover, Hovestadt and associates (1985) referenced several criterion-related studies that strengthen the validity of the FOS. Reliability estimates are found in Table 1.

The *Personal Authority in the Family System Questionnaire* (PAFS) (Bray, Williamson, & Malone, 1984a, 1984b) is a self-report instrument designed to assess relationships in the three-generational family system. The PAFS contains 132 items and each item is rated on a 5-point Likert scale. The questionnaire contains five intergenerational scales: intergenerational fusion/individuation (INFUS), the degree to which parents and children are dependent on each other versus being more independent and autonomous; intergenerational intimacy (ININT), the quality and degree of satisfaction one has in his or her relationship with parents; intergenerational triangulation (INTRI), the degree to which individuals become "triangled" into their parents' relationship; intergenerational intimidation (INTIM), the degree of personal intimidation experienced in relation to parents; and personal authority (PERAUT), the ability to maintain intimate contact with parents while also remaining individuated. Concurrent validity of the PAFS is strengthened by a significant correlation between the ININT and the Family Adaptability and

Cohesion Evaluation Scales (FACES) (Olson, Bell, & Portner, 1978). In addition, low correlations were found between the FACES Social Desirability Scale and two intergenerational scales: INTRI and INTIM. Construct validity is bolstered by a factor analysis that provides empirical support for the PAFS scales. Reliability estimates are found in Table 1 (Bray et al., 1984b).

Whereas the FOS describes an individual's family of origin as he or she remembers it, the PAFS describes an individual's current interaction with his or her family of origin. The FOS subscales evolved from theoretical constructs developed by Lewis et al. (1976), whereas the PAFS subscales evolved from the work of family systems theorists like Bowen (1978), Boszormenyi-Nagy and Ulrich (1981), and Williamson (1981, 1982). Both inventories focus on relationship patterns and styles of interaction with one's family of origin, and in that regard they highlight systemic theory.

Discussion

Assessment and diagnosis have not received a great deal of attention in family therapy (Liddle, 1983). Keeney (1983) argued that in conducting an assessment, it is important to distinguish among three basic levels of the family system: the individual level, the level of dyadic relationships, and the level of the family as a whole social group. He also mentioned that when selecting an assessment procedure, there should be congruence between the level of the system responding to the assessment and the level to which inferences are being made. For instance, the self-report inventories described in this article focus on dyadic relationships and the family as a social group. These instruments, however, are responded to or completed by an individual family member, and thus some inconsistency exists. That is, assessment data are obtained from an individual level while references are made to dyadic relationships or the family as a whole.

The incongruence that Keeney (1983) speaks of is problematic because systemic data collected through self-report inventories reflect an individual family member's perceptual biases. Of the inventories described in this article, four exceptions to the incongruency problem exist. They include assessment information gathered with the Inventory of Marital Conflicts (IMC), the Kvebaek Family Sculpture Technique

(KFST), the Beavers-Timberlawn Family Evaluation Scale (BT), and the Centripetal/Centrifugal Family Style Scale (CP/CF). These assessment techniques attempt to control for perceptual biases of individual family members. The IMC evaluates levels of influence in a couple's relationship according to demonstrated ability to resolve differences, the KFST allows perceptions of closeness within the family to be consensually validated, and the BT and CP/CF arrange for outside observers to rate family interaction.

Keeney (1983) also noted that "no system level is ever completely independent or autonomous from other system levels in the every day flow of action" and "the interconnectedness of levels of system suggests that information obtained from any level of system can be used to make inferences about the relation of that system to other levels of system" (p. 161). This seems in line with a conclusion by Cromwell and associates (1980) suggesting that a member's perceptions of the family contributes to the very nature of that system. It would seem then that counselors may elect to use self-report inventories in clinical practice and research, but they should remember that reports of systemic family processes are colored and limited by the perceptions of the individual respondent. Cromwell and associates (1976b) suggested that a multi-method approach to assessment furnishes a more comprehensive picture of the family and, consequently, counselors may decide to combine data from self-reports and observations when completing an assessment.

Although marriage and family assessment requires a firm grasp of family systems theory, it would also seem that assessment can be used to help acquire a more thorough understanding of systems theory. Students have been offered an opportunity to complete a battery of family inventories. Using data generated from the inventories, they are provided with a written assignment. This assignment directs them to describe structural dynamics in their families (e.g., boundaries and hierarchical arrangements) as well as rules reflected in the family structure (e.g., who can talk with whom and about what). The students also discuss how the family structure and rules have encouraged or interfered with movement through the life cycle and how these dynamics might influence working as a family therapist (e.g., influencing the ability to identify, challenge, or reinforce particular family patterns). Indeed, for research, practice, and teaching purposes, it seems essential that counselor educators have an understanding of marriage and family assessment.

References

Bloom, B. L. (1985). A factor analysis of self-report measures of family functioning. *Family Process, 24*, 225–239.

Boszormenyi-Nagy, I., & Ulrich, D. N. (1981). Contextual family therapy. In A. S. Gurman & D. P. Kniskern (Eds.), *Handbook of family therapy* (pp. 159–186). New York: Brunner/Mazel.

Bowen, M. (1978). *Family therapy in clinical practice*. New York: Jason Aronson.

Bray, J. H., Williamson, D. S., & Malone, P. E. (1984a). *Personal authority in the family system questionnaire manual*. Houston: Texas Woman's University.

Bray, J. H., Williamson, D. S., & Malone, P. E. (1984b). Personal authority in the family system: Development of a questionnaire to measure personal authority in intergenerational family processes. *Journal of Marital and Family Therapy, 10*, 167–178.

Brock, G. W., & Barnard, C. P. (1988). *Procedures in family therapy*. Boston: Allyn & Bacon.

Christensen, B., & Scoresby, A. L. (1975). *The measurement of complementary, symmetrical, and parallel interaction in family dyads*. Unpublished manuscript, Brigham Young University, Provo, Utah.

Cromwell, R., Fournier, D., & Kvebaek, D. (1980). *The family sculpture technique: A diagnostic and research tool in family therapy*. Jonesboro, TN: Pilgrimage.

Cromwell, R., Olson, D., & Fournier, D. (1976a). Diagnosis and evaluation in marriage and family counseling. In D. H. Olson (Ed.), *Treating relationships* (pp. 517–551). Lake Hills, IA: Graphic Press.

Cromwell, R., Olson, D., & Fournier, D. (1976b). Tools and techniques for diagnosis and evaluation in marital and family therapy. *Family Process, 15*, 1–49.

Crowne, D. P., & Marlowe, D. (1964). *The approved motive: Studies in evaluative dependence*. New York: Wiley.

Duhl, F., Kantor, D., & Duhl, B. (1974). Learning, space and action. In D. A. Block (Ed.), *Techniques of family psychotherapy* (pp. 47–63). New York: Grune and Stratton.

Epstein, N. B., Baldwin, L. M., & Bishop, D. S. (1983). The McMaster Family Assessment Device. *Journal of Marital and Family Therapy, 9*, 171–180.

Epstein, N. B., & Bishop, D. S. (1981). Problem centered systems therapy of the family. In A. S. Gurman & D. P. Kniskern (Eds.),

Handbook of family therapy (pp. 444–482). New York: Brunner/Mazel.

Gladding, S. T., Burggraf, M., & Fenell, D. L. (1987). Marriage and family counseling in counselor education: National trends and implications. *Journal of Counseling and Development, 66*, 90–92.

Goldenberg, I., & Goldenberg, H. (1985). *Family therapy: An overview* (2nd ed.). Monterey, CA: Brooks/Cole.

Haley, J. (1963). *Strategies of psychotherapy.* New York: Grune & Stratton.

Haley, J. (1976). *Problem-solving therapy: New strategies for effective family therapy.* San Francisco: Jossey-Bass.

Harper, J. M., Scoresby, A. L., & Boyce, W. D. (1977). The logical levels of complementary, symmetrical, and parallel interaction classes in family dyads. *Family Process, 16*, 199–209.

Hovestadt, A. J., Anderson, W. T., Piercy, F. P., Cochran, S. W., & Fine, M. (1985). A family-of-origin scale. *Journal of Marital and Family Therapy, 11*, 287–297.

Hulgus, Y. F., Hampson, R. B., Beavers, W. R., & Beavers, J. (1985). *The Beavers systems model of family assessment: Norms, validity, and reliability.* Dallas: Southwest Family Institute.

Keeney, B. P. (1983). Ecological assessment. In J. C. Hansen & B. P. Keeney (Eds.), *Diagnosis and assessment in family therapy* (pp. 155–169). Rockville, MD: Aspen.

Lederer, W. J., & Jackson, D. D. (1968). *The mirages of marriage.* New York: W. W. Norton.

Lewis, J. M., Beavers, W. R., Gossett, J. T., & Phillips, V. A. (1976). *No single thread: Psychological health in family systems.* New York: Brunner/Mazel.

Liddle, H. A. (1983). Diagnosis and assessment in family therapy: A comparative analysis of six schools of thought. In J. C. Hansen & B. P. Keeney (Eds.), *Diagnosis and assessment in family therapy* (pp. 1–33). Rockville, MD: Aspen.

Locke, H. J., & Wallace, K. M. (1959). Short marital-adjustment and prediction tests: Their reliability and validity. *Marriage and Family Living, 21*, 251–255.

Madanes, C. (1981). *Strategic family therapy.* San Francisco: Jossey-Bass.

Meadows, M. E., & Hetrick, H. H. (1982). Roles for counselor education departments in marriage and family counseling: Current status and projections. *Counselor Education and Supervision, 22*, 47–54.

Miller, I. W., Epstein, N. B., Bishop, D. S., & Keitner, G. I. (1985). The McMaster Family Assessment Device: Reliability and validity. *Journal of Marital and Family Therapy, 11*, 345–356.

Moos, R. H., & Moos, B. S. (1981). *Family Environment Scale manual.* Palo Alto, CA: Consulting Psychologists Press.

Moos, R. H., & Moos, B. S. (1983). Clinical applications of the Family Environment Scale. In E. E. Filsinger (Ed.), *Marriage and family assessment: A sourcebook for family therapy* (pp. 253–273). Beverly Hills, CA: Sage.

Nichols, M. P. (1984). *Family therapy: Concepts and methods.* New York: Gardner.

Olson, D. H., Bell, R., & Portner, J. (1978). *FACES-I: Family adaptability and cohesion evaluation scales.* St. Paul, MN: Family Social Science, University of Minnesota.

Olson, D. H., & Ryder, R. G. (1970). Inventory of Marital Conflicts (IMC): An experimental interaction procedure. *Journal of Marriage and the Family, 32*, 443–448.

Olson, D. H., McCubbin, H. I., Barnes, H., Larsen, A., Muxen, M., & Wilson, M. (1985). *Family inventories: Inventories used in a national survey of families across the family life cycle.* St. Paul, MN: Family Social Science, University of Minnesota.

Papp, P., Silverstein, O., & Carter, E. (1973). Family sculpting in preventive work with well families. *Family Process, 12*, 197–212.

Peltier, S. W., & Vale, S. O. (1986). A national survey of counselor education departments: Course offerings on marriage and family. *Counselor Education and Supervision, 25*, 313–319.

Pratt, D. M., & Hansen, J. C. (1987). A test of the curvilinear hypothesis with FACES II and III. *Journal of Marital and Family Therapy, 13*, 387–392.

Ritter, K. Y., West, J. D., & Trotzer, J. P. (1984, March). *Comparing family counseling and group counseling: An interview with George Gazda, James Hansen, and Alan Hovestadt.* An interview conducted at the American Association for Counseling and Development Convention, Houston, Texas.

Russell, C. S. (1980). A methodological study of family cohesion and adaptability. *Journal of Marital and Family Therapy, 6*, 459–470.

Scoresby, A. L. (1975). *Introduction to the Relationship Style Inventory.* Unpublished manuscript, Brigham Young University, Child Development and Family Relations, Provo, Utah.

Scoresby, A. L., & Christensen, B. (1976). Differences in interaction and environmental conditions of clinic and non-clinic families: Implications for counselors. *Journal of Marriage and Family Counseling, 2*, 63–71.

Simon, R. (1972). Sculpting the family. *Family Process, 11*, 49–57.

Skinner, H. A., Steinhauer, P. D., & Santa-Barbara, J. (1983). The Family Assessment Measure. *Canadian Journal of Community Mental Health, 2*, 91–105.

Steinhauer, P. D., Santa-Barbara, J., & Skinner, H. A. (1984). The Process Model of Family Functioning. *Canadian Journal of Psychiatry, 29*, 77–88.

Van der Veen, F., Howard, K., & Austria, A. (1970). Stability and equivalence of scores based on three different response formats. *Proceedings of the 78th Annual Convention of the American Psychological Association, 5*, 99–100.

Van der Veen, F., & Olson, R. (1981). *Manual and handbook for the family concept assessment method.* Unpublished manuscript.

Watzlawick, P., Beavin, J. H., & Jackson, D. D. (1967). *Pragmatics of human communication: A study of interactional patterns, pathologies, and paradoxes.* New York: W. W. Norton.

West, J. D., Hosie, T. W., & Zarski, J. J. (1987). Family dynamics and substance abuse: A preliminary study. *Journal of Counseling and Development, 65*, 487–490.

Williamson, D. S. (1981). Personal authority via termination of the intergenerational hierarchical boundary: A "new " stage in the family life cycle. *Journal of Marital and Family Therapy, 7*, 441–452.

Williamson, D. S. (1982). Personal authority in family experience via termination of the intergenerational hierarchical boundary: Part III—personal authority defined, and the power of play in the change process. *Journal of Marital and Family Therapy, 8*, 309–323.

A Beginner's Guide to the Problem-Oriented First Family Interview

Timothy Weber
James E. McKeever
Susan H. McDaniel

The beginning family therapist is confronted with a peculiar problem. The burgeoning family therapy field has spawned a wide array of books, journals, training programs, and workshops. However, the volume and diversity of these excellent resources, instead of bringing further clarity, can produce an unsettling confusion in many family therapy trainees.

This confusion is often most apparent at the point of the first meeting with a family when bewildered and anxious trainees are obliged to take leadership, condensing the mass of clinical options into a practical, sensible, well-organized interview with a group of strangers. Understandably, trainees often will ask prior to meeting with a family for the first time, "How do I proceed?"; "Where do I begin?"; "What do I do after I begin?"; "What should I try to accomplish?" Although the questions trainees ask about getting started may seem elementary to the seasoned therapist, trainees may have a fresh sense of a fundamental point Haley (1978) has noted: "If therapy is to end properly, it must begin properly—by negotiating a solvable problem and discovering the social situation that makes the problem necessary" (p. 9). "Beginning properly," without drifting and getting muddled in irrelevant details, is an imposing challenge to both the beginning therapist and more experienced therapists.

Recognizing the pivotal importance of the first interview with a family, Haley (1978) wrote his important and influential chapter on "Conducting the First Interview" that appeared in the publication *Problem Solving Therapy*. Several other authors have focused on procedures for conducting this initial meeting (Anderson & Stewart, 1983; Bross, 1983; De Shazer, 1982; Fisch, Weakland, & Segal, 1982; Minuchin, 1974; Selvini-Palazzoli, Boscolo, Cecchin, & Prata, 1980; Stierlin, Rucker-Embden, Wetzel, & Wirsching, 1980). These presentations, and the structural and strategic theories on which they are based, have been especially valuable for beginning trainees who, in our experience, tend to work most effectively using a concrete, problem-oriented framework (McDaniel, Weber, & McKeever, 1983). Nevertheless, as useful as these theoretical and clinical discussions have been, they may not meet the needs of trainees who are in search of a concise, step-by-step guide for negotiating the rugged territory of the first interview.

The purpose of this paper is to present a concrete, step-by-step, beginner's guide to the problem-oriented first family interview. This guide is an integration of procedures from a variety of approaches rooted in the structural and strategic orientations. As family therapy supervisors, we have found the guide to be useful in our work with beginning trainees in a variety of training contexts. We want to emphasize that this guide should be used only in the context of comprehensive training and supervision in family theory and therapy.

In keeping with our goal of making the guide as brief as possible, we have avoided commenting on the theoretical premises for these tasks and have limited our discussion of the many procedural variations that are bound to arise in working with any family. Such matters are more effectively addressed through background reading and direct supervision, indispensable supports for beginning family therapists. Also, our intention has not been to provide extensive and exhaustive examples of each task. Rather, we have stayed within the narrow bounds of presenting an overview of those tasks we believe constitute a crisp and efficient problem-oriented first family interview. Finally, our goal has not been to provide a detailed review of the literature, citing references to support the guidelines. We have listed sources at the conclusion of this paper that the beginner may find helpful in understanding both the theory and techniques of the problem-oriented first family interview.

Four primary goals shape the work of the first interview:

1. Join the family, accommodating to the style of family members and creating an environment in which family members will feel supported.
2. Organize the interview so that family members will begin to gain confidence in the therapist's leadership.
3. Gather information about the problem in such a way that the family's transactions around the problem become clearer.
4. Negotiate a therapy contract, emphasizing the family's initiative in defining goals and desired changes.

Our guide for the first interview is a compendium of specific tasks designed to accomplish the four goals. It is oriented toward a family interview, although it can easily be adapted for a couple or family-oriented individual session. Note that the full context of the first interview includes both pre-interview and post-interview tasks. The initial contact with the family over the telephone is a crucial process that helps the therapist build tentative hypotheses based on preliminary information and sets the tone and pattern of inquiry for the first meeting. Likewise, after the interview, it is essential to review the information gathered, evaluate how the interview was conducted, and organize a treatment plan so that therapy can proceed most effectively. These essential tasks help polish the therapist's thinking and work in subsequent meetings. With some exceptions (Anderson & Stewart, 1983; De Shazer, 1982; Fisch, Weakland, & Segal, 1982; Selvini-Palazzoli, Boscolo, Cecchin, & Prata, 1980; Stanton & Todd, 1981), far too little attention has been given to these fundamental preparatory and review tasks and how they can be integrated with the family interview.

In order to underscore the importance of thinking about the first interview as an integrated process incorporating both pre- and post-interview tasks, we have outlined the 12 phases of the first interview: (1) telephoning; (2) forming hypotheses; (3) the greeting; (4) the social phase; (5) identifying the problem; (6) observing family patterns; (7) defining goals; (8) contracting; (9) checklist; (10) revising hypotheses; (11) contacting the referral person; and (12) gathering records. These stages of the interview itself are similar to Haley's (1978) outline. However, we have added additional phases, including pre- and post-interview tasks and have integrated techniques from other approaches that we have found useful.

Although the phases are clearly demarcated, and phases within the interview itself are assigned approximate time frames for clarity and pacing, the actual process of interviewing demands a good measure of sensitivity to the "natural flow" of moving from one phase to another. Phases can overlap or take place concurrently in an actual interview. The sensitivity and flexibility required to adjust to the various tasks usually grow as therapists gain more experience in working with families.

The following guide is intended for use by trainees *in conjunction with close supervision*. It may also serve as a refresher for experienced family therapists.

Phases of First Interview

1. Telephoning

The goal of the telephone call is to make contact with the family and to contract for the first interview.

1. Gather basic information, including names, addresses, and phone numbers.
2. Ask for a brief description of the problem.
3. Identify members of the household and other people involved with the problem (including the referral source).
4. Contract for the first interview, including:
   a. Who will attend (if the contact person resists bringing the entire family—members of the household—to the first session, treatment options vary; either meet with the family members most concerned about the problem or insist that all family members must attend; prior to the phone call, the supervisor should be consulted regarding possible options).
   b. Date and time of the interview.
   c. Where it is to take place, including directions to the facility and check-in procedures.
   d. Fee for the initial session.
5. If the family is not self-referred and the referring person calls before the family:
   a. Inquire about the referring person's understanding of the problem.
   b. Clarify what the referring person is requesting (e.g., consultation or referral for therapy).
   c. Agree on how follow-up information will be given to the referring person. Regardless of whether or not the referring person calls before the interview, contact should be made following the interview.

2. Forming Hypotheses

The purpose of this phase is to develop initial hypotheses to help guide the exploration of issues in the first interview.

1. Develop tentative hypotheses to be tested in the interview (these hypotheses will be expanded and revised as new information is gathered throughout treatment).
   a. Begin by determining the life-cycle stage of the family and the predicted problems and tasks of that life-cycle stage.
   b. On this foundation, build hypotheses using other data such as the nature of the referral, the emotional tone conveyed by the contact person on the telephone, and the family member identified as "the patient." A background in family theory and close supervision are essential in forming crisp and testable hypotheses. Beginners should not expect themselves immediately to provide sharp hypotheses. This skill develops with experience and supervision.
2. Develop a strategy for the first interview, including specific questions, observations, or tasks that will facilitate data-gathering and help test the hypotheses (the strategy will help prevent muddled thinking and drifting in the session).
3. Having developed initial hypotheses and a working strategy, be careful to remain open to the uniqueness of the family and to information that supports alternative hypotheses.

3. The Greeting (approximately 5 minutes)

Because it is difficult for most people to come into treatment, the goal of this phase is to welcome and identify the family members and begin to introduce them to the setting and to the therapist.

1. Introduce yourself to the contact person and to other adults in the household. Shake hands and greet each member of the family (greetings should be age-appropriate, i.e., use formal names for adults, at least initially; be sure to greet and make contact with all children attending, no matter what their age).
2. Invite the family members to sit where they wish (use this information diagnostically).
3. Orient the family to the room (e.g., videotaping, observation mirrors, where toys for children are located, etc.) and to the format of the session (e.g., length of the meeting, split session, etc.).
4. If you are audio or videotaping, obtain oral permission from adult members. (Signatures on the consent form can be gathered at the end of the interview.)

4. The Social Phase (approximately 5 minutes)

The goal of the social phase is to build a nonthreatening setting for the family, to get to know them better, and to help them become more comfortable.

1. Help the family to get comfortable by engaging in informal conversation, followed by introducing the agenda: "It would help me if I first got some further information about you."
2. Increase contact with each family member by requesting demographic information from each of them such as their age, work/school activity, education, length of marriage, etc. Try to find something in each person that is interesting. Find an opportunity to be human and generally less intimidating to the family (e.g., by following up on a family member's job or interests).
3. While talking to the family, remember to give special attention and respect to the adult leader/spokesperson of the family. Make special efforts to engage those in the family who are distant, especially the parent who did not make the initial contact.
4. Note each family member's language and nonverbal behavior and attempt to match and use this style and language in subsequent sessions when working with this family member.

5. Identifying the Problem (approximately 15 minutes)

The goal of this phase is to explore each family member's view of the problem in specific behavioral terms, as well as the solutions that have been attempted.

1. Continue defining the agenda: "Often in families people have different views about what the problem is. Today I would like to hear from each of you about how you see the problem."
2. Address each member of the family, usually beginning with the adult who appears to be most distant to the problem.
3. Help family members be more concrete and specific by asking, "How is this a problem for you?"; "When did the problem begin?"; "What prompted you to come in now?"
4. Find out how members of the family have attempted to solve the problem and what the results of these attempted solutions have been.

5. Explore the involvement of others in the problem: "Have you been given advice from other people about this problem?"; "What do you think of their advice?" (Include inquiries about previous therapists and other professionals.)
6. Ask about recent changes in the family, such as moves, illness, death, occupational shifts, or exits and entrances of members into the family organization. While keeping a focus on the presenting problem, be aware of contextual changes in the family system that influence and are influenced by the presenting problem.
7. Process reminders:
   a. Encourage family members to be specific; ask for examples.
   b. Help family members to clarify their thoughts.
   c. Maintain an empathic and noncritical stance with each person.
   d. Affirm the importance of each person's contribution.
   e. At this point, don't offer advice or interpretations even if asked.
   f. Block interruptions from others if persistent.
   g. Note, but don't emphasize disagreements among family members.
   h. Go slowly!

6. Observing Family Patterns (approximately 15 minutes)

The goal of this phase is to "bring the problem into the room" so that the therapist and the family can get a clearer picture of the behavioral patterns of family members around the problem.

1. Have family members clarify a specific, behavioral aspect of the presenting problem in one of several ways:
   a. Ask specific family members (e.g., father and mother, father and son, brother and sister, etc.) to talk to each other about the problem and how it has been handled.
   b. Have family members describe the interactions of *other* family members as they respond to the problem. ("John, when you get into a fight with your sister, what does your mother do?" "And when your mother does that, what does your father do?")
   c. Have family members re-enact an example of the problem (e.g., "Show me what happens in your house when Susie comes home late").

2. Step back, observe, and listen to the family in order to make an interactional assessment, especially noting particular repetitive behavior sequences that occur around the problem.
3. If any change in the family's interaction is proposed, this change should be based on clear therapeutic goals and family's behavior in the session (e.g., if mother is the parent who is busily managing the children in the session while the father remains quiet and distant, the therapist may suggest: "John could you help your children find something to play with so that you, Mary, and I can continue talking over here.").
4. Compliment specific family members on concrete actions that were positive (e.g., "Mary, you seem to have some good ideas as to how to get your dad to hear you.").

7. Defining Goals (approximately 5 minutes)

The goal of this phase is to crystallize the goals of treatment as viewed by each family member in specific and realistic behavioral terms.

1. Ask each family member to summarize what he or she would like to see changed (notice similarities and differences among the goals of different family members).
2. Define the changes in terms of specific positive behaviors other than negative behaviors (e.g., "I'd like Dad to help me with my English assignments" rather than "I'd like Dad to stop nagging me about my homework.").
3. Underscore the strengths of the family by asking, "I'm sure there is a lot you do together that you would like to keep doing. What is it that you would like *not* to change?" (This question may be given to family members as a task for them to think about before the next session.)
4. Help the family members to specify their expectations more clearly and realistically by asking, "What would be the smallest change that might indicate that things are moving in a better direction?"
5. Part of calming an anxious family is slowing them down. Sometimes a homework assignment, such as asking them to gather more information about the problem, is useful at this point.

8. Contracting (approximately 5 minutes)

The goal of this phase is to reach an agreement regarding the continuation of therapy and its structure.

1. At the end of the interview ask the family about the next step, emphasizing their initiative (e.g., "What is the plan for proceeding?").
2. If the family does not elect to continue, offer a referral to another therapist or agency or indicate how they might return to therapy in the future. If they elect to continue, arrange for the next appointment and determine who will attend (the structure of treatment is the therapist's responsibility).
3. Some families may want to contract for a specific number of sessions. This option should be considered since some families may work more effectively when therapy is time-limited.
4. Review the business agreement including fees, insurance information, etc.
5. Ask the adults to sign the taping consent forms and the necessary release of information forms for gathering relevant information from other practitioners and agencies (physicians, schools, previous therapists, etc.).
6. Ask if family members have any questions.
7. Conclude the interview.

9. First Interview Checklist

Use the following checklist to evaluate the process of the first interview. Did the therapist:

1. Make contact with each member of the family and help him or her feel as comfortable as possible.
2. Establish leadership by clearly structuring the interview.
3. Develop a working relationship with the family without being either too "professional" or too personal.
4. Recognize strengths in the family and in family members.
5. Maintain an empathic position, supporting family members and avoiding blaming or criticizing.
6. Identify the specific problems the family bring to treatment and their previous attempted solutions;

7. Start to learn the family's view of the world and each family member's language, style, and perspective on the problem.
8. Begin to understand the family's repetitive interactions around the problem behavior.
9. Gather information about significant other family friends and professionals involved with the problem.
10. Negotiate a contract with the family that is mutually acceptable.

10. Revising Hypotheses

Use the information gathered in the first interview to revise and refine the pre-interview hypotheses and plan for the next interview.

11. Contacting the Referral Person

If the referral person was not present for the first family interview, contact the referral person.

1. Indicate that the family has been seen and communicate any treatment contract that has been negotiated.
2. Get the referral person's perspective on the problem.
3. Share a brief, initial assessment of the family and its problem. Supervision is important here in helping to determine what information should be shared with the referring person depending on that person's position in the system.
4. Lay the groundwork for any collaboration necessary for carrying out the treatment strategy.

12. Gathering Records

Write for school records, records of previous treatments, or any other relevant information from professionals or social agencies.

Summary

Our goal in this paper has been to provide beginning therapists and their supervisors with a highly structured, simplified, and practical guide for conducting a problem-oriented first family interview. This guide is intended to be a basis from which beginning therapists can develop their personal styles. Each initial interview is unique, requiring the therapists to be flexible in order to accomplish the interview goals. This guide provides the trainee with a framework for conceptualizing appropriate goals, the behavioral tasks needed to reach those goals, and approximate time limits within which these goals may be accomplished. With supervision and experience, the beginning trainee may then tackle the multiple subtleties involved in each stage of the first interview.

References

Anderson, C. M., & Stewart, S. (1983). *Mastering resistance: A practical guide to family therapy.* New York: Guilford Press.

Bross, A. (Ed.) (1983). *Family therapy: Principles of strategic practice.* New York: Guilford Press.

De Shazer, S. (1982). *Patterns of brief family therapy: An ecosystemic approach.* New York: Guilford Press.

Fisch, R., Weakland, J. H., & Segal, L. (1982). *The tactics of change: Doing therapy briefly.* San Francisco: Jossey-Bass.

Haley, J. (1978). *Problem-solving therapy.* San Francisco: Jossey-Bass.

McDaniel, S. H., Weber, T., & McKeever, J. (1983). Multiple theoretical approaches to supervision: Choices in family therapy training. *Family Process, 22,* 491–500.

Minuchin, S. (1974). *Families and family therapy.* Cambridge, MA: Harvard University Press.

Selvini-Palazzoli, M., Boscolo, L., Cecchin, G., & Prata, G. (1980). Hypothesized—circularity—neutrality: Three guidelines for the conductor of the session. *Family Process, 19,* 3–13.

Stanton, M. D., & Todd, T. C. (1981). Engaging "resistant" families in treatment: Principles and techniques in recruitment. *Family Process, 20,* 261–280.

Stierlin, H., Rucker-Embden, L, Wetzel, N., & Wirsching, M. (1980). *The first interview with the family.* New York: Brunner/Mazel.

This article was originally published in *Family Process,* Vol. 24, 1985, pp. 357–364. Reprint permission granted by Family Process, Inc.

The Use of Strategic Family Therapy in the School Setting: A Case Study

George Stone
Barbara Peeks

School counselors face the fundamental choice of whether to solve students' problems by using an individual counseling approach or by using a family-based approach that involves the students' parents. The approach described here is based on strategic family therapy (Madanes, 1981). Counselors working from this perspective assume that when a child presents a problem, it is because his or her parents do not agree on some issue. As the parents struggle through this issue, the child may develop a problem as a way of helping his or her parents; that is, by creating a crisis the child forces the parents to focus on him or her and put aside their differences.

Madanes (1984) suggested that when a child develops a problem, it can be helpful to his or her parents in an indirect way; the child's authority is exaggerated in relation to the parents, and a dual hierarchy develops, one in which the parents are in charge of their child and another in which the child is in charge of the parents. The school counselor, by focusing on the presenting problem, helps parents agree on a solution to that problem. When the parents agree, they can act effectively, and the family reorganizes around the clear authority of the new parental relationship instead of the problem of the child.

The purpose of this article is to present a family-based way of thinking that can be used by school counselors in solving family and school problems. The use of strategic family therapy in the school setting can best be illustrated by describing a case in which a school counselor helped parents reestablish their authority over their intelligent, 17-year-old son, a senior in high school. The counselor was employed in a 1,300-student high school in a midwestern town of 25,000.

Although he did not have a history of causing problems, this young man displayed uncooperative and disruptive behavior in one of his classes during the first week of school. The teacher took prompt action and met with the student's father. The young man's troublemaking increased, and by the third week of school the school counselor and the vice principal were involved.

The counselor met with the boy repeatedly, using an individualized counseling method that was based on creating a helping relationship to resolve the young man's inappropriate behavior (Rogers, 1961). During the next 7 months, however, his troublemaking slowly but steadily escalated, spreading to all but one of his classes. After some weeks without success with the young man alone, the counselor recommended to the father that he seek family counseling at a community agency. The father declined, saying, "He is not a problem at home" and "It is the teacher's fault."

During this time the young man misbehaved in various ways. For example, he often would enter the class and stand on his chair; he would stand up abruptly in class and say things in a loud voice that others had difficulty understanding and that were out of context in the situation; he would then just as abruptly sit down, put his head on his desk, and refuse to join the class proceedings; he would crawl in and out of a window in a classroom; he would leave the room during the middle of class without permission; and he disrupted his band class by purposely misplacing his instrument or by not attending. When he did not attend band class he would make an unscheduled appearance in another class; after a sports event, he walked on top of his father's car. Another student's father reported to the counselor that he suspected the young man of stealing money and clothes from his son. Perhaps most alarming, he came to school on four successive Mondays with an abrasion in exactly the same spot on his cheek. When asked about this, he gave four different bizarre stories about how each had occurred. He later accused his father of beating him, but when the counselor and vice principal investigated this allegation with the father, they found it to be untrue.

The father, perhaps as a result of being accused of abuse by his son, requested psychological testing for him. On the basis of this testing, the psychologist recommended to the father that he seek immediate assistance for his son in the form of psychiatric hospitalization. Again, the father declined and the young man continued to make trouble.

In late March he was suspended for 5 days. The principal was supported by the superintendent, who wrote a letter informing the parents that their son had been placed on probation and that if he were involved in one more incident, he would be expelled. The father still refused family counseling. School personnel, accepting the father's position as representative of both he and his wife, made no attempt to contact the young man's mother.

The father's refusal to accept the counselor's referral even in the face of the suspension prompted the counselor to abandon her individual counseling method and employ a strategic approach. Because neither she nor the other two counselors in her building had used such an approach before, she contacted a consultant who lived 200 miles away and was known to be experienced in strategic family therapy. She had attended two workshops given by the consultant and had begun a study of the approach. Because it was not possible for the consultant-counselor team to work in the way recommended by Montalvo (1973), using live supervision and videotaping counselor-family interactions for study, contact between them was by telephone and letter. (Counselors inexperienced in strategic family therapy should receive supervision and training before using the procedures described here. In this case, when seeking consultation, the counselor had attended two 1-day workshops and had read two books on the approach [Haley, 1977; Madanes, 1981]. After receiving additional training, the counselor has used strategic family therapy with a wide range of school and family problems.)

When the counselor contacted the consultant, she outlined the details described above. She added that the young man was an avid participant in the fantasy game Dungeons and Dragons®. (Dungeons and Dragons® is a role-playing adventure game. Individuals play the roles of characters in a fantasy world where heroes search for fame and fortune in the face of dangerous obstacles. Some view the game as satanic, causing problems for young people, We believe problems attributed solely to the game are part of a larger social context that includes the game.) The counselor and others in the school community feared he had overidentified with a character he portrayed and that he had begun living and acting as that character. She had begun a study of the game so that she could talk him back to reality.

Recommendations of the Consultant

After hearing the details of the presenting problem, the consultant was most concerned with managing what Montalvo (1973) called the "elusive interplay between contexts" (p. 353)—in this situation, between the counselor and the father. The father's refusals of the school's referrals for family counseling made him seem unreasonable. But was he? Perhaps there was something about the offers that made them intolerable to him. From this perspective, the initial problem for the consultant was to devise a strategy that would change the sequence of events between the counselor and the father from a sequence of adversity (offer-refusal) to a sequence of cooperation (offer-acceptance).

In the formulation of such a strategy, it was important to develop a hypothesis about the function of the symptom to the family organization. Because the details of the family organization were not known in this case, the consultant made the following assumptions: (a) the parents were in disagreement with each other, possibly because the father had changed jobs twice in a year; (b) the young man was misbehaving as a way of helping his parents by distracting them from their disagreement; (c) the son would soon leave home and was making trouble as a way of staying involved with his parents; and (d) the father's unwillingness to accept family counseling was taken as a message that he would not tolerate any counseling approach that attempted to deal directly with his presumed marital problems.

These assumptions led the consultant to recommend the following strategy: (a) the counselor would handle the problem herself in the school setting rather than make a referral; (b) the counselor would not continue to push for family counseling but focus her efforts on the young man's problems; (c) the counselor would stay away from a psychological definition of the problem and frame the young man's problem as one of discipline; (d) the counselor would ask the father's permission to call his wife to invite her to a family meeting at school; and (e) the counselor would use an ordeal, a specific application of strategic family therapy, as the way to change the young man's behavior directly while helping the parental relationship indirectly. The particular ordeal recommended by the consultant is a procedure devised by Jay Haley (1984), and it was presented to the parents by the counselor in this way:

> When your son misbehaves at school the faculty member who observes his misbehavior will send him, along with a written explanation of the event, to me [counselor]. I will call you [father] at your office. You are to leave your office immediately, pick him up at school, escort him home, and supervise his digging a hole 3 ft × 3 ft × 3 ft in a flowerbed in your backyard. When the hole is of the proper size, your son is to place one of his record albums in it. Still under your supervision, he is to replace and stomp the dirt

> and clean the shovel. Upon his completing this task, you will escort him back to me and I will return him to his scheduled class. At the end of each day your are to talk with your wife about your son's behavior that day.

Finally, the consultant recommended that the counselor clear the plan with her administrator before presenting the ordeal to the family and request that he forego the suspension if the parents agreed to cooperate. He consented to this altered approach, clarifying the lines of authority within the school and giving the counselor a point of leverage with the parents.

The Strategic Intervention

In the first family meeting the parents said, "We will do anything to help our son graduate." Once they had made that commitment, the counselor revealed the ordeal and they agreed to carry it out. With the young man, the counselor used terminology and ideas from Dungeons and Dragons®, as she had originally planned to do; the idea was to stimulate his participation rather than lead him out of a psychological wilderness. For example, she used the challenge aspect of the game to present herself as a "worthy adversary," which she subsequently proved by gaining his parents' cooperation.

Then the counselor told the boy's teachers: "If he even looks like he might cause trouble, send him to me." Because the teachers viewed the counselor as a person responsible for solving the problem, they readily cooperated with her request.

On March 31 the young man misbehaved, and the ordeal was invoked for the first time. The father returned with him to the counselor's office, however, reporting that the hole had not been dug because he and his son had argued over whether the record album could be wrapped in plastic before burial. Because having the father supervise the son was the crucial point in the procedure, the counselor avoided an exploration of the argument and its meaning and instead protected the father by taking personal responsibility for the argument. She apologized for not being specific enough in her instructions and told him to have his son wrap the album in "foil" before burial. Then she sent the man home to supervise his son's digging, which he did.

The young man misbehaved again in about 1 week. It had just rained and the earth was a sea of mud. As he had promised, the father supervised the proper digging of the hole. It was over 3 weeks before the young man caused trouble again; the ordeal was invoked for a third and final time.

In the last family meeting on May 3, it was clear to everyone that the young man was over his problem and would graduate. In that meeting the parents tentatively stated their hopes for their son to work or go to school after his graduation. He said he wanted to go into military service in the fall and emphatically stated his plan to "bum around" until then. The counselor asked the parents what might happen if they allowed their son to bum around. They replied that they did not like the possible results of that course of action. The counselor took a strong stand in support of the parents and emphasized that she did not think they were being unreasonable in asking their son to be productive. Before the family left her office, she gave the parents a college catalogue. Following the counselor's example, the parents also took a strong stand on this issue. In addition, the counselor supported the young man's desire to enter the military after hearing his parents voice no objection to the plan.

From the time the plan was set up in late March until May 3, the counselor met with the family five times. These family meetings were brief, never exceeding 15 minutes, and focused on a review of the plan. The counselor neither explored family relationships nor encouraged communication. The counselor spent about a total of 2 hours with the family.

The young man stopped causing trouble and both parents expressed surprise that their son's behavior had "improved at home, too," even though the father had initially protested that there were no problems at home. After high school graduation the young man not only completed a full summer session and one regular semester of college, but he also earned the good grades he was capable of receiving and did not make trouble. He entered the service 7 months after graduation and reported in letters home his success and satisfaction with his decision. On leave some months later, he spoke to his church youth group about why it is important to respect parents.

Discussion

The strategic intervention was both successful and cost effective. The counselor had earlier spent about 30 hours failing to resolve the presenting problem—10 hours with the young man in individual counseling sessions and about 20 hours in teacher and administrative meetings. Other school personnel also invested great amounts of time: lost classroom time devoted to correcting his misbehavior, many administrative meetings, and psychological testing. When implementing the strategic intervention, however, the counselor invested slightly over 5 hours in guiding the plan to success—3 with her colleagues and only 2 with the family members.

Details of the family's organization are not presented in this article, because they were not known. Yet, the presenting problem was resolved and a follow-up indicates that the improvement has been stable for over 3 years. The consultant's strategy respected the family's privacy; however, the consultant was fully prepared to have the counselor explore the family's organization and formulate another plan of action if the initial plan failed.

What is emphasized in this article, instead of the family's organizational complexity, is (a) the way the school professionals initially thought about the problem, (b) the complexity of the relationship between the family and the school, and (c) the contrasting way the consultant thought about the problem and planned a solution.

The school professionals initially thought about the problem as if it were contained within the boy and as if their own actions had nothing to do with maintaining the problem situation. The continuation of the young man's problem was blamed on the father's refusal to seek family counseling. Haley (1977) suggested that "once a therapist thinks in organizational terms, he must think of himself as a part of the social system, that is the client's problem" (p. 6).

A sequence of adversity had developed between the father and school personnel, probably beginning in the first contact between the teacher and the father. The counselor was a participant in that sequence, and so her attempts to help inadvertently led to the father refusing to accept help in the form she recommended. The counselor's actions thereby contributed to the maintenance of the problem rather than to its solution. The consultant chose an ordeal as a way to break the sequence of adversity because he believed both parents would cooperate more readily when their need for privacy was met and when the focus was on their son's misbehavior rather than on their marital disagreement. As the counselor changed her counseling approach with the young man and his family according to the consultant's recommendations, the family also changed.

Haley (1984) emphasized that an ordeal should (a) be more severe than the symptom, (b) be good for the person(s) involved, (c) change the structure of the family or situation, and (d) be metaphorical to the problem situation. This ordeal met these criteria.

The ordeal was more severe than the symptom for the father because once he was committed to it, he had to leave work to deal with his son. This made it difficult for him at work. What did he tell his boss and co-workers? How did he plan his work day? When did he make up his lost work time? It was also inconvenient to drive to school, drive his son home, stand by while his son dug the hole, drive him back to school, and return to work. At the same time, the ordeal was beneficial for the father because he enforced an effective discipline with his son, correcting the authority within the family organization in relation to himself, not in relation to the counselor.

From the young man's point of view, the ordeal was more severe than the symptom because it was work to dig a hole and because he had to give a record album for each offense. Digging the hole was beneficial to the boy because it provided good exercise and, from a strategic perspective, he now had to behave to protect his father from the consequences of the ordeal rather than misbehave to distract his father from the marital disagreement. The ordeal normalized the young man's problems because digging a hole is a reasonable discipline for someone who makes trouble. This approach avoided stigmatizing him "emotionally disturbed."

The family structure was changed as the father and mother began to cooperate with each other and with the counselor. When the young man delayed entering the service for a semester, he seemed to be testing his parents' ability to maintain their cooperation after his troublemaking stopped, he was free to leave home.

The structure of the school was also altered: A traditional procedure involving individual counseling, administrative meetings, and suspension was discarded, and a new, more effective one was substituted. The ordeal gave the counselor a positive and concrete plan of action with which to approach her principal. Without this alternative plan, the principal would have invoked expulsion and the young man would have failed to graduate.

The consultant selected an album for burial because of the frequency of the disruptions in band class, which highlighted music as special to this young man. Was he metaphorically sacrificing the music in his life to help his parents deal with their difficulties? If so, the ordeal made his metaphorical sacrifice literal.

This case illustrates that strategic family therapy can be used in the school setting to help create important, lasting changes in a student's family. The ordeal, rather than individual counseling, made it possible for this family to move to a new stage of its life cycle, one in which an adult son completed high school and left home. It also allowed the parents to deal directly with their son's problem by accepting the responsibility, which the counselor affirmed was theirs, for the problem's resolution.

The school is the best resource for parents when a problem with a child develops. Therefore, school counselors who think about problems in this strategic, family-based manner are in a good position to aid parents in the reestablishment of their natural authority over their children. At the same time, this process benefits the school by making costly special placements unnecessary.

References

Haley, J. (1977). *Problem-solving therapy.* New York: Harper & Row.

Haley, J. (1984). *Ordeal therapy.* San Francisco: Jossey-Bass.

Madanes, C. (1981). *Strategic family therapy.* San Francisco: Jossey-Bass.

Madanes, C. (1984). *Behind the one-way mirror: Advances in the practice of strategic therapy.* San Francisco: Jossey-Bass.

Montalvo, B. (1973). Aspects of live supervision. *Family Process, 12,* 343–359.

Rogers, C. (1961). *On becoming a person.* Boston: Houghton Mifflin.

The Use of Circular Questioning in Marriage and Family Counseling/Therapy

Robert L. Smith
Jean A. Griffin
Karen Thys
Elaine Ryan

Many marriage and family therapists view the family as a system of interlocking relationships that contributes to the present functioning of the family. To investigate this systemic model, family therapists have introduced several methods for exploring the changes and differences which affect the family system. One such approach, circular questioning, provides the family with an opportunity to view itself systemically (Fleurides, Nelson, & Rosenthal, 1986). The use of circular questioning or circular interviewing "alone, can and does, trigger therapeutic change" (Tomm, 1987, p. 5) in the family system. A review of circular questioning is provided in this article in an attempt to enhance the readers with insight regarding its potential use when counseling with families.

What is Circular Questioning?

Four Italian psychiatrists, Mara Selvini-Palazzoli, Luigi Boscolo, Gianfranco Cecchin, and Giuliana Prata—collectively called the Milan Group—are credited with the development of circular questioning (Tomm, 1984a). They base their approach on systems theory, cybernetics, and information theory.

Specifically, circular questioning is a method of conducting an interview. Responses by the therapist are primarily questions (Tomm, 1984b). The questions are asked in order to generate information for the family about their relationships with each other. Within this process is the illumination of pattern—the systemic nature of the family. The typical family myth of the identified patient owning the presenting problem is gently disputed by asking relevant questions about family relationships and differences among them (Selvini-Palazzoli et al., 1980). The focus is on the recursiveness of the system—what happens over and over again involving the presenting problem (Tomm, 1984a).

The systemic therapist resists giving opinions and directives although the family may invite or expect this behavior. Hence, goal setting by the therapist is avoided (Matthews, 1984). The quality of family functioning is both defined and determined by the family.

Use of Circular Questioning

In order for circular questioning to be helpful in uncovering relevant information about the family, the Milan Group offers three guidelines: hypothesizing, circularity, and neutrality (Selvini-Palazzoli et al., 1980). The guidelines provide a structure for the circular questioning; otherwise the aimless therapist may appear unskilled or biased.

Before a therapist greets a family, some information is available from the initial contact about their concern. All information from that contact is considered useful in developing a hypothesis which will influence the choice of questions the therapist asks in the first interview. It is important to note that the Milan Group suggests that the therapist receive the initial contact so that circular questioning, and thus information gathering, begins immediately (Tomm, 1984b). This practice circumvents the validation of the family's linear view of the presenting problem. Through this method, a wide range of perceptions and issues that take a circular characteristic are presented, rather than one of two immediate issues that are often seen as cause/effect (linear).

Though it is important for the therapist to have a hypothesis about the family's functioning before the first interview, it is equally important to loosely hold that hypothesis. Hypotheses should always be evolving on the basis of feedback from the family. Therapists are cautioned to avoid being so rigid in their thinking that a hypothesis becomes a belief, for therein lies judgment and personal values (Tomm, 1984b).

Circularity is defined by the Milan Group as being "...the capacity of the therapist to conduct his investigation on the basis of feedback from the family in response to the information he solicits about relationships and, therefore, about difference and change" (Selvini-Palazzoli, et al., 1980, p. 8). Circularity provides the rationalc for the search of relational patterns through the use of circular questioning. The family, with a lineal epistemology, typically presents a small arc in the circular pattern (i.e., A causes B) (Tomm, 1984a). A family with a lineal epistemology sees one or two events or issues causing all of the family's problems. The therapist should recognize that this is but one place to start, or punctuate, the full sequence of events, according to the premise of circularity.

The third guideline, neutrality, is perhaps the most difficult to employ. The therapist displaying neutrality conveys acceptance, respect, and a desire for understanding. Suggesting change, blaming, or taking sides is avoided. Ideally, the therapist shows acceptance by listening and gently cloaks challenges by creative, but useful questions. At the end of an interview, the family members should not be able to describe, without confusions and disagreement, the therapist's involvement in coalitions or one's opinion about the family members (Tomm, 1984b).

Types of Circular Questioning

Through the use of circular questioning, a therapist may determine how the present pattern of functioning developed, when it became troublesome, and what previous pattern existed. In this exploration of family relationships, "what" is happening is more useful than "why" it is happening.

There are basically five types of circular questions that aid in collecting this information (Selvini-Palazzoli et al., 1980; Tomm, unpublished draft). Each type probes for either the revelation of differences or pattern. What follows is a more detailed description of each type.

Pattern Questions:

1. By questioning the pattern of events, the therapist focuses on plotting the circular sequence of interaction. What is happening in the family?
   Examples: When your wife makes a sexual overture, what do you do? What does your mother do when your father has been drinking?
2. By questioning the meaning associated with the pattern of events, family members are now asked their interpretation and opinions about what they see is happening in the family.

Examples: What does she do when you believe she is trying to get her way? When he plans a vacation without your knowledge, what does that mean?

Difference Questions

3. Questioning the difference in behavior, attitude, relationships, etc. between family members is useful in mapping alignments and coalitions in the family.
   Examples: Who shows more anger when your brother comes home late, mom or dad?
4. Through the use of questioning, the therapist investigates the difference in behavior, attitude, relationships, etc. between family members in regard to rank, by asking a family member who exhibits the most or least of some quality. Then, one is asked who would be next in line, and so on. Several family members should be asked their ranking on the same quality to discover family positions.
   Examples: Who was the first to notice your brother's unhappiness? Then who, etc.? Who most strongly believes that you show disrespect? Who believes this the second most strongly…etc.?
5. Questioning the difference in behavior, attitude, relationships, etc. between family members over time purposely identifies shifts in family alignments and loyalties, and when they occurred.
   Examples: Was there more arguing before or after the birth of your first child? Since your brother moved back home, are you more or less distant with your father?

Though it is important to help the family determine their previous, as well as their present pattern of interaction, it is also useful to ask about the future (Penn, 1985). By virtue of directing a future-oriented question to the family, the assumption is conveyed that they are volitional beings. Hence, they begin to realize that change is of their choosing.

> *Examples:* When your daughter goes to college, who will be more concerned for the other, you or your daughter? After the divorce, will you be more or less independent?

These examples provide evidence of the careful purposefulness or rationale behind the use of specific questions. Random questioning is not encouraged. Well-thought-out questions become natural after much experience in hypothesis building and preparation.

Conclusions

As illustrated, circular questioning can be helpful in uncovering significant information about a family. This information can be gathered in a relatively brief period of time while providing family members with interesting and different perceptions that may not have been shared previously. As such, circular questioning departs from the traditional approach in counseling which rejects the use of excessive questions.

Although implications for counselors/therapists working with families are obvious, precautions are warranted. Questions should be well thought out and not random in nature. The questioning of patterns, meaning, and differences requires a clear focus and needs to be intentional and direct. Additional background reading concerning the use of circular questions is recommended. Supervision of the use of circular questioning is also recommended prior to implementing this practice in one's own therapeutic work.

References

Fleurides, C., Nelson, T. S., & Rosenthal, D. M. (1986). The evolution of circular questions: Training family therapists. *Journal of Marital and Family Therapy, 12*(2), 113–127.

Matthews, W. M. (1984). Ericksonian and Milan therapy: An intersection between circular questioning and therapeutic metaphor. *Journal of Strategic & Systemic Therapies, 34*(4), 16–25.

O'Brien, C., & Bruggen, P. (1985). Our personal and professional lives: Learning positive connotation and circular questioning. *Family Process, 24*(3), 311–322.

Penn, P. (1982). Circular questioning. *Family Process, 21*(3), 267–280.

Selvini-Palazzoli, M., Boscolo, L., Cecchin, G., & Prata, G. (1980). Hypothesizing—circularity—neutrality: Three guidelines for the conductor of the session. *Family Process, 19*, 3–12.

Tomm, K. (1984a). One perspective on the Milan system approach: 1. Overview of development, theory, and practice. *Journal of Marital and Family Therapy, 10*(2), 113–125.

Tomm, K. (1984b). One perspective on the Milan systemic approach: 2. Description of session format, interviewing style, and interventions. *Journal of Marital and Family Therapy*, *10*(3), 253–271.

Tomm, K. (1987). Interventive interviewing: Part 1. Strategizing as a fourth guideline for the therapist. *Family Process*, *26*, 3–13.

This article was originally published in *Awareness: The Journal of the Colorado Association for Counseling and Development*, Vol. 18, 1990, pp. 17–19. Reprint permission granted by the Editor.

The Genogram as Process

Robert L. Beck

We are often prisoners of content. Our clients come to us anxious, depressed, hurting in one way or another, and in the initial interview tell us an elaborate story about the etiology of their difficulties. We listen attentively, gather data with interest, and in observing their affect, may or may not attempt to integrate the content with the expressed or unexpressed feelings. The construction of the genogram is a widely utilized process among mental health practitioners and family physicians The interviewer's data gathering often focuses primarily on its content-oriented components. Genogram development usually addresses itself to content, and even mental health practitioners may deemphasize process when constructing a genogram.

This paper reviews the literature on the genogram and underscores the importance of utilizing this teaching and diagnostic tool as a mechanism for enhancing understanding of the individual or family dynamics in process. It will go beyond consideration of the technical, content-oriented component of genogram construction to include the process component of the data gathering, its impact on the student or the client, the family-of-origin group, or the client and therapist relationship.

Clinical Applications of Family Diagraming

The literature on the genogram appears in the journals of a variety of professional disciplines including nursing (Starkey, 1981), family medicine (Gerson & McGoldrick, 1985; Jolly, Froom, & Rosen, 1980; Milhorn, 1981; Rogers & Durkin, 1984; Sproul & Gallagher, 1982), and, of course, family psychotherapy (Guerin & Fogarty, 1972; Guerin & Pendagast, 1976; McGoldrick & Gerson, 1985). Most of the family practice and family treatment literature addresses the utilization of the genogram as a fact-finding device.

Jolly et al. (1980), family practitioners, examine the genogram purely as a device for accumulation of data. Kramer (1985) addresses the utilization of the "family diagram" in her book on teaching family therapists and family treatment. She alludes to the process component of this data gathering in referring to it as a "discovery process" and states that it is often a "satisfying...integrating" but at times "upsetting experience" for a family member (p. 34). She returns to the content focus as she describes data gathering or collecting facts in interviewing family members. Guerin and Fogarty (1972) address the mechanisms of the genogram in use but do not elaborate on the response or participation of the family or family member to the process of the information gathering.

Hartman (1978) views the genogram as a data-gathering device which later serves the course of treatment. She goes a step further by describing the use of the data in the assessment phase by asking clients to "associate" to emerging material and in marital treatment to "increase empathy between the marital pair" (p. 476). Guerin and Pendagast (1976) suggest the possibility that the developing genogram can have some impact on the process of engagement between therapist and client.

Rogers and Durkin (1984), family physicians, describe the "other benefits" of genogram construction: "The act of taking a family history may contribute to the establishment of rapport between doctors and patients, thereby building a foundation for productive doctor-patient relationships" (p. 17).

Their observation is unique in the scant literature on the genogram appearing in family medicine. It underscores the implications for attention to process in psychotherapy where the client-therapist relationship is of particular importance.

The literature points to a wide variety of applications of genogram construction with individuals and families, including:

1. A tool for engagement in treatment;
2. A vehicle for building the therapeutic alliance;
3. A bridge to the client and therapist's mutual understanding of the goals of treatment;
4. A diagnostic tool;
5. A tool for subliminal learning—to enable the client(s) to begin to work toward self-understanding;
6. A data-gathering device; and
7. A structured beginning in treatment.

This review affirms that the uses of the genogram that receive the most attention are those that focus on the nondynamic process-oriented applications. This paper will focus primarily upon the first five of these applications, all of which deal with the dynamic component of the genogram's impact on the treatment process.

The Paucity of Process

The authors cited above do not make a direct connection between the process of genogram building and the potential for addressing the client's feelings about the genogram itself. In McGoldrick and Gerson's (1985) comprehensive book on the genogram, the emotional implications of this information gathering for the family are given limited attention. While they state that genogram development does provide a way to "join" with families (p. 2), and acknowledge the potentially painful experience in sharing family material (p. 36), they do not delve further into the process-related issues which are frequently present as the genogram is constructed. Gurman (1979) discusses the "problem with family genograms" and describes the "organizational" aspects of genogram construction. He states that the process of dealing with "unspoken feelings" is an endeavor that will occur outside of the therapy session (p. 74). While emotional interchanges will occur outside the therapy setting, is it not the function of the therapist to elicit and work with these feelings within the treatment environment? Gurman's view is consistent with a variety of nondynamic models, yet it hints at the difficulties that may arise when the process is not addressed in the here and now. Finally, Bradt (1980), who refers to the family as a "living, regenerating organism" (p. 24), does not focus on the dynamic processes in genogram development.

This inattention by psychotherapists to dynamics may be a function of Bowen theory perspective, which does not attend to process. In many of these papers, there is little consideration given to the client's response to the therapist's intrusive pursuit of data, or the impact of one family member's presentation on the others. How, for example, does a wife feel about her husband's description of his role in his family, which in her view is a distortion? In clinical practice, attention to a family member's nonverbal responses to another's presentation can be as important as the data. The significance of a husband presenting more detail than his wife about her family, and the implication of their suppression of the historical elements, if noted, can be helpful in broadening the diagnostic understanding of the marital relationship. The children's responses as the parents reflect for the first time on who this family is in relation to their families-of-origin is obviously educative and can reinforce a greater degree of self-reflection. Would not an adolescent identified client benefit from hearing about a grandfather and uncle who have followed the same path of self-destruction? Therapists who do not address these issues may relay a message to their clients that attending to the emotions of the moment is not appropriate and may put a lid on productive use of relevant material.

Other authors have considered the use of the genogram from a broader process perspective. Lieberman (1979) touches upon the impact of the genogram construction on the interaction of the family "outside the session" (p. 63). Wachtel (1982) views the genogram as a vehicle for "getting out emotions," "cooling off...heated exchanges," "joining...with the reluctant parent in family sessions," and as a "map to the unconscious" (pp. 339–341). She ably discusses this added dimension of the focus on dynamics. It is noteworthy that while this paper precedes a number of recent publications by 3 or 4 years, subsequent articles have not picked up on Wachtel's important ideas.

Why Process?

Bowen (1978) admonishes practitioners not to attend to the dynamic component of their interface with family members and states that it is "theoretically possible to leave the intensity of the (therapeutic) relationship between the original family members...to work toward avoiding the transferences" (p. 346). He alludes repeatedly to the "overimportance" assigned the transference and the "emotional process" that goes with it (p. 346). Many of his disciples subscribe to this view as they too avoid the process-oriented or transferential phenomena frequently observed in therapy. From their perspective, it can be argued that process is in the eyes of the beholder, and indeed, to ignore it is to diminish its visibility, but not its existence. In an earlier paper (Beck, 1982), I spoke to the process component of family-of-origin groups and suggested that ignoring this material denied its existence and limited potential learning and growth for group members. The same can be said for the integration of process observations and interventions in constructing genograms. According to Bowen theory, a dyad will, over time, face the prospect of interchanges that are less than satisfactory on an emotional level. As Bowen (1978) states:

> A two-person system may be stable as long as it is calm, but when anxiety increases, it immediately involves the most vulnerable other person to become a triangle...The emotional forces within the triangle are constantly in motion from moment to moment, even in periods of calm. (p. 373)

Therefore, if we subscribe to the Bowen triangling theory, it can be postulated that when no attention is paid to the growing dyadic tension in the therapy arena, the twosome will focus outside of this dyadic relationship to establish a triangle. The inattention to growing tension in a family or group of individuals who are constructing genograms and presenting highly charged material will thus support the emergence of triangling as the individuals attempt to defuse and focus on reinforcing the identified patient's role, or on other issues or individuals. The process which emerges to tone down the intense affect or interchange, thus works against the detriangling process that is being encouraged by the therapist.

It is inevitable that the dyadic system will, at one time or another, attempt to defuse its tension by triangling or focusing outside of the intense interactional field. To ignore the tension in a group, a family, or a couple's therapy session as genogram construction is underway begs for trouble, as unresolved dyadic tension has no place to go but to the triangled party.

Thus, ignoring process subtly encourages triangling despite the therapist's attempts to contain the tension and channel it back to the family-of-origin. Often, clients are not enthusiastic about venturing forth in their family-of-origin, despite the therapist's compelling argument that they do so. Even if they accept the therapist's conceptualization of the problem(s), they may very well struggle against the returning home process that is suggested. It is here that the therapist can work with the clients as they construct genograms and assist them in understanding the nature of the emotional processes which are emerging. If these processes are not addressed, at minimum, something is lost, though perhaps not irretrievably. If the process is addressed, the therapist is providing the client an added dimension for self-understanding and change, as well as a boost toward freeing the individual to ultimately reenter the family and accomplish the necessary tasks.

The Genogram in Process

Genogram construction in and of itself is a technique for gathering data. Yet there is a creative quality in going beyond the accumulation of facts to develop an understanding of the meaning of triangling patterns, their impact on the client, and their maintenance. The creative component is best addressed through the therapist's monitoring of the interview itself, attending as he or she usually does in treatment to the mood, affect, and posturing of the client. As the genogram is being developed, and as the therapist inquires about the client's parents, attention is best given both to the verbal response, for example, "My mother lives in Omaha and my father in Milwaukee," and to the affective presentation of the reporting of, for example, a divorced parental system. The therapist will hopefully ask for an elaboration of the facts:

Therapist: Why do they live in different cities?
Client: Oh, they divorced in 1972.
Therapist: You were 12 then.
Client: Yes.

Is this affirmative response offered with blank affect or with tearfulness or sadness? The interviewer might then comment on the affect and inquire further as to the individual's residual feelings about the divorced parents. The benefits are obvious: the building of a bond between therapist and client and an important bit of affective material for future reference. To proceed by inquiring about the sad affect will, of course, temporarily derail the initial task of data collection. Yet to ignore the affective response potentially impedes the development of the alliance as the therapist may appear to be nonempathic, cool, or removed. The data will always be there, but the particular affective response may be fleeting and not easily retrieved.

Case Example

Barbara, a 38-year-old mother of one, presented with concerns about her 15-year marriage and her husband's apparent distancing. The therapist suggested that she help him build a clearer picture of the structure of her family, and a genogram was undertaken. This process began with a charting of family-of-origin material, including parental and sibling systems. Barbara's controlled yet somewhat anxious presentation began to shift and she appeared more thoughtful and sad. The therapist responded to these shifts and commented on her sad affect as the data were gathered.

She began to describe her relationship with her parents, "Well, actually, it was pretty good until high school." Becoming tearful she said, "My God, I can't believe I'm doing this." She described a relationship in high school with a boy one year younger, who had not met with her parents' approval, and having to give up the relationship to calm the tension in her family. She began to cry softly, frequently punctuating her tears with amazement that she had held on to feelings about this for so long.

The therapist moved back and forth between collecting data and commenting on the affective component of the presentation as he inquired about her parents' relationship (distant), her relationship with her older sibling (distant), and her relationship with her parents in the past (in touch but emotionally distant). She commented, "We never kiss or touch," and that her current relationships "only go so far."

The therapist moved actively between the role of statistician and affective monitor as he worked with Barbara to develop a broader understanding of her difficulties in her marriage. It appeared that her distant relationship with her husband was paralleled by her family-of-origin relationships. Moving back and forth between the genogram construction phase of the therapy and the emotional processes which were present enabled Barbara and the therapist to put together a more complete picture of her concerns and strengthen the working alliance.

Not to have proceeded with Barbara in an alternatively emotionally focused and data-gathering manner would possibly have reinforced her focusing primarily on her disappointment in her marriage. Considering that Barbara and her husband had lived a highly constricted and distant life together for over 15 years, any tools which would support the therapist's work in addressing the affect or emotional content and model attending to this material could help them break their unrewarding pattern of relating. While in time the therapist might have helped Barbara reach similar conclusions about the interplay of the family-of-origin issues and her current marital difficulties, it would have been accomplished in an affective vacuum—a vacuum which was paralleled by her marriage, family-of-origin, and other personal relationships.

The Byproducts of Process

The first byproduct of attention to process in genogram development is *building or strengthening the therapeutic alliance*. The therapist's empathic acknowledgment of the pain associated with the presentation of a loss of a parent addresses both the existence of the loss itself and the individual's sense of abandonment and an awareness that the therapist is a resource for understanding. This goal is not inconsistent with the Bowen theory, as the alliance will aid in the process of encouraging the client to consider the frightening possibility of assuming an initially vulnerable "I" position in the family-of-origin. Even when the alliance is built in such a manner, the therapist can continue to remain detriangled and not become part of the emotional field.

Attention to the process in genogram building provides a second important byproduct. The affective expression of the historical presentation provides a vehicle for increased bonding of the family group, the marital pair, or the training group members. Those who have participated in or have led psychotherapy groups can testify to the powerful pull of shared emotional experiences which have been highlighted by the group leader or therapist. This bonding need not cross the line to enmeshment and will likely result instead in a stronger attachment between, for example, the marital pair whose strengthened relationship is built upon an understanding of each's roots, struggles, and individual needs.

Third, attention to the process provides the therapist with the experience of *recreating the family dynamics*. For example, a wife in couple treatment presents material about the loss of a parent and does so with no apparent affect. Therapist A dutifully records the material, asks for clarification or further data, issues an assessment of the shift that took place in the family following the loss, and proceeds with the construction of the genogram. Therapist B also records the data, but wonders out loud about this woman's flat affect as she reports the event. She indicates that this is the way she was taught to manage painful experiences and that it has always worked for her. She states that her parents' style was not to let life's periodic crises get them down, or at least not to show their feelings when under pressure. She affirms that, in effect, she was just doing what she was taught. Her husband states, "But you know, that's a big issue with us. I feel I can't come to you with even my biggest problems—you just won't respond."

Surely this process would have taken place later in treatment, yet here it is integrated with the earliest stages of the therapeutic process. It provides a vehicle for building the therapeutic alliance, and it enables the therapist to broaden his or her understanding of the marriage and its difficulties. In terms of the Bowen theory and its application, a therapist who inquires about the absence of emotion when data is presented aims at understanding the level of emotional tension related to the intergenerational issues. This will not necessarily shift the focus irreversibly to the therapeutic environment, but it will relate the emotional component to the family issues under discussion.

Fourth, process-oriented genogram construction offers the client an opportunity of actively *participating in the formulative phase of treatment.* An interactional process where history, dynamics, and here-and-now affect are being graphically laid out for all to see will reinforce the individual's, couple's, or family's active study of both the history and their part in it. The therapist's attempts to underscore seemingly significant transgenerational themes is more likely to be integrated and utilized if they are brought together in an interactional process. This process brings the work to the client, who is more likely to comprehend his or her role in the family structure if actively involved in the construction of the genogram. Consistent with the Bowen theory, while emotions are addressed, they are not examined as a primary change agent and the therapist can, in Bowen's words, "remain free of the emotional field" (1978, p. 251) as the formulative work is accomplished.

Finally, attention to process in the genogram development phase of family-of-origin work may do nothing more than *enhance the overall experience.* In this family systems framework, we are dealing with the whole person, his or her relationships, distortions, desires, fears, and emotions. The merging of data collection and organization, the rapt attention of the therapist, which includes his or her empathic responses and acknowledgment of the client's feelings, assists the development of an environment that appears both professional and safe. Additionally, a partial process focus in genogram construction can teach "the functioning of emotional systems" (Bowen, 1978, p. 251), as the system is described and illustrated by the client through the expression of feelings as well as facts.

Conclusions

The beauty of the Bowen theory is in its adaptability to various treatment structures. Family-of-origin concepts can be effectively integrated into dynamically oriented individual, marital, family, or group work. Bowen has served us well in presenting the overall design through his elaborate theoretical discussions. Yet, despite his suggestions that process is not necessary, his model begs us to use ourselves in creative ways in applying family-of-origin concepts in practice. Is this not the mark of the differentiated therapist?

References

Beck, R. L. (1982). Process and content in the family-of-origin group. *International Journal of Group Psychotherapy*, *32*(2), 233–244.

Bowen, M. (1978). *Family therapy in clinical practice.* New York: Jason Aronson.

Bradt, J. O. (1980). *The family diagram: Method, technique and use in family therapy.* Washington, DC: Groome Center.

Gerson, R., & McGoldrick, M. (1985). The computerized genogram. *Primary Care*, *12*(3), 535–545.

Guerin, P. J., & Fogarty, T. (1972). Study your own family. In A. Ferber, M. Mendelsohn, & A. Napier (Eds.), *The book of family therapy* (pp. 445–467). New York: Science House.

Guerin, P. J., & Pendagast, E. G. (1976). Evaluation of family system and genogram. In P. J. Guerin (Ed.), *Family therapy* (pp. 450–464). New York: Gardner Press.

Gurman, A. S. (1979). Research and clinical exchange. *American Journal of Family Therapy*, *7*(3), 74–76.

Hartman, A. (1978). Diagrammatic assessment of family relationships. *Social Casework*, *59*, 465–476.

Jolly, W., Froom, J., & Rosen, M. G. (1980). The genogram. *The Journal of Family Practice*, *10*(2), 251–255.

Kramer, J. R. (1985). *Family interfaces: Transgenerational patterns.* New York: Brunner/Mazel.

Lieberman, S. (1979). Transgenerational analysis. *Journal of Family Therapy*, *1*, 51–64.

McGoldrick, M., & Gerson, R. (1985). *Genograms in family assessment.* New York: W. W. Norton.

Milhorn, H. T. (1981). The genogram: A structured approach to the family history. *Journal of the Mississippi State Medical Association, 10,* 250–252.

Rogers, J., & Durkin, M. (1984). The semi-structured genogram interview: I. Protocol; II. Evaluation. *Family Systems Medicine, 2*(1), 176–187.

Sproul, M. S., & Gallagher, R. M. (1982). The genogram as an aid to crisis intervention. *The Journal of Family Practice, 14*(5), 959–960.

Starkey, P. J. (1981). Genograms: A guide to understanding one's own family system. *Perspectives in Psychiatric Care, 19*(5 & 6), 165–173.

Wachtel, E. F. (1982). The family psyche over three generations: The genogram revisited. *Journal of Marital and Family Therapy, 8*(3), 334–343.

This article was originally published in *American Journal of Family Therapy,* Vo. 15, No. 4, 1987, pp. 343–351. Reprint permission granted by Brunner/Mazel Publishers.

Chapter Four

Training Marriage and Family Counselors/Therapists

The future of a profession can be viewed as grounded in its training. Therefore, careful attention needs to be directed toward specific training activities and proposed training models. Such is true when considering the training of marriage and family counselors/therapists. To this end, the authors examine critical issues and concerns about training. The section begins by focusing on gender issues in training. In the discussion of gender issues and marriage and family counseling/therapy training, the argument is made for a greater awareness by trainers, as well as trainees. Models of implementing gender issue concepts within the curriculum are discussed ranging from free-standing courses to an integration within existing curricular requirements. Rich and Sampson discuss the importance of intensive simulations in family therapy training. Seen as a way to enhance training and better prepare practitioners, the authors advocate that a variety of simulated family systems be used in training. Costa describes how family sculpting can be implemented within marriage and family counselor training programs.

Three articles—Gladding, Burggraf, and Fenell; Domoko-Cheng Ham; and Sheverbush and Ward—look at trends and models in training marriage and family counselors/therapists. The Gladding article surveyed counselor education programs and revealed a major growth in comprehensive programs in marriage and family counseling, and an increase in curricular experiences in this area. Additional directives concerning accreditation and other issues were obtained. Domoko-Cheng Ham creatively reviews the "art" of teaching family therapy in a traditional academic program, and Sheverbush and Ward provide a model for implementing marriage and family counselor training in conjunction with the community/agency training model.

Additional training issues not included in this text range from training epistemology as related to marriage and family therapy to specific models of supervision and supervisor style. Lengthy discussion of these issues are provided elsewhere and will continue to be discussed in academic settings and within professional associations.

Gender Issues in Training: Implications for Counselor Training Programs

Patricia Stevens-Smith

The importance of counselors/therapists being aware of gender issues has been documented (Avis, 1986; Goldner, 1985; Hare-Mustin, 1978; Margolin, Fernandez, Talovic, & Onorato, 1983; Walters, Papp, Carter, & Goldstein, 1991), as has been the shift in male and female roles in society and the changing structure of the American family over the past 40 years (Degler, 1980; Hewlett, 1986; Kimmel & Messner, 1989). Yet, few counselor education training programs systematically incorporate gender issues into their courses and fewer have specific courses listed as such in their curriculum.

It is necessary to examine both family systems theory and the feminist prospective in order to understand the necessity of addressing gender issues within the graduate program. This article presents an argument for incorporating gender into the curriculum and suggests methods for integration.

Systems-Based Family Theory

Systems-based theories are advocated as an effective framework for facilitating change and growth within the family. Inherent in this model is that human problems are defined within family interactions and their developmental history. Therefore, change in the family system creates change in the individual and/or change in the individual changes the family system. Accordingly, systems are "self-regulating and self-maintaining" with members contributing equally to the system's maintenance through the concept of circular causality. Power to initiate change is seen as equal for all family members: male, female, adult or child. Appropriate hierarchical structure and boundaries are considered integral concepts in the maintenance of family health. Families are often evaluated and counseled with only slight regard for the outside social and political structures that affect the family (Smith, 1991).

Feminist Family Therapy

Feminist family therapy is not a theory of family therapy but rather a unique philosophical approach to working with existing theories of family therapy. Techniques from other theories are recognized and utilized in the practice of feminist family therapy. Feminist family therapy is different from traditional systems theory since it recognizes the effects that social and political influences have had throughout history on the roles taken by men and women within the family (Walters, Papp, Carter, & Goldstein, 1991).

Gender Inequality

Gender inequality, along with society's preservation of this inequality, is the missing concept in systems-based family theory (Avis, 1989; Hare-Mustin, 1978; Walters et al, 1991). With the integration of a feminist perspective, the systems-based family framework of therapy becomes a more complete structure for working with today's families. Integrating feminist perspective into family therapy theory means acknowledging the effect of society on the family in regard to work, reproduction, and societally ascribed gender roles. It also means accepting the fact that power is not equal within the family. The counselor must then be able to develop an effective strategy based upon the effect of these facts on the client/family.

The Changing American Family

One cannot adequately address today's family system without addressing the societal changes both in gender roles and in the family structure (Smith & Stevens, 1992). Less than 27% of today's families are "traditional" two-parent families (U.S. Bureau of the Census, 1988). The increasing number of single parent female-headed households, remarriage creating step or blended families, same-sex households, and childless dual-career couples are only a few of the families in today's society (Goldenberg & Goldenberg, 1990).

Despite these many changes in women's roles and the family system, family therapists continue to see the family as the "traditional nuclear system" and deny the continued struggle of women living in a patriarchal society. At the same time not enough attention is given to inequities that exist in the workplace and in the division of labor within the home or to the "feminization of poverty" which is often a result of divorce for women (Faludi, 1991; Hewlett, 1986; Hochschild, 1989). Holding to traditional pejorative beliefs about the family further denies the reality of today's family.

To effectively prepare counselors/therapists for working with families, it is necessary that they have an understanding of the effect of society on both gender roles and the family. Counselor trainees, in addition, must also be aware of their own biases and prejudices regarding gender issues.

Integrating Gender Issues in Training

Integrating gender into counselor training involves developing an awareness of how gender affects all aspects of an individual's life—personal, professional, economic, and political. For example, counselor trainees need a greater awareness of the economic consequences of divorce; the different effect on men and women of battering, sexual violence, and incest; as well as an awareness of the daily differences in male and female world views.

Avis (1989) states that two assumptions are inherent within an integrated training curriculum. The first and major assumption is that we are all sexist. This assumption is supported by Schaef (1985) who states that we cannot grow up in this culture without being both sexist and racist.

Avis' second assumption is that the inclusion of gender awareness into the curriculum is an ethical issue. It is not ethical to deny that prejudice exists. To admit its existence and increase one's awareness of how these prejudices are integrated into personal and professional lives, is the ethical solution.

Steps Toward Integration

In order to facilitate an awareness by counselor trainees, counselor educators must themselves be aware. Counselor educators should address their own misunderstandings of feminism, examine their own gender biases, and share their experiences and learning both with peers and students. Given the political nature of gender awareness and the emotional intensity connected with challenging these roles, there could be a prevailing resistance to the incorporation of these issues within the curriculum. Avis (1989) suggests asking colleagues to read and discuss gender issues. She states that it may be necessary to be patient, persuasive, and persistent with one's peers.

After colleagues increase their own awareness of gender issues, the curriculum can be modified in two ways (Avis, 1989). The first is through an introduction of gender awareness into existing courses. Many courses within a typical counselor training curriculum lend themselves well to the integration of gender issues. Counseling foundation courses and basic techniques courses in individual and family counseling/therapy have components relating to building the counseling relationship as well as addressing one's own biases in working with different populations. Discussing gender issues within this context is both desirable and practical for training. The career development course is an ideal setting to examine women's and men's changing roles in the workplace. Multicultural classes naturally lend themselves to the discussion of changing lifestyles for men and women. A course in professional/ethical issues would be incomplete without addressing ethical implications of counselor biases. Human development coursework and gender issues also integrate easily.

The second method of integration is to develop a course in gender awareness. Although this course could be taught as an elective within the curriculum or as a workshop, its importance calls for it to be a required curricular experience (see Appendix A).

A combination of a required course and an integration within existing courses would be of maximum benefit to the students. This allows both an intensive study of the issues and an integration into other aspects of counseling.

Specific Techniques for Raising Awareness Within the Curriculum

Since the discussion of gender issues can be extremely emotional and life-changing, it is important to provide a safe environment for growth and exploration. This necessitates that the counselor educator become comfortable with one's own gender issues and be willing to self-disclose personal growth and development in this area as well as one's mistaken notions. For students, a personal journal assignment may be most helpful to express feelings generated by this course material. A number of gender awareness exercises can be incorporated into classes. Roberts (1991) developed exercises that assist in the articulation of gender survival messages, followed by a comparison of differences between males and females. Roberts recommends exercises that heighten awareness of how male/female role ideas develop.

A tool for bringing gender into classroom discussions or counseling sessions is the construction of circular questions concerning previous or current role constructs (Roberts, 1991). Circular questioning is an effective therapeutic tool that counselor/therapists use for many different issues (Smith, 1990).

The use of media as a tool to demonstrate gender bias is also suggested. For example, students could be required to trace the changes in gender and family issues in the last ten years of a professional journal. Observing gender roles and communication patterns on television (Saturday morning cartoons or daily soap operas) and in current films is enlightening (personal communication, Don W. Locke, 1991). Print advertisements also are useful tools for defining gender expectations in society. Participation in these activities heightens students' awareness of the gender messages given and received daily.

Another use of media is to observe taped counseling sessions for subtle gender messages given by the therapist to the client. Observing student counselors in training and providing feedback on gender message is also helpful.

Completing a family genogram is a standard awareness exercise for counselor trainees. To examine three generations of same-sex relatives in their family of origin in the areas of: health (physical and emotional), work (in and out of the home), and male/female family roles can be an effective method of examining gender expectations (Ault-Riche, 1988).

Counselors who have taken an interest in assisting men and women in establishing a clearer personal identity and developing positive interpersonal relationships find it essential that they themselves become educated in the complexity of gender issues. The diversity of these roles, developed over the past two decades, have created a difficult challenge for even the most experienced counselor. It is the counselor educators' responsibility to provide counselor trainees with opportunities to understand and experience diverse gender roles and family types.

References

Ault-Riche, M. (1988). Teaching an integrated model of family therapy: Women as students, women as supervisors. In L. Braverman (Ed.), *Women, feminism and family therapy* (pp. 175–189). New York: Haworth.

Avis, J. (1986). Feminist issues in family therapy. In F. Piercy & D. Sprenkle (Eds.), Family therapy sourcebook (pp. 213–242). New York: Guilford Press.

Avis, J. M. (1989). Reference guide to feminism and family therapy. *Journal of Feminist Family Therapy, 1*(1), 94–100.

Degler, C. N. (1980). *At odds*. New York: Oxford Press.

Faludi, S. (1991). *Backlash: The undeclared war against American women*. New York: Crown Publishers.

Goldenberg, H., & Goldenberg, I. (1990). *Counseling today's families*. Pacific Grove, CA: Brooks/Cole Publishing Company.

Goldner, V. (1985). Feminism and family therapy. *Family Process, 24*, 31–47.

Hare-Mustin, R. (1978). A feminist approach to family therapy. *Family Process, 17*, 181–193.

Hewlett, S. A. (1986). *A lesser life: The myth of women's liberation in America*. New York: Warner Books.

Hochschild, A. (1989). *The second shift*. New York: Viking Press.

Kimmel, M. S., & Messner, M. A. (Eds.). (1989). *Men's lives*. New York: Macmillan Publishing

Margolin, G., Fernandez, V., Talovic, S., & Onorato, R. (1983). Sex role considerations and behavioral marital therapy: Equal does not mean identical. *Journal of Marital and Family Therapy, 9*, 131–145.

Roberts, J. M. (1991). Sugar and spice, toads and mice: Gender issues in family therapy training. *Journal of Marital and Family Therapy, 17*(2), 121–132.

Schaef, A. W. (1985). *Women's reality: An emerging female system in a white male society*. San Francisco: Harper and Row.

Smith, R. L. (1990). The use of circular questioning in marriage and family counseling/therapy. *The Journal of the Colorado Association for Counseling and Development, 18*, 17–19.

Smith, R. L. (1991). Marital and family therapy: Direction, theory and practice. *Counseling and Human Development, 23*, 1–12.

Smith, R. L., & Stevens, P. W. (1992). A critique of healthy family functioning. *Topics in Family Psychology and Counseling, 1*, 6–14.

U.S. Bureau of the Census. (1988). *Household, families, marital status, and living arrangements*. Washington, DC: Author.

Walters, M. A., Papp, P., Carter, B., & Goldstein, O. (1991). *The invisible web*. New York: Guilford Press.

Appendix A
Gender Course Sample Outline

Component One: Gender, Race, Ethnicity, and Social Class

Focus: Self-examination, reflection, reaction, and awareness

Suggested selected readings:

Bernard, J. (1990). The good provider roles: Its rise and fall. In Michael S. Kimmel and Michael A. Messner (Eds.), *Men's lives* (pp. 223–240). New York: Macmillan Publishing Company.

Chodorow, N. (1978). *The reproduction of mothering: Psychoanalysis and the sociology of gender.* Berkeley: University of California Press.

Davenport, P. S., & Yurich, J. M. (1991). Multicultural gender issues. *Journal of Counseling and Development, 70*, 64–71.

Degler, C. N. (1980). *At odds*. New York: Oxford University Press.

Hood, E. (1984). Black women, white women: Separate paths to liberation. In Jagger and Rothenberg (Eds.), *Feminist frameworks* (pp. 189–202). New York: McGraw-Hill.

Rotundo, E. A. (1985). American fatherhood. *American Behavioral Scientist, 29*(1), 7–23.

Component Two: Women's Psychology and Thinking

Focus: Equality, differences, similarities, stereotypes; moral development, affiliation and caring; epistemological development

Suggested selected readings:

Belensky, M. F., Clenchy, B. M., Goldberger, N. R., & Tarule, J. M. (1986). *Women's way of knowing*. Glenview: Basic Books.

Gilligan, C. (1982). *In a different voice.* Cambridge: Harvard University Press.

Schaef, A. W. (1985). *Women's reality: An emerging female system in a white male society.* San Francisco: Harper and Row.

Component Three: Implications and Applications

Focus: Counseling theory and practice; professional integration

Suggested selected readings:

Hare-Mustin, R. (1978). A feminist approach to family therapy. *Family Process, 17,* 181–194.

Hare-Mustin, R. (1988). Family change and gender differences: Implications for theory and practice. *Family Relations,* pp. 36–47.

McNamara, K., & Pichard, K. (1989). Feminist identity development: Implications for feminist therapy for women. *Journal of Counseling and Development,* pp. 184–189.

Pittman, F. (1985). Gender myths. *The Family Therapy Networker, 9*(6), 24–33.

Walters, M. A., Papp, P., Carter, B., & Goldstein, O. (1991). *The invisible web.* New York: Guilford Press.

Component Four: Synthesis

Focus: Counseling theory and practice; professional integration

---

This article was originally published in *Awareness: The Journal of the Colorado Association for Counseling and Development,* Vol. 20, 1992, pp. 12–20. Reprint permission granted by the Editor.

Building Intensive Simulations in Family-Therapy Training

Robert O. Rich
Dick T. Sampson

Intensive family simulation is part of a process for training family therapists. It emphasizes trainee participation in a simulated family. The goal of this technique is training students to make structured observations and intervention plans that culminate in their active intervention in a simulated family. Continual supervision through a one-way mirror with direct telephone communication is a major element of the technique.

Graduate students beginning family-therapy training need family situations in which they can apply and evaluate their newly acquired skills and knowledge. Students often report that classroom role playing for this purpose feels artificial. On the other hand, all but the most advanced students are often intimidated by actual families presenting real problems. The literature (Berg, 1978; Bardill, 1976; Fulmer, 1983; Raasoch & Laqueur, 1979; Sigal & Levin, 1976; Weingarten, 1979) suggests family simulation as an intermediate step between classroom role plays and conducting actual family therapy. Intensive family simulation was developed to provide trainers with a structured, step-by-step technique for accomplishing this intermediate step.

Issues in the Development of Simulation

Four important issues emerged as the intensive family simulation curriculum component was developed: (a) The simulated family and family therapy needed to be realistic enough for learning to be generalized to the real world; (b) The experience needed to be safe enough to protect the simulated family participants from overidentification with the experiences; (c) The student therapists needed a training experience that allowed them to safely experiment with and evaluate the use of themselves as therapeutic instruments; and (d) The simulated families needed to be established, develop history and dynamics, experience several therapy sessions, and be appropriately terminated within a 12-week period.

Hartley, Ritchie, and Fitzsimons (1981) commented on the matter of realism. They found that too little realism in a game simulation is experienced by participants as artificial or contrived. Intensive family simulation approached this issue by including family-building exercises at the beginning of the simulation process. The exercises focused on individual and family role taking. Participants were instructed to act as if the roles they took were actually their own and often drew on their own life experiences in creating their simulated roles. Specific exercises (described later) were also introduced to facilitate the role-taking process and increase the participants' feeling of reality during the simulation. When these procedures were followed, intensive simulations became close enough to reality to be powerful learning tools generalizable to actual family therapy.

Sigal and Levin (1976) noted the importance of safety for participants in the simulated family. They suggested that roles in simulated families sometimes become so realistic that participants may lose themselves in the identity of the role. They solved this problem by having the instructor directly intervene to protect the student from emotional harm. They recommended referring to participants by role rather than by name and/or shifting to the cognitive mode by discussing the simulated family's dynamics in an abstract or generalized way. Sigal and Levin used these interventions to lower intensity and provide distance between the participants and their roles in the simulated families. During intensive simulations, the instructors have worked whenever possible through the therapists in the simulation. This was accomplished through continual observation of the interaction through one-way glass and communication with the therapists via direct phone lines. Direct intervention with the simulated family by instructors was needed quite infrequently. Sessions also were *debriefed* and *deroled* to provide closure for participants. This process is described in detail later as one of the phases of simulation. Debriefing focused on the participants becoming more aware of their present surroundings than they were during the role play. It emphasized the differences between the students' own identities and their simulated roles. Although intensive family simulations often have become powerful experiences for their members, they have been sufficiently bounded by purpose (educational), time (2 hours or less per week), and space (supervised laboratory) constraints to adequately protect the participants. Instructors also exercised control over admission to the course. Intensive family simulations would be inappropriate in most undergraduate courses and for some graduate students. Keeping the class size below 25 and team teaching it, with both instructors typically present during sessions, provided further programmatic safety features.

Intensive family simulations were developed over a 12-week time span, with members of the simulated family meeting from 15 minutes to 2 hours in any given week. The simulated families were capable of growth and development of significant family history within these time constraints. For example, a simulated child may say to her "mother": "Of course I'm not important to you! You didn't want children in the first place!" (Referring to experiences during formulation of simulated-families.) Through techniques described in subsequent sections, the simulated families expanded and contracted as members were gained or launched. These changing patterns provided a richness in the therapy sessions not possible in one-shot family-therapy role plays. Because the simulated interaction occurred in an intensely observed and supervised setting, the dynamics evolved but still were controlled by the constraints of the simulation.

Research Support

The literature review found little research on the use of simulations in teaching family dynamics and family therapy. Weingarten's (1979) students ranked participation in the simulated families as the most effective among eight learning activities in a nonclinical family-dynamics course. She concluded that traditional teaching methods, combined with family simulation techniques in the classroom, had much to offer in teaching students about family dynamics. Raasoch and Laqueur (1979) suggested that the use of simulations dramatically accelerated the family-therapy training process.

Fulmer's (1983) review of the family-simulation literature supported increasing emotional intensity as one of the primary advantages of the technique over classroom role plays. Berg (1978) found, contrary to her original expectations, that students permitted processes to evolve naturally in simulations rather than acting out the dynamics described in their textbooks. On the other hand, Fletcher (1971) found that the consequences encountered in simulations may also inhibit participants from experimenting with new behaviors. His comments were specifically directed toward scientific game simulations but could have significance for family simulations as well. If Fletcher (1971) is correct, the responses by others in intensive family simulations may inhibit trainees from attempting newly learned interventions, but probably to a lesser extent than they would be inhibited by actual families in therapy. Our observations suggest that although students did become involved in the intensive family simulations as both family members and therapists, they were extremely willing to experiment with new techniques and strategies. In addition, even though some "textbook" dynamics occurred in intensive family simulations, for the most part family rules and roles emerged naturally as the dynamics of simulated families developed. For example, family mottos such as "We'll stay together even if it kills us" were often quoted by members of a simulated family to explain some aspect of their behavior. Family mottos also remained quite consistent for a given simulated family over the 10 to 12 weeks of its existence.

Phases of Intensive Simulation

Intensive simulation in family-therapy training consists of three separate phases: (a) Family Building, (b) Therapy Simulation, and (c) Debriefing. The dynamics of these phases are similar to the Hollander (1978) Psychodrama Curve in that they develop along continuums of temporal and emotional intensity. The goal of the Family Building Phase is to allow the family to develop a history and structure from which to create a family-therapy simulation. This phase offers students the opportunity to prepare for the development of emotional intensity. Providing "warm-up" time allows members of simulated families members to adopt their roles in more realistic and spontaneous ways. The second phase, Therapy Simulation, is the actual use of the simulated family for student-therapist intervention. The goal of this phase is to give students the opportunity to observe, experience, and practice family-therapy intervention. Emphasis is placed on a cycle of observation, planning, intervention, and feedback. It is during the family-simulation phase that emotional intensity reaches its peak. The major goal of the third phase, Debriefing, is cognitive integration of the simulation's experiential data through discussion. This phase also allows for lowering and integrating emotional intensity. Each of these phases is necessary to the total development and use of an intensive family simulation. The sequence of activities described below facilitates the movement of students through the phases of intensive simulation.

Family Building Phase

This phase consists of encounter, family member selection, family scene setting, and family history building.

Encounter activities. Encounter activities allow the class members to meet, make contact, and share feelings and ideas. This step is structured in the following manner:

- *Please form a circle.* The purpose of this activity is to learn the names of your class members. Starting with the person to my (leader's) left, state your name and tell us something about yourself. Then repeat the names of the persons who have previously introduced themselves. The person on my (leader's) immediate right will be required to name the total group.

After completion of this activity, the students are next instructed to:

- *Please stand up.* Without talking, mill through the group. Your goal in this activity is to explore the process of making contact with another person. Meet as many people in the class as time allows.

At the end of the milling exercise, the students are placed in pairs to share their reactions to the activity and discuss the process of making contact with others.

Family member selection. Selection activities are aimed at pairing and preparing for family growth. The activities in this section were adapted from exercises described by Fulmer (1983, pp. 56–58). Several members of the class are selected to become family builders. These members are told:

- *You have been chosen to select a simulated mate.* You are now free to court other members of the class. When you find a person you think you might like to pair with for this exercise, you may propose to them. They have the right to accept or reject your proposal.

This process is observed and later discussed by the members of the class.

After completion of the pairing process, most family builders should have a simulated mate. Some students selected for this process may elect to remain single, formulate simulated same-sex relationships or be asked by the instructors to be simulated single parents. The family builders and their partners are asked to select a last name other than their own for the simulated family. They are instructed then to share their feelings about the exercise. The remainder of the class is then assembled in a separate room to share their reactions about the exercise with each other.

Following directions in Fulmer (1983, p. 58), preparation for family growth is facilitated by instructing the simulated couples and single family builders as follows:

- *Please prepare an advertisement for a child.* Your ad should include the qualities you consider desirable in a child (i.e., sex, positive qualities, physical attributes, etc.). You may also list the qualities you have to offer the child.

Those not already selected for families remain in a separate room. Their instructions are:

- *Prepare a situation-wanted ad* that expresses the qualities you would like in the simulated family you will join.

The birth process is simulated by placing the names of all the class members not in the couples group in a selection box. A family is then chosen by the leader. The family is asked to draw a name from the selection box. The leader then brings the person named into the room and formally announces the birth, as follows.

- *A baby boy or girl has been born to the ____________ family.* Some couples may be kept childless, but others are expanded by planned or unplanned births. Couples may also negotiate adoptions or foster arrangements.

Those members not randomly selected as children are then assigned various roles by the leaders and join their assigned family (i.e., grandparent, aunt, foster child, tenant, ex-spouse, friend, etc.). Each student then negotiates with his or her simulated family for an age and name, while maintaining the randomly selected birth order.

Family scene setting. Scene-setting activities focus on such areas as role development, family themes, and a family problem statement.

To set the family scene, members are given the opportunity to develop the role they will play within the family. An adaptation of the role card game described by Ogden and Zevin (1976) and later by Masson and O'Byrne (1984, pp. 129–130) has been particularly effective in family role development. A deck of 39 note cards is prepared for each simulated family. On each card is either an interactional role (negotiator) or household role (cook). Families are asked to sit in a circle on the floor or around a table. The parents are given the deck of role cards and told:

- *Your family is not to talk during this phase of the activity.* Place the 39 role cards face up in the center of your family. Each member is to examine all the cards to determine which roles they would most like to play in the family.

After sufficient time is allowed for card examination, the families are instructed as follows:

- *Family members may now choose the cards that describe the roles they would like to play in the family.* Be sure to pick at least one interactional role and one household role. When all members have chosen their roles, you may begin discussing your role selections.

The discussion will terminate with each family member having a deck of cards that will describe his or her family role for the remainder of the training. At the completion of this role-defining activity, the students are asked to close their eyes and experience themselves in their roles within the family. When the students open their eyes they are to assume their age and role definitions. The family is now ready to develop the theme and dynamics of the family through the following activity originally described by Fulmer (1983).

> Parents, your family is now to develop a family coat of arms. This coat of arms should explicitly state your family motto and address your family's wishes, strengths, and weaknesses. Please remember to stay in your role while developing your coat of arms. Paper and colored marking pens will be provided. (p. 59)

Each family is instructed to post its coat of arms on the wall of the training room. Family members are then asked to develop a problem statement for this family while staying in role.

Family history building. Activities for building the family history should be designed to allow the family opportunities to practice and experience its interactional dynamics. These activities make up the experiential history of the family. They also set the stage for the development of intensity.

The authors use a family budget outing to encourage the development of each family's history. Each family member is asked to bring a certain amount of money to the next class session. These sums vary from $.25 to $1.00 based on the family's simulated social characteristics and the role of the family member. The families are given the following instructions:

- *Parents, take your family to a restaurant, student union building, or similar place for a family outing*. The outing is to last 45 minutes. The goal is for your family to stay in role and to experience the historical development of your family as deeply as possible. Spend no more than the total amount of money assigned to your family.

The activities described here for the Family Building Phase are by no means exhaustive. Alternative activities may be found in Okun and Rappaport (1980) and Masson and O'Byrne (1984). But the activities described have been found to be especially useful in the development of a simulated history and of emotional intensity. They provide the warm-up necessary for the therapy simulation phase of the training cycle.

Therapy Simulation Phase

This phase involves the students as simulated family members, therapists in training, and observers. The supervisor-instructor is also key to the simulation. This phase is similar to the Hollander (1978) stage of enactment in that emotional intensity will reach its peak during the simulation phase.

The simulated family is placed in an interview room equipped with one-way glass, remote-control video cameras, and a phone connection to the observation room. Family members are asked to close their eyes and visualize their role and the historical development of their simulated family. Upon opening their eyes, family members are to assume their roles and begin spontaneously interacting. Two other class members are selected to function as co-therapists.

The co-therapists are given a short case history of the family. They are then asked to join with the family. After initiating the joining process, the therapists are asked to intervene in the family in a growth-promoting way.

The observers are placed in pairs to process their observations and to discuss how they might intervene in the family. Each pair of observers may be given an evaluation sheet to guide the focus of their observations. Throughout the simulation, the observers are involved in a dialogue with the instructors. The observers are also informed that their pair may be asked to intervene in the family at any time during the simulation.

The instructors act as facilitators for the observation group and as supervisors for the trainees. They focus on activation of the cycle of observation, planning, intervention, and feedback. They look for those transitions in the therapy simulation during which observation pairs may enter as new therapists. They give feedback to trainees who are returning to the observation group from the therapy simulation. They intervene in the therapy simulation based on their training goals. Team teaching by two instructors permits simultaneous active supervision of the therapy process and dialogue with the observers or debriefing of previous therapists.

The process of the therapy simulation moves from joining, to the application of an intervention by the trainees, to the supervisors facilitating the reality-processing experiences of all class members, to the purposeful, positive ending of the simulation.

The reality-processing stage is key to the learning objectives of the simulation. The instructors' efforts are aimed at expanding the student therapist's ability to observe the family "dance," design interventions, process and track the simulated family's reaction to their interventions, and use feedback to encourage further growth of the simulated family. Instructors intervene by briefing each pair of trainees on potentially effective strategies to use before they enter the therapy room and by active coaching of trainees during sessions via closed telephone lines. Occasionally, one or both instructors will enter during a session to demonstrate a technique or conduct a full session while being observed by the trainees.

The key to effective completion of the family simulation is a purposeful ending. It is important that the simulation phase conclude by providing creative and productive objectives for both the family and the acting therapists. This step leads to the debriefing phase of the simulation.

Debriefing Phase

Debriefing is a critical aspect of training with intensive family simulations. Other authors advocating the use of simulations have been quite uniform in stressing the importance of debriefing (Bardill, 1976; Lederman, 1984; Raasoch & Laqueur, 1979). They have described the importance of debriefing as a vehicle for helping students to integrate their learning and gain closure on their experience in the simulation. Debriefing in intensive family simulations has normally included in-role and out-of-role discussions of personal reactions to simulation experiences at the end of each session. After especially intensive simulations, formal deroling through reality-focusing exercises, guided imagery, and relaxation exercises have been used with good effect. The last class meeting is devoted to feedback, dialogue, and summarization to provide closure and integrate learning for the overall experience.

Evaluation

Course evaluations were conducted during the final session of each class by administering a standard evaluation form to participants. One question on the evaluation form asked students to list the two or three most effective instructional techniques used in the course. Of 63 students completing evaluation forms, 53 (84%) responded to this question by listing conducting therapy with simulated families, participating as a member of a simulated family, or both. The data reported were collected in 1984, 1987, and 1988. Data for 1985 and 1986 were not available. The following is typical of student comments:

> Practice with "real" simulated families was valuable. The opportunity to be a therapist with simulated families brought information and techniques into reality. Simulated families are a powerful way to practice two things at once—therapeutic interventions and being in a family. The family simulation provided us with a safe place to explore.

The instructors' subjective impressions about the intensive family simulation process were congruent with student feedback. These impressions suggested that the simulation process led to increased skill development by students.

Summary

Intensive family simulations were developed to allow therapists-in-training to learn family-therapy techniques and strategies under real-time active supervision in a safe environment. Several activities were used to increase the emotional intensity of the simulated family, thus facilitating development of family history and dynamics. The Hollander (1978) Psychodrama Curve provided an excellent model for adaptation to intensive family therapy simulations. Simulations move through three distinct phases: (a) family building, (b) therapy simulation, and (c) debriefing. The authors found that encouraging student movement through the phases of simulation increased student ability to creatively intervene in families. Simulation also encouraged the integration of theory, technique, and application.

References

Bardill, D. (1976). The simulated family as an aid to learning family group treatment. *Child Welfare, 55,* 703–708.

Berg, B. (1978). Learning family therapy through simulation. *Psychotherapy: Theory, Research and Practice, 15,* 56–60.

Fletcher, J. (1971). The effectiveness of simulation games as learning environments. *Simulation and Games, 2,* 425–453.

Fulmer, R. (1983). Teaching the family life cycle: A guide for a workshop using simulated families. *American Journal of Family Therapy, 11,* 55–63.

Hartley, D., Ritchie, E., & Fitzsimons, E. (1981). The design of large-scale training games. *Simulation and Games, 12,* 141–152.

Hollander, C. (1978). *A process for psychodrama training: The Hollander psychodrama curve.* Denver: Snow Lion.

Lederman, L. (1984). Debriefing: A critical reexamination of the past-experience analytic process with simulations for its effective use. *Simulation and Games, 15,* 417–431.

Masson, H., & O'Byrme, P. (1984). *Applying family therapy: A practical guide for social workers.* Elmsford, NY: Pergamon.

Ogden, G., & Zevin, A. (1976). *When a family needs therapy.* Boston: Beacon Press.

Okun, B., & Rappaport, L. (1980). *Exercises for working with families.* North Scituate, MA: Duxbury.

Raasoch, J., & Laqueur, H. (1979). Learning multiple family therapy through simulated workshops. *Family Process, 18,* 95–98.

Sigal, J., & Levin, S. (1976). Teaching family therapy by simulation. *Canada's Mental Health, 24*(2), 6–8.

Weingarten, K. (1979). Family awareness for nonclinicians: Participation in a simulated family as a teaching technique. *Family Process, 18,* 143–150.

Family Sculpting in the Training of Marriage and Family Counselors

Luann Costa

Family sculpting is an expressive technique emerging from the experiential approach to family counseling. Experiential Family Counseling (Goldenberg & Goldenberg, 1991) is derived from existential, humanistic, and phenomenological psychology that was developed as the so-called third force in reaction to psychoanalysis and behaviorism. Representative experiential family therapists include Whitaker, Kempler, Satir, and Bunny and Fred Duhl (Becvar & Becvar, 1988; Goldenberg & Goldenberg, 1991; Nichols, 1984). This article presents the assumptions underlying Experiential Family Counseling, identifies the techniques associated with the experiential approach, describes in detail how one technique can be taught, and provides implications for marriage and family counseling trainers in counselor education departments.

While individual differences exist among counselors, three basic assumptions are common to all experiential family counselors: (a) an atheoretical stance, (b) a focus on the present, and (c) an emphasis on existential encounter (Goldenberg & Goldenberg, 1991). First, beyond the theory espoused by the existential, humanistic, and phenomenological derivations of the approach, experiential family counselors adopt a relatively atheoretical stance and shun theory as a hindrance. They believe change occurs through a growth experience and not merely through intellectual interpretation, insight, or the uncovering of the past. Openness, self-awareness, spontaneity, freedom of expression, creativity, action, intuition, self-fulfillment, process, confrontation, and personal integrity are valued rather than theory. These values constitute the essence of the experiential approach to families. The counselor is viewed as a facilitator, a resource person, an observer, a detective, and a model for effective communication (Becvar & Becvar, 1988). The ability to respond in an intuitive spontaneous manner and the counselor's use of self as a person are the necessary conditions that determine a successful therapeutic experience.

Second, the focus or major time frame in Experiential Family Counseling is the present, the here-and-now data from immediate experience (Goldenberg & Goldenberg, 1991) and action in the present rather than interpretation of the past. Alienation of experience, suppression of feelings, and denial of impulses lead to behavior disorders. Dysfunctional family systems are self-protective, mechanical, and rigid, avoid risk taking whether they are enmeshed or disengaged (Becvar & Becvar, 1988), and are characterized by an atmosphere of emotional deadness (Satir, 1972). The primary goal of counseling is seen as encouraging the process of growth leading to increased self-awareness through action in the here-and-now.

Third, the existential encounter is the *sine qua non* of Experiential Family Counseling and results in increased awareness and authenticity, leading to a reintegration of repressed or disowned parts of the self. The counselor provides an opportunity for intimate personal experience—an existential encounter—that is the primary force and key to growth in the psychotherapeutic process. Consistent with phenomenological psychology, behavior is determined by personal experience and individual perception rather than by external reality (Goldenberg & Goldenberg, 1991).

The expressive and often innovative techniques associated with Experiential Family Counseling include family drawing (Bing, 1970), spatialization (e.g., a metaphorical representation in space of the problem), sculpting (Duhl, Kantor, & Duhl, 1973; Jefferson, 1978; Papp, Silverstein, & Carter, 1973), psychodrama, choreography (Papp, 1976), role-playing, family puppet interviews (Duhl, Kantor, & Duhl, 1973), family floor plan (Coppersmith, 1980), and the use of metaphors, games, humor, and almost any behavior comfortable for the counselor (Becvar & Becvar, 1988). Experiential Family Counseling, however, can be divided into two groups in regard to therapeutic techniques. Some counselors (e.g., Satir, Papp, Duhl, and Duhl) employ highly structured devices such as sculpting and choreography to stimulate affective intensity, while others (e.g., Whitaker) rely on their own personality, spontaneity, and creativity. Nevertheless, despite diverse methods, this article provides detailed guidelines for conducting one structured technique in Experiential Family Counseling—family sculpting—that can also be used in marriage and family counselor training.

Family Sculpting

Family sculpting is a visual, spatial, metaphorical representation that reveals a person's perceptual map of their family of origin. The recently established environmental and specialty standards for marriage and family counseling or therapy (Council for Accreditation of Counseling and Related Educational Programs [CACREP], 1990) require trainee knowledge of family of origin and related influencing factors that can cause personal blocks in professional growth and development. This technique may be one method of partially meeting that requirement. Because CACREP-accredited (1990) marriage and family counseling training programs require family-of-origin experience of their trainees, it may be used as a training technique to demonstrate expressive experiential methods and is especially useful as a tool to cut through excessive verbalizations, intellectualization, defensiveness, and projection of blame when students examine their own family of origin. It is also an effective therapeutic procedure to ameliorate countertransference problems in the clinical practice of marriage and family counseling. Only to the extent that marriage and family therapy trainees come to terms with their family-of-origin experiences can they be effective in maintaining therapeutic objectivity when confronted with highly resistant families (Lawson, 1988; Lawson & Gaushell, 1988) demonstrating severe symptomatology.

Family sculpting consists of creating an arrangement, portrait, or tableau of family members placed in various physical positions that represent their relation to each other at a particular moment in time. Satir (Goldenberg & Goldenberg, 1991; Nerin, 1986; Satir & Baldwin, 1983) developed the technique of family reconstruction, or spatialization of the issue, during the 1960s, which is a similar therapeutic procedure wherein family members reenact their multigenerational drama thereby changing entrenched perceptions, feelings, and beliefs. The intervention technique may be used at any point in clinical assessment and diagnosis during the ongoing therapeutic process, although it is preferable to use it relatively early in a student's training program to enhance ongoing personal growth and development.

Due to its flexibility of implementation, sculpting forces a process focus, ownership and responsibility for feelings, and new choices and options for change and personal growth. For example, one trainee resigned from her job and went into therapy after sculpting her alcoholic family of origin and became conscious of the powerful emotional connection between work and her family of origin. In both contexts, she was overwhelmed by the same feelings of "confusion, chaos, and a need to break out." The job was "killing me, draining me." She further stated, "The sculpting also made me more receptive to the healing I needed to do with my mother." Issues of confidentiality and professional ethics, of course, must be addressed by the trainer.

All sculpting should be done on a voluntary basis and confidentiality must be guaranteed for the volunteer. Because the experience often elicits powerful emotional intensity, a small class of between 8 and 10 students is recommended and an alternative assignment should be given for those who do not wish to participate. Adequate time for processing the experience and providing appropriate closure must be available before beginning the experience.

In addition, sculpting can foster the reduction of students' countertransference reactions that potentially may immobilize the therapeutic process. Sculpting allows students to convert their inner perceptions of family boundaries, coalitions, alliances, subsystems, roles, and triangles into a graphic active mode of expression, or more simply, to put feelings into action. Family choreography (Papp, 1976) is an extension of family sculpting including movement to show dynamic shifting transactional patterns. Papp referred to family choreography as a "fluid form of realigning relationships" (cited in Nichols, 1984, p. 286). Family patterns are thus brought into conscious awareness and scapegoating or blaming of one member often becomes unnecessary. Satir (cited in Becvar & Becvar, 1988) referred to body, mind, and feelings as a significant triad. Body parts can become metaphors for psychological meanings, and, thus, physical symptoms are often an expression of emotional illness. Sculpting allows trainees, as well as clients, to experience themselves in a safe environment and to expand their awareness, thus arriving at a new integration and reinterpretation of experience. Overall, the rationale is to expand awareness by fostering the experience of a growth process through action in the present in order to emphasize new possibilities and empower the trainee for change.

Guidelines

The guidelines for conducting the family sculpture are relatively simple, although the technique is sometimes difficult to implement successfully. The sculpture consists of four roles (Duhl, Kantor, & Duhl, 1973) and four steps originally developed by Moreno and Elefthery (1975). The roles include (a) the *sculptor* (often called the director) of the family portrait, the trainee or client, or the individual who volunteers to sculpt his or her family of origin; (b) the *facilitator,* therapist, or professor, who guides the sculptor, thus providing clarity and protection during the unfolding process; (c) the *actors* or role-players who are chosen by the sculptor to portray members of the family of origin; and (d) the *audience* or remaining class members who observe and comment on the process in the feedback stage. If the class is relatively small and the family sculpted is large (e.g., one of my trainees sculpted her family of 10, which left few observers), inanimate objects such as chairs, pillows, or stuffed animals may be used to serve as players.

After the roles are chosen by the sculptor, the following four steps are monitored by the facilitator:

1. *Setting the scene.* The facilitator and sculptor stand, and the facilitator helps the sculptor establish a particular situation he or she wishes to explore. The facilitator requests the sculptor to select a particular event or point in time (e.g., 6 years old) that arouses intense feelings. The facilitator may use visualization if appropriate and ask the sculptor to close his or her eyes and describe an image or several images. When the sculptor visualizes a scene, questions may elicit information about the scene including the following: (a) the size and shape of the room, house, or context; (b) the coloring, atmosphere, light and darkness, warmth, texture of floor and walls; and (c) any significant objects in the room (e.g., a stereo, dining room table, and so forth). This is similar to establishing a stage setting. The facilitator can mirror or repeat back the setting to the sculptor checking for accuracy and clarification.

2. *Choosing the role-players.* The sculptor chooses other individuals in the class to portray family members in the family of origin (e.g., mother, father, brothers, sisters, and self). Often the sculptor chooses people whose personal or physical characteristics are similar to the original family members. Anyone living in the house may be included in the sculpting such as grandparents, other relatives, or any significant others. Deceased family members are also included.

3. *Creating the sculpture.* The facilitator instructs the sculptor to tell each player what they need to know to play a certain person, and then the sculptor places them in a specific spatial metaphorical position, gesture, or pattern of movement in relation to self and other family members. Distance, closeness, touching, facial expression, and positioning of arms and legs are significant indicators of the sculptor's

perception of the family. The facilitator may say, "I'd like you to arrange each member in a position that seems to describe something about them. Go up to each person and arrange them in terms of how *you* see them, how *you* envision them. In other words, create a picture or a tableau of your family as you see them at this point in time in your picture or visualization." Possible facilitative questions include the following:

1. Where should mother stand? Your father?
2. What position does your mother assume (sitting, standing, kneeling, lying down, and so forth)? Your father?
3. What is the expression on your mother's face? Your father's?
4. How close are they? Are they touching one another? How? Where?
5. What are they saying to one another, if anything?
6. What is the title of your sculpture?
7. How long has this sculpture been this way?
8. What is going to happen in this sculpture?
9. How does it feel to be in this place in this family?
10. Do you agree this is how the family functions?

Similar questions are then asked regarding the relative placement of siblings and other significant family members including the positioning of the person portraying the sculptor. Movement or choreography may be added. This procedure continues until all family-of-origin members have been sculpted into specific positions, postures, or gestures. In encouraging movement and action without words, the facilitator ritualizes the emotional essence of the family. The scene can be played, however, with or without words, whichever procedure enhances the existential encounter. The facilitator may also exaggerate the family sculpture and use repetition to increase intensity of affect. I found that Satir's (1972) technique of anchoring the sculptor kinesthetically with one hand in the small of the back and occasionally encouraging the sculptor to breathe deeply throughout the process, as well as using a soothing tone of voice, provides ongoing support, safety, and sensitivity. The facilitator keenly observes the sculptor for any signs of increasing affect and gently fosters the process, continually protecting the sculptor from possible overload or from being used by the group to serve vicarious needs. The facilitator must maintain the utmost respect for the trainee, blocking any attempts by others to analyze or cognitively disrupt the experiential process of the sculptor. At that moment, all attention and concentration must be on the needs of the sculptor.

4. *Processing the sculpture.* The facilitator develops the meaning of the sculpture from the sculptor's perspective during this step. The sculptor and the other participants are debriefed and deroled in order to bring them back to the current reality. As the exercise progresses, new insights may increase the sculptor's perceptions, interpretations, and reactions of what has occurred in the particular family of origin. Patterns of relationships, boundaries, triangles, alliances, and coalitions can be clearly shown. Feedback is given by the surrogates, group members, and facilitator thus providing support and validation for the sculptor's experience. Alternatives are generated for the sculptor to reencounter the family of origin with his or her new learning. Depending on the goals of the sculptor, however, the process would be different if differentiation or individuation is sought rather than closeness or connectedness.

The role of the trainer or professor should be one of facilitation (L'Abate, Ganahl, & Hansen, 1986). Facilitators should refrain from giving an interpretation as a means of reframing the sculptor's reality because insight is more powerful if achieved by the sculptor alone rather than the facilitator intruding or imposing meaning from the outside. The sculptor should be given complete freedom, respect, and validation of his or her own perception with appropriate guidance and support. It is important to allow student sculptors to comment on their own experience first and then ask more leading questions or suggest hypotheses later.

Additional suggestions (L'Abate et al., 1986; Sherman & Fredman, 1986) for variations of sculpting exercises include comparisons between current and ideal reality; past, present, and future perceptions; the same scene or related scenes to build intensity of affect; before-and-after life cycle shifts and losses of family members such as the death of a child or parent and the divorce of a spouse; the family of origin and the current family at particular nodal life cycle events such as births, deaths, and children leaving, to see patterns that connect the past to the present. For training purposes, dominant-submissive or disengaged-enmeshed couples can also be metaphorically represented. The variations are infinite and limited only by the creativity and intuition of the trainer.

Suggested questions to process the new family sculpture depending on emergent affect and specific issues could include the following: What title would you give your tableau or what phrase describes your family creation? What changes would you like to see? What patterns do you want to keep? What do you need to have happen in this family? How would you sculpt them to show how you would like them to be? It is a good idea if time permits to have the sculptor create a new sculpture depicting a more healthy or functional arrangement, thus emphasizing increased choice, hope, and empowerment of the sculptor. Rushing the sculptor or pushing for premature closure before the creative process has emerged should be avoided. There is no substitute for timing, rapport, and respect, and the sculptor's experience should always be validated.

In the final step, each role-player provides feedback for the sculptor by verbalizing how it felt to be in the role and position assigned by the sculptor. Observers describe the verbal or nonverbal behavior of the players and the sculptor and check out inner experiences revealed in action. It is a good idea to have the student observers share feelings or experiences triggered within themselves rather than evaluating the sculptor's experience. In order to encourage transfer and generalization of learning and to promote more productive interactions between family members, it is critical that options for acting on the new insights with the student's family of origin are discussed as well as new insights of self as a trainee in marriage and family counseling.

Case Study

Susan was a middle-aged graduate student completing her master's degree in marriage and family counseling. During a beginning marriage and family counseling course, Susan volunteered to sculpt her family of origin.

Susan sculpted a conflict in her family of origin when she was 17 years of age. The family was seated around the dining room table and included her two younger sisters and both her parents. She described her sister Sally, the 13-year-old middle child, as "dramatic, histrionic, acting out, with a 'chip on her shoulder,' and continually complaining and arguing with Dad." Then she described her 9-year-old youngest sister Lisa as "quiet, a 'Tom Boy' aligned with Dad, the boy he always wanted; she always stayed out of it." She described her father as "glaring at Sally, somewhat removed" (she moved that chair farther back from the others at the table) and "angry at Mom for protecting Sally." Her mother was "accommodating, pacifying, trying to please everyone especially Sally, and on guard, waiting, but trying to prevent a blow-up." Susan characterized herself as "tense, nervous, uptight, 'Miss goody goody,' but irritated and uncomfortable, glaring and rolling her eyes at Sally, but yet feeling glad that Sally was in trouble again." She further stated, "I stayed out of it because Sally did it all for us. We competed for

Mother's attention; I was mad because she was getting attention, but on the other hand, I wanted her to get in trouble." All family members were tense and uptight, waiting for the inevitable confrontation. As the conflict progressed, Susan stated that Sally burst into tears, shouted, "I hate this family and I'm leaving," threw her chair down, and ran from the table.

This scene was sculpted first, then choreographed, or put into motion, with words and without words exaggerating the affect and intensity each time. Throughout the sculpting, Susan was wringing her hands nervously as she observed the family sculpture she had created at the dinner table. Father was sitting back glaring rigidly; Lisa was rocking back and forth while smiling slightly; Mother was patting Sally on the back, attempting to pacify her; and Sally was shouting and pounding on the table. She said the family had been this way in all of her 17 years, and she titled the family tableau sarcastically "Fun at Dinner."

Then Susan created a new sculpture according to needed changes or how she would like the family to be. In this arrangement, everyone could discuss, disagree rationally, accept feelings, and maintain their own position without disruption. Her mother would be less accommodating and avoid saying "honey" so often, and Susan herself would speak up more. When the facilitator asked Susan to close her eyes, to exaggerate wringing her hands, and to share what she was feeling, Susan, after fighting the sadness for a time, shared that her sister Sally had died a few months before, and she was immediately overcome with intense sobs and profound grief.

At this point, the facilitator switched to a Gestalt technique of assisting Susan through her grief and unfinished business with her sister. Susan was able to say many things she had wanted to say to her sister before she died such as, "I'm sorry we never really talked; I'm sorry you had to carry the burden for the family; I'm sorry I didn't speak up; I'm sorry I didn't understand you; it wasn't fair you had to die when you have so much talent and that you have to leave your 2-year-old daughter." The individual portraying Susan's sister was able to provide empathy, support, forgiveness, and healing to Susan as did others in the class. Susan was able to grieve in a safe environment when other immediate members of her family had not allowed her to grieve, insisting she must get on with her life. Susan was able to make decisions that would honor her sister, such as helping to raise her sister's daughter and establishing a closer relationship with her remaining sister and parents. All role-players demonstrated support and empathy for Susan by sharing their own losses including two members whose fathers had recently died and one member who had been sexually abused. The facilitator extended the class in order to ensure a healthy and therapeutic closure to Susan's existential encounter. She left with supportive friends and in a follow-up telephone call the next day, she indicated that she felt relieved, positive, and grateful for the experience. She was planning to follow through on several suggested alternatives that had emerged during the experience and to reencounter her family of origin interacting differently (e.g., increased differentiation, less triangulation) according to her new insights. She stated that her overall training and personal development as a marriage and family counselor was enhanced by the existential encounter with her family of origin because several troublesome counter-transference issues were alleviated.

Implications for Counselor Educators

The success of this training technique lies in the sensitivity and spontaneity of the facilitator or counselor educator. To provide a healthy existential encounter, and an optimal training experience, the counselor educator must be able to focus intently on the needs and reactions of the sculptor, keep the process present-oriented, and avoid attempts of all players to intellectualize, distract, or disrespect the sculptor in any way. All attention, concentration, and control must be in the protective service of the sculptor's uniqueness. Timing, pacing, flow of process, and knowing when to push and when to back off are crucial. The integrity, professionalism, and ethical stance of the counselor educator are critical concerns in providing the opportunity for an intimate personal experience that is a key to growth. Issues of confidentiality, trust, and a safe environment need to be addressed and modeled by the instructor. This approach may not be appropriate or comfortable for some family counseling trainers or counselor educators but I have used it often enough to assert with confidence that it is a powerful and effective expressive training technique in demonstrating Experiential Family Counseling to trainees to examine and to reintegrate trainees' perceptions of their own family of origin. Isomorphically, it is also an effective therapeutic procedure that may ameliorate counter-transference problems in the clinical practice of marriage and family counseling. With careful and sensitive supervision, adequate experience, and ongoing professional growth and development of *both* counselor educators and trainees, this experiential expressive technique can be a powerful therapeutic tool to use with clinical families in actual family practice.

References

Becvar, D. S., & Becvar, R. J. (1988). *Family therapy: A systemic integration*. Boston: Allyn & Bacon.

Bing, E. (1970). The conjoint family drawing. *Family Process, 9*, 173–194.

Coppersmith, E. (1980). The family floor plan: A tool of training, assessment, and intervention in family therapy. *Journal of Marital and Family Therapy, 6*, 141–145.

Council for Accreditation of Counseling and Related Educational Programs. (1990). *Environmental and specialty standards for marriage and family counseling/therapy*. Alexandria, VA: Author.

Duhl, F. J., Kantor, D., & Duhl, B. S. (1973). Learning, space, and action in family therapy: A primer of sculpture. In D. A. Bloch (Ed.), *Techniques of family psychotherapy* (pp. 69–76). New York: Grune & Stratton.

Goldenberg, I., & Goldenberg, H. (1991). *Family therapy: An overview* (3rd ed.). Monterey, CA: Brooks/Cole.

Jefferson, C. (1978). Some notes on the use of family sculpture in therapy. *Family Process, 17*, 69–76.

L'Abate, L., Ganahl, G., & Hansen, J. (1986). *Methods of family therapy*. Englewood Cliffs, NJ: Prentice-Hall.

Lawson, D. M. (1988). Using family sculpting and choreography in a student growth group. *Journal of Counseling & Development, 66*, 246–247.

Lawson, D. M., & Gaushell, H. (1988). Family autobiography: A useful method for enhancing counselors' personal development. *Counselor Education and Supervision, 28*, 162–167.

Moreno, J. L., & Elefthery, D. G. (1975). An introduction to group psychodrama. In G. M. Gazda (Ed.), *Basic approaches to group psychotherapy and group counseling* (pp. 69–100). Springfield, IL: Thomas.

Nerin, W. F. (1986). *Family reconstruction: Long day's journey into light*. New York: Norton.

Nichols, W. (1984). *Family therapy: Concepts and methods*. Boston: Allyn & Bacon.

Papp, P. (1976). Family choreography. In P. Guerin, Jr. (Ed.), *Family therapy: Theory and practice*. New York: Gardner.

Papp, P., Silverstein, O., & Carter, E. (1973). Family sculpting in preventive work with "well families." *Family Process, 12*, 197–212.

Satir, V. M. (1972). *Peoplemaking*. Palo Alto, CA: Science and Behavior Books.

Satir, V., & Baldwin, M. (1983). *Satir step by step: A guide to creating change in families*. Palo Alto, CA: Science and Behavior Books.

Sherman, R., & Fredman, N. (1986). *Handbook of structural techniques in marriage and family therapy*. New York: Brunner/Mazel.

Marriage and Family Counseling in Counselor Education: National Trends and Implications

Samuel T. Gladding
Margaret Burggraf
David L. Fenell

Interest in the American Association for Counseling and Development (AACD) in the area of marriage and family counseling (MFC) has increased dramatically during the 1980s. The association sponsored a National Conference on the Family in 1986 and has highlighted marriage and family counseling in theme sessions at recent national conventions. Three AACD divisions, the Association for Counselor Education and Supervision (ACES), the American Mental Health Counselors Association (AMHCA), and the Association for Specialists in Group Work (ASGW), have formed interest networks in marriage and family counseling. Two divisions (ACES and ASGW) have also sponsored workshops concerning the role that counselor training programs should assume in the preparation of marriage and family counselors. Also, ACES sponsored the publication of a monograph (Okun & Gladding, 1983) focusing on marriage and family counselor education and has promoted the marketing, through AACD, of a series of five videotapes demonstrating 50 specific family counseling skills (Piercy & Laird, 1985).

Professional interest in marriage and family counseling has been reflected in other ways. Hollis and Wantz (1983) indicated that marriage and family counseling courses have been added to the curriculum of counselor training programs at a rate three times faster than that of the next most frequent category, geriatric counseling. During the period from 1980 to 1983, 140 courses in marriage and family counseling were added to curricula. Approximately two-thirds of all counselor education departments now offer such courses (Peltier & Vale, 1986). Also, there is interest among some AACD members in forming a division for marriage and family counselors.

The strong interest in marriage and family counseling in AACD and in departments of counselor education has led to the publication of is suggested (Fenell & Hovestadt, 1986; Hovestadt, Fenell, & Piercy, 1983). In the three-level model outlined by these authors, marriage and family counselor training are integrated into programs of counselor education. At the first level, a degree in this specialty is offered. At the second level, a concentration is provided within a currently existing degree. At the third level, elective courses are made available without any attempt to integrate them systematically with other degree requirements.

Few authors have conducted research to determine the actual directions that counselor training institutions are taking in the development of programs in marriage and family counseling. Two notable exceptions are studies by Meadows and Hetrick (1982) and Peltier and Vale (1986), in which there has been an attempt to identify the marriage and family counseling courses offered by counselor education programs.

Meadows and Hetrick (1982) surveyed the chairpersons of a representative, random sample of 114 counselor preparation programs. They found that 55% of these programs offered one or more courses that the chairpersons described as related to marriage and family counseling preparation. Furthermore, they found a strong agreement among the participants regarding 30 marriage and family counseling competencies that they believed were appropriate for general counselors.

In another national survey of chairpersons of counselor preparation programs, Peltier and Vale (1986) found that of 244 chairpersons who returned questionnaires, 154 (63%) reported that marriage and family counseling courses were available in their departments. Family counseling was the most frequently offered course (taught in approximately half of the departments). As did Meadows and Hetrick, they also found that many marriage and family counseling courses are available to students in other departments, such as sociology, psychology, and home economics. Although informative, these two studies have only supplied preliminary data on the interest of counselor educators in marriage and family counseling and on the availability of offerings in their departments.

The purpose of this study was to build on previous interest and data by surveying a national sample of leaders in counselor education to determine their current attitudes about marriage and family counselor preparation programs and future trends in designated areas. Specifically, answers to the following questions (addressed by earlier studies) were sought: What percentage of counselor education programs provide training in MFC? What types of MFC programs are currently available at counselor training institutions? What MFC courses are currently being offered in counselor training programs?

New information was obtained through answers to the following questions: What types of support and continuing education (e.g., training films, curriculum suggestions, and training guidelines) do counselor education programs need to enhance MFC training? What types of employment opportunities (e.g., private practice, mental health centers, hospital-health centers, hospital-health agencies) exist for counselors with MFC training? What are the opinions of counselor educators regarding accreditation of MFC programs? What factors are keeping some programs from offering courses in MFC? We also examined (a) the number of participants with plans to develop MFC course work in their programs in the immediate or near future and (b) the educational qualifications of faculty members currently teaching MFC courses.

Method

Sample

The sample for this study was drawn from department chairpersons identified for each of the 510 counselor preparation programs listed in the fifth edition of Hollis and Wantz's (1983) *Counselor Preparation 1983-1985* directory. Department chairpersons were selected because of their leadership roles and because of their knowledge of the directions in which their programs are developing. Participants returned a total of 285 questionnaires for an overall response rate of 56%. Of the questionnaires returned, 11 were excluded from the data analysis: 3 were returned with no responses recorded and 8 were returned with a notification that the counselor education program or department no longer existed. There were 274 usable questionnaires.

Instrument

Eight members of the ACES Interest Network for Marriage and Family Counseling constructed the 18-item survey instrument using the Peltier and Vale (1986) questionnaire as an initial guide. Each question was written in a uniform style, edited, revised, and field tested twice on a randomly selected sample ($n = 10$) of counselor educators who were members of the ACES MFC Interest Network and not involved in the construction of the survey. These members reviewed the instrument for face validity and offered criticism on the content and clarity of the items.

Procedure

A copy of the survey questionnaire was mailed to each counselor preparation program chairperson. In a cover letter sent with the questionnaire, the purpose of the survey was explained and cooperation in the research was requested. A follow-up letter was sent to chairpersons who had not responded 4 weeks later in an attempt to increase the response rate.

Results

Descriptive Data

The 274 surveys returned represented all four regions of AACD. Of the respondents, 42 (15%) were from the North Atlantic region, 76 (28%) from the North Central region, 94 (34%) from the Southern region, and 62 (23%) from the Western region. Of the departments, 226 awarded at least master's degrees, 68 offered specialist degree programs, and 89 had doctoral programs.

Responses to the Questionnaire

Of the 274 programs, 195 (71.2%) offered courses in marriage and family counseling, 78 (28.4%) did not offer MFC courses, and 1 (0.4%) did not respond. Also, 78 (28%) of the department chairpersons indicated that they currently had a major in marriage and family counseling, 157 (57%) offered no such major, and 39 (14%) did not respond. Of the 157 programs not currently offering a marriage and family counseling major, 40 (25%) indicated that they anticipated establishing such a major in the next 5 years, 96 (61%) responded that no such program was planned, 6 (4%) replied maybe, and 15 (10%) did not respond. Those not engaged in such training cited three reasons: (a) insufficient faculty resources ($n=30$), (b) insufficient funds ($n=31$), and (c) availability of courses in MFC in other departments ($n=31$).

Respondents reported (see Table 1) that the MFC courses most likely to be available in counselor training programs were (a) family counseling, offered in 140 programs (51%); (b) marriage counseling, offered in 104 programs (38%); and (c) practicums in marriage and family counseling, offered in 88 programs (32%). The MFC courses least likely to be provided in counselor education departments were (a) family enrichment, offered in 19 programs (7%); (b) family health and pathology, offered in 21 programs (8%); and (c) family counseling with special populations, offered in 30 programs (11%). Graduates of MFC programs were likely to find employment in three primary settings: community mental health centers, private practice, and hospitals or health agencies.

The number of faculty members teaching MFC courses were as follows: 102 (37%) departments had 1 faculty member, 55 (20%) had 2 faculty members, 22 (8%) had 3, 14 (5%) had 4, and 81 (30%) had 5 or more. Of the faculty members teaching MFC courses, 27 (10%) were graduates of programs approved by the American Association for Marriage and Family Therapy (AAMFT), 143 (52%) were not graduates of such a program, and 104 (38%) did not indicate the qualifications of their faculty members to teach MFC courses. Of the faculty members, 83 (30%) were AAMFT clinical members or approved supervisors.

When the chairpersons were asked whether support from AACD (e.g., guidelines for clinical supervision) would be helpful in the development of their MFC training programs, more than 76% ($n = 210$) said yes. Respondents indicated they could particularly use help in the areas of family counseling (68%), marriage counseling (61%), divorce counseling (59%), marital and family relations (52%), and systems theory (50%).

When asked their opinions regarding the accreditation of marriage and family counseling programs, 52% of the respondents believed that training guidelines should be provided by the Council for the Accreditation of Counseling and Related Programs (CACREP), the accrediting body of AACD. Other respondents (22%) reported that marriage and family counseling should be accredited by the Commission on Accreditation of Marriage and Family Therapy Education, the accrediting body of AAMFT. The other respondents (19%) to this question believed that accreditation of marriage and family counseling programs was not necessary in counselor training programs (7% of the respondents did not answer this question).

Discussion

The results of this survey are similar to those of the earlier studies of Meadows and Hetrick (1982) and Peltier and Vale (1986) in that all three revealed (a) a high interest among counselor education chairpersons in marriage and family counseling and (b) increased attention in counselor

Table 1
Marriage and Family Courses Offered in Counselor Education Departments and Other Departments Accessible to Counselor Education

Offered in Counselor Education Departments			Offered in Other Departments	
n	%	Course	*n*	%
47	(17)	Marriage and Family Relations	76	(28)
21	(8)	Family Health and Pathology	34	(12)
61	(22)	Human Sexuality	90	(33)
104	(38)	Marriage Counseling	21	(8)
140	(51)	Family Counseling	29	(11)
29	(11)	Research in Marriage/Family Counseling	24	(9)
41	(15)	Sex Therapy	25	(9)
19	(7)	Family Enrichment	19	(7)
60	(22)	Structural/Strategic Family Therapy	23	(8)
35	(13)	Transgenerational Family Therapy	8	(3)
46	(17)	Parent Education	28	(10)
58	(21)	Professional/Ethical Issues in Marriage/Family Counseling	15	(6)
30	(11)	Family Therapy/Special Population	11	(4)
88	(32)	Practicum in Marriage/Family Counseling	17	(6)
63	(23)	Internship in Marriage/Family Counseling	12	(4)
34	(12)	Divorce Counseling	12	(4)

Note. The percentages listed in parentheses are based on $n = 274$.

education departments to offering courses and programs in this specialty, especially family counseling courses. The study also revealed that, as previously reported, MFC courses are accessible to counselor education students through other departments.

The results of this survey indicated that a higher number and percentage of MFC courses are now offered in counselor education departments than were found in Peltier and Vale's (1986) study: 195 (71%) versus 154 (63%). Also, there has been an increase in the number of departments offering majors in MFC: 78 (28%) as compared to 52 (21%) reported by Peltier and Vale (1986). Also, 40 more programs are planning to start such a major within 5 years. Because only a limited number of questionnaires were returned in this survey, as was true in previous surveys, these numbers must be considered with caution. Still, a trend toward more emphasis in MFC courses and majors in counselor education programs seems evident.

Although interest and program development are high, respondents are unsure of what organization should accredit programs in MFC (i.e., AAMFT or CACREP). This confusion could be attributable to the relatively new nature of MFC courses and programs in counselor education departments and to the differing backgrounds and qualifications of faculty members who teach in these departments. Peltier and Vale (1986) suggested that a joint meeting between AAMFT and ACES to discuss standards for accreditation would be helpful. We suggest that a meeting between AAMFT and CACREP representatives may be more beneficial in exploring models for accrediting MFC programs in counselor education departments. The three-tier system, as outlined by Hovestadt et al. (1983) and Fenell and Hovestadt (1986), deserves consideration as a possible model for accreditation. This model provides more flexibility for recognition of quality and quantity of course offerings than does any other model. The link between types of accreditation, licensure, and employment opportunities requires further exploration.

Another finding of this survey that needs to be emphasized is the desire by counselor education chairpersons for additional support to improve their marriage and family counselor training programs. Such support, they suggested, could be provided through resources developed by AACD in the form of training films, curriculum guide suggestions, workshops, and monographs. The exact types of resources that MFC courses and programs want and need, and whether they differ by size and emphasis of a counselor education program, still must be investigated. Also, it is important to know how the availability of such resources may affect programs currently unable to provide MFC courses.

As Meadows and Hetrick (1982) stated, "providing services to couples and families can clearly be a societal contribution of counselors" (p. 53). Before these services can be conducted properly, however, it is vital that investigators discover more about the direction of courses or programs in counselor education departments and take steps to ensure the qualitative aspects of these offerings.

References

Fenell, D. L., & Hovestadt, A. J. (1986). Family therapy as a profession of professional specialty: Implications for training. *Journal of Psychotherapy and the Family, 1*, 25–40.

Hollis, J. W., & Wantz, R. A. (1983). *Counselor preparation 1983–1985.* Muncie, IN: Accelerated Development.

Hovestadt, A. J., Fenell, D. L., & Piercy, F. P. (1983). Integrating marriage and family therapy within counselor education: A three level model. In B. F. Okun & S. T. Gladding (Eds.), *Issues in training marriage and family therapists* (pp. 29–42). Ann Arbor, MI: ERIC/CAPS.

Meadows, M. E., & Hetrick, H. H. (1982). Roles for counselor education departments in marriage and family counseling: Current status and projections. *Counselor Education and Supervision, 22*, 47–54.

Okun, B. F., & Gladding, S. T. (Eds.). (1983). *Issues in training marriage and family therapists.* Ann Arbor, MI: ERIC/CAPS.

Peltier, S. W., & Vale, S. O. (1986). A national survey of counselor education departments: Course offerings on marriage and family. *Counselor Education and Supervision, 25*, 313–319.

Piercy, F. P., & Laird, R. (1985). *Skills of family therapy.* Alexandria, VA: American Association for Counseling and Development.

Teaching Family Therapy in an Academic Counselor Training Program: A Productive Paradox

MaryAnna Domokos-Cheng Ham

A dilemma often exists for counselor educators who teach family therapy in a general counselor training program. This dilemma is a predicament involving a choice between integrating and not integrating family therapy courses into the general counseling curriculum. Whereas many counseling courses focus on interactive skill training (Egan, 1990; Ivey, 1988), family therapy courses, based on the interactional perspective of systems theory, highlight circular and reciprocal interactions as a way to understand family behaviors and dynamics.

As a counselor educator who teaches family therapy courses (and this dilemma produces a tension for me) I feel as if I am pulled from one perspective to another, as if I must choose between a focus of only systems theory and one of melded theoretical perspectives. This tension is not new to educators of family therapy, who experience an isolation of family therapy from the general thrust of academic training and who have found differences heightened between family therapy and other counseling approaches (Framo, 1979; Ganahl, Ferguson, & L'Abate, 1985a, 1985b; Lebow, 1987; Ribordy, 1987; Sugarman, 1984).

In order to understand and deal with this tension, I have begun to view this dilemma as a paradox that allows me to work productively with contradictory theoretical assumptions and educational tasks. The tension is actually a sign of a pervading paradox, a subjective phenomenon with contradictory differences that must be held together as a single entity (Dell, 1981a). As evidence of this paradox, I identify aspects of family therapy theory and approaches for teaching family therapy skills that incorporate three crucial components from the definition of paradox: dilemma, multiple truths, and coexistence of contradictions.

Three Conditions That Define a Paradox

The term *paradox* has been found in a variety of contexts: in philosophical and psychological theories as well as in prescriptions for individual, group, and family therapy treatment. The overly inclusive use of the term has led to misunderstandings and perhaps a carelessness in its definition (Seltzer, 1986). In order to focus this discussion, the definition of paradox provided by Watzlawick, Bavelas, and Jackson (1967) will be used: "Paradox may be defined as a contradiction that follows correct deduction from consistent premises" (p. 188).

Three conditions exist in a paradoxical situation. The first condition is that dilemmas are exposed (Dell, 1981a). Dilemma, as a dimension of paradox, arises from multiple choices where no choice is right or wrong. A second condition for paradox is that multiple truths allow many, often different, perspectives of a situation to coexist and be simultaneously meaningful (Goldberg, 1980). A third condition for paradox is the acknowledgement of the other two conditions, dilemma and multiple truths, and the acceptance of their coexisting contradictions. This third condition emphasizes the importance of considering all feedback, both positive and negative, so that interaction among contradictory choices can be maintained and even encouraged (Dell, 1981b). In my teaching of family therapy in an academic setting, I have recognized these three conditions of paradox as part of the process of integrating family therapy courses into a counseling program.

Dilemma

Family therapists become aware of this first condition of paradox as a resistance to including family therapy instruction in the general counseling curriculum. If family training is not a primary focus of an institution, then resistance to family therapy instruction is expressed by administrative decisions to have family therapy courses taught by other academic departments or training sites outside the institution (Framo, 1976; Henry, Sprenkle, & Sheehan, 1986; LaPerriere, 1979; Lebow, 1987; Pinsof, 1983; Ribordy, 1987; Sugarman, 1984). The Council for Accreditation of Counseling and Related Educational Programs (CACREP) has acknowledged the resistance to having family therapy curricula isolated from or external to general counseling courses. CACREP has taken action to integrate family therapy curricula into counseling programs. The Spring 1990 issue of the *CACREP Connection* reported that Marriage and Family Counseling Standards for accreditation of curricula had been adopted, in principle, by the council with the understanding that the subcommittee would revise and reformat them for compatibility with current standards for counselor training curricula. The final draft was submitted and approved by the council in October 1990.

Even as the resistance to integration continues, family therapy is increasingly included in university and college counseling programs (Gladding, Burggraf, & Fenell, 1987), and new dilemmas arise as more family therapy courses are included in academic settings. The following questions reflect a few of these dilemmas:

1. Should family therapy courses be integrated into a general counseling curriculum, or should an independent department of family counseling be created? How should integration be managed?
2. If family therapy courses are included as part of a general counseling curriculum, should the family therapy content be included as a unit in a course on counseling theory and practice, or should that content be offered in separate and discrete courses?
3. If family therapy courses are not integrated into the general curriculum, should students (a) enroll in didactic courses in other departments, such as sociology, child and family development, or anthropology, or (b) receive experiential family therapy training in family institute settings outside the academic institution?

These questions pose a dilemma by forcing choices. A counselor educator may conclude that a particular response to any one of these questions excludes an alternative response. There is no best choice.

For any counselor educator, dilemmas arise around decisions about course content and teaching methods. For the counselor educator who teaches family therapy courses, additional, specific dilemmas are created in developing teaching methods to convey theory, content, and family therapy skills while in the process of evaluating the students' competence.

Faculty teaching family therapy theory in a counseling program are faced with differences between the theoretical premises underpinning many counseling approaches and those for family therapy. Often, faculty teaching family therapy courses are caught in the dilemma of either highlighting differences or seeking similarities between counseling and family therapy theories.

Ganahl, Ferguson, and L'Abate (1985a) emphasize differences between the theoretical approaches of counseling and family therapy. The different theoretical premises affect implementation of three basic educational tasks: theory building, skill development, and evaluation. Family therapy faculty who are trained and experienced in counselor training courses may find they encounter problems in performing these tasks resulting from these different theoretical bases. Problems encountered include (a) relying on linear epistemology and overemphasizing the supposed inherent and relatively immutable characteristics of families or individuals, (b) ignoring the principle of summativity, the notion that any system as an integrated, coherent entity is not more than the composite of independent elements, and (c) emphasizing the evaluation and testing of individuals and de-emphasizing the effect of relationship between individuals (Ganahl et al., 1985a).

As a response to these differing theoretical premises, Liddle and Saba (1982) describe their "generic objective or meta-goal" as a teaching model for an entry-level graduate family therapy course. Their approach offers a means for encouraging students to shift to an interpersonal or systemic paradigm to increase students' capacity to conceptualize human problems and their solutions in interactional rather than individualistic ways. Through this approach, the content of family therapy courses can lead students from the atomistic, reductionary, linear world view to one of wholeness, patterns, and relationships (Liddle & Saba, 1982).

Often I experience the conflict expressed by Ganahl et al. (1985a) and teach family therapy from the theoretical premises of many counseling approaches. However, I also use the teaching model described by Liddle and Saba (1982) and recognize that counseling theory, used as an underpinning for acquiring skills in working with individuals in an interactive approach, incorporates principles of systems theory. Yet, I continue to sense the dilemma of being caught between theoretical choices when deciding how to teach family therapy. For example, the decision to present course material in a lecture format where I, as the teacher, am imparting specific and discrete information to students creates a dilemma. The implication in this traditional academic method of teaching is that the teacher will have the answer and will be the "expert," whereas in interactive family therapy there is no "expert" and no right answer.

Although counseling faculty use a broad variety of teaching methods, Ganahl et al. (1985b) indicate that a wide range of additional methods for teaching family therapy continue to be discussed, developed, and implemented. Such traditional teaching methods as written assignments and oral presentations are coupled with videotape observations (Falicov, Constantine, & Breunlin, 1981; Green & Saeger, 1982) as a way to teach systems theory concepts. Live observation and videotape have been suggested as useful vehicles for teaching intervention and executive skills (Boscolo & Cecchin, 1982; Garrigan & Bambrick, 1977). Several family therapy educators have suggested students' involvement through self-exploration of their own genograms and personal histories (Ferguson, 1979) and through articulation of their own personal theories of family functioning (Constantine, 1976).

Evaluation is a normal part of any teaching assignment that is generally required within a traditional academic counselor training program. In my own experience teaching family therapy, I find that evaluation poses the most difficult dilemma of all the educational tasks because of the implication that an answer is either "right" or "wrong." Often an academic institution requires the faculty to define educational objectives and to evaluate whether students have met these objectives. In addition, students often want their achievements to be specifically documented to show employers or other educational institutions. Even though the teaching of relational skills has been defined quantitatively (Carkhuff, 1969; Carkhuff & Truax, 1965; Gazda et al., 1973), family therapy educators may experience incongruence in a linear and discrete approach to evaluating nonlinear content and methods.

Multiple Truths

The choices made by a counselor educator teaching family therapy in response to the questions in the previous section contain the "multiple truths" that constitute an aspect of the paradox. Each choice is based on a particular set of assumptions, a particular perspective and world view. The philosophical framework of family therapy is constructed from an epistemology that invites multiple truths. This epistemology provides rules, or maps of assumptions, that govern the theoretical underpinning of course content and teaching methods (Auerswald, 1985). This epistemological approach of family therapy, taken from both modern physics and Batesonian evolution, reflects (a) a monistic universe, a condition of the coexistence of multiple choices, (b) no established causative relationships between events, (c) abstract ideas of the mind as part of the field of study, and (d) no certainty (Auerswald, 1985). This Batesonian approach, advocating the existence of multiple truths, is in juxtaposition to another set of assumptions adapted from theories of Newtonian physics and Darwinian evolution. Although counseling curricula include several conceptual perspectives, all of their perspectives derive from these more traditional assumptions. The assumptions from this perspective include (a) a dualistic universe, an either/or choice, (b) one event as causative in relation to the next event, (c) the field of study as separate from the studying mind, (d) the examination of entities as atomistic and the progression of events as linear, and (e) truth as absolute (Auerswald, 1985).

In all tasks of teaching family therapy, the counselor educator may need to acknowledge the reality of multiple truths in order to be consistent with the underlying epistemology of family therapy. The systemic perspective leads the family therapy educator to address the multiplicity of approaches to theory, methods of teaching, and evaluation as a coexistent condition rather than only as a dilemma.

However, there are occasions when the family therapy educator may feel compelled by a situation to choose one alternative over another and, thus, become stuck with the tension created by a forced choice, a dilemma. For example, when I use videotapes of family therapy sessions to demonstrate theories and methods of family therapy, students often begin to "analyze" the family interactions from a linear theoretical perspective by hypothesizing what the family's "problem" is and who has "caused" it. In response to students who want validation of their approach to observing families, I sometimes feel compelled to offer solutions to "problems" and to provide absolute criteria for decision making. I then feel that I have lost sight of a systems perspective and sense that I am conveying linear concepts to the students.

In contrast to being caught in a dilemma, I respond to students' linear statements and questions by inviting them to discuss their perceptions about the family with one another in small groups or the entire class. Students have expressed to me that this latter teaching method encourages an exchange of multiple perspectives, truths from all the participants, and their representative world views.

Coexistence of Contradictions

The final condition of paradox involves the coexistence of contradictory truths where multiple perspectives are valid even if they are contradictory. This condition of paradox requires living with competing demands and tension created by the pull of opposites. For counselor educators teaching family therapy, living with competing philosophical perspectives will mean tolerating the coexistence of different curricula. For both traditional counselor training and family therapy faculties, required teaching skills demand an empathic realization of all perspectives present in a situation (Seltzer, 1986). In fact, faculty who are able to place themselves in other perspectives may be better able to tolerate the coexistence of multiple truths.

Because there can be no single approach for helping and understanding human beings (Watzlawick, Bavelas, & Jackson, 1967), counseling faculty, including family therapy faculty, must entertain the belief that choice is an "illusion" (Weakland & Jackson, 1958), a situation where neither choice is "right" or "wrong." Even though traditional counselor training and family therapy curricula have sets of theoretical assumptions and a logical development of concepts that lead to solutions, neither is totally correct or incorrect. Each has consistent logical assumptions, and yet the assumptions for one are incompatible with the other.

In my own teaching experience I have found that students become confused, tense, and sometimes angry when I "claim" one set of assumptions and then behave with another. For example, I often say to students that I believe they have the skills to know the answers to questions I pose and that I will gladly accept multiple answers if they will tell me how they arrived at their answers. Yet, when I hear their logic for arriving at an answer, I question the components they use in developing their argument and suggest they arrive at a solution in another way. The students are then confused because they have believed my directive, that I will accept their answer if they can explain it, but then I have suggested that one solution may be better than another rather than that all solutions have equal importance.

The coexistence of contradictory ways of thinking is essential for family therapy curricula to reside within a traditional counselor training program. Moreover, the counselor educator who teaches family therapy must be able to tolerate the dilemmas inherent when several theoretical frameworks reside together in one overall counseling program. The faculties of both traditional counselor training and family therapy find they are "living a paradox," a contradiction where no real choices exist, because both are correct.

Conclusion

From my own experience of teaching family therapy in a counselor education program, I offer the following suggestions for "living with paradox" and with the coexistence of contradictory philosophical assumptions and educational tasks:

1. Acknowledge the *differences* as well as the *similarities* between the basic philosophical assumptions and the curricular realities of the two approaches.
2. Acknowledge the *context* of course content and educational tasks—that is, the meaning each curriculum approach gives to and assumes for the course content and teaching methods (Tomm, 1984).

Both these suggestions require interaction among all faculty members, which leads to collaborative thinking. This approach describes, rather than criticizes, events and enlarges, rather than narrows, the overall perspectives of all faculty. In particular, differences and similarities between theoretical, epistemological premises can be explored. For example, a discussion with students about similarities and differences between the use of empathic understanding in an individual counseling process and its use in family therapy can highlight how the concept of empathy alters in meaning when context changes.

Many students come to family therapy courses with some skepticism about an interactional approach to counseling after completing several introductory counseling courses. These initial counseling courses often focus on a linear approach to understanding human behavior—in particular, the unitary characteristics within an individual, not the interactive characteristics of an individual within a group or family. However, students' skepticism about a nonlinear approach to counseling can be addressed through multidimensional classroom experiences in these introductory counseling courses. For example, students who participate in role play and engage in a self-analysis of their role play recorded on videotape often report that such a multidimensional experience encourages them to view themselves and their experience from many perspectives. In this case, one teaching method elucidates both linear and nonlinear theory.

Even evaluation of objectives can be approached from different perspectives. For example, an evaluation exercise can be given to students at the beginning of a course sequence, at the middle, and at the end.

Although evaluation may not be defined as collaborative, in this evaluation of the process over time, the students can provide feedback to the teacher. The teacher can then adjust course content in relation to the student responses. In this approach both student and teacher are evaluating each other and themselves as the person who learns and the person who teaches. Both discover specific information where misunderstanding may have occurred in their learning and teaching. Yet, each explores in an open-ended manner where one is capable of expanding information the other has offered.

Family therapy faculty who teach in counseling programs continue to be confronted with a dilemma. This dilemma evolves from an awareness by family therapy faculty of the differences and contradictions between the theoretical foundations of many counseling courses and family therapy. Once the family therapy faculty recognize that the multiple truths of different and contradictory theories can coexist, they engage in a paradoxical process. This process, a productive paradox, can lead to a creative and constructive coexistence for family therapy faculty to teach and reside within an academic counseling program.

References

Auerswald, E. H. (1985). Thinking about thinking in family therapy. *Family Process, 24*, 1–2.

Boscolo, L., & Cecchin, G. (1982). Training in a systemic therapy at the Milan Center. In R. Whiffen & J. Byng-Hall (Eds.), *Family therapy supervision: Recent developments in practice*. London: Academic Press.

Carkhuff, R. R. (1969). *Helping and human relations: A primer for lay and professional helpers*. (Vol. 1: Selection and training). New York: Holt, Rinehart & Winston.

Carkhuff, R. R., & Truax, C. (1965). Training in counseling and psychotherapy: An evaluation of an integrated didactic and experiential approach. *Journal of Counseling Psychology, 29*, 333–336.

Constantine, L. (1976). Designed experience: A multiple, goal directed training program in family therapy. *Family Process, 15*, 373–396.

Dell, P. F. (1981a). Paradox redux. *Journal of Marital and Family Therapy, 7*, 127–134.

Dell, P. F. (1981b). Some irreverent thoughts on paradox. *Family Process, 20*, 37–51.

Egan, G. (1990). *The skilled helper: A systematic approach to effective helping* (4th ed.). Pacific Grove, CA: Brooks/Cole.

Falicov, C., Constantine, J., & Breunlin, D. (1981). Teaching family therapy: A program based on learning objectives. *Journal of Marital and Family Therapy, 7*, 497–506.

Ferguson, L. R. (1979). The family life cycle: Orientation for interdisciplinary training. *Professional Psychology, 10*, 863–867.

Framo, J. L. (1976). Chronicle of a struggle to establish a family unit within a community mental health center. In P. J. Guerin (Ed.), *Family therapy: Theory and practice* (pp. 23-39). New York: Gardner.

Framo J. L. (1979). A personal viewpoint on training in marital and family therapy. *Professional Psychology, 10*, 868–875.

Ganahl, G. F., Ferguson, L. R., & L'Abate, L. (1985a). Training in family psychology. In L. L'Abate (Ed.), *The handbook of family psychology and therapy* (Vol. 2, pp. 1248–1280). Homewood, IL: Dorsey.

Ganahl, G. F., Ferguson, L. R., & L'Abate, L. (1985b). Training in family therapy. In L. L'Abate (Ed.), *The handbook of family psychology and therapy* (Vol 2, pp. 1281–1317). Homewood, IL: Dorsey.

Garrigan, J., & Bambrick, A. (1977). Introducing novice therapists to "go-between" techniques of family therapy. *Family Process, 16*, 237–246.

Gazda, G. M., Asbury, F. R., Balzer, F. S., Childers, W. C., Deselle, R. E., & Walters, R. P. (1973). *Human relations development: A manual for educators*. Newton, MA: Allyn & Bacon.

Gladding, S. T., Burggraf, M., & Fenell, D. L. (1987). Marriage and family counseling in counselor education: National trends and implications. *Journal of Counseling and Development, 66*, 90–92.

Goldberg, C. (1980). The utilization and limitations of paradoxical intervention in group psychotherapy. *International Journal of Group Psychotherapy, 30*, 287–297.

Green, R. J., & Saeger, K. E. (1982). Learning to "think systems": Five writing assignments. *Journal of Marital and Family Therapy, 8*, 285–294.

Henry, P., Sprenkle, D., & Sheehan, R. (1986). Family therapy training: Student and faculty perceptions. *Journal of Marital and Family Therapy, 12*, 249–258.

Ivey, A. (1988). *Intentional interviewing and counseling* (2nd ed.). Pacific Grove, CA: Brooks/Cole.

La Perriere, K. (1979). Toward the training of broad-range family therapists. *Professional Psychology, 10*, 880–883.

Lebow, J. F. (1987). Training psychologists in family therapy in family institute settings. *Journal of Family Psychology, 1*, 219–231.

Liddle, H. A., & Saba, G. W. (1982). Teaching family therapy at the introductory level: A conceptual model emphasizing a pattern which connects training and therapy. *Journal of Marital and Family Therapy, 8*, 63–73.

Pinsof, W. M. (1983). Integrative problem-centered therapy: Toward the synthesis of family and individual psychotherapies. *Journal of Marital and Family Therapy, 9*, 19–35.

Ribordy, D. L. (1987). Training family therapists within an academic setting. *Journal of Family Psychology, 1*, 204–218.

Seltzer, L. F. (1986). *Paradoxical strategies in psychotherapy: A comprehensive overview and guidebook*. New York: Wiley.

Sugarman, S. (1984). Integrating family therapy training into psychiatry residency programs: Policy and alternatives. *Family Process, 23*, 23–32.

Tomm, K. (1984, March). *Two lines of enquiry which foster change: Circular and reflexive questioning*. Lecture at a conference organized by the Family Institute of Cambridge at Harvard University.

Watzlawick, P., Bavelas, J. B., & Jackson, D. D. (1967). *Pragmatics of human communication: A study of interactional patterns, pathologies, and paradoxes*. New York: Norton.

Weakland, J. H., & Jackson, D. D. (1958). Patient and therapist observations on the circumstances of a schizophrenic episode. *Archives of Neurology and Psychiatry, 79*, 554–574.

This article was originally published in *Journal of Mental Health Counseling*, Vol. 13, 1991, pp. 211–220. Reprint permission granted by Sage Publications.

Adding a Family Counseling Training Component to a Community Agency Counseling Master's Degree

Robert L. Sheverbush
Donald E. Ward

Counselor education programs increasingly face strong challenges both to maintain standardized generic counseling curricula and training methods and to incorporate new, sophisticated specialty knowledge and skill requirements necessary for counselors in the field. The demands upon counselor educators to retrain and extend their skills in new areas in order to integrate new ideas into their training programs may be especially difficult for small to medium-sized programs in regional institutions.

The Department of Psychology and Counseling at Pittsburg State University, Kansas, created an innovative program for family counseling training to expand curriculum offerings and to provide professional development for counselor educators and professional counselors. There were several innovative features of the program with regard to counselor education, professional development of counselor education faculty and area mental health professionals, and improvement of departmental relations both within and outside the university that may be helpful to others planning to develop similar or related programs.

Conceptualization of the New Program Component

A community agency counseling major was added to the traditional school counseling training program at Pittsburg State in the 1970s. It has recently been revised to meet CACREP standards. The need for training in at least one specialty area was identified as a necessary component of a high quality contemporary community agency counseling training program.

As we surveyed our own students, graduates, their employers, and the literature, it became apparent that the area of family counseling is perhaps the most sought-after specialty in the field. In fact, in one survey mental health agency administrators most often identified family interventions as a preferred skill (Cook, Berman, Genco, Pepka, & Shrider, 1986). Fifty-seven percent of the counselor education department chairpersons responding to a national survey indicated that only one or two faculty members taught marriage and family courses, and only 30% of all these teaching courses in this area held AAMFT Clinical Membership or approved Supervisor status (Gladding, Burggraf, & Fenell, 1987). Hollis and Wantz (1986) report that marriage and family counseling courses were added more frequently to counseling program curricula than any other type of courses in 1980, 1983, and in 1984-1987. We therefore decided that family counseling was the specialty area we wanted to develop.

Several issues became apparent as we worked to conceptualize and plan the family counseling specialty component. One of these concerns the emergence of family counseling as a discipline. Although our counseling faculty had engaged in family counseling in the past, most of our work was either an extension of our individual and group counseling training or based upon experience and continuing education, rather than upon formal training in family systems. In addition, many professional counselors and other mental health workers in area agencies and schools engaged in or wanted to increase their use of family counseling but most considered themselves only minimally trained and were eager to acquire additional training in family work.

We chose to view family counseling as a specialty area that could be included within a traditional counselor training program, rather than using the ASMFT model of training family therapists as a distinct program (Fenell & Hovestadt, 1986). Since there was little likelihood of the department gaining an additional faculty position with a family counseling specialization at the time, we decided to explore the possibility of retraining existing faculty members in family counseling. We also decided to include counselors and mental health workers, many of whom have served as practicum and internship site supervisors, from area agencies and schools with us in a collegial, systematic professional development program.

Program Planning and Organization

It was evident that a program could not be developed with the limited numbers and resources of the department faculty. Therefore, from its planning and inception stages, the project has itself had a larger systemic perspective. One external system that was contacted and included was the Family Institute of Kansas City as the primary retraining agency. The first author was awarded sabbatical leave during the spring semester of 1985, during which he laid the groundwork for the program and attended training sessions at the Family Institute.

Securing funding was a crucial issue in the planning and organization stage. Departmental alumni were solicited, and a small grant was obtained from the university foundation for the remodeling of a large counseling laboratory room to accommodate videotaping, live supervision, and a treatment team approach to working with families and training/retraining family counselors and to pay the costs of contracting with the Family Institute. Professional counselors from agencies and schools in the area constituted the other major component of the system and joined university faculty members in a cooperative learning team.

The First Year

A two-course sequence was designed to accommodate the varying knowledge and experience levels of the participants, both sequences meeting on Monday evening. Approximately 60 students enrolled in the first course, covering the theory of family counseling from a systems perspective. This course continued for the entire academic year, met the needs of current graduate students desiring an introduction to family counseling, and was a corequisite for those concurrently enrolled in the Practicum in Family Counseling.

The Practicum in Family Counseling was an advanced supervised experience for counselor educators and counseling and mental health professionals. Taught and supervised by AAMFT-approved supervisors from the Family Institute, the 20 class members included half of the 10 regular faculty members in the Department of Psychology and Counseling, two university deans, both of whom had counseling and/or behavioral sciences backgrounds, and 13 professionals from community mental health centers, school psychology cooperatives, a hospital chaplain's office, private practice, a residential youth center, and so forth. The class time was devoted to demonstrations, case staffings, and to live supervision of families.

During most 3-hour weekly class meetings, two families were seen by co-counselor class members. A major feature of the family counseling sessions conducted during class time was the use of live supervision with the entire class serving as a consultation treatment team. The class and supervisors viewed the family counseling interview through a one-way mirror and on a video monitor. Recommendations for interventions from the team were called in during the session using a telephone system. A break was scheduled approximately two-thirds of the way through the family counseling interview, during which the co-counselors went to a different room to consult with the supervision-treatment team and to develop recommendations for end-of-session homework interventions.

The Second Year

By the beginning of the 1986-87 academic year, the five regular departmental faculty involved in family counseling training had completed the academic and supervised family counseling practice (including previous years of experience) requirements for AAMFT clinical membership, and both authors had been granted clinical status. During the second year of the training program, a new group of 25 students began the two-semester sequence in the theories course. The first author assumed responsibility for teaching the course and expanded the formal course requirements. Faculty members who had completed the package of first-year training experiences were also able to assume supervision responsibility for the family counseling practicum during the second year. We again contracted with the Family Institute of Kansas City, although the supervision at this point was conducted in half-day and all-day sessions at the Family Institute and was directed at overseeing our supervision of students in our training program. Half of the original 20 practicum class members continued their involvement to gain more hours of supervised experience toward AAMFT clinical membership. Ten new people became involved. Since the special funding commitments had lapsed, participants paid the equivalent of instate tuition for the training experience, which was then used to pay the Family Institute of Kansas City directly for the supervision.

The Third Year

During the 1987-1988 academic year, the family counseling theories and practicum courses were integrated into the regular graduate program curricula. Since the family counseling courses are taught and supervised by those of our own faculty who are now AAMFT Approved Supervisors, all work completed by participants in the program will count toward their own AAMFT certification requirements.

Conclusion

As with other aspects of the training model, the team teaching and supervision approach, with responsibility shared by five faculty members, was both challenging and very rewarding. At several points there were hierarchical issues to be worked through in relation to those who had been fellow students the first year now serving as supervisors of the treatment team members during the second year. However, the general team approach and the open consultative communication model served to establish an excellent atmosphere in which those issues could be addressed and productively resolved. In fact, the quality of both the family counseling and the training experience improved due to the year of experience working with family systems approaches and the team supervision and treatment model.

Our relationships with area agencies have improved. By having joined our family counseling training program, many counselors in practice are both highly qualified and receptive to making and accepting referrals and to providing field supervision of our practicum and internship students. Our image in the community and university has also been enhanced, as evidenced by the allocation of additional resources in both settings. At least seven professionals from the first two years' practicum have been granted AAMFT clinical status themselves. Several recent graduates of our program with the family specialization have been sought after, and practicums created in area agencies specifically to emphasize their family counseling skills.

By initiating a family counseling training component in our master's program, we have been able to achieve several important goals. In the first, a strong family counseling specialty component, one of the most sought-after training specialties, is now solidly in place and available to our own students from nationally accredited faculty supervisors. In addition, a major professional development effort for half of our department faculty involving hundreds of hours of high-quality collegial learning experiences has resulted in broadening and extending our skills, in stimulating and revitalizing us professionally, and in two levels of AAMFT credentialing. The innovative elements of the family systems training model stimulated us to approach counselor education and supervision from a more sophisticated and innovative perspective, challenging us to integrate new skills, theoretical assumptions, and supervision ideas into our professional styles.

References

Cook, E. P., Berman, E., Genco, K., Repka, F., & Shrider, J. (1986). Essential characteristics of master's level counselors: Perceptions of agency administrators. *Counselor Education and Supervision, 26*, 146–152.

Fenell, D. L., & Hovestadt, A. J. (1986). Family therapy as a profession or professional specialty: Implications for training. *Journal of Psychotherapy and the Family, 2*, 25–40.

Gladding, S. T., Burggraf, M., & Fenell, D. L. (1987). Marriage and family counseling in counselor education: National trends and implications. *Journal of Counseling and Development, 66*, 90–92.

Hollis, J. W., & Wantz, R. A. (1986). *Counselor preparation 1986-89: Programs, personnel, trends*. Muncie, IN: Accelerated Development.

Chapter 5

Issues and Topics in Family Therapy

A number of diverse issues currently face individuals practicing marriage and family counseling and therapy. Many concerns are unique to the field as they reflect societal issues today. Some of the standard issues addressed include: ethics in marriage and family therapy, research, supervision, and curriculum standards. Specific issues also covered include: feminism and family therapy, counseling ethnic minorities, remarriage, treating marital violence, the AIDS family, critiquing family systems, and examining the use of paradoxical techniques.

Ethical considerations have taken on great relevance in the field since marriage and family therapy has ethical concerns that differ from individual therapy. One of the most basic concerns having both ethical and legal implications is the question of "Who is the client?" Systems theory indicates that the family system is the client and this philosophy colors how the therapist handles issues such as secrets, custody proceedings, and divorce.

The first two articles, one by Smith, and the other by Wendorf and Wendorf, address these issues. Another ethical concern discussed by Sexton is the use of paradoxical intervention in therapy. Although an accepted technique in strategic family therapy, it must be used with discretion and only after appropriate training in order to avoid ethical and legal problems.

The ever-changing structure of today's families has been previously discussed in Chapter 1. However, London and Devore bring to our attention the unique understanding necessary in order to work with ethnic minority families. Therapy is now available to greater numbers of the population and families who are culturally different from the therapist are much more likely to be seen now than in the past. It is imperative that training programs incorporate multicultural counseling into their curriculum.

As individuals, families, and society struggle to redefine themselves, issues of gender role confusion, domestic violence, AIDS families, and remarriage myths must be dealt with. Dramatic shifts have occurred within the past 50 years in what is expected of males and females. It appears, however, that many of the traditional beliefs about gender role identity still exist. Enns' article on the feminist perspective in family therapy examines this area. She believes that traditional family therapy theories ignore the inequality in power that continues to exist in families as well as society. Enns believes that to ignore this inequity and to counsel the family "as if" power is equal is dangerous. She offers an alternative to "examine and critique" sex roles and "brainstorm" with clients' methods of achieving equality. Enns also encourages therapists to become involved in the bigger system of society in order to continue to make changes.

Important issues, relapse prevention and treatment adherence, often ignored in marital therapy are addressed by Carlson, Sperry, and Ward Howell. The authors of this article state clearly their belief that "counselors have front-loaded the helping processes." They raise the issue of counselors placing almost all of their resources with identification, diagnosis, and remediation, rather than with treatment adherence and relapse prevention.

Ethical Issues in Marital and Family Therapy: Who is the Client?

Robert L. Smith

In view of "the increasing numbers of psychotherapists engaging in marital and family therapy, there is a need for ethical guidelines when therapy is considered with more than one family member" (Margolin, 1982). This statement made in the early 80s, published in the *American Psychologist*, is viewed by the author as being of even greater significance in the 1990s. Ethical standards advocated by professional organizations seem to still focus on relationships existing between one therapist and one client. Even the standards promulgated by AAMFT specifically for marriage and family therapists leave many questions and concerns unaddressed, creating confusion and a void concerning suggested ethical principles and guidelines when working with couples and families. This article addresses some of the current ethical issues in marital and family therapy and presents suggestions for clarification. It is intended that issues examined and suggestions made will assist psychologists and therapists who face ethical dilemmas frequently when working with multiple clients in marital and family systems.

A major ethical concern discussed by Margolin involves "who is the client" when working with couples and families. The question centers upon whether the therapist's allegiance is to the family system, identified patient, individuals who initiate therapy, or alternately between specific individuals during the course of therapy. This dilemma is further complicated when the therapist moves from individual to family therapy and vice versa. A clear and articulated statement of "who is the client" can help clear the way for dealing with many ethical dilemmas in marital and family therapy.

The concern of "who is the client" surfaces frequently both during and after therapy. For example, who holds the right to waive privileged communication after a couple terminates therapy? Is it an individual or do both partners need to agree? This issue becomes very real when child custody cases are involved.

Hare-Mustin (1980) stated that family therapy may be dangerous for your health. This is not an over exaggeration when considering the dynamics of marital and family therapy and subsequent risks for individuals in the family system. Unfortunately, too often one family member's needs are satisfactorily addressed while another member may view therapy as not proceeding according to personal expectation or need. Occurrences as this often exist even when the therapist clearly articulates that the family system is the client.

Further evidence of the importance of making a determination of "who is the client" involves the handling of secrets both prior to and during treatment. For example, how are phone conversations, written letters and other means of personal communication handled by the therapist who is seeing the entire family? Are secrets kept from the family during treatment and who makes this decision?

Interestingly enough, survey research (Green & Hansen, 1989) explored reactions of family therapists to ethical dilemmas similar to those discussed in this article. Although a high rate of consensus was obtained regarding therapists response to several of the ethical issues, some confusion still existed. For example, when presented with a dilemma involving confidentiality and the sharing of family secrets mixed responses were obtained ranging from announcing that no secrets will be tolerated during therapy to leaving the final decision to the individual who shared the secret. A second dilemma involving privileged communication also obtained a wide range of responses. Although the greatest number of respondents would refuse testimony unless all family members agreed to waive privileges, an interestingly large number of practicing family therapists stated they would just refuse to testify, or would ask the children what they wanted.

Findings as those by Green and Hansen (1989) support the need for greater attention to ethical issues in marital and family therapy. This includes (1) addressing ethical issues and legal concerns in a clearer and broader manner through professional codes of ethics, (2) emphasizing ethical issues and concerns at state, regional and national meetings through seminars and roundtable discussions, and (3) providing clearer examples of informed consent statements when working with couples and families. In addition, research needs to be conducted on ethical, legal and professional issues in family therapy. Piercy and Sprenkle (1986) state that such a lack of research stems from the relatively early stage of that field. The author believes it is now time for action. We owe this much to ourselves, the profession, and more importantly, to the couples and families involved in treatment.

References

Green, S. L., & Hanson, J. C. (1989). Ethical dilemmas faced by family therapists. *Journal of Marital and Family Therapy, 15*(2), 139–158.

Hare-Mustin, R. T. (1980). Family therapy may be dangerous for your health. *Professional Psychology, 11*, 935–938.

Margolin, G. (1982). Ethical and legal considerations in marital and family therapy. *American Psychologist, 37*, 788–801.

Piercy, F. P., & Sprenkle, D. H. (1986). Ethical, legal and professional issues. In F. P. Piercy & D. H. Sprenkle, *Family Therapy Sourcebook.* New York: Guilford Press.

This article was originally published in *The Family Psychologist,* Vol. 7, 1991, p. 16. Reprint permission granted by the Editor.

A Systemic View of Family Therapy Ethics

Donald J. Wendorf
Robert J. Wendorf

The relatively young field of family therapy can be proud that part of its evolution as a profession has included a willingness to examine its own ethical conduct. It seems reasonable to assume that our understanding of the ethics of family therapy should expand as our knowledge of theory and techniques expands. However, we do not find that the area of ethics has kept abreast of the rest of the field in its appreciation for and utilization of systems principles as a conceptual base. Therefore, we will offer a brief critical review of the literature on family therapy ethics to aid in developing our own ethical principles, using more systemic thinking. We will examine ways in which the field has maintained a limited, nonsystemic viewpoint with regard to problems, the family, the therapy system, and the societal context of therapy. We will discuss these principles as applied to three practical, ethical questions of family secrets, therapist deceptiveness, and therapist advocacy of (feminist) values.

During the 1960s, several authors raised ethical concerns related to family therapy, one example being Hurvitz's (1967) paper on "Marital Problems Following Psychotherapy with One Spouse." Grosser and Paul (1964) presented an early but comprehensive treatment of "Ethical Issues in Family Group Therapy," addressing several questions still quite relevant to today's practice. They dealt with the potentially harmful disclosure of extremely negative affect within the family, the possible undermining of authority as parental failures are brought out in therapy, and the disclosure of personal sexual data. Their discussion of secrets wrestled with the problems of individual versus family confidentiality and reflected the field's uncertainty as to who is the patient, whether concurrent individual treatment is a necessary part of "conjoint patient-family treatment," and whether symptoms represent intrapsychic or family dysfunctions. By today's standards this pioneering effort was not systemically oriented, but it was certainly challenging and called attention to the complexity of ethical issues deriving from the new therapies.

A major contributor to the field of family therapy ethics was Jay Haley (1976) who dealt with many thorny areas of the therapist-patient relationship. Haley explored the ethics of the "benevolent lie" and the effect on the patient of therapist manipulativeness, paradoxical truths, concealing versus forcing insight, the goals of therapists versus client, the power differential inherent in therapy, the need to take and change sides, and the relativity of what is "reality." Haley built a strong case for the ethical legitimacy of strategically saying things for the benevolent effect they can have, rather than for a literal, nonsystemic, or simplistic view of what is true. He argued further that the therapist should take a great deal of responsibility for the process and outcome of therapy.

Although not an article centering on ethics, Whitaker and Miller's (1969) discussion of divorce as a possible outcome of treating only one partner in a troubled marriage certainly raised ethical concerns. The question of whom it is ethical to treat, given an individual presentation for treatment, has cropped up again and again (Halleck, 1971; Hurvitz, 1967) as part of that larger question of who is the patient in family therapy. Hare-Mustin (1980) objected to the routine involvement by therapists of the entire family despite the actuality that some members have successfully disengaged from an enmeshed family. Also, she complained that children's needs and goals may be subordinated to those of the more powerful adults in therapy, that therapists may take sides, and that involving the whole family complicates confidentiality problems. These are certainly critical questions. The article suggested to Wendorf (1984), however, that Hare-Mustin made several questionable assumptions: that family therapy is a unitary modality characterized by forcing all members to sit in the same room, that total disengagement from an enmeshed system is either possible or desirable, that children should hold the same power and rights as adults in a successful family hierarchy (or lack thereof), and that deterioration rates increase with an increase in the number of members attending (some data suggest the opposite, as cited by Gurman and Kniskern [1981]).

A number of prominent theorists have presented persuasive clinical evidence that family problems must be understood as involving two or even three generations (Boszormenyi-Nagy & Ulrich, 1981; Framo, 1981). Although it has not been clearly argued that it is unethical to consider less than several generations, Boszormenyi-Nagy and Ulrich (1981) do maintain that "the future life prospects of young and even yet unborn children represent the highest ethical priority" (p. 182) for their parents in therapy.

Hare-Mustin coauthored another classic paper in the ethics literature with Paulette Hines (Hines & Hare-Mustin, 1978). These authors concentrated on three areas: the goal of maximizing the growth of the entire family, confidentiality, and the intrusion of the therapist's values on the therapeutic work. They questioned when and to whom a therapist may reveal secrets told to the therapist in the course of treatment. They also made the excellent points that therapist's values influence the therapy in terms of assessment, goals, and intervention strategies and that therapists must be responsible for clarifying their values for themselves and their patients. However, we will argue later that these authors used a limiting, nonsystemic view of secrets and that Hare-Mustin (1978) appears to have violated her own ethical principle in advocacy of her feminist values as part of family therapy.

One of the most comprehensive treatments of family therapy ethics was offered by Margolin (1982), who dealt with therapist responsibility, confidentiality, patient privilege, informed consent and the right to refuse treatment, therapist values, sex roles, and training and supervision. She, too, however, presented a rather interpersonal, behavioral-social learning conceptualization of family therapy that limited this approach to simple communications training and cognitive or attitudinal reorientation. She, too, seemed to treat family therapy as merely a treatment "modality" that differs from more traditional approaches only in including more than one family member in the room. She remained on a level of concrete, overt, dyadic interactions. Thus, she did not appear to view symptoms as the behaviors of a system per se operating to maintain itself (homeostatic function), to solve current problems, and to develop new patterns of organization to accommodate to new situations (evolutionary function). We believe this hampered her analysis of the ethical issues raised.

For example, Margolin took the often-voiced position that the confidentiality issue is one of whether to reveal "secrets" told in individual sessions to the rest of the family, whether to refuse to let anything be told in confidence, and whether this would prevent the therapist from gaining needed information. She seemed to assume that "secrets" belong only within the mind of one person, acting as an isolated individual rather than also viewing secret-telling as part of a system's functioning as a whole. She further assumed that secrets can be known by the therapist only on a factual, literal level, ignoring possible metaphorical or transactional levels of meaning. Thus, she was oriented toward handling secrets on a content level rather than dealing with the dysfunctional family processes they reflect. This led to her unclear recommendations to the therapist to "(1) determine a policy that is compatible with his or her method of conducting therapy and, (2) convey that policy to the family" (p. 793). She put herself in the awkward position of deciding what to do about secrets based only on uncertain predictions of the outcome of disclosing or not. She even wound up talking about child advocacy and keeping information obtained in individual child sessions from the parents. Within this linear viewpoint, the choice for the therapist is: (a) not to offer confidentiality but to lose information, or (b) to promise to maintain confidentiality but be rendered impotent to act on the information gained. We will argue later that a more systemic view escapes this dilemma and allows secrets to be dealt with on a process level.

Similarly, Margolin's approach to the issues of therapist deception and manipulativeness did not come to grips with the difficulty of defining "truth" in light of the self-recursive nature of circular patterns of causality. How does one provide opportunity for informed consent when something becomes "more real" or "different" by virtue of the therapist saying it in the context of the therapeutic relationship? For example, when a probation officer advises his probationer not to consider him totally trustworthy because of his enforcement role, he probably makes himself *more* trustworthy to the probationer. When the probationer discloses a confidence, has the probation officer then secured informed participation in counseling, or has he manipulated his client by making a remark that becomes less true by virtue of its context? As most authors have done, Margolin also looked in only one linear direction at the effect of therapist interventions: the level of therapist to client. What about the effect of such interventions on the therapist? Is our probation officer turning himself into a "con artist" or becoming a better counselor for his client?

A commendable effort to address the unmet needs in the ethics literature was provided by a book edited by Luciano L'Abate (1982), which included several chapters devoted to ethics and values. O'Shea and Jessee (1982) examined ethical problems arising from the clash between systems thinking with its "reciprocal determinism," individually oriented theories of pathology and therapy, and social institutions and the cultural standards espousing individualism. For example, they discussed refusing treatment (from Napier and Whitaker) unless everyone comes; confidentiality, especially outside the nuclear family; paradox and presenting "factually skewed" information; and therapist-family-societal conflicts such as feminist values. However, they took few direct stands on the issues beyond positions previously stated by others and none that considered all levels of the therapy system.

Another relevant chapter in L'Abate's volume, that of Taggart (1982), presented the thesis that "the values discussion among family therapists has suffered because of a reluctance to bring values under the same systems epistemology as informs other aspects of their work" (p. 25). Taggart examined the difficulties of formulating a systems ethics based on the multilevel aspect of systems; a process rather than a structural view of reality; assumptions of order through fluctuation rather than homeostasis and adaptation; and an acceptance of continuous evolution rather than the traditional belief in unchanging absolutes, institutions, and "unmoved movers." This excellent presentation, unfortunately, did not apply these insights to answering ethical questions of everyday clinical work, admittedly an extremely difficult task, which we, too, can only begin here.

In her book on training in systems thinking, Duhl (1983) offered the notions that the values inherent in therapy not only affect the client but also affect the therapist trainee, her role, relationship, standards, and behaviors. She also noted in passing that the values of society influence therapy theorists who, in turn, help shape the way our society views people. She cited popularly held Freudian sexual views as an example of this circular process but did not state any clear ethical principles implied by this analysis.

One therapy approach, that of Boszormenyi-Nagy's "Contextual Family Therapy" (Boszormenyi-Nagy & Ulrich, 1981) has ethical principles as the very core of its precepts. This approach is built around the concept of "relational ethics," which involves "equitability": "that everyone is entitled to have his or her welfare interests considered in a way that is fair from a multilateral perspective" (p. 160). Relational ethics is taken to be "a fundamental dynamic force, holding family and societal relationships together through mutuality and trustworthiness of relationship" (p. 160). This concept forms the basis for therapist actions that aim at helping each individual take responsibility for balancing the family's three-generational fairness "ledger" by considering each person's welfare.

Although ethics are indeed the base of this influential therapy school, it should be recognized that it is an ethical theory of human relationships of our clients, but not an ethics of doing family therapy. Two interesting exceptions to this statement, however, are that one "evidence of its power" (i.e., the efficacy of this therapeutic approach) is its "effects in the lives of contextual therapists" (p. 185) and that the equitability principle is a "safeguard against the intrusion of the values of the therapist" (p. 160). These statements imply a clear awareness of a system of mutual influences affecting both client and therapist.

In summary, we see the previous literature on family therapy ethics as having identified and examined a number of key issues that directly affect the day-to-day practice of therapists. This work needs to be updated, however, to keep abreast of our evolving understanding of systems concepts and their implications. We will begin this process by stating our own ethical base, one that we believe to be more systemic than that of previous orientations: We believe that the therapist's task is to help people become more competent in solving their problems as individuals and as systems. This problem-solving should always include the presenting problem but should also consider the problem in its broader patterns, or isomorphic transactions. In addition, this problem-solving should maintain a regard for the short- and long-term needs, growth, and welfare of the other individuals and subsystems that are involved in this mutually recursive system of influence. To be considered are the effects of actions both on and by the therapists and on and by the society in the system of family-therapist-society that forms the context in which family therapy occurs. This requires broad, systemic thinking. (At times, other levels or sublevels, in addition to family-therapist-society, may need to be included here, such as with a trainee or training group or with involvement of particular groups such as schools, social agencies, businesses, etc. In addition, the therapist must always be attuned to the possibility of dysfunction arising at the level of the biological substratum.)

It is our contention that in several ways the family therapy field has not approached ethical questions with a systemic viewpoint.

1. Family therapists view particular *problems* nonsystemically (Wendorf & Wendorf, 1981). Many approaches such as those of Haley (1976), the MRI brief therapists (Wendorf, 1981), most behaviorists (e.g., Margolin, 1982), and others tend to see the symptomatic behavior interactions themselves as the problem *in*

toto. They fail to examine adequately either the broader context of other family members' behaviors beyond a dyadic or triadic level, the same pattern of behaviors in other content areas, or the behaviors of the therapist. Although this does not appear to limit their immediate therapeutic effectiveness in dealing with the identified problem, it does limit their analyses of ethical issues, as we discuss below, e.g., in the use of isomorphic transactions to help with the problem of secrets.

2. Family therapists view the *family* nonsystemically by neglecting to consider the extended family and other generations. They may forget the individuals involved in a system, forget that the family is an entity in itself and not simply a collection of individuals, or forget that each family is unique within the broader societal context. These errors can lead to ethical problems, as we discuss below, e.g., when secret-telling behaviors are seen as belonging only to individuals or when therapists' values about society override the importance of helping a particular family.
3. Family therapists have a limited view of the *therapy system* as they usually ignore the recursive effects of therapy on the therapist. We discuss this in connection with the issue of therapist deceptiveness and therapist advocacy of values in therapy.
4. Family therapists do not think systemically about the *therapy context*. They tend to forget that society affects the family and therapist and that therapists and the practice of therapy affect the society. This is one of the issues in our section on therapists' values.

In contrast to these nonsystemic views, we understand "systemic" thinking as a view of human persons that recognizes not only their biological and intrapsychic individuality but also the inherent inclusion of their unique "personalities" in larger collections of individuals who are all involved in regular patterns of reciprocal influence. These persons and relationships constitute a system that can be seen to function as an entity in itself. Behaviors by any individual or group are affected by and, in turn, affect the others, so that behaviors are seen as occurring in an interpersonal and transactional context, not as isolated acts.

As examples of the application of our principles and propositions, we would like to re-examine the questions of family secrets, therapist deceptiveness, and therapist advocacy of their (feminist) values.

Family Secrets

Our position is that therapists should openly state a policy of keeping or revealing confidences according to therapy needs and not only the request of one individual. We should consider how all the levels in the complex therapy system will be affected by our actions. To begin with, when the therapist reserves the right to use clients' disclosures based on the good of all concerned, we find that most clients decide to reveal their secrets anyway. Thus, little information is lost to the therapist from this policy, as Margolin (1982) feared. Furthermore, we find that these "secrets" are usually known to most family members already, including the children. They may not be known at a content level of specific facts, but the basic issues involved are known as they are experienced in the relationships carried on around them. In any case, it is essential that the therapist be free to look at *all* levels of the individual-family-therapist-society system in deciding what confidences to keep or to reveal. Simply deciding to advocate the best interest of any one level (e.g., the patient or the family system as a whole) resolves the conflicts of interest inherent in a multilevel system only by denying that it is such a system and by ignoring other interests.

One common objection to this policy is that this will prevent the therapist from gaining access to all the relevant data available (Karpel, 1980; Margolin, 1982). However, just as other family members "know" the secret in some ways, so can the systemic-thinking therapist be aware of the basic clinical issue underlying the secret. It can be experienced in the therapist's interactions with the family as they work on changing, and it can be known on analogical, metaphorical, and intuitive levels. Furthermore, the basic problems, of which the secret is an expression, can be observed and acted upon as they are operative in behavioral patterns or transactions isomorphic (Maclusky & Naftolin, 1981; Wendorf & Wendorf, 1981) to that of the secret.

For example, most authors (cited above) describe as problematic the situation of one spouse confiding an extramarital affair to the marital therapist. But one can view sustained outside relationships as the joint efforts of a couple to triangulate in order to regulate their distance and closeness (Elbaum, 1981). This pattern would be visible in many of their other interactions affected by the marital dysfunction. For instance, we know of a case in which the wife revealed through a previous therapist her once-a-year homosexual affair with a friend in another city. The present therapist and the husband already knew that intimacy and the wife's self-esteem as a woman were problems in this marriage. They dealt with these issues in isomorphic transactions such as the couple's problems in sharing leisure activities and parenting responsibilities. There was no need to reveal the literal details of the affair to the husband because the problems, of which the affair was only one instance, were dealt with by way of other marital transactions (Elbaum, 1981).

This view, however, still overlooks the other basic issue of why a "secret" is *not* told to other family members and *is* told to the therapist. At times this private revelation may be quite appropriate and really not a secret at all. For example, the information may be truly "private," as with the details of a spouse's previous relationships that have no important implications for the current situation (Boszormenyi-Nagy & Ulrich, 1981; Karpel, 1980). Or, parents may appropriately divulge material to the therapist, and not to their children, to protect the children or to maintain the needed generational boundary around their marital relationship (Margolin, 1982). Automatic prohibition against these disclosures would serve no ethical purpose and could needlessly interfere with the therapy by, for example, undermining the societally sanctioned authority of parents. Society has recognized the value to itself of allowing individuals the right to privileged communication even though society at large may suffer in isolated instances (e.g., when crime is concealed and therefore goes unpunished).

At other times, the disclosure of secrets only to the therapist may be a part of the very clinical issues necessitating therapy, that is, symptomatic of the family system's pathology. Selvini-Palazzoli and Prata (1982) pointed out that accepting this revelation means "accepting a denied coalition with the person who offers the revelation against" (p. 447) somebody else. As Grosser and Paul (1964) explained, "More often than not, the material is not the charged issue, but rather the patient's wish to be special in having a secret with the therapist" (p. 881). To accept the secret then constitutes turning over to the client the initiative for appropriate side-taking and ignoring the basic problems underlying this behavior. This could leave the therapist impotent and triangulated without a means of using this information therapeutically. In this situation, the needs of good therapy dictate an ethical stance that permits the therapist to violate an inappropriate confidence.

It is important, then, to view the problems of secrets systemically. One must include the therapist in the formulation, both as to how he or she affects the family and is affected in return. Similarly, societal values of honesty, openness, and privacy need to be considered. A systems view also offers a route to learning about issues and intervening through the family-therapist relationship and in patterns isomorphic to the secret. Again, we suggest that the most ethical way to handle "secrets" is to inform the family that confidences will be used by the therapist in the best interest of the entire family system. The system (and its members as individuals) can then decide what to tell. And the therapist, thinking systemically, can decide when it is appropriate to keep or reveal the secret.

Therapist Deceptiveness

Haley (1976), cited previously, has provided convincing arguments that indirect manipulations such as so-called "paradoxes" and reframings (Grunebaum & Chasin, 1978) are not only harmless but helpful and, indeed, often somewhat obvious and easily acceptable to clients. Papp (1980) added the concept that a paradoxical statement speaks to what is true on a systemic level, if not on a literal, factual level. The Palo Alto MRI therapists (Watzlawick, Weakland, & Fisch, 1974) contributed the idea that such statements speak to what *may be true* by virtue of being said, as in the above example of the probation officer's trustworthiness. It may, in fact, be the case that these approaches are beneficial to clients without danger of being harmful to them and therefore pose little ethical problem in regard to hurting the family. However, we would like to pose the question of what effects these benevolent deceptions have on the *therapist* in the self-recursive, therapist-family system and on the society that forms the context for this therapy.

How do we as therapists begin to think of ourselves as helping persons? What becomes our view of our clients who can so easily be deceived? What role do we come to see ourselves playing in therapy and in society in general: manipulators; definers of reality; moral philosophers; benevolent societal decision makers; culturally sanctioned parents for the problematic; all-knowing and all-powerful healers; objective, outside mechanics repairing troubled systems rather than people? Will we then endanger our therapeutic relationships by communicating this sort of "con artist" attitude by nonverbal slips, or will we simply become good liars? Clearly, this dramatic blowup into absurdity does not appear to happen often. Yet, if we do not consider the long-term effects of our deceptiveness on ourselves and the view of us thus presented to the rest of the mental health community, students in training, and society in general, we may be running a risk of disillusioning many people, including ourselves. This could affect how we handle our future cases as well as putting our stamp of approval on an ethic for the culture to adopt. The greatest danger would seem to be a tendency to think arrogantly that we are superior to our patients, outside the usual rules, so we can be "tricky," and that the end justifies our means.

This situation is not only problematic but unnecessary. To begin with, a paradox is more a reflection of the ambivalence in a system than the cleverness of a therapists' strategy. It is misleading for the therapist to think of himself as "paradoxing" someone rather than presenting a systemic view to a client who is stuck in a linear punctuation of the same reality. We also see deceptive paradoxes as unnecessary, since literal truth is just as useful.

We suggest that our field is well enough developed to afford therapists a variety of choices of many techniques for being truthful on a number of different levels, not just the systemic level. For example, a frequent practice in strategic, brief, and systemic therapies (De Shazer, 1982; Papp, 1980; Selvini-Palazzoli, Boscolo, Cecchin, & Prata, 1978) is to use a cotherapy team behind a one-way mirror. The therapist in the room can accentuate polarities or ambivalences, tap loyalties to the therapists, or help the family overcome their resistance to change by delivering one message from the team, or a faction of it, and the opposite from the therapist or other faction. The therapists are said to be in disagreement on what should be done when actually they fully agree that they should *say* they disagree for the helpful effect this will have. A variation of this theme is to report on what one's "team" said even when one actually has no team (Fisch, Weakland, & Segal, 1982) behind the mirror.

In addition to believing we have to see ourselves as part of the system we call "resistant" (Goolishian & Anderson, 1980), we believe the same sort of approach could be used as effectively and more honestly by simply delivering the two messages as both coming from the therapist. "On the one hand, I understand that you need to change to meet this need. But, on the other hand, I recognize these risks in not continuing as you have for these other reasons. How will you get out of this bind?" If this proved to be as effective, would it not be preferable for the impact it has on the therapist as a moral person participating in the therapeutic enterprise? This is a minor example. Nevertheless, the issue of the effects of our work on ourselves is important and largely unaddressed.

In fact, we propose that we should begin revamping our outcome research to explore the long-range effects on the therapist of doing particular types of therapy and interventions. Therapists have a complicated role in our society, combining aspects of parenting, problem-solving, grandparenting, secular ministering, scientific investigating, representing cultural values, enforcing norms, and so forth. They need to examine in greater depth, and on many levels, their goals and reasons for practicing therapy. We believe we should use therapy not only to help clients solve immediate problems but to enhance their overall competency as well. The conduct of therapy should also contribute to our own growth and should consider cultural needs, expectations, values, and development. We should choose therapy approaches not only for their efficiency and effectiveness in changing clients' behavior but also for what they offer on the additional levels (Wendorf, 1984) of affecting therapists and society.

Therapist Advocacy of (Feminist) Values

It is difficult to decide what is ethical conduct when we can "know" so strongly that we are "right" on a particular set of values and we can "see" how people are hurt when a family, or even our culture as a whole, espouses a different set of values. We will discuss this concern as it pertains to family therapist advocacy of feminist values, but the same issues are relevant to many other values such as antiwar, antiracism, or pro-Christian values, etc. Several writers have cautioned against the imposition by therapists of their own special causes, beliefs, or values on clients (Becvar, Becvar, & Bender, 1982; Hare-Mustin, 1978; Margolin, 1982). Yet, we see some of these same authors (Hare-Mustin; Margolin) as guilty of exactly that fault in their advocacy of feminist values in family therapy.

Hare-Mustin (1978) for example, proposed a "feminist approach to family therapy," claiming that "all family members can benefit from consciousness-raising as a part of family therapy" and that "family therapy provides opportunities for social change unavailable in other therapeutic approaches" (p. 187). Thus, she claims, therapists should do such things as modeling a nonstereotypic female role model, making the family aware of their sexist communication patterns and power differentials, and supporting male-female equality through androgynous personality types and roles.

Similarly, Margolin (1982) offers suggestions on "how to utilize the therapy situation to change the oppressive consequences of stereotyped roles and expectations in the family" (pp. 798-799). Like Hare-Mustin, she cautions therapists to examine their own values so that they can avoid imposing their traditional sex-role biases on clients. Both advocate that therapists be aware of their own sexist ("wrong") values and how they may unwittingly impose them on clients; yet, both seem to feel this imposition is acceptable in the case of their own nonsexist ("right") values.

We personally agree with these therapists on most of their ideas about the needed changes in sex roles in our society. We disagree, however, that therapists should decide which values are acceptable and use therapy as a means to campaign for the revisions they favor. First, there is little or no scientific or clinical evidence that feminist family therapy is necessary for the treatment of the presenting problems or that the feminist hypothesis that symptoms are "manifestations of oppression in a sexist society" (Libow, Ruskin, & Caust, 1982, p. 7) is valid. Further, we find this to be a linear, monocausal view of a systemic, multicausal, circular pattern. For instance, it is quite reasonable to suggest that the chemical and neurological difference between women and men biologically disposes them toward somewhat unique or different (not necessarily "unequal"—another *value* judgment) gender roles rather than purely androgynous roles (Ehrhardt & Meyer-Bahlburg, 1981; Lacoste-Utamsing & Holloway, 1982; Maclusky & Naftolin, 1981). It is also unsystemic to forget that women are a part of the cultural system that assigns a "lesser" role to them. And, as therapists, are we employed by clients to help solve their problems or to liberate them? We believe that we are culturally sanctioned to be healers but not crusaders.

On the other hand, we recognize that we are not identical with our culture. We also do therapy as individuals. In fact, we agree with the many therapists who maintain that it is through our personal relationship with a client that all our techniques are empowered. We bring our entire selves into this relationship: our competency, skills, emotions, needs, knowledge, and values. Even if we try not to, our values will have an impact on our clients to some degree. Are not our clients expecting us to be real people and true to our own beliefs? Does not our culture expect us to be leaders in providing solutions to many of society's ills?

Clearly, these are difficult questions. Our position is that as we apply our systems thinking to analyzing these problems, we should include our cultural context and the effects on ourselves as individuals as additional levels in the analysis (an insightful treatment of feminist values in family therapy was provided by Libow, Ruskin, and Caust [1982]). Feminist therapists recognize the harmful impact of the larger system of therapist and community on the marital dyad where stereotyped sex roles are concerned. They do not seem to evaluate the negative aspects of pushing their own values. We must first be honest with ourselves about our values. Is there scientific, clinical, or theoretical evidence to support them, or are we responding to a popular trend, a biased sample of problematic families, personal preferences, or our intuitions? Have we prematurely decided and closed our minds to alternatives? Are we too sure of ourselves and becoming rigid, dogmatic, or arrogant? Are we beginning to see ourselves as the moral judges of our society with answers for every question? Certainly we do not want this sort of hubris to be our operating base in therapy.

We must be aware of the impact we make on our clients and their impact in return on us, as well as how our therapy fits into the larger context of our culture. Our view is that we should be cautious in any attempt to affect societal values through our therapy, as the result can negatively affect the particular family in therapy, ourselves as therapists, and society (Duhl, 1983). We should help solve the problems brought to us and not use clients to push personal causes, no matter how "right" they appear to be; yet, we should be ourselves and be responsible in sharing with our society the knowledge we possess. Foremost, we believe that we are ethically bound to be honest and forthright with our clients, clearly informing them of their choices, our biases, and our professional judgments. When we find a value or pattern that works for a particular family, whatever our biases, at least we ought not to make their lives more difficult or their problems worse. Even with the "informed consent" of a clear explication of our beliefs *as* beliefs, we must remain cognizant of the tremendous influence we have as "experts" in human relations. We must be extremely careful not to abuse our power, both for the family's protection and, lest we begin to perceive ourselves as God-like, for our own protection. As therapists we may ethically strive to change society, but at the level of society, not of the individual family, with whom we contract as therapist not moralist.

References

Becvar, R. J., Becvar, D. S., & Bender, A. E. (1982). Let us first do no harm. *Journal of Marriage and Family Therapy, 8*, 385 391.

Boszormenyi-Nagy, I., & Ulrich, D. N. (1981). Contextual family therapy. In A. S. Gurman & D. P. Kniskern (Eds.), *Handbook of family therapy*. New York: Brunner/Mazel.

De Shazer, S. (1982). *Patterns of brief family therapy: An ecosystemic approach*. New York: Guilford Press.

Duhl, B. S. (1983). *From the inside out and other metaphors*. New York: Brunner/Mazel.

Elbaum, P. L. (1981). The dynamics, implications, and treatment of extramarital sexual relationships for the family therapist. *Journal of Marriage and Family Therapy, 7*, 489–495.

Ehrhardt, A. A., & Meyer-Bahlburg, F. L. (1981). Effects of prenatal sex hormones on gender-related behavior. *Science, 211*, 1312–1318.

Fisch, R., Weakland, J. H., & Segal, L. (1982). *The tactics of change—doing therapy briefly*. San Francisco: Jossey-Bass.

Framo, J. L. (1981). The integration of marital therapy with sessions with family of origin. In A. S. Gurman & D. P. Kniskern (Eds.), *Handbook of family therapy*. New York: Brunner/Mazel.

Goolishian, H., & Anderson, H. (1980, November). *Strategic interventions with resistant families*. Workshop presented at the 38th Annual Conference of the American Association for Marriage and Family Therapy, Toronto, Canada.

Grosser, G. H., & Paul, N . L. (1964). Ethical issues in family group therapy. *American Journal of Orthopsychiatry, 34*, 875–884.

Grunebaum, H., & Chasin, R. (1978). Relabeling and reframing reconsidered: The beneficial effects of a pathological label. *Family Process, 17*, 449–456.

Gurman, A. S., & Kniskern, D. P. (Eds.). (1981). *Handbook of family therapy*. New York: Brunner/Mazel.

Haley, J. (1976). *Problem-solving therapy*. San Francisco: Jossey-Bass.

Halleck, S. L. (1971). *The politics of therapy*. San Francisco: Jossey-Bass.

Hare-Mustin, R. T. (1978). A feminist approach to family therapy. *Family Process, 17*, 181–194.

Hare-Mustin, R. T. (1980). Family therapy may be dangerous for your health. *Professional Psychology, 11*, 935–938.

Hines, P. M., & Hare-Mustin, R. T. (1978). Ethical concerns in family therapy. *Professional Psychology, 9*, 165–171.

Hurvitz, N. (1967). Marital problems following psychotherapy with one spouse. *Journal of Consulting and Clinical Psychology, 31*, 38–47.

Karpel, M. A. (1980). Family secrets: 1. Conceptual and ethical issues in the relational context. 2. Ethical and practical considerations in therapeutic management. *Family Process, 19*, 295–306.

L'Abate, L. (Ed.). (1982). *Values, ethics, legalities and the family therapist*. Rockville, MD: Aspen Publications.

Lacoste-Utamsing, C. D., & Holloway, R. L. (1982). Sexual dimorphism in the human corpus callosum. *Science, 216*, 1431–1432.

Libow, J. A., Ruskin, P. A., & Caust, B. L. (1982). Feminist and family systems therapy: Are they irreconcilable? *American Journal of Family Therapy, 10*, 3–12.

Maclusky, N. J., & Naftolin, F. (1981). Sexual differentiation of the central nervous system. *Science, 211*, 1294–1302.

Margolin, G. (1982). Ethical and legal considerations in marital and family therapy. *American Psychologist, 37*, 788–801.

Minuchin, S. (1974). *Families and family therapy*. Cambridge, MA: Harvard University Press.

O'Shea, M., & Jessee, E. (1982). Ethical, value and professional conflicts. In L. L'Abate, (Ed.), *Values, ethics, legalities and the family therapist*. Rockville, MD: Aspen Publications.

Papp, P. (1980). The Greek chorus and other techniques of family therapy. *Family Process, 19*, 45–57.

Selvini-Palazzoli, M., Boscolo, L., Cecchin, G., & Prata, G. (1978). *Paradox and counterparadox*. New York: Jason Aronson.

Selvini-Palazzoli, M., & Prata, G. (1982). Snares in family therapy. *Journal of Marital and Family Therapy, 8*, 443–450.

Taggart, M. (1982). Linear versus systemic values: Implications for family therapy. In L. L'Abate (Ed.), *Values, ethics, legalities and the family therapist*. Rockville, MD: Aspen Publications.

Watzlawick, P., Weakland, J., & Fisch, R. (1974). *Change: Principles of problem formation and problem resolution*. New York: Norton.

Wendorf, D. J. (1981). A data-based reply to Hare-Mustin on family therapy perils. *Professional Psychology, 12*, 665–666.

Wendorf, D. J. (1984). A practical, challenging model for training practicing professionals in family therapy. *Journal of Marital and Family Therapy, 10*, 31–41.

Wendorf, R. J., & Wendorf, D. J. (1981). Problems with family therapy in a community mental health center. *Hospital Community Psychiatry, 32*, 852–855.

Whitaker, C. A., & Miller, M. H. (1969). A re-evaluation of psychiatric help when divorce impends. *American Journal of Psychiatry, 126*, 57–64.

This article was originally published in *Family Process*, Vol. 24, 1985, pp. 443–453. Reprint permission granted by Family Process, Inc.

Issues in the Application of Paradoxical Techniques: Ethical, Legal and Therapeutic Perspectives

Thomas L. Sexton

Paradoxical techniques have a long history in counseling and psychotherapy. The earliest systemic family counseling models were based on the cybernetic perspective within which paradox was a powerful tool in disrupting and treating relational systems within families (Haley, 1976, Selvini-Palazzoli, Boscolo, Cecchin, & Prata, 1978; Weeks & L'Abate, 1982). Families were told to increase the very behavior they may have identified as problematic, or decrease actions they believed to be helpful. Similarly, other clients may have been directed to appreciate the very events they believed to be be the source of their concern.

Clinical presentations of paradoxical procedures are often met with great fascination and even laughter as the paradoxical bind is developed, the client struggles, and change ultimately occurs. Usually, clients are presented with directives without any information about the therapeutic or logical rationale behind the intervention so that the therapeutic bind will remain effective (Haley, 1976). Many marriage and family counseling practitioners have increasingly embraced the use of paradox as an important and useful clinical tool.

Given the clinical potential and great popularity of paradoxical techniques, it is surprising how little critical attention has been given to their application. In fact, marriage and family counselors have endorsed paradoxical procedures largely because they "fit" theoretically with the prevalent family systems view or because they have been proposed to be "effective." However, there may be more considerations than just theoretical fit or a clinical effectiveness when selecting a counseling technique. Marriage and family practitioners using paradoxical techniques also face a number of unique concerns that are unlike those issues faced by counselors who use more standard counseling techniques. This chapter will focus on the unique therapeutic, ethical, and legal issues that are important for marriage and family practitioners to consider when using paradoxical counseling techniques.

Ethical Considerations

Paradoxical techniques have the potential to be useful clinical tools particularly when presented within a trusting counseling relationship and accompanied by an informing treatment rationale. However, the use of any counseling technique must also be considered within the professional context in which it is used. The ethical codes provide professional guidelines to determine the limits within which a counselor should operate and thus, compose a major part of the professional context within which practitioners are expected to make appropriate clinical decisions (Woody, 1990).

Like no other set of techniques, paradox has generated a long standing ethical debate. Client manipulation and deception are the most common ethical issues raised in regard to paradoxical procedures (Brown & Slee, 1986; Okun & Rapapport, 1980). Along this line, a major concern is the extent to which the counselor should mislead or deceive a client in the interest of providing therapeutic help. Paradoxical opponents have promoted the notion that upholding the principles embodied in the ethical codes entails a commitment to promote and protect the rights and welfare of the client (Hare-Mustin, Marecek, Kaplan, Liss-Levinson, 1979; Whan, 1983). Some have also suggested that the therapeutic relationship should be the prototype of a healthy relationship, and thus, should be characterized by respect for client autonomy, trust, honesty and loyalty (Ramsey, 1970; Whan, 1983). Brown and Slee (1986) argued that the indirect and oppositional actions of paradoxical counselors are in contradiction to the stated goals of the client and are thus, manipulative and deceitful. Whan (1983) suggested that under such conditions the welfare and free will of the client is at risk. Not surprisingly, from this ethical perspective, therapeutic practices that involve deceit or manipulation, even if done in the client's best interest, are in opposition to these ethical ideals.

Informed consent, another guiding principle for ethical practice of counseling, has also been of concern in regard to the use of paradox. The principle of informed consent states that clients should have sufficient information about procedures, goals, side effects, qualifications of the counselor, and alternative sources of help to make informed choices about whether to begin and continue in counseling (American Association for Counseling and Development, 1988; American Association for Marriage and Family Therapy, 1988; American Psychological Association, 1989). Consequently, clients are entitled to an explanation of the procedures and purposes of counseling, the possible benefits as well as discomforts and risks, counseling alternatives, and the right to question or withdraw from counseling at any time (Hare-Mustin et al., 1979). Does a practitioner using paradoxical techniques have the right to violate respect for the client's autonomy and or his/her right to be fully informed and give consent to treatment for the sake of their chosen clinical technique? Judged by these standards, marriage and family counselors who factually skew, intentionally ignore, distort, deemphasize, or overemphasize information may be engaging in unethical practice.

Proponents of paradoxical techniques have taken a different view of these ethical concerns. Most advocates have adopted a "utilitarian" ethical stance, suggesting that it is the efficacy of an approach that should determine the legitimacy of its use (Haley, 1976; Watterson, Gallesch, & Hanson, 1987). Proponents have noted that paradoxical techniques are not unethical but are, at worst, unusual and therefore misunderstood by critics (Dowd & Milne, 1986). Watzlawick et al., (1974) argued that the crucial question is actually one of beneficial versus harmful dishonesty. From this perspective, it has been argued that there are a number of different perspectives of any life event and the counselor using paradoxical procedures only provides an alternative view of these events (Watzlawick et al., 1974). Thus, paradoxical counselors are honest and ethical, but from the standpoint of cybernetic versus linear logic. Similarly, Fisher, Anderson, and Jones (1981) contend that paradoxical techniques that work are truthful in the sense that they accurately embody the patient's phenomenological experience.

Paradoxical proponents have also argued that the issue of informed consent is no more of a problem in paradoxical counseling than in any other approach (Haley, 1976; Weeks & L'Abate, 1982). They argued that practitioners using more traditional counseling approaches do not disclose their procedures any more than those practitioners using paradoxical methods. Margolin (1981) agreed that paradoxical techniques inherently involve a degree of manipulation that limits informed consent and free choice. However, according to Margolin, complete objectivity and openness in counseling is not possible. In fact, Haley (1976) contended that informed consent is counter-therapeutic in many cases in which paradox is used. Finally, Weeks and L'Abate (1982) argued that the lack of informed consent may be less of an ethical problem when viewed within the context of treatment effectiveness.

The definition of paradox held by the practitioner may be one important factor when considering these ethical concerns. Those marriage and family counselors who conceptualize paradox as "unexpected" counselor behavior are at risk to fall into the ethical trap of providing potentially manipulative, deceitful and ill-considered treatment interventions without a theoretical foundation or treatment rationale. If, for example, counselors consider their behavior as "paradoxing" or "just doing something different" rather than presenting an accurate interactional perspective, they may believe themselves unbound by ethical restraint because the "ends justify the means" (Wendorf & Wendorf, 1985). On the other hand, those counselors who have a solid theoretical understanding of paradox may not view these procedures as paradoxical, and thus, feel no need to critically consider these ethical issues. Regardless of the theoretical perspective of the clinician, all practitioners must still operate within the guidelines of the profession and uphold the principles of client welfare and safety.

Another important concern may lie with the attitude of the counselor. It is probably important for marriage and family counselors to consider their personal reasons for using paradoxical techniques. Paradoxical techniques are powerful counseling interventions that may put the counselor in a position to direct and manipulate the client to engage in actions based on hidden agendas. Because the purposes of these interventions are often hidden, the counselor may not be as accountable as they may be with other, more direct techniques. Other times practitioners may use paradox as a last try with a difficult client. At such times the choice of paradox may be made out of frustration and struggle on the part of the counselor to find an effective intervention. However, paradoxical techniques used in a kneejerk and cavalier fashion or used to mask a lack of counselor skill in difficult clinical situations is similarly unethical (Fisher et al., 1981; Stuart, 1980).

The key to operating ethically while utilizing paradoxical approaches resides with the clinician, not with the technique or the ethical codes. Wilbach (1989) suggested that ethically aware counselors need to include ethical considerations as an integral part of all treatment planning. For example, rather than relying solely on a "utilitarian" stance clinicians should consider both the specific ethical codes as well as the higher ethical principles when making clinical decisions (Woody, 1990). Kitchener (1981) suggested that a useful ethical principle is that of producing the maximum good with the maximum protection of the welfare of all involved.

Additionally, responsible use of these techniques requires the counselor to be competent in their use (American Association for Counseling and Development, 1988; American Association for Marriage and Family Therapy, 1988; American Psychological Association, 1989). In order to be competent the practitioner should have an understanding of the role of the symptom for each family member, obtain adequate supervision, use a therapeutic style conducive to the technique, and base the intervention on a conceptual rationale that supports the choice of intervention (Fisher et al., 1981; Tennen, Rohrbaugh, Press, & White, 1981). Consequently, paradoxical techniques should be based in the clinician's theoretical background and used only after supervision and training in the clinical application of paradox. Providing treatment rationales to clients will not only insure informed consent but may serve to actually enhance therapeutic cooperation (Selvini-Palazzoli et al., 1978).

Legal Considerations

Therapeutic problems and ethical issues are important professional concerns to weigh when using any counseling intervention. But marriage and family counselors also operate in a legal context. For practitioners a major concern is the relationship between their treatment decisions and the manner in which the judicial system may evaluate those choices. If practitioners using paradoxical procedures operate from a systemic theoretical perspective, they may be misunderstood by the linear-based legal system. For example, while the marriage and family counselor is concerned about understanding a relational system in a non-causal manner, the legal system is primarily concerned with ascertaining responsibility for action and the determination of guilt (Roswell, 1988). Regardless of ones' theoretical approach or the efficacy of ones' clinical procedures, the actions of counselors are primarily judged upon the legal standards, case law and state licensing requirements (Van Hoose & Kottler, 1985).

The legal standard by which professional behavior is judged is the tort of negligence. In cases involving professional negligence, it must be shown that: (1) the counselor had a legal duty to the client, (2) the counselor's performance of that duty did not conform to accepted practices, (3) there was a causal relationship between the counselor's conduct and the alleged harm to the client, and (4) actual harm to the client occurred (Roswell, 1988). There is no simple way of determining whether the use of a particular technique, such as paradox, constitutes negligence or malpractice. However, a number of legal standards/principles have emerged from the medical practice literature that are particularly relevant to the marriage and family practitioner using paradoxical techniques.

For example, the courts have ruled that voluntary informed consent is an essential part of the treatment process (Meisel et al., 1977). Insuring informed consent is complicated by the fact that there is no one criterion for judging whether voluntary consent has been given. Roth, Meisel, and Lidz (1977) suggested that in situations in which a high cost/risk to benefit ratio exists for the client, a conservative approach to informed consent is appropriate. High cost/risk situations exist when (1) the client is competent, (2) there is an emergency, (3) the procedure is either viewed as experimental or untested relative to other procedures, or (4) if there are questions of peer and/or social acceptance for the procedures (Roth et al., 1977). Paradoxical procedures fall into the high cost/risk category because they may be viewed by many as experimental and because of questions of social acceptance based on treatment acceptability. Consequently, it may be prudent for the marriage and family counselor to proceed with a conservative approach to informed consent when utilizing paradoxical techniques.

The directive, counter-attitudinal nature of defiance-based paradoxical techniques has raised an additional legal concern, that of the community standard of care. In any legal conflict, the appropriateness of a counselor's actions would be judged against the standard of care, or the type and level of care that would be given by a similar professional to a similar client with a similar problem (Huber & Baruth, 1987). In the case of a legal challenge to a marriage and family counselor who had used paradoxical techniques, his/her actions would be compared by the court to other types of treatments useful for the client's presenting problem. Since most forms of counseling are based on linear-causal assumptions (Strong & Claiborn, 1982), marriage and family counselors using paradox may suddenly find themselves outside what the professional community would judge as appropriate. Similarly, since paradoxical techniques are generally active and directive in nature, Roswell (1988) suggested that it may be easier for a court to perceive a link between the counselor action and the proposed client injury. As relatively new and untested procedures without clear research support, paradoxical procedures may also raise more legal questions than other established treatment procedures.

These legal concerns are not intended to suggest that paradoxical procedures should or cannot be used within the linear-based, legal world. However, as with both the therapeutic and ethical arenas, the marriage and family counselor using such procedures must take particular precautions to protect themselves from the legal system. One of the most important legal protections may be for counselors to insure they abide by the ethical guidelines established by their professional group (Hare-Mustin et al., 1979). By including an ethical dimension to treatment planning counselors gain support from the profession as a whole, in light of any legal conflict.

Many marriage and family counselors appear to employ paradoxical procedures without following accepted procedures of informed consent because of the belief that such information may render the technique inactive. However, since the research evidence suggests that client understanding and knowledge may in fact facilitate change and the legal system insists on voluntary information to insure client's right to self determination, this practice seems unwarranted. Given the specificity of the medical negligence literature, it would also seem unwise to construe the client's request for help as an indication of global informed consent. Instead, the informed consent guidelines suggested by Everstine, Everstine, Heyman, True, Frey, Johnson, and Seldon (1980) could be a useful guide for the marriage and family counselor. According to these guidelines the marriage and family counselor would provide specific information about the risks, benefits, availability of alternative treatments as well as the appropriate rationales for use of these procedures to the client.

In order to accomplish these informed consent guidelines, it may be useful for the marriage and family counselor to obtain signed consent from all parties, including parents, spouses and/or siblings of the initially identified client. Similarly, it would be useful for the practitioner to conceptualize informed consent as a process rather than as an event (Roswell, 1988). Thus, information would be given about procedures and client's consent would be gathered on an ongoing basis. While serving as a legal protection, this model of informed consent may additionally serve as a method to enhance treatment acceptability. Finally, when paradoxical procedures are based on comprehensive, documented treatment plans that clearly addresses the client's presenting problem, practitioners can document the justification for their treatment decisions (Roswell, 1988). With complete treatment notes, counselors can track the course of their conversations with clients, noting instances of consent, and documenting treatment justification.

Conclusion

Paradoxical techniques in the practice of marriage and family counseling have great potential to produce client change. The issues identified here are not intended to suggest that paradoxical techniques are ineffective or that the techniques should not be used by the marriage and family practitioner. In the past, paradoxical procedures have been used because they were said to work, because they were powerful, and because they were theoretically correct. Contrary to the position suggested by many paradoxical proponents, a variety of unique therapeutic, ethical and legal challenges await marriage and family practitioners who use paradox. When the issues of treatment efficacy and acceptability, professional ethics, and legal challenges are considered, the position that "the ends justify the means" is no longer a prudent professional rationale upon which to make counseling decisions. Without thoughtful consideration of the issues involved in the application of paradoxical procedures, the potential utility of these techniques may never be realized and the practitioner may be ethically and legally at risk. However, when used within a therapeutic relationship with appropriate treatment rationales, using informed consent and backed by complete treatment documentation, paradoxical techniques can be an important addition for any marriage and family therapist. In addition to professional use, continued research and theoretical consideration are needed in order to more fully understand the change mechanism and the moderating variables that may mitigate the use of paradoxical counseling procedures.

References

American Association for Counseling and Development. (1988). *Ethical standards* (rev. ed.). Falls Church, VA: Author.

American Association for Marriage and Family Therapy. (1985). *AAMFT code of ethical principles for marriage and family therapists*. Washington, DC: Author.

American Psychological Association. (1989). *Ethical standards of psychologists* (rev. ed.). Washington, DC: Author.

Brown, J. E., & Slee, P. T. (1986). Paradoxical strategies: The ethics of intervention. *Professional Psychology Research and Practice, 17,* 487–491.

Dowd, E. T., & Milne, C. R. (1986). Paradoxical interventions in counseling psychology. *The Counseling Psychologist, 14*(2), 237–282.

Everstine, L., Everstine, D. S., Heyman, G. M., True, R. H., Frey, D. H., Johnson, H. G., & Seldon, R. H. (1980). Privacy and confidentiality in psychotherapy. *American Psychologist, 35*(9), 828–840.

Fischer, L., Anderson, A., & Jones, J. E. (1981). Types of paradoxical interventions and indications and contra indications. *Family Process, 20,* 25–35.

Haley, J. (1976). *Problem-solving therapy.* San Francisco: Jossey-Bass.

Hare-Mustin, R. T., Marecek, J., Kaplan, A. G., & Liss-Levinson, N. (1979). Rights of clients, responsibilities of therapists. *American Psychologist, 34,* 3–16.

Huber, C. H., & Baruth, L. G. (1987). *Ethical, legal and professional issues in the practice of marriage and family therapy.* Columbus, OH: Merrill.

Kitchener, K. S. (1981). Intuition, critical evaluation and ethical principles: The foundation of ethical decisions in counseling psychology. *The Counseling Psychologist, 12,* 43–45.

Margolin, G. (1981). Ethical and legal considerations in marital and family therapy. *American Psychologist, 37,* 788–801.

Meisel, A., Roth, L. H., & Lidz, C. W. (1977). Toward a model of the legal doctrine of informed consent. *The American Journal of Psychiatry, 43,* 285–289.

Okun, B., & Rapapport, L. (1980). *Working with families: An introduction to family therapy.* North Scituate, MA: Duxbury Press.

Ramsey, P. (1970). *The patient as a person.* New Haven, CT: Yale.

Roswell, V. A. (1988). Professional liability: Issues for behavior therapists in the 1980s and 1990s. *The Behavior Therapist, 11,* 163–171.

Roth, L. H., Meisel, A., & Lidz, C. W. (1977). Tests of competency to consent to treatment. *The American Journal of Psychiatry, 134,* 279–284.

Selvini-Palazzoli, M., Boscolo, L., Cecchin, G., & Prata, G. (1978). *Paradox and counterparadox.* New York: Jason Aronson.

Strong, S. R., & Claiborn, C. D. (1982). *Change through interaction: Social psychological processes of counseling and psychotherapy.* New York: Wiley-Interscience.

Tennen, H., Rohrbaugh, M., Press, S., & White, L. (1981). Reactance theory and therapeutic paradox: A Compliance-defiance mode. *Psychotherapy: Theory, Research and Practice, 18,* 14–22.

Van Hoose, W. H., & Kottler, J. A. (1985). *Ethical and legal issues in counseling and psychotherapy.* San Francisco: Jossey-Bass.

Watterson, J. A., Gallesch, J. M., & Hanson, G. R. (1987, August). *Family therapists' ethical concerns regarding the use of paradoxical techniques.* Paper presented at the annual convention of the American Psychological Association, New York, NY.

Watzlawick, P., Weakland, J., & Fisch, R. (1974). *Change: Principles of problem formation and problem resolution.* New York: Norton.

Weeks, G. R., & L'Abate, L. (1982). *Paradoxical psychotherapy: Theory and practice with individuals, couples and families.* New York: Brunner/Mazel.

Wendorf, D. J., & Wendorf, R. J. (1985). A systemic view of family therapy ethics. *Family Process, 24,* 443–453.

Whan, M. (1983). Tricks of the trade: Questionable theory and practice in family therapy. *British Journal of Social Work, 13,* 321–337.

Wilbach, D. (1989). Ethics and family therapy: The case management of family violence. *Journal of Marital and Family Therapy, 15,* 43–52.

Woody, J. D. (1990). Resolving ethical concerns in clinical practice: Toward a pragmatic model. *Journal of Marital and Family Therapy, 16,* 133–150.

Research in Marriage and Family Therapy

David L. Fenell
Barry K. Weinhold

In 1952 Hans Eysenck shook the world of psychotherapy with the results of his research on psychotherapy effectiveness. Eysenck (1952) reported that, according to his analysis, about 67% of neurotic patients improved within two years whether they received therapy or not. Eysenck challenged psychotherapists to demonstrate the effectiveness of their approaches or to concede that these approaches were not useful.

Bergin (1967, 1971) was the first to respond to Eysenck's criticism. Bergin's re-evaluation of Eysenck's data revealed that psychotherapy was at least moderately effective with neurotic patients, as 65% improved within two years with psychotherapy, while 43% of untreated neurotic patients improved within two years.

Despite Bergin's findings, the challenge to demonstrate the effectiveness of psychotherapy remains. As ethical practitioners, psychotherapists seek to provide the most beneficial treatment to clients. How can we know what kinds of treatment are most beneficial unless effective research is conducted to demonstrate the results of various approaches? As ethical therapists, we want to know, within the limits available, whether the treatment works (Levant, 1984).

Paul (1967) phrased a question that described what psychotherapy research attempts to discover. His question clearly identified the complexities involved in conducting psychotherapy research. Paul asked: "What treatment, by whom, is most effective for this individual with that specific problem, and under what set of circumstances?" Attempting to respond to Paul's question has been and will continue to be a major challenge for psychotherapy researchers.

Following the publication of Bergin's findings (1967, 1971), investigators began to identify deterioration in clients as a result of psychotherapy (Lambert, Bergin, & Collins, 1977). Deterioration occurs when the client becomes worse as a result of therapy. It was discovered that deterioration occurred in less than 10% of the clients treated, with the rate higher for more disturbed clients.

Several research projects were conducted investigating the effects of the level of therapist empathy, warmth, and genuineness on the outcome of therapy (Mitchell, Bozarth, & Kraft, 1977; Rogers, 1957; Truax & Carkhuff, 1967; Truax & Mitchell, 1971). Although the results of these studies consistently suggested that these therapist qualities are important factors in client change, the mechanism for these results, as well as how widely the findings can be generalized, has been questioned (Mitchell, Bozarth, & Kraft, 1977). Nonetheless, when various theories of counseling are compared, results indicate that one approach is generally just as effective as another (Luborsky, Singer, & Luborsky, 1975; Smith & Glass, 1977; Strupp & Hadley, 1979). Thus, researchers have not been able to conclude precisely what it is about psychotherapy that brings about improvement. These studies lend indirect support to those researchers who have concluded that the therapist qualities of empathy, warmth, and genuineness are factors that facilitate change.

Later studies by Bergin and Lambert (1978) suggested that short-term therapy lasting 6 months or less was effective in providing symptom relief for the client. Smith and Glass (1977) completed a meta-analysis of 375 controlled-outcome studies that suggested that the typical client in therapy is better off than 75% of individuals with similar problems who are not treated. Thus, a fairly solid body of research has been compiled suggesting that psychotherapy is effective.

The preceding summary of some of the important findings in psychotherapy for individuals sets the stage for a review of the research in marriage and family therapy. The same problems that exist in research with individual clients exist in family therapy research, but with additional complications. In marriage and family therapy research, change is more difficult to assess. Are we looking for change in the identified patient? Other family members? Family subsystems? The family system itself? Without knowing what to look for, it is difficult to assess change (Gurman & Kniskern, 1981). Olson, Russell, and Sprenkle (1980) stated that to evaluate family therapy, researchers need ways to identify and measure family system changes. A significant amount of work remains to be completed before researchers are able to reliably identify and accurately measure system change.

Four major reviews of the research concerning the outcome of marriage and family therapy have been conducted by DeWitt (1978);

Gurman and Kniskern (1978a); Olson, Russell, and Sprenkle (1980); and Wells and Dezen (1978). Of these, the Gurman and Kniskern review is most often cited in the marriage and family therapy literature. Specific findings based on these comprehensive reviews indicate the following conclusions:

1. Improvement rates in marriage and family therapy are similar to improvement rates in individual therapy.
2. Deterioration rates in marriage and family therapy are similar to deterioration rates in individual therapy.
3. Deterioration may occur because:
   a. The therapist has poor interpersonal skills;
   b. The therapist moves too quickly into sensitive topic areas and does not handle the situation well;
   c. The therapist allows family conflict to become exacerbated without moderating therapeutic intervention;
   d. The therapist does not provide adequate structure in the early stages of therapy; and
   e. The therapist does not support family members (Gurman & Kniskern, 1981).
4. Conjoint marital therapy (with both partners present) is the treatment of choice over individual therapy for couples experiencing marital problems. Low improvement rates and high deterioration rates are found when couples are treated separately for marital problems (Gurman & Kniskern, 1978b).
5. Family therapy is as effective, if not more so, as individual therapy for problems involving marital and family conflict and even for treating an individual's problems.
6. Brief therapy limited to about 20 sessions seems to be as effective as open-ended therapy.
7. Participation of the father in family therapy increases the probability of successful outcome.
8. Co-therapy has not been shown to be more effective than one-therapist family therapy.
9. Therapist relationship skills have an influence on the outcome of therapy. Good relationship skills produce positive outcomes and poor relationship skills may produce deterioration.
10. When the identified patient has severe psychological problems, a successful outcome is less probable.

11. Modified structural family therapy has been used to successfully treat psychosomatic problems (Minuchin, Rosman, & Baker, 1978) and drug and alcohol problems (Stanton, 1978; Stanton & Todd, 1979, 1981).
12. Family type, family interaction style, and family demographic factors have not been demonstrated to be related to the outcome of family therapy.

These findings reflect the synthesis of numerous studies conducted over the past 20 years. Psychotherapy research is still in a relatively primitive state of the art, and these findings should be considered with this limitation in mind.

Future research should focus on evaluating specific aspects of treatment on specific targets in the family system. This research will be important because specific therapist behaviors to produce change may have little relation to the family therapy theory being practiced. Identifying these specific, change-producing, theory-neutral factors will be important for all practitioners.

Future research designs should use a control group so that findings can be generalized as much as possible. In addition, findings should be significant in practical ways to clinicians as well as statistically significant to researchers. Another need is for researchers to conduct follow-up evaluations of their subjects to determine long-term effects of treatment (Gurman & Kniskern, 1981).

In addition to providing practicing clinicians with information about the efficacy of certain treatment approaches, psychotherapy research provides a continuous flow of information to the increasingly critical public concerning the effects of treatment for psychological difficulties.

Summary

This article has introduced some of the critical issues in marriage and family therapy that will be of interest to the psychotherapist beginning work with couples and families. It is important for family therapists to know about professional associations because they provide information about the profession as well as opportunities for professional interactions with others interested in family therapy . A knowledge of the ethical and legal issues that are pertinent to the practice of family therapy ensures that clients receive the quality of therapy to which they are entitled.

Finally, a knowledge of the research in marriage and family therapy is important so that clinicians will be aware of the strengths and limitations of family therapy.

References

Bergin, A. (1967). Some implications of psychotherapy research for therapeutic practice. *International Journal of Psychiatry, 3,* 136–150.

Bergin, A. (1971). The evaluation of therapeutic outcomes. In A. Bergin & S. Garfield (Eds.), *Handbook of psychotherapy and behavior change.* New York: John Wiley.

Bergin, A., & Lambert, M. (1978). The evaluation of therapeutic outcomes. In A. Bergin & S. Lambert (Eds.), *Handbook of psychotherapy and behavior change: An empirical analysis* (2nd ed.). New York: John Wiley.

Dewitt, K. (1978). The effectiveness of family therapy: A review of the outcome research. *Archives of General Psychiatry, 35,* 549–561.

Eysenck, H. (1952). The effects of psychotherapy: An evaluation. *Journal of Consulting Psychology, 16,* 319–324.

Gurman, A. S., & Kniskern, D. P. (1978a). Deterioration in marriage and family therapy: Empirical, clinical and conceptual issues. *Family Process, 17,* 3–20.

Gurman, A. S., & Kniskern, D. P. (1978b). Research on marital and family therapy: Progress, perspective and prospect. In S. L. Garfield & A. E. Lambert (Eds.), *Handbook of psychotherapy and behavior change: An empirical analysis* (2nd ed.). New York: John Wiley.

Gurman, A. S., & Kniskern, D. P. (Eds.). (1981). *Handbook of family therapy.* New York: Brunner/Mazel.

Lambert, M. J., Bergin, A. E., & Collins, J. L. (1977). Therapist induced deterioration in psychotherapy. In A. S. Gurman & A. M. Razin (Eds.), *Effective psychotherapy: A handbook of research.* New York: Pergamon Press.

Levant, R. (1984). *Family therapy: A comprehensive overview.* Englewood Cliffs, NJ: Prentice-Hall.

Luborsky, L., Singer, B., & Luborsky, L. (1973). Comparative studies of psychotherapies. *Archives of General Psychiatry, 29,* 719–729.

Minuchin, S., Rosman, B., & Baker, L. (1978). *Psychosomatic families: Anorexia Nervosa in context.* Cambridge, MA: Harvard University Press.

Mitchell, K. M., Bozarth, J. D., & Kraft, C. C. (1977). A reappraisal of the therapeutic effectiveness of accurate empathy, nonpossessive warmth, and genuineness. In A. S. Gurman & A. M. Razin (Eds.), *Effective psychotherapy: A handbook of research*. New York: Pergamon Press.

Olson, D. H., Russell, C., & Sprenkle, D. H. (1980). Marriage and family therapy: A decade review. *Journal of Marriage and the Family, 42*, 973–993.

Paul, G. L. (1967). Strategy of outcome research in psychotherapy. *Journal of Consulting Psychology, 31*, 109–118.

Rogers, C. R. (1957). The necessary and sufficient conditions of therapeutic personality change. *Journal of Consulting Psychology, 21*, 95–103.

Smith, M. L., & Glass, G. V. (1977). Meta-analysis of psychotherapy outcome studies. *American Psychologist, 32*, 752–760.

Stanton, M. D. (1978). Some outcome results and aspects of structural family therapy with drug addicts. In D. Smith, S. Anderson, M. Buxton, T. Chung, N. Gotlieb, & W. Harvey (Eds.), *A multicultural view of drug abuse*. Cambridge, MA: Schenkman.

Stanton, M. D., & Todd, T. (1979). Structural family therapy with drug addicts. In E. Kaufman & P. Kaufman (Eds.), *The family therapy of drug and alcohol abuse*. New York: Gardner Press.

Stanton, M. D., & Todd, T. (1981). Family treatment approaches to drug abuse problems. *Family Process, 18*, 251–280.

Strupp, H. H., & Hadley, S. W. (1979). Specific vs. nonspecific factors in psychotherapy: A controlled study of outcome. *Archives of General Psychiatry, 36*, 1125–1136.

Truax, C. B., & Carkhuff, R. R. (1967). *Toward effective counseling and psychotherapy: Training and practice*. Chicago: Aldine.

Truax, C. B., & Mitchell, K. M. (1971). Research on certain therapist interpersonal skills in relation to process and outcome. In A. E. Bergin & S. L. Garfield (Eds.), *Handbook on psychotherapy and behavior change: An empirical analysis*. New York: John Wiley.

Wells, R. A., & Dezen, A. E. (1978). The results of family therapy revisited: The non-behavioral methods. *Family Process, 17*, 251–274.

Suggested Readings

Gurman, A. S., & Kniskern, D. P. (1981). Family therapy outcome research: Knowns and unknowns. In A. S. Gurman and D. P. Kniskern (Eds.), *Handbook of Family Therapy*. New York: Brunner/Mazel.

Huber, C., & Baruth, L. (1987). *Ethical, legal and professional issues in the practice of marriage and family therapy.* Columbus, OH: Merrill.

Margolin, G. (1982). Ethical and legal considerations in family therapy. *American Psychologist, 7*, 788–801.

Okun, B. F., & Gladding, S. T. (Eds.). (1983). *Issues in training marriage and family therapists.* Ann Arbor, MI: ERIC Counseling and Personnel Services Clearinghouse, The University of Michigan.

This article was originally published in *Counseling Families: An Introduction to Marriage and Family Therapy,* 1989, pp. 300–304. Reprint permission granted by Love Publishing.

Dilemmas of Power and Equality in Marital and Family Counseling: Proposals for a Feminist Perspective

Carolyn Zerbe Enns

In recent counseling history, feminist and family systems counselors have changed the face of many counseling experiences by moving beyond the traditional intrapsychic understandings of personal and family distress and proposing that problems in living are embedded in the context in which individuals behave. Feminist counselors presume clients' health, competence, and ability to act proactively in their environments. They stress the interrelationship of individual problems, environmental factors, socialization, and oppression and emphasize the importance of active change of these factors rather than adjustment to status quo definitions of well being (Butler, 1985; Gilbert, 1980; Rawlings & Carter, 1977). Feminist counselors represent a wide range of theoretical orientations but are drawn together by their recognition that sexism limits the psychological well being of women and men, by their advocacy of equality in relationships and society, and by their refusal to use any counseling methods or explanatory concepts that promote bias (Thomas, 1977).

Family systems counselors view family functioning as a complex process in which the behavior of every individual is related to and dependent on the behavior of all other individuals in a system. Each interpersonal event is considered to be multiply determined by mutual interactions within a family system, and no individual or specific interaction is seen as the cause of family problems (Koman & Stechler, 1985; Nichols, 1984). Systems thinking is recognized as the cornerstone or hallmark of family counseling, and Nichols (1984) indicated that not believing in systems is a bit like not believing in the flag, apple pie, and motherhood.

Most family and couples counseling approaches, with their emphasis on viewing problems in context instead of as anchored in internal personality deficiencies, tender a friendly overture to feminist perspectives on relationships. There is a common recognition that personal issues and social environments are inextricably linked. Both feminist and family systems counselors show commitment to helping individuals and families investigate creative, original ways of incorporating change into their lives and affirm the capacity of persons to choose and act on new and rewarding behavioral alternatives.

Despite these parallels and commonalities, a more careful scrutiny reveals significant differences between the philosophical substrates of feminist counseling and couples and family counseling, particularly as they relate to power and sex role concerns. The purpose of this article is to explicate power and equality issues in couples-family counseling as reflected in (a) problem definitions, (b) family sex role issues, and (c) the therapeutic relationship. After each section, suggestions for reconciling family systems and feminist perspectives are provided.

Problem Definitions in Family and Couples Counseling

Focus of Definitions: The Nuclear Family or Social Systems?

Libow, Raskin, and Caust (1982) indicated that both systems and feminist therapists are "appreciators" of symptoms as growing pains with a communicative, coping, or adaptive purpose; they are not considered to be personal flaws that must be overhauled, cured, or removed. They also acknowledged, however, that although family systems counselors define problems as manifestations of interaction within the family unit, feminist counselors call for a wider view of the social environment, one in which symptoms are perceived as emerging from restrictive assumptions about appropriate sex role behavior and the oppressiveness of a sexist society. These authors maintained that a family systems orientation may be preferable to a feminist orientation because it allows counselors to introduce changes into a family "without directly introducing ideas (such as oppression and feminism) that would create alarm or resistance in all or some of the members" (Libow et al., 1982, p. 10). Most feminist counselors, however, believe that dealing solely with the inner structure of the family leads to limited change, which may reinforce traditional norms and hinder the potential of women and men.

Family systems counselors have been criticized for their reductionistic conception of family functioning, an account that considers the family as an interpersonal event or closed system, "particularizes" family issues, and neglects to account for pervasive social and historical forces that impinge on the family (Gurman & Klein, 1980; James & McIntyre, 1983). Goldner (1985) and Taggart (1985) criticized family counselors for assuming that once nuclear family systems are fully "therapized," women's issues will disappear. Family counselors may perpetrate the same injustice as individually oriented therapists who focus on removing the problems of specific troubled children who bear the symptoms that result from negative family and parental interactions. Family systems counselors may treat the individual child of society, the nuclear family, and neglect to see family and couple interactions as related to social attitudes and problems (James & McIntyre, 1983).

Elkaim (1982) maintained that most family counselors merely focus on the visible part of the iceberg and neglect to consider the housing, job, school, and poverty concerns of a large segment of society. The typical systems approach is designed to "heal the cracked bones of a whole number of people rather than stop the hand of those delivering the blows" (Elkaim, 1982, p. 345). Elkaim's concerns are especially pertinent to women, who are much more likely than men to live in poverty and experience discrimination in the work force (Belle, 1984).

The resistance of some family counselors to dealing with the social milieu is epitomized by Minuchin's (1974) assertion that family counseling is "not a tool for humanistic revolution. It is often the opposite: one of the family's tasks is to provide continuity with a society which a family therapist, in his own value system, may consider restrictive. But the field for social change is not family therapy, but politics" (pp. 25–26).

Limitations of Circular Causality in Defining Problems

From a systems viewpoint, relationship problems represent "a mutually regulated dance between oppressor and oppressed, a dance maintained by the cyclical interaction sequences between the participants" (Libow et al., 1982, p. 8). The framework used here is one of circular causality, in which each event or individual is viewed as influencing every other aspect of a system in a complex, reciprocal, reinforcing process. No specific situation or person is considered the antecedent, cause, or effect of a problem. The concept of circular causality becomes especially problematic in issues of family violence, because it attributes abusiveness to the nature of interactions between partners (Taggart, 1985). Family systems thinking is helpful for understanding the sequences that accelerate abusiveness and comprehending how battering becomes a couple's only strategy for resolving conflict (Cook & Frantz-Cook, 1984; Margolin, 1979). Feminist counselors, however, consider unequal social power and sex role socialization as the sources and causes of many of women's problems, especially those involving emotional, sexual, and physical abuse.

Women are estimated to be the victims of aggressive and violent acts, such as battering, incest, and rape, in 30% to 50% of families (Carmen, Russo, & Miller, 1984; Rosewater, 1984). When social attitudes and forces that maintain oppressive sexist norms are not accounted for, problems of violence against women are likely to be poorly understood. Many counselors articulate views based primarily on structures *within* the nuclear family and personality dynamics, such as self-defeating patterns that exacerbate negative cycles. These definitions and themes have also been popularized for the public in self-help psychology books in which women's problems are linked to personal styles, such as "loving too much" (Norwood, 1985), engaging in "sweet suffering" (Shainess, 1984), or succumbing to the "Wendy dilemma" (Kiley, 1984). Even within the neutrality of systems thinking, women may be seen as legitimate victims of violence if self-defeating patterns and cyclical interactions become the sole focus of interventions (Taggart, 1985). According to Walker (1985):

> Whatever analysis is applied, unless the violence is seen as a function of a sexist and violent society—which ultimately only can be controlled and eliminated by changing the very structures of that society which reinforce individuals' violent behavior—we cannot be helpful to the victim/survivors. (p. 204)

Despite the prevalence, intensity, and long-term effects of abuse, both men and women tend to minimize, rationalize, and deny abusive behavior (Walker, 1985). The role of the counselor must include raising consciousness and educating clients about the incidence and unacceptability of both physical and emotional abuse in relationships. Also, a contextual view, which incorporates a social critique and social change model, is essential for validating victims-survivors of violence, minimizing self-blame, and facilitating emotional expression that motivates rather than paralyzes individuals.

Importance of Awareness and Insight to the Change Process

Although both systems and feminist counselors perceive symptoms as vehicles for understanding the mechanisms of individuals, they perceive the connection between client insight about these symptoms and change in different ways. Family systems counselors are usually more concerned about altering behavior than understanding the cause or source of problems (Koman & Stechler, 1985). Insight or understanding is encouraged when it fits into a particular intervention but is not considered a goal in its own right (Libow et al., 1982).

In contrast, feminist counselors believe that it is important for both clients and counselors to determine how symptoms may emerge from attempts to cope with unjust situations. Awareness of the nature, function, and effects of distress helps clients construct satisfying lifestyles based on principles of equality. Exploration and discovery of alternative realities is conducted through the use of sex role analysis (Rawlings & Carter, 1977), consciousness-raising techniques (Kaschak, 1981), and reframing methods (Smith & Siegel, 1985). When external issues are not considered, women are likely to assume personal blame for problems they have limited or no control over, such as job discrimination or sexual harassment.

Problem Definitions: Suggestions for a Feminist Response

Feminist family counselors can use family systems concepts to understand the dynamics that maintain sequences of behavior in the family. If couples and family counselors, however, ignore institutional precursors of distress and assume that the nuclear family is immune from societal messages that bombard it from outside, they may encourage adjustment to prevailing norms and reinforce longstanding inequities. Gentle questioning of unexamined assumptions and the appropriate sharing of statistics pointing to injustice and sexism (Carmen et al., 1984; Steil, 1984) are useful ways to help couples and families explore new definitions of their problems. Contrary to popular belief, many feminist concerns about the negative impact of traditional social values can be addressed without using labels, such as oppression, patriarchy, and sexism, that may be misunderstood or may trigger negative emotional reactions.

Although the provision of factual information about inequality and sex role socialization facilitates client decision making, counselors must be careful not to oversell employment as the primary means for women to gain independence and greater self-esteem, because many available jobs are repetitious, demeaning, marginally lucrative, and may substitute one form of oppression for another (Hare-Mustin, 1981). For example, women in dead-end jobs (along with young poor women heading households) have recently experienced the greatest increase in depression (Belle, 1980; Carmen et al., 1984).

As students of our culture and as change agents, feminist family counselors face the challenge of questioning traditional assumptions and proposing conceptualizations and solutions that recognize the inseparable nature of personal and social change. It will be difficult, however, to create positive alternatives unless institutional and employment policies allow for more opportunities to balance personal and professional lives. As a result, counselors should consider expanding their roles and increasing their impact by promoting political and legislative policies that support flexible family roles. Critical issues include paternity and maternity leave, flexible working hours, reentry educational opportunities, and affordable, quality child care (Norgren, 1984).

Sex Roles Within the Family

One of the apparent similarities between feminist and family systems approaches to counseling is their common reflection of traditional role prescriptions. A careful comparison reveals that although many family counselors advocate neutrality about role choices (Avis, 1985), feminist counselors actively promote the expansion of behavioral repertoires by helping both women and men move beyond sex role stereotypes and explore both instrumental and expressive aspects of themselves. Furthermore, feminist therapists advocate equality of personal power in intimate relationships (Rawlings & Carter, 1977). Some of the neutral family approaches may inadvertently reinforce, legitimize, and endorse traditional sex roles, thus perpetuating systems that limit the potential and life satisfaction of women and men (Avis, 1985; Margolin, Fernandez, Talovic, & Onorato, 1983).

Thinking, Feeling, and Communication Styles

Behavioral marital counselors, with their emphasis on instrumental problem solving, may neglect the impact of sex role socialization on women's tendency to choose affective styles and men's tendency to choose rational patterns of thinking and relating (Gilligan, 1982). A man's more powerful position in a relationship may be reinforced by objective problem-solving and decision-making processes that build on skills he has spent a lifetime cultivating (Jacobson, 1983; Margolin, 1982). Likewise, Bowen family systems counselors emphasize differentiation (Bowen, 1976), "thinking about emotional issues" (Singleton, 1982, p. 93), and rational decision making, processes that may fail to value the more emotional and intuitive strengths that are reinforced in many of women's life experiences (Belenky, Clinchy, Goldberger, & Tarule, 1986; Gurman & Klein, 1980). The explicit valuing of objective, intellectual processes may result in feelings of inadequacy and lowered self-esteem in some women. Whereas this section elaborates on the limitations of systems concepts that primarily emphasize individuation, skill building, and rational styles, a later section discusses how experiential family approaches, which value more affective methods, may be used to create balance in family work.

Many women may find it more difficult to use instrumental communication tools, such as assertive behaviors, unless they are convinced that they will be rewarded rather than punished (Fodor & Rothblum, 1984; Gurman & Klein, 1980). Whereas men's autonomy and assertiveness wins admiration, women's assertiveness and directness may be met with skepticism or rejection, reinforcing women's sense of danger (Miller, 1986). In one study, women who experimented with assertive behavior experienced increased feelings of self-respect but expressed misgivings about the potential of negative reactions such as being discounted, rejected, or ignored (Fiedler & Beach, 1978). Also, women's appropriate assertion has been a major factor associated with abusive spousal incidents (O'Leary, Curley, Rosenbaum, & Clarke, 1985), a reality that is likely to encourage battered women to use conciliation and acquiescence rather than direct communication. In addition to helping individuals learn new skills, counseling should focus on examining and altering expectations of what is appropriate male and female behavior.

The socialization experiences of women encourage them to be expressive, relational, and supportive, qualities that make them cooperative and motivated clients in family and marital counseling. Jean Baker Miller (1986) asserted that women in counseling more frequently confront themselves with questions about responding effectively to others and express deep fears and frustrations with themselves when they feel they are not "giving." They are also more likely than men to believe that all activity should lead to increased emotional connection with others. Some family systems concepts, however, such as fusion, enmeshment, differentiation, and boundaries, focus primarily on the importance of maintaining healthy separations from others. These concepts may be perceived by some women as creating distance rather than healthy closeness (Goodrich, Rampage, Ellman, & Halstead, 1988).

Because women are trained to place family harmony, cooperation, and communication higher on their list of priorities than many men, the counselor may inadvertently rely on women's commitment to relationships and expect more of them, reinforcing old patterns in which responsibility for relationship change is placed on women (Goldner, 1985; Jacobson, 1983). This reliance may create feelings of conflict in women who are encouraged to demonstrate more autonomy and instrumental skills, yet are involved, by virtue of their emotional commitment, as supportive allies of the counselor.

Women often come to counseling with an externally anchored sense of self-esteem and have difficulty distinguishing personal desires and wants as distinct from the needs of others (Klein, 1976; Siegel, 1983). It is not unusual for an exhausted, depressed, bored mother of small children to ask a counselor to make her a better wife and mother. She has no other image of herself (Lerner, 1984). Other women report knowing who they were prior to being in an intimate relationship but convey that in giving to another person they have lost a sense of who they are (Sanford & Donovan, 1984). Men, on the other hand, often express fear of being engulfed or entrapped in human relationships (Gilligan, 1982). Furthermore, Heriot (1983) asserted that when individuals attempt to integrate the strengths of empathy and sensitivity with autonomy and competence, they are often caught in a double bind by a society that does not recognize these roles as compatible. This dilemma may be fully resolvable only when social changes and loosening stereotypes allow for more integration of strengths that have been traditionally attributed to one sex.

Generational Boundaries and Power Within the Family

Given women's strong social injunctions to care for and nurture others, it is not surprising that family and marital counselors often define women as "overinvolved." When structural family counselors observe maternal "overinvolvement," they use powerful interventions to retrieve the disengaged man from the periphery of the family, extricate the woman from her intense involvement with her children, and realign her with her husband (Minuchin, 1974; Minuchin & Fishman, 1981). In one of

Minuchin's (1984) interviews, he made the following statements to the adult man:

> At some point your daughter needs to grow up. And your wife needs to start to grow up first.... You need to talk to your wife about keeping Loretta a little girl.... I think she has run the house for too long, you know. (pp. 107–109)

The adult male is given the central role, consolidating his power and heightening his status, potentially reducing the adult woman's self-esteem and discounting her limited authority (Hare-Mustin, 1981). Encouraging a father to take charge conveys a simplistic, functional view of family roles. It may also imply that the mother has failed, that the father can do a better job, and that an expert counselor must repair the damage (Goodrich et al., 1988).

Haley (1976) and Minuchin (1981, 1984) placed importance on "hierarchies" in families, and although they stress the necessity of joint executive authority between parents, they often treat the adult man as the central authority figure in their attempt to gain his alliance and commitment to family processes. The word *hierarchy* seems inappropriate in a family systems approach that claims neutrality about family functions.

Hare-Mustin's (1981) concept of "clear generational boundaries" is far more compatible with a feminist view of the family in which power differentials between people are minimized. The need for generational boundaries should be viewed from a perspective that examines their ability to enhance or detract from more flexible and rewarding sex roles in the family. Counselors may place special emphasis on the man's participation and comfort, especially if he has been disengaged in important aspects of family life. Although increasing the father's involvement, including a leadership role, facilitates family health, options other than authoritative roles should be explored. Also, attempts at building executive alliances with the adult man must not emphasize his participation without also exploring novel executive options for the adult woman in the family (Robbins, 1983).

Sex Roles: Suggestions for a Feminist Response

Counselors should, first of all, examine the impact of sex role stereotypes on their own motivation to work with families and couples, their choice of interventions, and their interpretation of what constitutes successful intervention (Goodrich et al., 1988; Hines & Hare-Mustin,

1978). They must also acknowledge that, if they adopt a neutral stance, they make a political statement by implying that marital choices, such as division of labor in the family, are purely matters of personal taste (Avis, 1985; Jacobson, 1983). In spite of dramatic social change and attempts by counselors to become open to creative family options, several research studies suggest that counselors continue to adhere to sex role stereotypes as the essence of normality. For example, counterstereotypical couples were labeled as more maladapted than stereotypical couples with identical problems (Woodruff & Conoley, 1985). Another analogue study found that more female than male protocols were expected to make concessions, such as compromising career ambitions, to achieve satisfactory relationships (Bowman, 1982). These research results inform counselors that they must continue to examine their own assumptions about intimate partnerships.

In addition to examining personal motivations, it is important for counselors to consistently use inclusive language and to avoid particularistic labels or terminology (Lerman, 1986). For example, phrases such as *clear generational boundaries* should be substituted for the term *hierarchies*, and *parenting or nurturing* should be substituted for *mothering*.

Third, family counselors concerned about the high costs associated with traditional family roles are encouraged to provide factual information and statistics that clarify the specific nature of inequality and sex role socialization. Avis (1985), for example, reviewed a number of studies demonstrating that traditional relationships are associated with emotional distress in women, including higher rates of depression (Weissman, 1980), lowered self-esteem (Birnbaum, 1975), and poorer marital communication and satisfaction (Burke & Weir, 1976).

Fourth, marriage and family counselors should consider engaging their clients in discussions of who controls financial and emotional resources in the family, who exerts power in the family, how power is communicated, and how equitable partners perceive their lives to be. Questions focusing on a cost-benefit analysis of sex role behaviors and expectations are likely to unveil central socialization influences that are frequently covert and to enhance exploration of more satisfying labor distributions in the family. For example, what are the rewards and costs of being solely responsible for the financial survival of the family or of carrying primary responsibility for the emotional growth and nurturance of the family? Where do these personal beliefs about appropriate roles come from? How can the overwhelming and positive aspects of one person's roles be shared by another, potentially enriching the other's life? If individuals are willing to risk greater individual development in nonstereotypical areas, they are likely to be less territorial about traditional roles and less likely to limit or restrict power-sharing activities.

Fifth, themes of independence and interdependence should be explored and integrated. Western industrial society has emphasized the importance of individual achievement and autonomy (Gilligan, 1982). Although relationship maintenance and the cultural values of instrumentality and independence are often seen as mutually exclusive (Heriot, 1983), more integrated views of health are available. Gilligan (1982) spoke to the importance of balancing self-development with responsiveness to others, and Kegan (1982) described differentiation and reintegration of connection and separateness as "the two greatest yearnings in human experience" (p. 107). In addition, the self-in-relation model of women's development (Jordan & Surrey, 1986) encourages counselors to emphasize relationship differentiation, the development of oneself within significant attachments, instead of separation-individuation, which centers on self-reliance and individual destiny (Jordan & Surrey, 1986).

Concepts such as personal differentiation and boundary setting have helped us understand how maturity and autonomy allow individuals to engage in satisfying relationships. In addition, close connections can provide the context for healthy mutual empowerment and personal development. The self-in-relation model (Jordan & Surrey, 1986) and Gilligan's (1982) morality of care provide ways of expanding on rather than replacing other notions of growth in relationships, such as Bowen's useful concept of individual differentiation.

Although many family counseling theorists emphasize rational thinking processes, others such as Satir (1982) and experiential family counselors (Nichols, 1984) perceive "emotional deadness" as a major factor in family problems. From their perspectives, the goals of counseling include the reintegration of disowned parts of the emotional self, enhancement of individual self-esteem and uniqueness, and spontaneous, nonrational experiencing of what individuals feel and think. Some of the experiential family counseling methods, such as family sculpture or drawings (Nichols, 1984) and Gestalt counseling techniques (Kempler, 1982), encourage family members to express individuality within the presence of others. In the spirit of integration, counselors should consider incorporating methods that promote both thinking and feeling processes, as well as those that examine the rewards of both independence and relatedness.

Sixth, counselors should make concerted efforts to build alliances with both adult partners in the family and to reinforce the competent acts and personal growth goals of each. For example, women should not merely be blocked from specific kinds of "overinvolvement" but should be encouraged to engage in self-nurturing activities that may have been neglected while they have been "giving" so completely to family members. Women's socialized ability to recognize the essential cooperative nature of existence, and to appreciate emotional and intuitive processes, must be acknowledged as strengths that can be shared with other family members (Belenky et al., 1986; Miller, 1986). Women may need particular help, however, in balancing personal needs and those of family members, because many women have never experienced a phase as single adults in which they formulated personal goals and established personal identities (Gluck, Dannefer, & Milea, 1980).

Men may need special assistance in developing power to express emotions and to validate themselves as persons, instead of as achievement and authority figures. Although increased family involvement in the form of executive influence represents a fairly straightforward task for men, emotional roles may be more difficult for them to assume because they have been encouraged to experience emotions vicariously through women and to gain personal validation from the support of women (Pleck, 1984). When partners are encouraged to explore undernourished and untapped aspects of themselves, they are more likely to express personal wants and dreams, positive leadership, and interests in positive connections with intimate others.

Power in the Therapeutic Relationship

Counselor's Role and Sources of Influence

From the inception of feminist therapy, feminist therapists have perceived clients as their own best experts and have promoted egalitarian relationships in which clients are encouraged to take responsibility for their own progress and growth (Butler, 1985; Gilbert, 1980; Rawlings & Carter, 1977). According to Libow et al. (1982), family systems counselors emphasize expert power, whereas feminist counselors rely on referent power that emerges from an emphasis on commonalities in the female experience, egalitarianism, and the redistribution of power in the therapeutic relationship. In a depiction of feminist counseling that seems narrow and restrictive, they implied that feminist counselors are confined to being equal partners in a consciousness-raising effort, thus limiting the effectiveness of feminist counselors.

Feminist counselor Douglas (1985), however, indicated that denying that power differentials exist in the therapeutic relationship is inappropriate and can be likened to the responses of counselors who deny that they make a political statement by their neutrality. Feminist counselors are aware that clients will attribute power to them because of their expertise, position, and heightened verbal and interpersonal skills. Feminist counselors use reward power when they provide support and encouragement, informational power when they highlight the effects of traditional sex role socialization, expert power when they devise resocialization experiences, referent power when they use modeling and self-disclosure, and legitimate power when they base their work on a contractual agreement with clients (Douglas, 1985).

Power and Informed Choice

In keeping with the feminist intent to empower clients and demystify the nature of therapy, counselors are encouraged to assure informed choice by defining agreements that outline goals, therapeutic procedures, and possible side effects of specific techniques. Contractual relationships clarify the nature and parameters of counseling, shift the balance of power in favor of greater equality, and provide a context for clients to take responsibility for their progress (Hare-Mustin, Marecek, Kaplan, & Liss-Levinson, 1979). For feminist counselors, manipulation and indirect suggestions are eschewed in this collaborative effort. On the other hand, family systems counselors may choose not to show the client their "full hand of cards" (Libow et al., 1982, p. 10). Some strategic family counselors place little value on informed choice and promote deception and covert manipulation as central to successful counseling (Widiger & Rorer, 1984). Strategic-paradoxical techniques are sometimes used to "shake up" a system, overcome resistance, and overpower a presenting symptom. At the same time, these techniques may fail to convey respect and understanding of family pain.

The strategic-paradoxical techniques of symptom escalation or exaggeration augment the power differentials between clients and counselors by emphasizing the counselor's control and the need to outmaneuver a resistant individual or family group. In keeping with symptom escalation, a strategic counselor might ask a woman to exaggerate her sense of powerlessness because her dependent role is necessary for family functioning. It is presumed that as a result of the counselor's injunction, the woman will no longer receive a payoff for her behavior, will abandon her stifling role, adopt a defiant, oppositional attitude, and make a 180 degree shift in her response style. Although paradoxical interventions are very potent, however, they are also risky (Fischer, Anderson, & Jones, 1981). Even when interventions work, as described in the example, individuals have no opportunity to internalize change or to process its meaning, especially as it relates to sex role issues.

Therapeutic Mutuality and Power: Suggestions for a Feminist Response

How can feminist family counselors respond to clients in a relationship that calls for counselor expertise, yet also strive for equality? Unequal power in the counseling relationship might promote a continuation of hierarchical family relationships that have reinforced powerlessness in women (Kaschak, 1981). It is sometimes difficult for counselors to determine how to balance their authority and personalities with respect and recognition of the family group as its own best expert. Although sometimes difficult to implement, a blending of expressive and authoritative roles is most compatible for feminist counselors who want to depict diverse, nonconventional, and flexible roles as both equal participants and active change agents (Kaplan et al., 1983).

Second, although shared power is a central attitude of feminist counselors, therapeutic mutuality and informed choice need not be considered "all or nothing" events, but a continuum of experiences that are based on a dynamic, growing, and deepening relationship. At entry into counseling, clients' crises, distress, or emotional volatility may make it difficult for them to absorb and use informed choice statements effectively. As clients assimilate new personal discoveries during counseling, they become increasingly capable of using information that conveys a rationale for the counselor's direction. As feminist counselors acknowledge the inevitable power differences in the therapeutic relationship, they may build in experiences to equalize power through ongoing efforts, rather than assuming that initial statements about the counselor's beliefs are sufficient to ensure that the rights of clients are protected.

Third, feminist marital and family counselors may choose "technical eclecticism" without accepting the philosophical assumptions of some therapies that convey limited respect for the client's capacities. For example, the strategic techniques of reframing and restraining can be compatible with a feminist perspective. In the case of women who feel helpless and use indirect, covert means of power, feminist counselors may use reframing to point out the goal directedness and energy associated with seemingly powerless behavior. "Weakness" of vulnerability, neediness, and helplessness can also be given positive connotations when they are associated with the strengths of sensitivity to others and the power of empathy (Miller, 1986). Counselors who use reframing in this way are not deceptive but help clients recognize that they *do* have power, allow them to let go of their guilt for relying on indirect means of influence, and free them to develop more effective, direct modes of expression (Smith & Siegel, 1985). In addition, counselors may use restraining methods (Weeks & L'Abate, 1982) to ask clients to count the cost of change before embracing new behaviors, especially when the responses of significant others may not be supportive of new modes of behaving.

Conclusion

This article has suggested that successful family interventions require attending to many levels of interaction: intrapersonal and interpersonal needs of individuals, small group interactions within a family system, and social forces that dramatically influence family life. The feminist family counselor who is committed to exploring methods for promoting equality in family members' lives must recognize how issues of power permeate personal and family life at each of these levels of experience. It is not enough to model neutrality, egalitarianism, and androgyny or to rely solely on skill-based or strategic methods for increasing the life satisfaction of partners. Although these efforts are useful, they are not powerful enough to counteract the cultural stereotypes that bombard the family. The feminist family counselor helps clients examine and critique constricting sex role expectations and brainstorms with them about methods for creating family identities based on healthy connections and power sharing. In addition, the counselor who is committed to social change and equality should consider acting on the feminist tenet that the "personal is political" by becoming involved in community and national policy issues that allow her or him to influence educational, occupational, and political systems.

References

Avis, J. M. (1985). The politics of functional family therapy: A feminist critique. *Journal of Marital and Family Therapy, 11*, 117–138.

Belenky, M. F., Clinchy, B., Goldberger, N. R., & Tarule, J. M. (1986). *Women's ways of knowing: The development of self, voice, and mind.* New York: Basic Books.

Belle, D. (1980). Who uses mental health facilities? In M. Guttentag, S. Salasin, & D. Belle (Eds.), *The mental health of women* (pp. 1–20). New York: Academic Press.

Belle, D. (1984). Inequality and mental health: Low income and minority women. In L. E. Walker (Ed.), *Women and mental health policy* (pp. 135–150). Beverly Hills, CA: Sage.

Birnbaum, J. A. (1975). Life patterns and self-esteem in gifted family-oriented and career-committed women. In M. Mednick, S. Tangri, & L. Hoffman (Eds.), *Women and achievement* (pp. 396–419). Washington, DC: Hemisphere.

Bowman, P. R. (1982). An analog study with beginning therapists suggesting bias against "activity" in women. *Psychotherapy: Theory, Research and Practice, 19*, 318–324.

Burke, R. J., & Weir, T. (1976). Relationship of wives' employment status to husband, wife and pair satisfaction and performance. *Journal of Marriage and the Family, 20*, 279–287.

Butler, M. (1985). Guidelines for feminist therapy. In L. B. Rosewater & L. E. A. Walker (Eds.), *Handbook of feminist therapy* (pp. 32–38). New York: Springer.

Carmen, E. H., Russo, N. F., & Miller, J. B. (1984). Inequality and women's mental health: An overview. In P. R. Rieker & E. H. Carmen (Eds.), *The gender gap in psychotherapy* (pp. 17–39). New York: Plenum Press.

Cook, D., & Frantz-Cook, A. (1984). A systematic treatment approach to wife battering. *Journal of Marital and Family Therapy, 7*, 171–180.

Douglas, M.A. (1985). The role of power in feminist therapy: A reformulation. In L. B. Rosewater & L. E. A. Walker (Eds.), *Handbook of feminist therapy* (pp. 241–249). New York: Springer.

Elkaim, M. (1982). From the family approach to the socio-political approach. In F. Kaslow (Ed.), *The International book of family therapy* (pp. 337–357). New York: Brunner/Mazel.

Fiedler, D., & Beach, L. R. (1978). On the decision to be assertive. *Journal of Consulting and Clinical Psychology, 46,* 537–546.

Fischer, L., Anderson, A., & Jones, J. E. (1981). Types of paradoxical interventions and indications/contraindications for use in clinical practice. *Family Process, 20,* 25–35.

Fodor, I., & Rothblum, E. D. (1984). Strategies for dealing with sex-role stereotypes. In C. Brody (Ed.), *Women therapists working with women* (pp. 86–95). New York: Springer.

Gilbert, L. A. (1980). Feminist therapy. In A. Brodsky & R. T. Hare-Mustin (Eds.), *Women and psychotherapy* (pp. 245–266). New York: Guilford Press.

Gilligan, C. (1982). *In a different voice.* Cambridge, MA: Harvard University Press.

Gluck, N. R., Dannefer, E., & Milea, K. (1980). Women in families. In E. A. Carter & M. McGoldrick (Eds.), *The family life cycle* (pp. 223–227). New York: Gardner Press.

Goldner, V. (1985). Feminism and family therapy. *Family Process, 24,* 31–47.

Goodrich, T. J., Rampage, C., Ellman, B., & Halstead, K. (1988). *Feminist family therapy.* New York: Norton.

Gurman, A. S., & Klein, M. (1980). Marital and family conflicts. In A. Brodsky & R. Hare-Mustin (Eds.), *Women and psychotherapy* (pp. 159–190). New York: Guilford Press.

Hare-Mustin, R. T. (1981). A feminist approach to family therapy. In G. D. Erickson & T. P. Hogan (Eds.), *Family therapy* (pp. 240–254). Monterey, CA: Brooks/Cole.

Heriot, J. (1983). The double bind: Healing the split. In J. H. Robbings & R. J. Siegel (Eds.), *Women changing therapy* (pp. 11–28). New York: The Haworth Press.

Hines, P. M., & Hare-Mustin, R. T. (1978). Ethical concerns in family therapy. *Professional Psychology, 9,* 165–171.

Jacobson, N. S. (1983). The politics of marital therapy. The American *Journal of Family Therapy, 11,* 11–24.

James, K., & McIntyre, D. (1983). The reproduction of families: The social role of family therapy? *Journal of Marital and Family Therapy, 9,* 119–129.

Jordan, J. V., & Surrey, J. L. (1986). The self-in-relation: Empathy and the mother-daughter relationship. In T. Bernay & D. W. Cantor (Eds.), *The psychology of today's woman: New psychoanalytic vision* (pp. 81–104). Hillsdale, NJ: Analytic Press.

Kaplan, A. G., Greif, A. C., Fibel, B., McComb, A., Sedney, M. A., & Shapiro, E. (1983). The process of sex role integration in psychotherapy: A contribution from a training perspective. *Psychotherapy: Theory, Research and Practice, 20,* 476–485.

Kaschak, E. (1981). Feminist psychotherapy: The first decade. In S. Cox (Ed.), *Female psychology: The emerging self* (pp. 387–401). New York: St. Martin's Press.

Kegan, R. (1982). *The evolving self.* Cambridge, MA: Harvard University Press.

Kempler, W. (1982). Gestalt family therapy. In A. M. Horne & M. M. Ohlsen (Eds.), *Family counseling and therapy* (pp. 141–174). Itasca, IL: Peacock.

Kiley, D. (1984). *The Wendy dilemma.* New York: Arbor House.

Klein, M. H. (1976). Feminist concepts of therapy outcome. *Psychotherapy: Theory, Research and Practice, 13,* 89–95.

Koman, S. L., & Stechler, G. (1985). Making the jump to systems. In M. P. Mirkin & S. L. Koman (Eds.), *Handbook of adolescents and family/therapy* (pp. 3–20). New York: Gardner Press.

Lerman, H. (1986). *A mote in Freud's eye.* New York: Springer.

Lerner, H. E. (1984). Special issues for women in psychotherapy. In P. R. Rieker & E. H. Carmen (Eds.), *The gender gap in psychotherapy* (pp. 271–284). New York: Plenum Press.

Libow, J. A., Raskin, P. A., & Caust, B. L. (1982). Feminist and family systems therapy: Are they irreconcilable? *American Journal of Family Therapy, 10,* 3–12.

Margolin, G. (1979). Conjoint marital therapy to enhance anger management and reduce spouse abuse. *American Journal of Family Therapy, 5,* 13–23.

Margolin, G. (1982). Ethical and legal considerations in marital and family therapy. *American Psychologist, 37,* 788–801.

Margolin, G., Talovic, S., Fernandez, V., & Onorato, R. (1983). Sex role considerations and behavioral marital therapy: Equal does not mean identical. *Journal of Marital and Family Therapy, 9,* 131–145.

Miller, J. B. (1986). *Toward a new psychology of women* (2nd ed.). Boston: Beacon Press.

Minuchin, S. (1974). *Families and family therapy*. Cambridge, MA: Harvard University Press.

Minuchin, S. (1984). *Family kaleidoscope*. Cambridge, MA: Harvard University Press.

Minuchin, S., & Fishman, H. C. (1981). *Family therapy techniques*. Cambridge, MA: Harvard University Press.

Nichols, M. P. (1984). *Family therapy: Concepts and methods*. New York: Gardner Press.

Norgren, J. (1984). Child care. In J. Freeman (Ed.), *Women: A feminist perspective* (pp. 139–153). Palo Alto, CA: Mayfield.

O'Leary, K. D., Curley, A., Rosenbaum, A., & Clarke, C. (1985). Assertion training for abused wives: A potentially hazardous treatment. *Journal of Marital and Family Therapy, 12*, 319–322.

Pleck, J. H. (1984). Men's power with women, other men, and society. In P. R. Rieder & E. H. Carmen (Eds.), *The gender gap in psychotherapy* (pp. 79–89). New York: Plenum.

Rawlings, E. I., & Carter, D. K. (1977). *Feminist and nonsexist psychotherapy for women*. Springfield, IL: Charles C Thomas.

Robbins, J. H. (1983). Complex triangles: Uncovering sexist bias in relationship counseling. In J. H. Robbins & R. J. Siegel (Eds.), *Women changing therapy* (pp. 159–169). New York: Haworth.

Rosewater, L. B. (1984). Feminist therapy: Implications for practitioners. In L. E. Walker (Ed.), *Women and mental health policy* (pp. 267–279). Beverly Hills, CA: Sage Publications.

Sanford, L. S., & Donovan, M. E. (1984). *Women and self-esteem*. New York: Penguin.

Satir, V. M. (1982). The therapist and family therapy: Process model. In A. M. Horne & M. M. Ohlsen (Eds.), *Family counseling and therapy* (pp. 12–42). Itasca, IL: Peacock.

Shainess, N. (1984). *Sweet suffering*. New York: Pocket Books.

Siegel, R. J. (1983). Accumulated inequalities: Problems in long-term marriages. In J. H. Robbins & R. J. Siegel (Eds.), *Women changing therapy* (pp. 171–178). New York: Haworth.

Singleton, G. (1982). Bowen family systems theory. In A. M. Horne & M. M. Ohlsen (Eds.), *Family counseling and therapy* (pp. 75–111). Itasca, IL: Peacock Publishers.

Smith, A. J., & Siegel, R. F. (1985). Feminist therapy: Redefining power for the powerless. In L. B. Rosewater & L. E. A. Walker (Eds.), *Handbook of feminist therapy* (pp. 203–214). New York: Springer.

Steil, J. M. (1984). Marital relationships and mental health: The psychic costs of inequality. In J. Freeman (Ed.), *Women: A feminist perspective* (pp. 113–138). Palo Alto, CA: Mayfield.

Taggart, M. (1985). The feminist critique in epistemological perspective: Questions of context in family therapy. *Journal of Marital and Family Therapy, 1*, 113–126.

Thomas, S. A. (1977). Theory and practice in feminist therapy. *Social Work, 22*, 447–454.

Walker, L. E. A. (1985). Feminist therapy with victim/survivors of interpersonal violence. In L. B. Rosewater & L. E. A. Walker (Eds.), *Handbook of feminist therapy* (pp. 203–214). New York: Springer.

Weeks, G. R., & L'Abate, L. (1982). *Paradoxical psychotherapy.* New York: Brunner/Mazel.

Weissman, M. M. (1980). Depression. In A. M. Brodsky & R. T. Hare-Mustin (Eds.), *Women and psychotherapy* (pp. 97–112). New York: Guilford Press.

Widiger, T. A., & Rorer, L. G. (1984). The responsible psychotherapist. *American Psychologist, 39*, 503–515.

Woodruff, J. G., & Conoley, C. W. (1985). *Sex-role stereotyping in marital counseling*. Paper presented at the 93rd annual convention of the American Psychological Association, Los Angeles.

Layers of Understanding: Counseling Ethnic Minority Families

Harlan London
Wynetta Devore

Practitioners in various disciplines must become sensitive to the uniqueness of ethnic minority families if they are to respond in ways that are helpful to clients. One cannot hold to the belief that current practices in mental health are adequate and appropriate for use with the many ethnic minority groups in this country. Nor can the practitioner forget that ethnicity is applicable to all individuals and families and is not limited to those who are identified as minority (Sue et al., 1982). The focus here is on particular groups of families who are at risk in our society due to their national origins and socioeconomic status. The primary aim is to provide a viable framework for practitioners to use as they seek to improve the human condition of minority families.

It is believed that such an effort is timely and needed for the following reasons: (a) the considerable complexity related to the status and conditions associated with minority family life in America, (b) minority families must negotiate and socialize their children to become self-sufficient, competent adults within the ambiguities of a cultural heritage that espouses a democratic equality for all citizens and a caste-like status for minority citizens (Peters, 1981), and (c) demands that result from having to cope within the American social context are multifaceted and inherently contradictory (Boykin & Toms, 1985).

To address some of these concerns, a schematic model is used to display the "Layers of Understanding" for practitioners working with ethnic minority families (Devore & Schlesinger, 1987). In the model (see Table 1) the two initial layers of understanding (a basic knowledge of human behavior and professional values) are introduced as basic requirements for all practitioners. In addition to these two layers, practitioners who work with ethnic minority families are expected to acquire the three additional layers of understanding. Together, the five layers offer the practitioner a practice orientation that recognizes the

Table 1
A Schematic Model Displaying the Layers of Understanding Required of Practitioners Working with Ethnic Minority Families

Basic Skills Required of All Practitioners	Additional Layers of Understanding Required of Practitioners Who Work with Ethnic Minority Families
1. A basic knowledge of human behavior	3. Self-awareness, knowledge of one's own ethnicity and its influence on practice
2. Professional values	4. Understanding the impact of ethnicity on the daily life of clients
	5. Modification and adaptation of skills in response to working with ethnic minority families

significance of human growth and development over the life cycle as well as those life experiences related to ethnicity.

A Basic Knowledge of Human Behavior

The competent practitioner should have a basic knowledge of human behavior with particular emphasis upon the developmental cycles of individuals and families. McGoldrick (1982) suggests that ethnicity interacts with individual development and the process of the family life cycle at every stage of development. This basic knowledge becomes the foundation upon which more specific knowledge and information about the experiences of ethnic minority families is built.

It is expected that all families, despite status or national origin, perform a variety of instrumental and expressive tasks such as the provision of food, clothing, shelter, and health as instrumental assignments; and nurture, love, and care as expressive tasks.

Billingsley's (1968) early work provides a discussion that may be generalized to other ethnic minority families. He suggests that most important among the instrumental functions is the expectation that families will be able to remain a stable unit and sustain themselves economically through their own efforts.

Such is not the experience for approximately 50% of ethnic minority families of color who often find themselves with only one parent (U.S. Bureau of Census, 1986). Many of these families need to look to public assistance agencies for financial support. This support provides minimal instrumental needs such as food, clothing, shelter, and medical care.

The fulfillment of these needs does not begin to address the affective or expressive function so necessary to positive family development. Several components of the expressive function are the tasks of: monitoring and fostering the relationship among family members, preparing and serving meals which is more than the provision of nutrition to the family, and child care which is more than feeding and clothing and providing shelter for children (Huber & Spitze, 1983).

These tasks are attended to throughout the life cycle of the family and require that the family change continually. At the same time, the family must interact with external forces—other people, groups, and institutions. These external forces do not necessarily contribute in positive ways. For example, they may respond to minority families in behaviors which reveal institutional racism (Knowles & Pruitt, 1969).

Development within minority families has an added level of complexity. As ethnic minority children go through the various stages of the life cycle, they must deal with the normal tasks of development *as well as those related to ethnicity*. Logan (1981), in a discussion of development in Black children calls for a concern for variables of race and race awareness as chief determinates of intellect and personal style of children. In addition, Logan suggests an acceptance of Black child studies into the education of practitioners and an acceptance of the color black as a symbol of pride, worth, and power.

Although attention is directed to the development of Black children, a similar perspective is appropriate as one considers the development of children in other ethnic minority groups. Logan asks for a willingness to reconceptualize one's scientific frame of reference regarding human growth and development, addressing the process through which it occurs (i.e., physical maturation and life experiences). This allows for a practice orientation that recognizes the significance of ethnic dispositions throughout the life cycle of ethnic minority individuals and families.

Professional Values

Practitioners bring to the encounter with ethnic minorities their own set of values that have been developed over a lifetime. Indications of one's values may be found in his/her beliefs, goals, attitudes, ethics, morals, feelings, thoughts, interests, and aspirations (Schulman, 1982). These values influence responses to ethnic minority families. One example of this can be detected in how much the practitioner operates within a traditional American mainstream value such as self-reliance. The practitioner's belief in self-reliance may hamper work with a Native American family, while acceptance of goals set by Asian parents for their children may contribute to greater participation in the helping process.

Professional organizations develop codes of ethics that reinforce the values upheld by the group. These codes serve as guidelines for professional behavior, but at another level they represent the imposition of a set of values that the practitioners may think "ought" to be followed in relation to client populations. Table 2 shows a composite code representing several professional organizations.

It is obvious that some of these codes are more salient to dealing with ethnic minority families than others, but taken as a whole, they provide a useful guide for practitioners' behavior in dealing with all client populations. Presumably, they are safeguards protecting both client and practitioner. Currently, the ethnic minority family is particularly protected as codes demand behavior that does not discriminate in relation to race or financial status. Clients expect responses that recognize their uniqueness without allowing these responses to present barriers to responsible practice.

Self Awareness, Knowledge of One's Own Ethnicity and Its Influence on Practice

Practitioners should have a knowledge of themselves which enables them to be aware of and to take responsibility for their own emotions and attitudes. Awareness is an essential area of knowledge. The disciplined and aware self is one of the practitioner's major tools for practice (Devore & Schlesinger, 1987). The questions to be answered

Table 2
Composite Code of Ethics and Professional Organizations who Adhere to the Code

Composite Code of Ethics	Professional Organizations					
	AAMFT[a]	COMHC[b]	AMA[c]	ANA[d]	APA[e]	NASW[f]
1. They shall accept as their first goal the performance of competent service.	x	x	x	x	x	x
2. They shall accept as their primary obligation the protection of the client's dignity and welfare.	x	x	x	x	x	x
3. They shall preserve the confidentiality and privacy of the information acquired concerning the client.	x	x	x	x	x	x
4. They shall not discriminate because of race, religion, age, sex, health, or national origin.						
5. They shall try to persuade the client to report to the appropriate authorities when the client's behavior tends to be destructive to him/herself or others.	x	x		x		
6. They shall use every resource available, including referral, to provide the best possible service for the client.	x	x	x	x	x	x
7. They shall safeguard the client from violations of human dignity and from physical and psychological harm.	x	x	x	x	x	x
8. They shall accept responsibility to the institution in which they are employed.	x	x	x	x	x	x
9. They shall participate in activities that contribute to the ongoing development of their professional knowledge and skill.	x	x	x	x	x	x
10. They shall be committed to increase the public's understanding of the needs and potentials of their clients.	x	x	x	x	x	x

Note. Adapted from Schulman, E. D. (1982). *Intervention in human services: A guide to skills and knowledge*. St. Louis: The C. V. Mosby Company.
[a]American Association for Marriage and Family Therapy; [b]Certified Clinical Mental Health Counselors; [c]American Medical Association; [d]American Nurses Association; [e]American Psychological Association; [f]National Association of Social Workers.

are, "Who am 1?" "Who am I in relation to my feelings about myself and others?" and in these instances discussed here, "Who am I in the ethnic sense?" This question may be followed by: "What does that mean to me?" and "How does it shape my perceptions of persons who are my clients?" (Devore & Schlesinger, 1987).

In a position paper describing the competent counselor, Sue et al. (1982) stated that the well-functioning practitioner is one who has moved from being culturally unaware to being aware and sensitive to his/her own cultural heritage and to valuing and respecting differences. Practitioners are reminded of the need for self-awareness and sensitivity to one's own ethnicity particularly in relation to the effect they may have on practice. Helping practitioners are reminded of the need for self-awareness and sensitivity to one's own ethnicity, particularly in relation to the effect it may have on practice.

The Impact of Ethnicity on the Daily Life of Clients

Each day American families must cope with the many forces that impinge on their lives. The impact of these external and internal forces will be modified by the ethnic values and characteristics of each family group. In the following pages our emphasis will be on the lives of Native American, Black and Asian families. Through this examination of family life, material is provided that should lead to a greater understanding of minority families and a more effective and sensitive response in the helping process.

Native American families. An examination of the value systems of various Native Americans will reveal universal themes within tribal specific expectations. While the Sioux value generosity in sharing with other members of the tribe, the Chippewa view this as "institutional giveaway." The Hopi call for strength, self-control, intelligence, and wisdom (Dillard, 1983), and the Plains Indians look to the purification rituals, the annual tribal Sun Dance, and the individual spiritual retreat to support their value of spiritual realization of the individual and the group (Brown, 1981). Dillard (1983) presents a general value system for Native American nations with the understanding that the system held by any tribe may not be adhered to by all of its members. Common among all tribal groups are: tribal loyalty, respect for elders, reticence, humility, avoidance of personal glory and gain, giving and sharing with as many as three generations of relatives, an abiding love for their land, and the attributions of human characteristics.

The Native American family serves as the repository of such values and guides behavior through all of the stages of the life cycle. The family system, often misunderstood by practitioners, may consist of three generations in a single household representing a variation on the nuclear model, sometimes referred to as a "stem family." Family composition may also be extended, consisting of several households, extending even to the clan. This extensive active kinship system provides a child with resources of parents, siblings, aunts, uncles, cousins, and grandparents (Red Horse, 1980). Such relationships appear to be blurred to the outsider, yet the system serves to protect children and to provide them with an assurance of love.

The practices which follow serve to illustrate the value placed on children among Native American families. Children are regarded as important to the family, and Native American adults seldom strike a child. Families engage only in those social activities where children are included. Talking loudly, while correcting a child, is greatly disapproved. Competition is considered acceptable as long as the object is not to get the best of or to hurt someone. Children are taught that the land is lent to them and is not for private exploitation (Burgess, 1980). The importance of ownership of private property is not an entrenched value as it is with families with Northeastern European background. The practitioner must understand the Native American family within this context, as counseling and services are provided.

Native American traditions are not difficult to carry out on the reservation but as families move into cities, life changes. At present, more Native Americans reside in cities than on the reservations and are separated from their traditional helping networks. In this non-Native American society, Native American family life and child-rearing mechanisms are at risk (Cross, 1986).

Government policy has also served to diminish the impact of the extended family. There has been a clear effort to detribalize and assimilate Native American populations. Byler (1977) has written of "The Destruction of Native American Families," explaining how federal policy has served to break up the extended family and the clan structure. As a result of these efforts, the loss of normal controls and protections has contributed to pathological response patterns on the part of the young. Cross (1986) speaks of health problems related to alcohol abuse such as fetal alcohol syndrome and a high percentage of alcohol-related deaths. Also, young adults have a high suicide rate, and many young children are left without protection.

These are the families for whom services by practitioners are needed. The practitioner must understand Native American family life in the present within the context of traditional values and child-rearing practices that have been besieged by federal policy and life in urban areas.

Black American families. A major source of information about Black families has been provided by dramatic illustrations of pathology and deficiencies found in these families. In the work of Frazier (1939) and the influential government-sponsored Moynihan report (1965), disorganization and dysfunction were emphasized. Black mothers were said to be responsible for the breakdown and pathology found in Black families. Much of this deficit perspective has infiltrated the academic and helping professions over the past 2 decades. Fortunately, many practitioners are beginning to recognize the cultural variations, functionality, and validity of Black family lifestyles. Many now realize that, like other ethnic or racial minorities, Black families cannot be seen as a homogeneous group (Allen, 1978). Yet, despite their diversity, there are common experiences in discrimination and prejudice. A sense of unity and support has served as a buffer against many of these experiences.

Martin and Martin (1985) examined the helping tradition, an essential element in the Black family, tracing its historical roots back to Africa and slavery in America. While the helping tradition remains, they suggest that it diminishes as the family confronts urban environments. When this tradition is intact, it reinforces a kin-structured network of relationships that provide economic and moral supports in daily living (Hall & King, 1982).

The practitioner must bear in mind the strong sense of collective consciousness regarding identity and kinship embedded in Black family values. Adaptable family roles would be included as well as high achievement and strong work incentives. Prominent in any listing of values would be religion. The church remains constant, providing a base for the spirituality that is a dominant force in the Black family and community.

Again, like Native American families, not all Black families hold these values. Interaction and assimilation in mainstream society often call for individual achievement and competition rather than kinship ties and strong group affiliation. Ethnic group membership is not exempt from stress upon the individual regardless of minority group status. Values held dearly by grandparents diminish over the generations.

Variations are also found in the structure of Black families. Included in these structures are: nuclear families, extended families, and augmented families. Families may comprise husband and wife, single parent (mother or father), child, and other relatives or nonrelatives (Furstenberg, Hershberg, & Modell, 1975; Billingsley, 1968). These families and the networks that they form serve as loan agencies, emergency food sources, nursing homes, transportation agents, models, and morale boosters (Hall & King, 1982).

The single-parent family headed by women has increased in number and commands considerable attention. Reports (Rainwater, 1966; Schulz, 1969) describe families in disarray. Yet there is evidence that some such families are able to fulfill the universal functions assigned to all American families. There is almost universal agreement that many Black family units of mothers and children are strengthened by the support networks of family and friends. Despite burdened, stressful, and restricted lives, many Black mothers have shown the ability to provide healthy psychological, physical, and social growth environments for their children (McAdoo, 1983). The children gained a sense of individual, family, and racial identity. Values stressing education and religion, racial pride, and family unity found in the larger Black community were found in these families as well. A variety of coping skills, crucial to survival in an urban setting were learned.

Foster (1974) and Kochman (1977) pointed out that many youngsters have developed survival skills and a mental toughness through sustained contact with a social environment which would be devastating to children from other groups. Many Black urban youngsters have to know how to deal effectively with pimps, corner grocers, bill collectors, and policeman. Many of these same youngsters are clever in "ribbin' and jivin'" with school personnel, welfare workers, juvenile authorities, and practitioners. The term ribbin' or ribbing is used to describe the verbal game of taunting, denigrating, or making fun of someone (e.g., people, their clothing, or parts of their body), whereas, jivin' or jiving refers to verbal coping and survival techniques which Black urban persons use to manipulate or persuade others. For example, "shuckin' and jivin'" often requires an ability to control and conceal one's true emotions. Youngsters realize early in life that they exist in an often hostile and complicated world, and verbal and physically aggressive games are only ways to deal with their pain and struggle. It must be emphasized that gamesmanship and verbal attacks are survival and coping techniques. These almost ritualized games are attempts to cope with and survive the severe economic constraints present in the urban environment.

The sensitive practitioner needs to understand the above-mentioned communication pattern. However, the practitioner should be aware that the name given a verbal contest in one city may be different in another location. Also, there may be some difference between the way the verbal contest is played on the street corner as compared with how it is played in school. For the practitioner the important issue is not the proper designation of verbal games among Black youth, but that the practitioner begins to understand these verbal games exist and recognizes them. These skills and adaptations to urban life are used by many Blacks. The skillful practitioner must be able to move through and beneath this level of verbal exchange and respond appropriately to the affect of Black individuals and families. Some suggested skills and techniques relative to the achievement of this goal are provided for the practitioner in the final section of this article.

Asian-American families. For the purposes of this discussion, Chinese, Japanese, and Vietnamese families are considered to be Asian families. The spectrum is larger including such groups as the Koreans, Filipinos, Pacific Islanders, East Indians, and Indochinese. The focus here on Vietnamese families examines briefly the more recent immigrant experience.

Asian family cultural values can be explained as desirable ideals founded upon the precepts of Confucianism. Traditional cultural values are related to the concepts of humanism, which is based on the belief that virtuous behavior is inherent in all people, and order and hierarchy relative to placing the proper emphasis on relationships between parent and child. Self-discipline is also emphasized and requires that a person should learn to control emotions in order to think logically. As an integral part of Asian cultural values, collectivity is emphasized. This concept places an emphasis on kinship ties and mutual dependence where children are required to pay homage and give unquestioning obedience to their parents. The elderly learned scholars and older sages are revered for their knowledge and wisdom. An individual is obliged not to bring dishonor or shame to the family (Suzuki, 1980).

As the family is influenced by mainstream society, many families will no longer be able to maintain traditional values. There is evidence that filial piety is waning as the elderly, who can command respect, choose to remain in the city when their children move to the suburbs. This separation removes supports that have been an integral part of cultural traditions. Parents can no longer expect complete obedience, as families become more democratic and move away from the patriarchal system of the past. Contemporary Asian-American families still appear to hold the values associated with ethical behavior, respect for authority, and modesty and politeness (Suzuki, 1980).

Modification and Adaptation of Skills in Response to Working with Ethnic Minority Families

This layer of understanding calls for adaptation and modification techniques in response to dispositions of ethnic minority families. Practitioners must be aware of prevailing group inclinations in relation to such issues as privacy, using formally organized helping institutions, self-disclosure, discussion of intimate matters with persons outside the family, and the context in which help is or should be offered (Devore & Schlesinger, 1987).

In presenting a framework for ethnic minority practice, Lum (1986) offers a familiar process that includes contact, problem definition, assessment, intervention, and termination. At the same time, he presents some practice issues related to minority clients. The initial contact phase includes issues about communication barriers, family and personal background, and ethnic community. Problems relative to identification present issues of disclosure, information, and understanding. Assessment requires consideration of social-environmental impacts as well as psycho-individual reactions. Practitioner and client issues are joined at the point of intervention as they select goals and plan strategies. Termination presents several questions that must be addressed: (a) Was an effort made to connect people to the positive elements of support in the ethnic minority community? and (b) did gaining a sense of self related to "ethnic self-hood" provide motivation for coping efforts?

The techniques for practice with ethnic minority families are familiar to practitioners as Lum has suggested, but the process must be influenced by knowledge of the families' experiences in America in addition to understanding the presenting problems they bring to the helping process.

Three important skills have been presented among the characteristics of culturally sensitive helping practitioners (Sue et al.,1982). First, the ability to generate a wide variety of verbal and nonverbal responses is very important. The wider the repertoire of responses, the greater the chances are for understanding the presenting problem. Second, another skill requires the ability to send and receive verbal and nonverbal messages "appropriately." Some ethnic groups have a high regard for subtlety and indirectness of communication while others prize directness and confrontation. The practitioner must understand the communication style of an ethnic in order to respond appropriately. Third, the practitioner must be able to exercise appropriate institutional intervention skills on behalf of the client system. This requires a perspective that views many problems and barriers to client success as part of the institutional systems.

Summary

No matter which model for intervention a practitioner may choose, there is a need to consider the layers of understanding: (a) adherence to a set of personal and professional practice values that affirm the qualities of uniqueness, (b) an understanding of development of individuals and families as they mature across the life cycle, in the context of their own ethnic groups, (c) insights into one's own ethnicity and an understanding of how this may affect professional practice, (d) a sensitivity to the experiences of ethnic minority families in America, and (e) the modification and adaptation of familiar techniques in response to the ethnic minority family. These elements can go a long way toward producing the kinds of outcomes which will prove most beneficial to society as well as to the families themselves.

References

Allen, W. (1978). The search for applicable theories of black family life. *Journal of Marriage and the Family, 40*, 117–129.

Billingsley, A. (1968). *Black families in White America.* Englewood Cliffs, NJ: Prentice Hall.

Boykin, A. W., & Toms, F. D. (1985). Black child socialization. In H. P. McAdoo (Ed.), *Black children: Social, educational, and parental environments* (pp. 33–51). Beverly Hills, CA: Sage Publications, Inc.

Brown, J. E. (1981). The persistence of essential values among North American Plains Indians. In R. H. Dana (Ed.), *Human services for cultural minorities* (pp. 5–13). Baltimore: University Park Press.

Burgess, B. M. (1980). Parenting in the Native American community. In M. D. Fantini & R. Cardenas (Eds.), *Parenting in a multicultural society* (pp. 63–73). New York: Longman.

Byler, W. (1977). The destruction of American Indian families. In S. Unger (Ed.), *The destruction of American Indian families* (pp. 1–11). New York: Association of American Indian Affairs.

Cross, T. L. (1986). Drawing on cultural tradition in Indian child welfare practice. *Social Casework, 37*, 283–298.

Devore, W., & Schlesinger, E. G. (1987). *Ethnic sensitive social work practice* (2nd ed.). Columbus: Merrill Publishing Company.

Dillard, J. M. (1983). *Multicultural counseling*. Chicago: Nelson-Hall.

Foster, H. L. (1974). *Ribbin', jivin', and playin' the dozens*. Cambridge, MA: Ballinger Publishing Company.

Frazier, E. F. (1939). *The Negro family in the United States*. Chicago: The University of Chicago Press.

Furstenberg, F. F., Jr., Hershberg, T., & Modell, J. (1975). The origins of the female-headed Black family: The impact of the urban experience. *Journal of Interdisciplinary History, 6*, 211–233.

Hall, E. H., & King, G. C. (1982). Working with the strengths of Black families. *Child Welfare, LXI*, 536–544.

Huber, J., & Spitze, G. (1983). *Sex stratification: Children, housework and jobs*. New York: Academic Press.

Knowles, L. L., & Pruitt, K. (1969). *Institutional racism in America*. Englewood Cliffs, NJ: Prentice-Hall.

Kochman, T. (1977). *Rappin' and stylin' out: Communication in urban Black America*. Urbana, IL: University of Illinois Press.

Logan, S. L. (1981). Race, identity, and Black children: A developmental perspective. *Social Casework, 62*, 47–56.

Lum, D. (1986). *Social work practice and people of color: A process-stage approach*. Monterey, CA: Brooks/Cole Publishing Company.

Martin, J. M., & Martin, E. P. (1985). *The helping tradition in the Black family and community*. Silver Springs, MD: National Association of Social Work.

McAdoo, H. P. (1983). Societal stress: The Black family. In H. I. McCubbin & C. R. Figley (Eds.), *Stress and the family: Vol. 1. Coping with normative transition* (pp. 178–187). New York: Brunner Mazel.

McGoldrick, M. (1982). Ethnicity and family therapy: An overview. In M. McGoldrick, J. Pearce, L& J. Giordano (Eds.), *Ethnicity and family therapy* (pp. 3–30). New York: The Guilford Press.

Moynihan, D. P. (1965). *The Negro family: The case for national action.* Washington, DC: U.S. Department of Labor.

Peters, M. F. (1978). Notes from the guest editor. *Journal of Marriage and the Family, 40,* 655–658.

Rainwater, L. (1966). Crucible of identity: The Negro lower-class family. *Daedalus, 95,* 172–216.

Red Horse, J. G. (1980). Family structure and value orientation in American Indians. *Social Casework, 61,* 462–467.

Schulman, E. D. (1982). *Intervention in human services: A guide to skills and knowledge.* St. Louis: The C. V. Mosby Company.

Schulz, D. (1969). *Coming up Black.* Englewood Cliffs, NJ: Prentice-Hall.

Sue, D. W., Bernier, J. E., Durran, A., Feinberg, L., Pederson, P., Smith, E. J., & Vasquez, E. (1982). Cross-cultural counseling competencies. *The Counseling Psychologist, 10,* 49–51.

Suzuki, B. H. (1980). The Asian-American family. In M. D. Fantini & R. Cardenas (Eds.), *Parenting in a multicultural society* (pp. 74–102). New York: Longman.

U.S. Bureau of Census. (1986). *Money, income and poverty status of families and persons in the United States: 1985,* (Current Population Reports, Series P-60, No. 154, Table 15, p. 21). Washington, DC: U.S. Government Printing Office.

This article was originally published in *Family Relations,* Vol. 37, No. 3, 1988, pp. 310–314. Reprint permission granted by The National Council on Family Relations.

Remarriage Myths: Implications for the Helping Professions

Marilyn Coleman
Lawrence H. Ganong

A little understood but rapidly growing phenomenon in our society is remarriage. By 1977, 41% of marriages involved the remarriage of one or both partners (Glick, 1980). Samuel Johnson reportedly said that "remarriage is the triumph of hope over experience." Obviously, given the number of remarriages, our society contains a high percentage of hopeful people. Despite this hope, 44% of remarriages end in divorce (Glick & Norton, 1977). There are many reasons why remarriages fail; a subtle contributor to these divorce statistics may be people's reliance on marriage and family mythology.

The Role of Myths in Marriage and Family Life

A *myth* has been defined as "an ill-founded belief held uncritically, especially by an interested group" (Webster's New Collegiate Dictionary, 1979), and as "a recurring theme...that appeals to the consciousness of a people by embodying its cultural ideals or by giving expression to deep, commonly felt emotions" (American Heritage Dictionary, 1973). Myths are oversimplified, but firmly held, beliefs that guide perceptions and expectations. Bernard (1981) pointed out that myths usually incorporate an element of truth, noting that, "If there were not some truth in a cultural myth, it would quickly lose its power" (p. 67). That myths are generally unfounded does not reduce their power to influence both attitudes and behavior. Problems develop when myths serve as blinders to actual experience and lead people into painful situations that could have been prevented.

Myths are particularly prevalent in the context of family life, in which many people form "an interested group" and in which emotions are perhaps felt more deeply and ideals are held more fervently than in any other area of American life. Mental health clinicians and family researchers often lack the empirical evidence necessary to provide indisputable facts. Therefore, the field of counseling is vulnerable to "cultural myths." For example, observers of families have identified widely held myths about sex (Neely, 1981), marriage (Lederer & Jackson, 1968), parenthood (LeMasters & Defrain, 1983), divorce (Bernard, 1981), single-parent families (Verzaro & Hannon, 1980), and stepfamilies (Schulman, 1972; Visher & Visher, 1979). According to LeMasters and Defrain (1983), there are a large number of myths regarding marriage and family life because cultural myths, or *scientific fallacies*, serve to organize people's perceptions by reducing their perceived complexity and uncertainty of the world. Myths help people understand mysteries that experts have not explained.

Counselors may find it difficult to identify myths that operate within their clients' constructs of reality. If they are members of the same culture as their clients, counselors may be unaware of the myths and perceive them instead as facts or realities. Insofar as stereotypes represent cultural myths, there is empirical evidence that counselors share beliefs with others in the broader culture (Broverman, Vogel, Broverman, Clarkson, & Rosenkrantz, 1970; Fielding & Evered, 1978; Wampold, Casas, & Atkinson, 1981).

Bernard (1981) warned counselors to disengage themselves from the prevailing cultural attitude that "divorce has inherent power to make people unhappy" (p. 67). In an insightful analysis, she compared eight marriage "rules" with their counterparts in divorce mythology (see Table 1).

Divorced clients may need assistance in identifying and refuting myths about the inherent power of divorce to make them unhappy. Bernard (1981) pointed out how unwitting adherence by counselors to divorce myths can create problems for clients experiencing divorce.

Remarriage Myths

There is little evidence to indicate that individuals who have suffered the consequences of belief in marriage and divorce myths are any better equipped to handle remarriage. Unfortunately, the rapidly increasing family lifestyle of remarriage has a rich mythology of its own. It is possible to examine this remarriage mythos as it corresponds to the marriage and divorce myths identified by Bernard (1981). The number of myths surrounding remarriage is so extensive that, in some instances,

Table 1
Marriage and Divorce Myths

Marriage Myth	Divorce Myth
Things will work out if we love each other.	Because we don't love each other anymore, nothing will work out.
Always consider the other person first.	Always consider oneself first.
Keep criticism to oneself and focus on the positive.	Criticize everything; focus on the negative.
If things aren't going well, focus on the future.	If things aren't going well, focus on the past.
See oneself as part of the couple first, as an individual second.	See yourself as an individual first, as part of a couple second.
What's mine is yours.	What's yours is mine.
Marriage makes people significantly happier.	Divorce makes people significantly unhappy.
What is best for the children will be best for us.	What is best for us must be devastating for the children.

several remarriage myths exist for each related marriage and divorce myth. The purpose of this article is to examine popular remarriage myths and to offer suggestions to counselors working with remarried individuals or couples. The discussion is based on the authors' several years of experience leading remarriage workshops, teaching graduate courses on remarriage and stepfamilies, and conducting remarriage research. The most common remarriage myths are discussed briefly.

1. *Things must work out.* For some couples the goal of remarriage is to "get it right" this time. Everything will work out because this time it is *really* love. Those who had a simple first wedding ceremony may opt this time for multiple bridesmaids, a long, white gown, and other trappings of a traditional wedding. Those who had a traditional first wedding ceremony may choose something simpler or just different in an attempt to change their luck and get it "right." This approach merely

incorporates the original marriage myth, with a note of added intensity or desperation.

2. *Always consider everybody first.* The remarriage version of the second myth may take several forms. Variations may include "always consider yourself first," "always consider the other person first," "always consider your marriage first," "always consider yourself and *your* children first" (as compared to your spouse and his or her children), and finally, "always consider everybody first." These mutually exclusive myths may all be operating at one time. Attempting to fulfill these conflicting myths may leave people feeling schizophrenic at worst and frustrated at best.

People who had few financial resources as single parents may have felt deprived. If they developed an assertive style of obtaining resources for themselves and their children during this period, then they may continue to use that style on behalf of their children after remarriage; however, they may feel guilty for not trusting their spouses and putting them first. Those in the legal professions contribute to this problem by encouraging people to legally and financially consider themselves and their children first and by advising them to arrange antenuptial agreements, marriage contracts, and trusts.

Stepfamilies often consist of a man living with a woman and her children. The stepfather is faced with the task of joining a single-parent family system that may have been functioning for some time. The woman, who is trying to put her children first, may feel protective and interfere when the stepfather disciplines them (Mowatt, 1972). She may then feel guilty because she has failed to consider her husband first (the original marriage myth). The children may resent having to share their mother's attention with the stepfather, and she may feel guilty about giving them less attention. Thus, trying to juggle everyone's needs is not only stressful, it is impossible.

Although stepmother families are less common than stepfather families, the mythology surrounding them is more pervasive and more negative. The myth that the biological parent and children must be considered first may be even stronger in these families, which leaves the stepmother in a very precarious situation (Engebretson, 1982).

An alternative myth often fostered by counselors—"always consider the marital relationship first" (Visher & Visher, 1979)—is related to the first remarriage myth: If the relationship does not come first, then the marriage may fail, and it *must* succeed. There is empirical evidence, however, supporting the idea that satisfaction with stepparent-stepchildren relationships is more important to family happiness than is satisfaction with the marital relationship (Crosbie-Burnett, 1984).

3. *Keep criticism to oneself and focus on the positive.* The third myth is a simple return to marriage myth number 3 (Table 1) and is a result of the desperate feeling that the marriage *must* be successful. Some remarried partners believe that if they had adhered to this myth in their first marriage they might still be married. Consequently, they return to this myth with a vengeance in remarriage. It may be even more difficult to adhere to in remarriage, however, because there often are more people and things to criticize (i.e., stepchildren, ex-spouses, ex-in-laws, new in-laws). This myth also incorporates the pseudomutuality that arises because of the intense fear of failure. The marriage remains frozen and static because poking and prodding might uncover a fatal flaw. Children also may support this myth by becoming overtly upset if their parents and stepparents argue or by being unnaturally "good" around stepparents.

Few would fault a couple who show strong determination to make their remarriage work. The problems occur when an intense fear of failure interferes with direct, open communication between the partners (Jacobson, 1979). Intimate relationships normally involve disagreements and conflict. It would be impossible to totally avoid conflict, yet to the person overly concerned with becoming a two-time loser, conflict may create extreme anxiety. The result is often a style of adaptation called *pseudomutuality.* Pseudomutuality among remarried people and stepfamilies is defined as the tendency to deny history, ambivalence, and conflict (Sager et al., 1983). Members of the new family may fear yet another marriage failure and, therefore, "walk on eggs" rather than confront, challenge, or argue with other family members. Pseudomutuality may lead to unhappiness and feelings of powerlessness and alienation rather than unity.

4. *If things are not going well, focus on what went wrong in the past and make sure it does not happen again.* This myth again pushes for pseudomutuality and denial rather than honest communication. It is a reworking of the old relationship to "get it right" instead of an attempt to build a new and unique relationship. A corollary myth is to "criticize the past and focus on the future." Couples who convince themselves that everything was negative in their previous marriages (proof of which is that the marriage failed) and that everything is going to be perfect in their new marriage are building a relationship based on denial. The first sign of any pattern resembling that of the previous marriage may cause

panic. Focusing on the negative aspects of the previous relationship may also constrict behaviors of the current spouse ("Her previous husband would never help with the dishes and she divorced him. I'd better help with the dishes, although I'd much rather cook.") Both of these myths place a restriction on the open communication necessary to maintain an intimate relationship.

5. *See oneself as part of the couple first, as an individual second; see oneself as an individual first, as part of a couple second.* This myth is actually a combination of two myths. The first version is identical to the marriage myth and is held by remarried persons who are attracted to the sense of security they perceive as a benefit of being married. These individuals may have rushed quickly into remarriage following divorce (or even following death of a spouse). Religion, extended family members, and friends may encourage this myth and its related beliefs.

The second version is identical to the divorce myth and is held by remarried persons who consider themselves sadder but wiser after their first marriages—the major lesson they learned is that one must look out for oneself. This attitude is often encouraged by attorneys, families, and friends. For remarried persons who have children, the emphasis in the single-parent phase may have been on the parental role ("see oneself as a parent first, as an individual second"). Remarried parents may have a difficult time abandoning this belief, and some never do. Those who reclaim the marriage myth find their children reacting negatively to their new stepparent or to the marriage.

6. *What is mine is mine, what is yours is yours.* This myth tends to move developmentally through family stages from marriage ("what is mine is yours"), to divorce ("what is yours is mine"), to single parenthood ("what is mine is mine"), to remarriage ("what is mine is mine, what is yours is yours"). A problem with this myth is the lack of an "ours" orientation. There may be good reason to maintain some individual control of financial assets, but establishing intimacy in an atmosphere of a business corporation may be difficult, if not impossible.

Fishman and Hamel (1983), in a descriptive study of 16 middle-class stepfamilies, reported that stepfamilies tend to organize their finances in one of two ways: *common pot* or *two pot.* In the common pot, family resources are pooled and distributed based on perceived or expressed needs. There is no distinction between yours and mine. The two-pot stepfamily continues the single-parent family theme "what is mine is mine," and the remarriage is often preceded by the involvement of lawyers, antenuptial agreements, and contracts.

Fishman and Hamel (1983) found the two-pot agreement to be satisfactory when both partners were contributing approximately equal resources to the household. They found it to be much less satisfactory when contributions were blatantly unequal and one set of children were obviously "richer" or "poorer" than the other. They also found that a couple's economic stability was a matter of perspective; sometimes one spouse perceives the family's economic stability as solid and the other views it as shaky. They believed that a shared perspective of the family financial situation was an important factor in step-family unity and that neither the common-pot nor the two-pot approach would guarantee a remarriage free of conflict over financial resources.

This myth is especially subscribed to by persons who perceive that they have been hurt emotionally, financially, or legally in the previous marital relationship. It is common practice for attorneys to advise *all* persons who are remarrying to make antenuptial agreements regarding financial responsibilities, inheritance, and ownership of property (Mellon, 1984). Although this may be sound legal advice, in some cases it works against the development of trust and commitment in the remarriage.

7. *Marriage makes people significantly happier.* This myth is dramatically reinstated at the time of remarriage. It is not only imperative that people be happy in their remarriages, but even happier than they were in their first marriages. A related remarriage myth is that if two people are happy and love each other enough, then everyone will be happy, including children, grandparents, and ex-spouses.

The myth of "instant love," or "if you love me you will love my children," often operates at the time of remarriage and can cause a great deal of grief and misunderstanding. The couple, caught up in the bliss of a new romantic love relationship, may at first be oblivious to the fact that other family members (e.g., children) are less enthralled. It takes extraordinary effort to love a stepchild who blatantly ignores your existence or who is cleverly rude. The following example of such a stepchild is from Russell Baker's (1982) memoir, *Growing Up*.

> The day Herb, my stepfather, moved into Lombard Street with us, I set out on one of those campaigns of silent resistance of which only adolescents and high-spirited nations under conquerors' occupation are capable. I gave no spoken sign of my dislike. I was too cunning for that. My policy was to ignore him as completely as possible. Without saying a word that could possibly offend

> him, I would let him know that so far as I was concerned, he did not exist. There were a hundred ways of doing this. In meal conversations I addressed myself only to my mother or Doris, my sister, always managing to omit him from the circle. When he interrupted to say, "Pass the potatoes," I passed the bowl silently without looking at him while continuing to talk to my mother and Doris. When he addressed me directly with some pleasant remark about the food, such as, "Isn't this the best applesauce you ever tasted?" I murmured, "It's all right" or "Not bad," and without looking at him began speaking to my mother on some subject I knew would shut him out of the table talk. (p. 175)

The wise couple may decide they cannot ensure the happiness of their children in the stepfamily. Rather than concentrating on making the children "happy," they should concentrate on providing structure and reasonable rules and limits so that the children are at least aware that they will not be allowed to dominate the family with their unhappiness.

There is evidence from clinical literature that the remarriage of one spouse rekindles the animosity of the ex-spouse created by the breakup of the previous marriage (Visher & Visher, 1979). Instead of being happy about the remarriage, the ex-spouse becomes more intrusive, jealous, and difficult (although some ex-spouses may be happier). Previous agreements may have to be renegotiated, including legal arrangements such as visitation and child support.

Remarriage may make the remarried couple significantly happier, but they may find their circle of marital bliss surrounded by unexpected ripples of discontent and unhappiness on the part of others. If the remarriage does not result in happiness quickly enough or great enough, believers in this myth may seek someone to blame (stepchildren are good candidates for scapegoats) or may begin to plan or anticipate the dissolution of the marriage.

8. *What is best for us must be harmful for the children.* The final remarriage myth is a watered-down version of the divorce myth. Although the effects of parental remarriage on children are typically not perceived as negative as are the effects of parental divorce on children, there is clearly a widespread belief in our society that all stepchildren have a difficult time. Support for this myth ranges from Grimm's fairy tales, to self-help books for stepfamilies, to the increasingly large body of literature written by clinicians. The empirical research on stepchildren, however, does not support the view that parental remarriage

has harmful effects on children (Ganong & Coleman, 1984), and one can cite many successful individuals (e.g., Abraham Lincoln, Gerald Ford, James McNeill Whistler) who grew up as stepchildren. Unfortunately, the majority view is quite at odds with these facts.

Paradoxically, many remarrying parents entertain both this myth and myths that seem to be diametric opposites. "Having a 'real' family again is best for everyone" and "what is best for us is best for the children" are remarriage myths that essentially are denials of the notion that children will have to make adjustments and experience stress when parents remarry. Adherents to these myths may really believe that their children have been harmed by their changing family structure but react by convincing themselves that a two-parent family is a panacea.

Supporters of the Remarriage Myths

There are many supporters of remarriage myths in our society. The legal system, religious organizations, the helping professions (e.g., counseling), the extended family, friends, and popular media are examples. The contribution of the legal system has already been cited in the discussions of myths 2, 5, and 6. Religious organizations tend to support the myths both directly and indirectly. Organized religions traditionally have been nonsupportive of divorce. Divorced individuals have sometimes reported feeling uncomfortable or out of place in church. Clergy often make references to the tragedy of broken homes in sermons; as a result, divorced people may feel second class. Following remarriage, the couple may resume the intact nuclear family role and become a complete family rather than a broken family. Stepfamilies, however, are different from intact nuclear families. For example, stepfamily members have different family histories, there are more than two adults in parenting roles, and children may be members of two households. If stepfamilies feel that they must be intact nuclear families to be acceptable in the eyes of the church, it is likely that they will cling tenaciously to remarriage myths because the marriage "must be worked out." If organized religion is only moderately tolerant toward divorce, then remarried individuals my fear that a second divorce would stretch that tolerance to the breaking point. For highly religious people, the threat of being unacceptable in the eyes of the church could be overwhelming.

Counselors may support the myths because of their own biases against stepfamilies (Bryan, Ganong, Coleman, & Bryan, 1985) or because of a lack of knowledge concerning remarriage and stepfamily functioning. If counselors treat remarried couples and stepfamilies in essentially the same way they treat intact nuclear families, they are conveying to them that the complexities with which they are coping are unimportant and should be manageable. Counselors may actually be supporting myths such as "always consider everybody first" and the various versions of myth 5 through their own lack of knowledge about stepfamily complexity. The self-help literature (authored by counselors and laypersons) paints a predominantly negative picture of stepfamily life that may reinforce the fear of failure and the development of pseudomutuality instead of a more positive and productive style of communication.

Extended family members and friends, like clergy and counselors, may be unaware of the unique dynamics of remarriage and stepfamily life. There is ample evidence that biases exist against remarriage and stepfamily members (Bryan et al., 1985; Bryan, Coleman, Ganong, & Bryan, in press; Ganong & Coleman, 1983). Because of these societal biases, well-meaning family members and friends may ignore the uniqueness of the step-family situation and pretend that the situation does not exist. Ex-spouses may never be mentioned or may be mentioned only in relation to myth 4. Family members and friends may join in criticizing the past (usually meaning the ex-spouse) and encouraging a focus on the future.

Media support the myths in numerous ways. Television shows such as "The Brady Bunch" and "Eight is Enough" present unrealistic models. Stepfamily members watching these programs may feel they are failures if they are not as idyllically happy as are members of the television families because "marriage makes people significantly happier." The self-help literature is often negative in tone and is focused almost totally on potential problems. Neither approach is helpful in refuting the myths surrounding remarriage and stepfamily living. Media actually increase the external pressures to succeed without providing guidance on how to be successful. Popular media put tremendous pressure on remarried individuals to subscribe to these remarriage myths. When this external pressure is combined with people's internal needs to organize perceptions and reduce the perceived complexity of their lives, it is not surprising that remarriage myths exert an influence on many remarried persons.

The Counselor's Role

Counselors can help clients view their situations more realistically and solve their problems more effectively by reducing or eliminating their belief in remarriage myths. As noted previously, however, counselors can just as easily be part of the problem by reinforcing these myths. Although there are no easy solutions, there are a number of ways in which counselors can help decrease the effect of remarriage myths on their clients' lives.

First, counselors must be aware of these myths and how they might influence their work with clients. Which of these myths does the counselor adhere to as "the truth"? What aspects of the counselor's practice reinforce these myths? How has belief in these myths influenced the counselor? Becoming aware of one's own belief system is often difficult, especially when the beliefs are deeply felt. Therefore, the first step is more difficult than it initially seems to be.

Second, counselors should consider how these myths might influence clients who are remarried or who plan to remarry. Several potential effects have been suggested in this article, but counselors should consider each client individually in order to identify even more effects of these myths on client behaviors and emotions. In considering each client, counselors could ask themselves the following questions: "What remarriage myths are relevant to my client's situation?" "Which of these myths does my client seem to believe in?" "How would abandoning these remarriage myths help my client?" and "Which myths should be focused on first?" This process is somewhat more complicated in counseling settings in which both partners are clients. In such cases counselors could ask themselves, "Do my clients share the same remarriage myths?" "Do they believe in competing myths?" and "Whose myths should be focused on first?" This step is basically one of assessing and planning. It is extremely important.

Educational approaches are probably most appropriate in assisting clients to reduce their belief in remarriage myths. These approaches to remarriage intervention have the advantage of being appropriate for use with groups. They are particularly appropriate for groups of people planning remarriages so that pitfalls in beliefs can be anticipated and altered before problems occur. Once counselors ascertain clients' myth structures, they can teach them the fallacy and inaccuracy of these myths. Because myths do contain some elements of truth and because they are considered to be factual by clients, it should be expected that clients will not give up their myths easily. In rare cases clients will take the counselor's word that these are myths that should be abandoned. Usually, however, they will resist this information; counselors may then wish to use standard reality-testing procedures to help clients refute their own myths (Ellis & Grieger, 1977).

Counselors could also present logical arguments and rationales for their anti-myth positions. They should be prepared to back up their assertions and rationales with supporting documentation, such as information from clinical experts and from empirical research on remarriage and stepfamilies. Some recommended book-length clinical resources are those by Visher and Visher (1979), Wald (1981), and Sager et al. (1983). Empirical research is harder for counselors to obtain because it is scattered in journals, book chapters, and unpublished dissertations and theses. It is our impression that the bulk of the research in the area of remarriage, particularly in recent years, fails to support the myths. Counselors can use this empirical work to educate their clients. An excellent source of relevant bibliographies is the Remarriage and Stepparenting Focus Group of the National Council on Family Relations. The Stepfamily Association also has compiled an annotated bibliography that is available for a fee. Both of the bibliographies list empirical studies and are excellent resources for counselors interested in putting to use the efforts of their research colleagues.

There are several points about myths that should be noted and that are salient for clinical application. First, remarriage myths, by and large, are not the same as marriage myths. There are some similarities (e.g., marriage and remarriage myths 3, 5, and 7 are identical) and some connections, but the remarriage mythos is generally different. This should not be surprising to those who realize that remarriages are different from first marriages. Unfortunately, many people erroneously assume that a marriage is a marriage, regardless of whether or not it is a first marriage or a remarriage. The problems inherent in using a first marriage, intact family model as a standard for remarriage and stepfamily living have been well documented (Ganong & Coleman, 1984; Visher & Visher, 1979). That the remarriage mythos is different from the marriage mythos underscores the uniqueness of the problems, advantages, and dynamics of remarriages.

Second, different members of the extended family system reinforce myths that sometimes are mutually exclusive or oppositional. For example, attorneys may give advice that is in opposition to that of counselors (e.g., myths 2 and 6). This creates turmoil because clients either try to follow the advice of both or try to decide who to believe. Counselors should be aware that clients may be receiving competing advice. It may be necessary for counselors to work together and to hold conjoint meetings with attorneys. Other professional viewpoints (e.g., clergy versus counselors, clergy versus attorneys) may differ as well. Incompatible reinforcement of remarriage myths may also come from family and friends; counselors should be aware that their perspectives may be at odds with those of clients' significant others.

Finally, it should be noted that the eight remarriage myths discussed here are not exhaustive. There are probably hundreds of scientific fallacies related to remarriage and hundreds more related to broader stepfamily issues. Counselors must keep their eyes and ears open for other potential myths that disrupt the lives of their clients.

References

American Heritage Publishing. (1973). *American Heritage Dictionary.* New York: Author.

Baker, R. (1982). *Growing up*. New York: New American Library.

Bernard, J. (1981). The divorce myth. *Personnel and Guidance Journal, 60*, 67–71.

Broverman, L., Vogel, S., Broverman, D., Clarkson, F., & Rosenkrantz, P. (1972). Sex role stereotypes: A current appraisal. *Journal of Social Issues, 28*, 59–78.

Bryan, H., Ganong, L., Coleman, M., & Bryan, L. (1985). Counselors' perceptions of stepparents and stepchildren. *Journal of Counseling Psychology, 32*, 279–282.

Bryan, L., Coleman, M., Ganong, L., & Bryan, H. (in press). Person-perception: Family structure as a cue for stereotyping. *Journal of Marriage and the Family.*

Crosbie-Burnett, M. (1984). The centrality of the step relationship: A challenge to family theory and practice. *Family Relations, 33*, 459–464.

Ellis, A., & Grieger, R. (Eds.). (1977). *Handbook of rational-emotive therapy.* New York: Springer.

Engebretson, J. (1982). Stepmothers as first-time parents: Their needs and problems. *Pediatric Nursing, 8*, 387–390.

Fielding, G., & Evered, C. (1978). An exploratory experimental study of the influence of patients' social background upon diagnostic process and outcome. *Psychiatric Clinica, 11*, 61–86.

Fishman, B., & Hamel, B. (1983). The economic behavior of step-families. *Family Relations, 32*, 359–366.

Ganong, L., & Coleman, M. (1983). Stepparent: A pejorative term? *Psychological Reports, 52*, 919–922.

Ganong, L., & Coleman, M. (1984). Effects of remarriage on children: A review of the empirical literature. *Family Relations, 33*, 389–406.

Glick, P. (1980). Remarriage: Some recent changes and variations. *Journal of Family Issues, 1*, 455–478.

Glick, P., & Norton, A. (1977). Marrying, divorcing, and living together in the United States today. *Population Bulletin, 32*(5), 4–8.

Jacobson, D. (1979). Stepfamilies: Myths and realities. *Social Work, 24*, 202–207.

Lederer, W. J., & Jackson, D. D. (1968). *The mirages of marriage*. New York: Norton.

LeMasters, E. E., & DeFrain, J. (1983). *Parents in contemporary America* (4th ed.). Homewood, IL: Dorsey Press.

Mellon, S. (1984, February). *Legal issues as they relate to all members of the families*. Paper presented at the Iowa Conference on the Blended Family, Iowa City.

Mowatt, M. (1972). Group psychotherapy for stepfathers and their wives. *Psychotherapy: Theory, Research and Practice, 9*, 328–331.

Neely, J. C. (1981). *Gender: The myth of equality*. New York: Simon and Schuster.

Sager, C., Brown, H., Crohn, H., Engel, T., Rodstein, E., & Walker, L. (1983). *Treating the remarried family*. New York: Brunner/Mazel.

Schulman, G. L. (1972). Myths that intrude on the adaptation of the stepfamily. *Social Casework, 53*, 131–139.

Verzaro, M., & Hannon, C. B. (1980). Single-parent families: Myth and reality. *Journal of Home Economics, 72*(3), 31–33.

Visher, E. G., & Visher, J. S. (1979). *Stepfamilies: A guide to working with stepparents and stepchildren*. New York: Brunner/Mazel.

Wald, E. (1981). *The remarried family*. New York: Family Service Association of America.

Wampold, B., Casas, J., & Atkinson, D. (1981). Ethnic bias in counseling: An information processing approach. *Journal of Counseling Psychology, 28*, 498–503.

Merriam-Webster. (1976). *Webster's new collegiate dictionary.* Springfield, MA: author.

Relapse Prevention and Treatment Adherence in Marital Therapy

Jon Carlson
Len Sperry
Candace Ward Howell

Counselors are traditionally trained to identify, diagnose, and remediate the full spectrum of psychopathology. The traditional treatment model is to take a couple from problems to absence of problems. The counselor then accepts another couple as the client and guides them back to fuller levels of functioning. Unfortunately, research tells us that taking couples from symptoms to no symptoms without developing a clear follow-up program leads to an eventual return to a dysfunctional relationship in one-half of the cases (Jacobson, Schmaling, & Holtzworth-Munroe, 1987; Jacobson, 1989; Sperry & Carlson, 1991). *Counselors have front-loaded the helping processes* by putting all of their resources into identification, diagnosis, and remediation and very little into treatment adherence and relapse prevention.

Relapse Prevention

The concept of relapse prevention (RP) has become a central focus of research and practice in health psychology and behavioral medicine. Because non-adherence (previously called non-compliance) with treatment is so high, ranging from 30-80 percent (Sperry, 1985), clinicians have sought ways to reverse this phenomenon.

Relapse prevention is an intervention consisting of specific skills and cognitive strategies that prepare clients/patients in advance to cope with the inevitable "slips" or relapses in compliance to a change program (Marlatt, 1985). Although the early work on relapse prevention developed in alcohol and drug treatment programs where relapse and return to the addictive substance is very high, relapse prevention principles have been applied to smoking cessation, pain control, weight management, sleep disorders, exercise adherence, and other health promotion areas

(Lewis, Sperry, Carlson, in press). With the possible exception of Jacobson and Holtzworth-Munroe (1988), relapse prevention has not been introduced into the family psychology literature.

Daley (1989) describes five different relapse prevention models of which Marlatt's is the most well-known and researched. Marlatt (1985) has developed a cognitive behavioral model which emphasizes the following:

- identification of individual high-risk situations;
- development of coping skills for high-risk situations;
- practice in coping with potential lapses; and
- the development of cognitive coping strategies for use immediately after relapse.

Marlatt notes that the majority of relapse in adults occurs in response to stressful situations involving negative emotional states often following interpersonal conflict or social pressure. He stresses that reframing the relapse as a mistake rather than a factual error or moral shortcoming is an important preventive measure which can help the individual get back on track and learn from the experience. Relapse prevention helps the individual apply the "brakes" so that once a slip occurs it does not escalate into a full-blown relapse.

Relapse prevention has many potential applications in all areas of family psychology. One of the more obvious involves counseling couples in marriage maintenance, in which the counselors will not only predict relapses, but preventively intervene by preparing the couple for them.

Effective intervention involves engaging couples in the counseling process and helping them to actively and collaboratively participate through complying with homework assignments. Success seems to be based on couples' level of involvement in and adherence to therapy. Researchers consistently discover that the level of client involvement is related to therapy outcome (Holtzworth-Munroe, Jacobson, DeKlyen, & Whisman, 1989). Active collaboration in the tasks appropriate to the treatment process may be conceptualized as treatment alliance.

An important consideration is the need to predict external stressors in the relationship. These stressors are often related to the stages of marriage and family life and are predictable. Research indicates that planned booster sessions and training in stress management can be very helpful (Jacobson, 1989). However, just the use of booster sessions in the treatment philosophy does not appear to be enough to prevent relapse.

Relapse prevention programming must be initiated in the early stages of marital counseling and must be sequential rather than waiting for a problem to occur.

Perhaps the most important determinant of relapse is whether or not effective marital skill training has occurred and whether or not these strategies were tailored to the couple's needs and occurred in advance of stressful situations. In this article, we highlight the skills important in preventing relapse and facilitating treatment adherence.

Skills of Effective Marriage

To have a strong, effective, and healthy marriage and family life, people must have skills. The following six skills of effective marriage are among the most important:

1. making the relationship a priority;
2. communicating regularly;
3. practicing encouragement;
4. having marriage meetings and choices;
5. setting up negotiations, rules, and conflict resolution; and
6. having regular fun

Commitment, involvement, and full participation are the key concepts basic in every successful marriage. The commitment that couples make on their wedding day is seldom remembered and renewed. As a couple matures, involvement shifts from focusing on their relationship to focusing on children, careers, education, social activities, religion, sports, or other interests.

Making the Relationship a Priority

Counselors can help couples use the following two steps to make marriage a priority.

Step 1: Ask the couple to take an inventory of all the various responsibilities and commitments in their lives and then place marriage at the top of that list. Once they do that they will be aware of how parenting, athletics, and other areas affect their marriage relationship. In too many instances the marriage is at the bottom of the list.

Step 2: Ask the couple to check their date book. If they don't have one, get one. In this date book they can list the time for a weekly marriage meeting; times during the week for a regular dialogue with their partner; specific plans for fun activities in the marriage; and times that they will decide to do things that they enjoy together.

Some couples may think this process makes marriage too organized and systematic. In practice, we have found that the couples that receive the greatest amount of satisfaction and enjoyment from their marital relationships are those that are willing to make a commitment to that relationship, not only verbally but in actual time.

Ask the couple to put marriage maintenance on their schedule. Just as they schedule their child's Little League practice, dance lesson, or their own dental appointments, they should understand the importance of taking time for love. It was obviously important to make time for love when they first met and were courting. Now it is even more important.

Communication

Communication is the process of regularly and consistently making oneself open, honest, and congruent to their partner. We recommend couples set aside a minimum of ten minutes a day for dialogue. Dialogue is the basis of the marriage relationship. This would allow a minimum of five minutes for each to express their feelings. When they become comfortable with the dialogue they may want to extend the time period.

Have couples ask the following:

- Am I honestly and openly expressing both my thoughts and feelings?
- Are my attitudes and beliefs promoting open communication, or do I have limiting beliefs such as "I am right," "It's your problem," or "Talk will only make it worse"?
- Do I share my feelings and intentions, and affirm myself?
- Do I encourage my partner, and are we both open to feedback?

Regularly Planned Marriage Meetings

We believe that successful coupling requires regularly scheduled marriage meetings. Help the couple to schedule these meetings at a time when they will not be interrupted. The counselor needs to help the couple establish the minimum amount of time they feel will be productive, anywhere from 30 minutes to one hour.

Each meeting needs an agenda of items to be discussed. This agenda needs to be posted prior to the meeting and should be kept in a notebook. Counselors need to suggest that the couples include the following points:

- What I like about our relationship, what I like that I am doing, and what I like that my partner is doing. (Always begin with the positive or what is working.)
- What I would like to see improve in the relationship or what I think could go better.
- What I am willing to do to improve the relationship.
- Positive things I like in the relationship.
- A discussion of work and chores.
- Plans for fun.
- Problems and challenges.

At the marriage meeting, each partner needs to be urged to speak honestly and openly and listen to the other with empathy. Each person needs to participate as an equal. Have the couple plan an enjoyable activity each week that can be shared. The focus should be on encouraging one another by pointing out what is positive and what is going well. Urge the couple not to focus early meetings on highly controversial subjects that are designed to create conflict in the relationship. A marriage meeting is not a frill or an experiment but something that is very basic to improving and maintaining the marriage relationship.

Negotiating Change Through Conflict Resolution

When conflict occurs, couples have several choices. They can fight, avoid the conflict, or resolve the conflict. Energy devoted to fighting and establishing who is right and who is the winner is never productive. The conflict remains unresolved. When couples avoid the issue in conflict, it usually comes back at a later time in a much more severe form. The only reasonable alternative is conflict resolution. Change is based on the willingness of the partners to deal with the issue. Because conflicts hold real potential for damaging the relationship, it is important that they be resolved.

Conflicts may revolve around a variety of issues. Some frequent causes of conflict are the sexual relationship, social relationships, finances, recreation and leisure, parenting and children, in-laws, religion, friends, and alcohol and drugs. There is an endless variety of issues that may be the basis of conflicts. A simple but systematic procedure can be applied to the resolution of any conflict (Dinkmeyer & Carlson, 1984). The steps are:

1. Show mutual respect.
2. Pinpoint the real issues, not the superficial one.
3. Seek areas of agreement; things you are willing to do.
4. Mutually participate in decisions.

To explore the real issues couples need to consider some of their partner's goals and priorities.

Encouragement and Affirmation

One of the challenges in any relationship is self-esteem. When one person (or both) in a marriage has low self-esteem, it affects the system and the relationship. Very often people who lack self-esteem tend to believe that it is their partner's responsibility to make them feel good about themselves.

The encouraged partner ignores or refuses to believe negative self-depreciating statements such as "I am stupid," or "Nobody likes me." Being self-affirming is being a friend to oneself.

Encouragement can also be extended to one's partner. This helps couples to celebrate and recognize the positive in both the partner and the marital system. To keep marriage properly maintained, we suggest that couples focus on the strengths of each other.

Regularly Planned Fun

During the courtship period, the couple spends a lot of time doing things that are mutually enjoyable. They have lots of time planned together, places to go, and things to do and share.

A regular part of the marriage relationship involves planned time for activities that both partners enjoy, as well as planned time for activities that may interest only one partner. At the weekly marriage meeting, couples can schedule activities they may be doing together or separately during the coming week—for example, attending or rehearsing plays or musicals, or watching or playing sports such as golf, tennis, volleyball, walking, or hiking.

Summary

Effective marriage is not a privilege, rather a responsibility. Couples and their counselors need to understand how to create and maintain effective relationships. Traditional methods of helping focus on the front end of change, rather than on the maintenance of a successful intervention. We urge psychologists and counselors who work with couples to be aware of the important strategies to prevent relapse and increase treatment adherence:

1. engage couple and involve them in homework assignments throughout therapy;
2. match strategies to the couple's unique needs;
3. use booster sessions and plan procedures to handle normal external stress; and
4. train couples in the essential skills of marriage (Carlson, Sperry, & Dinkmeyer, 1992).

References

Daley, D. C. (1989). *Relapse prevention.* Blue Ridge Summit, PA: TAB Books.

Dinkmeyer, D., & Carlson, J. (1984). *Time for a better marriage.* Circle Pines, MN: American Guidance Service.

Holtzworth-Munroe, A., Jacobson, N. S., DeKlyen, M., & Whisman, M. A. (1989). Relationship between behavioral marital therapy outcome and process variables. *Journal of Consulting and Clinical Psychology, 57*(5), 658–662.

Jacobson, N. S. (1989). The maintenance of treatment gains following social learning-based marital therapy. *Behavior Therapy, 20,* 325–336.

Jacobson, N. S., & Holtzworth-Munroe, A. (1988). Marital therapy: A social learning-cognitive perspective. In N. S. Jacobson & A. S. Gurman (Eds.), *Clinical handbook of marital therapy.* New York: Guilford Press.

Jacobson, N. S., Schmaling, K. B., & Holtzworth-Munroe, A. (1987). Component analysis of behavioral marital therapy: Two year follow-up and prediction of relapse. *Journal of Marital and Family Therapy, 13,* 187–195.

Lewis, J., Sperry, L., & Carlson, J. (In Press). *Health counseling*. Pacific Grove, CA: Brooks/Cole.

Marlatt, G. A. (1985). Relapse prevention: Theoretical rationale and overview of the model. In G. A. Marlatt & J. R. Gordon (Eds.). *Relapse prevention*. New York: Guilford Press.

Sperry, L. (1985). Treatment noncompliance and cooperation: Implications for psychotherapeutic, medical, and lifestyle change approaches. *Individual Psychology, 41*, 228–236.

Sperry, L., & Carlson, J. (1991). Introducing relapse prevention into family psychology. *The Family Psychologist, 6*, 28–29.

Considerations for the Treatment of Marital Violence

Luann Costa
Debra Holliday

Introduction

Marital violence has received increasing public attention during recent years. The women's movement and the mass media have largely been responsible for communicating the message that it is not okay to be hit or abused—even by those you love—which has led people to become more willing to report abuse (Mathias, 1986).

Margolin (1979) suggests that marital violence is a pattern that involves both spouses, wherein the violent behavior of one spouse produces a degree of compliance from the other spouse, and that this causes a counterresponse that is directed toward the aggressor. This in turn leads to an escalation of hostility within the relationship.

As the subject becomes more openly discussed and explored, researchers and therapists are grappling with questions such as "What causes marital violence and what is the best treatment approach?"

Although there is a difference of opinion as to the course of treatment that should be taken, most experts who have worked in the field seem to agree on certain general "rules" to be followed. This article provides a model whereby therapists can assess the process of counseling clients involved in marital abuse in a step-by-step manner.

Background

It first helps to examine marital violence from a conceptual stance. One of the most comprehensive studies of battered women was conducted by Lenore Walker in the early 1980s. In her book, *The Battered Woman* (1980), she describes the cycle of violence which identifies three stages in the pattern: (1) the tension-building period, (2) the battering incident, and (3) the tension reduction—or "hearts and flowers" period. She feels this pattern is predictable, and that it is the last stage, or "hearts and flowers" stage, that often keeps the woman entangled in the relationship. During this phase, the batterer is contrite and exhibits kind, loving behavior, which often convinces the woman that this is his "true" self.

Although spouse abuse can involve violence by the woman towards the man, the overwhelming majority of violence is perpetrated by the man towards the woman. When it is a case of mutual battering, the woman may be self-defending. In addition, the physical damage to wives caused by husbands is usually greater than the physical damage to husbands by wives (Rosenbaum & O'Leary, 1986). According to the U.S. Department of Justice (1983), almost one third of all female homicide victims are killed by their husbands or boyfriends. In this article, we will consider only male abuse toward females.

Marital violence occurs in every socioeconomic, racial, religious and ethnic group. It has been found to be more probable in interracial or interreligious marriages and in couples where there is status incompatibility (Rosenbaum et al., 1986).

There seems to be a correlation between men who witness abuse as a child and men who grow up to be batterers themselves; however, no such correlation was found between women who witness abuse as a child and women who are abused by spouses as adults (Marshall & Rose, 1988).

Hotaling and Sugarman (1986) found that batterers are exposed early in life to family violence, are less assertive, and possess fewer educational and economic resources than nonviolent men. In addition, they found that male batterers are much more likely to engage in other forms of antisocial behavior than men who are not violent toward their wives. Hastings and Hamberger (1988) found that male abusers were less likely to be employed, to be in intact relationships and were less well educated.

Furthermore, the use of alcohol may also play a part in battering. Alcohol abuse has been identified as a common feature of domestic violence cases (Byles, 1978).

Assessment

Therapists may be confronted with an abusive situation in a variety of ways. Often, a man will be ordered by the courts to seek therapy for battering. Or perhaps a couple will come into therapy on their own as a result of marital violence. Sometimes, a woman in individual therapy will bring up the problem at some point in the course of treatment.

At this time, it is important for therapists to examine their own expertise in the area. The treatment of domestic violence requires careful assessment and specialized training on the part of the therapist, especially in view of the complicated and often dangerous nature of the situation. Therapists who treat this problem must be knowledgeable about all aspects of assessing and treating the problem. If this is not the case, a referral should be made.

The first decision the therapist must make after deciding to take the case is whether to treat the pair individually or as a couple. Most experts agree that the first priority must be the woman's safety. If it is a crisis situation, the therapist is ethically obligated to see that the woman has access to all the support services available to her, including the police, a victims' assistant, legal aid, and counselors from a battered women's shelter if needed.

It is important that the therapist meet with the woman alone at least once, as the woman may be intimidated by the presence of the abuser and not feel free to discuss the situation with the therapist.

At this point, the woman must make a decision. If she wants to separate from the abuser, the counselor can assist with practical measures to be taken, including obtaining a restraining order if indicated. The counselor's job would then be to support the woman in individual or group therapy, and the woman alone would be his or her client, while the abuser is referred to a men's group for violence control, such as Abusive Men Exploring New Directions (AMEND).

This seems simple and straightforward. In actuality, however, this path can be filled with surprises and frustrations. Goodrich & Rampage (1988) cite the pitfalls of counseling an abused woman. In many cases, the values of the therapist and client may clash, causing the therapist to agonize over whether to accept the client's values or try to change them. For example, a therapist who comes from a feminist perspective and values independence for women may have difficulty counseling a client whose culture emphasizes submissive behavior for women.

At the same time, the predicament of the client can bring out dependency issues from the therapist's life, complicating the situation. If a therapist has worked hard to change her own individual view and society's traditional view of women, care must be taken to avoid viewing clients who have been abused as symbols—unassertive, forbearing, and downtrodden—a type which feminists would like to see made obsolete.

Another source of conflict may result from attempting to label the woman as somehow participating in the abuse, as in systemic thinking, which views the victim and victimizer as equally responsible for the violence.

Earlier thoughts on the subject seemed to be that the woman stayed in the abusive relationship because of a personality defect and that she participated in the abuse in an unconscious manner (Feldman, 1982). More recently, however, feminist therapists have challenged this concept, calling it a case of "blaming the victim" and pointing out that there are many reasons a woman may stay with an abuser. Hilberman (1980) identifies a specific stress syndrome that results from violent abuse. Its symptoms include pervading anxiety and fear of the unexpected, chronic apprehension of imminent doom, vigilance, overwhelming passivity and inability to act, a view of themselves as incompetent and unworthy, guilt and denial of anger, concern about loss of control, and feelings of powerlessness to make changes. Financial dependence may also play a part in a woman's inability to leave.

Although these views conflict, they may each have merit. Cotroneo (1988) suggests that women who are victims of abuse have a problem with parentification, which means that as children these women took on the role of parenting their own parents, and have continued this role with their spouses. She feels that abused women, for the most part, have learned that it is "selfish" to take care of themselves and that it is their duty to take care of their spouses. This responsibility-taking by the wife for the husband's emotional well-being is also mentioned by other experts as contributing to the acceptance of marital violence (Mathias, 1986).

Although this may account for a woman's tolerating abuse, it is important for her to recognize that she did not cause the abuse, and that the abuser clearly made the choice to abuse her. It can be pointed out that the abuser may lack the skills for effective communication and negotiation, and uses violence instead. If possible, it may help to encourage the woman to discuss this with friends and family, thereby challenging and dispelling any beliefs that would put the blame with her.

In some cases, the woman will decide to remain with or go back to the abuser, even though the abuser refuses to acknowledge responsibility for the attacks or to seek help. In these cases, therapy becomes individual, although the abuser will loom large in the background of the therapy (Goodrich et al., 1988).

In any case, it is imperative that specialized training and careful assessment be used in order to provide the most appropriate treatment.

Case Study # 1

Case Study

Carol came into therapy at the suggestion of a county victims' advocate. She had been in an abusive relationship for 5 years, during which time she had been treated often at the local emergency room for injuries inflicted by her husband, Wayne. One week prior to her therapy session, Wayne had broken her right arm. He was arrested by the police and taken to jail. After being treated at the hospital and talking to the victims' advocate, Carol decided that she wanted to end the relationship with Wayne. She moved in with her sister, consulted a lawyer, initiated a restraining order against Wayne, and started divorce proceedings.

During the first session, Carol repeated her conviction that there was no hope for the relationship and the marriage should be ended. She discussed her plans for the future and her desire to be independent.

However, after a few sessions, Carol's confidence seemed to disappear. She began missing sessions, and during the sessions she did attend, the therapist felt she was holding something back. When confronted, Carol admitted that she had moved back in with Wayne. She explained that he had been threatening suicide, telling her how sorry he was that he had hurt her, and that he couldn't live without her.

After this confession, the therapist first spoke with Carol about an escape plan in case Wayne became violent again. Carol assured the therapist that she had a safety plan, but felt she would not need it—that Wayne had promised to stop the abuse.

The therapist continued to treat Carol for three more sessions, working on the issues of Carol's self-esteem and exploring her basic ideas about the roles of men and women in relationships.

Carol admitted that she was fearful of her own ability to survive by herself—both financially and emotionally. She also began to see that she felt responsible for Wayne's emotional well-being, and often put herself in the position of seeming inferior to him in order to build up his fragile ego.

But it was obvious to the therapist that Carol was uncomfortable with these insights, and before any further therapy could take place, Carol abruptly quit her therapy sessions altogether.

Discussion

This case points out the strong hold that these relationships can impose and the sometimes frustrating nature of counseling battered women who are severely conflicted about leaving the abuser.

In many cases, the abused women choose to stay with their abusers and work on the relationship in therapy as a couple. This presents therapists with many challenges. The topic of whether or not couples involved in marital violence can be counseled conjointly is a difficult one. Once again, the subject of safety becomes a priority.

If the woman chooses to stay with the batterer, the counselor must ensure that she has a plan of action should a dangerous situation occur. This includes having appropriate emergency phone numbers close at hand and identifying places or people she could ask for help if needed. This also includes having money, an extra set of car keys, important papers, and other essentials in a hidden but easily accessible place should she need to leave in a hurry.

The need to make these arrangements, although of course not the actual arrangements themselves, should be discussed with the abuser and he should be helped to understand the necessity for these plans.

Before any conjoint therapy can take place, the therapist must insist upon a "no-violence contract" for the couple. Most experts agree that this is essential to insure the safety of the wife (Rosenbaum, 1986; Willbach, 1989; Cook & Frantz-Cook, 1984). One of the most effective ways to stop spouse abuse is to establish consequences (Bograd, 1986). By making it clear that he or she will stop couples treatment if the violence recurs, the therapist is sending an important message to both husband and wife—that abuse will not be tolerated.

If the abuser refuses to sign the contract, couples therapy should end. The expert can continue to see either one or both of the spouses individually, but not conjointly. Group counseling is often recommended for abusers in this case.

Once these important safety precautions are met, the therapist's job is that of helping the abuser accept total responsibility for the violence while not alienating the abuser by appearing judgmental and accusatory.

This is a delicate balancing act, but both parties must understand that the abuser is responsible for his actions (Rosenbaum et al., 1986).

Often, a woman will declare that she made him hit her by flirting with other men, or nagging. It must be made clear that although the man cannot control his feelings, he can control his actions (Rosenbaum, et al., 1986). This conflicts somewhat with family systems therapy, which opposes placing blame and requires the therapist to remain neutral. However, most experts agree that in the case of violence, where the health and sometimes the very life of a person may be at stake, it is important to make clear the lines of responsibility (Cook et al., 1984).

After this is established, therapy can then deal with issues such as differentiation of the individuals; identifying sequences, cues, and themes; and coaching alternative responses.

Case Study #2

Case Study

Tom and Jill came to therapy because the previous week they had gotten into a fight and Tom had knocked Jill to the ground. Although it was common for him to throw objects and punch walls when they fought, he had never before touched or hurt Jill during one of these episodes. The incident had frightened Jill, and she had insisted that they come for marriage counseling. Tom had reluctantly agreed.

The therapist first asked about Jill's immediate safety. When she determined that this had been a one-time happening, she explained the need for Jill to have a safety plan, then discussed the "no-violence contract." Tom willingly agreed to sign it, and the stage was set for further therapy.

Tom and Jill came to therapy for a total of 26 sessions. Throughout the course of therapy, although there were many angry feelings and confrontations, Tom kept his promise of "no violence."

The therapy explored various issues, including Jill's pattern, begun in childhood, of placating men, and Tom's long-held, although carefully hidden belief that he was entitled to be treated as superior to Jill.

One of the main problems dealt with was Tom's insistence that he "just couldn't control his rage," that something just came over him periodically, and he would have to hit something or someone to release his anger. Tom attempted to use this excuse many times to explain his behavior, but each time the therapist focused on the necessity of his taking responsibility for his actions. Gradually, Tom accepted this. The therapist also worked with Tom on anger-reduction techniques, such as recognizing situations that triggered his outbursts and learning to utilize "time out" periods as a way to control his anger. At the same time Jill began to accept that she could not "make" Tom blow up by anything she did or said.

Tom and Jill spent many sessions examining family of origin issues, the marriages of their parents and the ideas and behaviors that were modeled for them regarding how men and women should act toward each other. Tom's father had physically abused his mother during Tom's formative years, and although Jill had not observed direct violence in her home, she began to examine her mother and father's relationship closely and see signs of psychological abuse in her own family of origin.

At the end of 6 months, it was mutually decided that Tom and Jill would terminate therapy. They returned for a follow-up session 4 months later and reported that no physical abuse had taken place during that time and that their relationship, while not perfect, was much better than it had ever been.

Discussion

This case illustrates the progress that can be made when both parties place the responsibility for violence where it belongs and then together explore the issues surrounding the violence.

Summary

In general, there are certain steps that can be followed by a therapist who is confronted with the issue of marital violence:

1. Determine if violence is occurring in the relationship. If so, provide the woman with information on safehouses, police numbers, etc.
2. Select treatment modality (individual, group, or conjoint therapy, or combination of these).
3. If individual therapy is decided upon, make arrangements to treat or refer; if conjoint therapy is decided upon:
   a. make sure the woman has a plan of action to assure safety.

b. obtain a no-violence contract.
c. focus on helping the man accept responsibility for violent behavior.
d. focus on self-esteem issues.
e. work with both spouses on issues of differentiation, identifying sequences that lead to violence, recognizing cues and themes, coaching alternative responses and teaching violence-control techniques.

Conclusion

It is hoped that as marital violence becomes confronted and demystified by society, mental health professionals, and the couples who are engaged in the violence, can make progress toward eliminating this humiliating and destructive problem.

References

Bograd, M. (1986). Holding the line: Confronting the abusive partner. *The Family Therapy Networker, 10*(4), 44–47.

Byles, J. A. (1978). Violence, alcohol problems and other problems in disintegrating families. *Journal of Studies on Alcohol, 39,* 551–553.

Cook, D., & Frantz-Cook, A. (1984). A systemic treatment approach to wife battering. *Journal of Marital and Family Therapy, 10,* 83–93.

Cotroneo, M. (1988). Women and abuse in the context of the family. In L. Braverman (Ed.), *A guide to feminist family therapy* (pp. 81–96). New York: Haworth.

Feldman, L. (1982). Dysfunctional marital conflict: An integrative interpersonal-intrapsychic model. *Journal of Marital and Family Therapy, 8*(4), 417–428.

Goodrich, T., & Rampage, C. (1988). *Feminist family therapy.* Markham, Ontario: Penguin.

Hastings, J. E., & Hamberger, L. K. (1988). Personality characteristics of spouse abusers: A controlled comparison. *Violence and Victims, 3,* 31–48.

Hilberman, E. (1980). Overview: The "wife-beater's wife" reconsidered. *American Journal of Psychiatry, 137,* 1336–1347.

Hotaling, G. T., & Sugarman, D. B. (1986). An analysis of risk markers in husband to wife violence: The current state of knowledge. *Violence and Victims, 1*(2), 101–124.

Margolin, G. (1987). The multiple forms of aggressiveness between marital partners: How do we identify them? *Journal of Marital and Family Therapy, 13*, 77–84.

Marshall, L., & Rose, P. (1988). Family of origin violence and courtship abuse. *Journal of Counseling and Development, 66*, 414–418.

Mathias, B. (1986). Lifting the shade on family violence. *The Family Therapy Networker, 10*(4), 20–29.

Rosenbaum, A., & O'Leary, K. (1986). The treatment of marital violence. In N. S. Jacobson & A. S. Gurman (Eds.), *Clinical handbook of marital therapy* (pp. 385–405). New York: Guilford.

U.S. Department of Justice. (1983). *Report to the nation on crime and justice*. Washington, D.C.: Bureau of Justice Statistics.

Walker, L. (1980). *The battered woman*. New York: Harper & Row.

Weingourt, R. (1985). Never to be alone: Existential therapy with battered women. *Journal of Psychosocial Nursing and Mental Health Services, 23*, 24–30.

Willbach, D. (1989). Ethics and family therapy: The case management of family violence. *Journal of Marital and Family Therapy, 15*, 43–52.

This article was accepted for publication in 1992 by *Journal of Mental Health Counseling*. Reprint permission granted by Sage Publications.

The AIDS Family: An Emerging Issue

Loretta J. Bradley
Mary A. Ostrovsky

As recently as 1981, few Americans had heard the term *acquired immunodeficiency syndrome* (AIDS), and the few Americans who had heard the term had little information about the disease's cause or prevalence. Yet today, only 8 years after the discovery of AIDS, there are definite signs that Americans not only are aware of, but also are very fearful of, AIDS.

In a recent study of the National Center of Health Statistics (1988), the Center reported that the U.S. public's awareness of AIDS includes virtually everyone. The study reported that 99% of adults 18 years and older have heard of AIDS. The majority of participants (90%) stated that they are certain that AIDS leads to death; 86% said they realize that AIDS has no cure; 78% said that they think anyone with the AIDS virus can transmit it through sexual intercourse; and 73% said they believe a pregnant woman can transmit AIDS to her baby.

With the increased awareness of AIDS, many Americans express fear and dread when the term AIDS is mentioned. The fear is real, especially when one recognizes that AIDS is spreading in epidemic proportions.

Prior to the discovery of AIDS, infectious disease was no longer considered a real threat for Americans. Although at one time infectious diseases such as typhoid, measles, diphtheria, and polio were definite health threats, these problems were conquered by the American health community—mainly with the advent of vaccines. During the past decade Americans have feared noninfectious diseases, such as heart attack, cancer, stroke, and diabetes, more than infectious diseases.

Consequently, for several years American health advances have been unprecedented in controlling infectious disease, and increased success had been achieved in controlling noninfectious disease. At least this was the scenario until the advent of AIDS. After many years of control over infectious disease, AIDS appeared. Suddenly Americans were thrust into the health arena with a new infectious disease that is spreading in epidemic proportions.

AIDS was formally recognized by the Center for Disease Control (CDC) in 1981. In less than 2 years from the initial report of five AIDS cases, CDC reported 5,550 AIDS cases in 1983. By 1985 more than 10,000 cases of AIDS had been reported. In mid May, 1988, CDC reported 62,200 cases of AIDS—a cumulative total of more than 2-1/2 times that of September, 1986 (Cooper, 1988). These data indicate that AIDS is spreading rapidly.

Kubler-Ross (1987) described the magnitude of AIDS cases as staggering, and she concluded that this is only the beginning. It has been predicted that by the end of 1991, an estimated 170,000 cases of AIDS will have occurred, and 179,000 persons will have died within the decade since the disease was first recognized (Koop, 1986). In the year 1991 an estimated 145,000 patients with AIDS will need health and support services, at a total cost of between $8 billion and $16 billion (Kubler-Ross, 1987).

To say that AIDS is just another medical problem is an understatement. With new AIDS cases doubling every 10 to 12 months (Mason, 1985) and with public opinion surveys reporting that AIDS ranks third (behind cancer and heart disease) as the disease most Americans fear they will acquire (Mills, 1986), certainly AIDS ranks among significant issues facing Americans.

Although researchers have made advances in establishing the cause of AIDS (Center for Disease Control, 1984; Gallo, 1987; Gallo & Montagnier, 1988), the origin of the AIDS virus (Essex & Kanki, 1988),the high risk factors associated with AIDS (Baltimore & Wolff, 1986; Bohm, 1987; Center for Disease Control, 1984; Ginzberg, 1984; Heyward & Curran, 1988; Mason, 1985; Witt, 1986), testing for the AIDS virus (Galea, Lewis, & Baker, 1988), and counseling with AIDS patients (Bor, Miller, & Perry, 1988; Coats, Temoshak, & Mandel, 1984; Gold, Seymour, & Sahl, 1986; Grant & Anns, 1988; Jaffe & Wortman, 1988; Krieger, 1988; Lomax & Sandler, 1988; Mejta, 1987; Morin, Charles, & Malyon, 1984; Nichols, 1985; Posey, 1988; Stevens & Muskin, 1987; Stulberg & Smith, 1988; Widen, 1987), little research has been devoted to the family of the AIDS patient. In a literature search we found only nine articles that even mentioned the family of the AIDS patient (Baer, Hall, Holm, & Lewitter-Koehler, 1987; Barret, 1989; Bruttn, 1989; Destounis, 1987; Deuchar, 1984; Faltz & Mandover, 1987; Flaskerud, 1987; Graham & Cates, 1987; Greif & Porembski, 1987), and only two focused on the AIDS family (Greif & Porembski, 1987; Robinson, Skeen, & Walters, 1987).

Given the incidence of increase of AIDS, by necessity many people are influenced by the presence of AIDS. Although most of the AIDS publications have focused on the medical aspects of AIDS or its impact on the AIDS patient, few studies have considered the effect of AIDS upon significant others. One group affected by the presence of AIDS is the family of the AIDS patient. Because of the paucity of information on the family of the AIDS patient, this article will focus on the family.

AIDS Overview

History

The Center for Disease Control (CDC) receives surveillance data from reports from state and local health departments. A report in June, 1981, alerted CDC to the presence of AIDS. The report described how in the past 8 months an extremely rare type of pneumonia caused by the protozoan *Pneumocystis carinii* had been diagnosed in Los Angeles. The disease was so rare that the drug given to treat it was experimental and was dispensed solely by the CDC. Between 1967 and 1979 only two cases of *P. carinii* pneumonia—a disease that usually attacks older persons whose immune systems have been profoundly impaired—had been reported. Yet in the five new cases in 1981, the pneumonia had struck five young homosexual men whose immune systems had no apparent reason for malfunctioning (Heyward & Curran, 1988).

Later in 1981 the CDC received reports of an increase in the incidence of a type of cancer called *Kaposi's sarcoma*. Prior to 1981 this type of cancer seldom had been seen in the United States, and when it was, it occurred mainly in elderly men and older patients receiving immuno-suppressive therapy. In a 30-month span, however, 26 cases of *Kaposi's sarcoma* had been diagnosed in homosexual men living in New York and California. Several of these men had also contracted *P. carinii* pneumonia. Also in 1981, clinicians and epidemiologists noted an increased occurrence in homosexual men of *lymphadenopathy* (disease with enlarged lymph nodes) and a rare malignancy called *diffuse, undifferentiated non-Hodgkin's lymphoma*. The common denominator in all cases was a severely impaired immune system. This collection of clinical syndromes was recognized as an entirely new syndrome that became known in 1982 as *acquired immunodeficiency syndrome*, or AIDS (Heyward & Curran, 1988).

Through control studies in late 1981, researchers had evidence to illustrate that the factor that differentiated homosexual patients with AIDS from homosexual controls was the number and frequency of sexual contacts. By 1982 researchers had evidence to strongly suggest that AIDS was transmitted by sexual relations in active homosexual males. Later in that year researchers had evidence indicating that other modes of transmission of AIDS existed. These included injection with blood or blood transfusions and were confirmed among hemophilia patients and intravenous (IV) drug abusers who shared hypodermic needles.

In December, 1982, a baby was born with AIDS. Thus, by the end of 1982, evidence strongly suggested that AIDS could be transmitted by sexual intercourse and blood. In January, 1983, researchers had evidence to illustrate the presence of AIDS cases in heterosexual partners of male IV drug abusers. Later in 1983, cases of AIDS were reported in central Africa and Haiti in persons without any homosexual or IV drug abuse history.

Because AIDS was known to be transmitted by sexual contact or blood, researchers were convinced that AIDS was caused by a class of infectious agents called retroviruses (Gallo & Montagnier, 1988). In two years, from mid-1982 to mid-1984, a new virus, the *human immunodeficiency virus* (HIV), was isolated by Montagnier and his colleagues at the Pasteur Institute in Paris and by Gallo and his colleagues at the National Cancer Institute. The HIV was isolated and shown to cause AIDS. Soon after the discovery of HIV, laboratory tests were developed to detect the presence of HIV in the blood (Heyward & Curran, 1988).

AIDS Risk

Ever since the AIDS pandemic was recognized, it has aroused mysterious dread in the United States. At first Americans believed they were safe if they were not homosexual or bisexual. As more information about AIDS has become known, however, it is apparent that several groups are at a higher risk for AIDS.

Table 1 presents data illustrating the distribution of AIDS among higher risk groups. Although the table presents data via type of group, the reader should be aware that individuals engaging in unprotected vaginal sex, oral sex, and IV drug use are at a higher risk for contracting AIDS regardless of whether the individual holds membership in one of the higher risk groups.

Table 1
Diagnosed Cases of AIDS by Risk Group (Adults)

Risk Group	% of Diagnosed AIDS Cases*
Homosexual or bisexual men	63%
Heterosexual IV drug abusers	19%
Homosexual or bisexual IV drug abusers	7%
Heterosexual men and women	4%
Recipients of blood or blood products	3%
Persons with hemophilia or other coagulation disorders	1%
Other or undetermined	3%

*Adapted from Center for Disease Control data as of 7/4/88.

As Table 1 indicates, 63% of the AIDS cases have occurred in homosexual or bisexual men, and 19% have occurred in heterosexual intravenous (IV) drug abusers. An additional 7% of the cases have occurred in homosexual or bisexual IV drug abusers. When the percents for those three groups are added, it becomes apparent that most of the AIDS cases have occurred in homosexual or bisexual men and IV drug abusers (89%). The 4% of the total AIDS cases attributed to heterosexual men and women occurred in persons who either had sexual contact with a person infected by HIV or were born in a country where heterosexual transmission of AIDS is the primary mode of transmission.

Further, Table 1 indicates that 3% of the AIDS cases occurred from blood contamination, and another 1% occurred in hemophiliacs. Because blood has been screened for the HIV since 1985, most of the AIDS transmission from blood transfusions occurred before 1985.

Contrary to popular belief, children constitute the fastest growing group of AIDS cases. In the past 12 months, Heyward and Curran (1988) reported 502 new cases of AIDS in children under 13 years of age; this represents a 114% increase over the past year. Table 2 presents data on the incidence of AIDS in children.

More than three-fourths (77%) of the children diagnosed with AIDS acquired it from their mother during the prenatal period, with the

Table 2
Diagnosed Cases of AIDS by Risk Group (Children)

Risk Group	% of Diagnosed AIDS Cases*
Children who contracted AIDS prenatally from their mothers	77%
Recipients of blood or blood products	13%
Persons with hemophilia or other coagulation disorders	6%
Other or undetermined	4%

*Adapted from Center for Disease Control data as of 7/4/88.

original mode of transmission being IV drug abuse on the part of the mother or her sexual partner. As this table further shows, 13% of the AIDS cases in children occurred among children who had received blood or blood transfusions, and 6% of the cases were found in children with hemophilia.

With regard to AIDS across race, the data show a disproportionate amount of AIDS infections in Blacks and Hispanics. Heyward and Curran (1988) reported:

> In the U.S. 59% of the reported AIDS cases among adults and 23% of the cases among children have been white; Blacks have accounted for 26% of adult cases and 53% of pediatric cases; and Hispanics for 14% of adult and 23% of pediatric cases. Such figures are in striking contrast to the respective percentage of Blacks (11.6%) and Hispanics (6.5%) in the general U.S. population. (p. 78)

Although gaps remain in understanding the transmission of AIDS, cumulative data indicate that some groups are at higher risk for AIDS transmission. Even so, no one should assume that because he or she does not hold membership in one of the higher risk groups, AIDS presents no threats.

The AIDS Family

Ozzie and Harriet Syndrome

For years Ozzie and Harriet represented the ideal American family. The Nelsons personified the American dream family. It included a husband, a wife, two bright, healthy children, a nice home, and a car. Dad (Ozzie) was the breadwinner of the family. Each day he left for work in a suit and tie with briefcase in hand, and accompanied by a happy smile. Mom (Harriet) was the loyal, loving wife who stayed home and cared for the family. Although her life centered on the family, she played bridge with neighbors and participated in volunteer work. She was always home when the children arrived from school, and she was available with her station wagon to transport her children and their friends to their after-school activities. When Dad arrived home from work she had a nice meal ready for him and the children to enjoy. The family frequently interacted with neighbors. The family was happy and enjoyed being together. Such was the American dream.

In reality, the American dream falls apart with only a cursory look at the data. Today many Americans are divorced, and single parenting is becoming more frequent (Craig, 1989). Many married couples are electing to remain childless. Women are no longer staying home but instead are entering the work force in increasing numbers. The American family is fast becoming a two-paycheck family. Although the idea of the American dream with its Ozzie and Harriet family may still be a *dream* for the American family, for most Americans it is only that and not reality.

One group that does not fit the traditional syndrome depicted by the Nelson family is the family whose child has AIDS—a disease the American family does not want to encounter. The dread of AIDS in American families is precipitated by a number of factors. Fear of a disease for which there is no known cure and dread of the social stigma associated with AIDS contribute to a large portion of the fear. Certainly AIDS in a family does not fit the American expectation. Consequently, many families have ignored the AIDS epidemic and have assumed that AIDS will not penetrate their family system. Erroneously, they have concluded that if their son is not gay or is not on drugs, AIDS should not be a concern for them. But try as the family might to ignore AIDS, it doesn't work. With more than 62,000 cases of AIDS diagnosed in 1988 and more than 260,000 cases projected by 1991 (Cooper, 1988), AIDS is a reality with which the American family must reckon.

Traditionally the American family consisted of father, mother, and children. But the AIDS family has caused Americans to re-examine and expand its traditional definition of the family to include not only the biological family but also lovers and friends. Family members of persons with AIDS (PWA) are usually from one of the following three groups: (a) biological family and spouses, lovers, and friends of homosexual and bisexual men, (b) biological family, spouses and lovers of IV drug users, and (c) spouses, lovers, and other family members of hemophiliacs (Donlou et al., 1985; Greif & Porembski, 1987; Mason, Olson, & Parish, 1988).

Common Family Responses

Upon learning that a family member has AIDS, the family typically experiences the following four reactions:

1. *Negative Reaction*. Learning that a family member has AIDS almost always evokes a negative response from family members. A common statement is, "I never expected this...this is awful."
2. *Surprise*. Although family members may realize that an individual may have been exposed to the AIDS virus via sexual contact or IV drug use, they nevertheless don't expect that person to contract AIDS. Upon being told that a family member has AIDS, the other members exhibit surprise and, in many cases, disbelief. They typically say, "I just can't believe that Jim has AIDS...surely this can't be true."
3. *Helplessness*. Upon learning that one of its members has AIDS, the family often experiences a feeling of helplessness. This is often manifested in their feeling of being out of control. A comment that typifies this feeling is, "Our Jim has AIDS, a disease without a known cure. Is there anything we can do? I feel so helpless."
4. *Loss*. Knowledge of an AIDS diagnosis often evokes a feeling of loss and a feeling that the loss doesn't seem to be right. Most parents expect to die before their child does, but with an AIDS diagnosis the child is likely to die before the parents do. Most spouses and lovers expect many years in a satisfying relationship,

> but with an AIDS diagnosis the relationship is likely to be shortened. With an AIDS diagnosis comes the inevitable feeling of impending loss. The feeling of loss if often verbalized as "I just can't believe that Jim is terminally ill and we're going to lose him."

Family of Origin of Homosexual and Bisexual Men

Because the greatest number of AIDS cases presently are in homosexual and bisexual men ages 20-40 years, most of their parents are 40–65 years old. According to developmental research conducted by Erikson and Erikson (1981), individuals between 40 and 65 years of age are dealing with the developmental task of establishing themselves as generative persons. Generativity is defined as *the effort to perpetuate oneself through something lasting and meaningful to the world.*

Some individuals express generativity through productivity in their work. Others may achieve generativity through creation and nurturance of a family (Craig, 1989). Thus, at this stage of life, parents usually are involved in rearing children and preparing for retirement. But AIDS may cause parents and other family members to return to earlier life roles, especially the role of caregiver. Kubler-Ross (1987) captures the essence of this predicament in summarizing the roles of mothers of AIDS victims: "They had to train themselves to be moms again for little helpless children in a grown-up body" (p. 32). Additionally, the prolonged illness of the PWA may drain family members emotionally and physically and deplete family resources (Flaskerud, 1987; Wolcott, Fawzy, & Pasnau, 1985).

Family members, especially parents, may find themselves geographically isolated from their child. Although they may want to offer their support, they may experience great situational stress in trying to find accommodations during visits or wanting to provide support and being unable to do so because of distance and finances. In other cases involving previous conflicts between the PWA and the family about issues concerning sexual preference and lifestyle, the family members may reject the PWA and desire greater geographic and psychological distance.

Because AIDS has attacked a minority group that lacks full acceptance by society, the family of the AIDS victim may feel as much stigma as the child does. This often is expressed in the form of anger, fear, guilt, and grief. Parents of a PWA frequently feel guilty because they erroneously believe that if they had reared their child differently, the child would have been neither gay nor ill (Wolcott, Fawzy, & Pasnau, 1985). The parents often admonish themselves by stating, "If only I had spent more time with him, this wouldn't have happened," or "Did I do something wrong to cause my son to be gay and contract AIDS?"

Although both fathers and mothers usually experience guilt, they do so for different reasons. Mothers feel guilt because they traditionally have been responsible for their children's actions (Flaskerud, 1987). Fathers experience guilt because they see their son's orientation as a reflection of their own masculinity. As might be anticipated, researchers have reported that gay men perceive their mothers as more supportive of their sexual orientation than their fathers (Skeen & Robinson, 1985).

Parents and other biological family members often grieve upon learning of the AIDS diagnosis. The grief is acute initially, and then, in the case of prolonged illness, chronic. The sequence is similar to the five stages of grief described by Kubler-Ross (1969) as denial, anger, bargaining, depression, and acceptance. The case of John depicts the grief process, as well as some of the family dynamics involved.

Case Illustration: John

John, a 23-year-old male, has just been diagnosed with AIDS. One of his greatest fears is telling his family that he has AIDS. He still remembers the trauma of 8 years ago when he told his family he was gay. On hearing that his son is gay, John's father at first was shocked and then outraged. His mother, although sad that her son is gay, tried to be understanding, but even she was often influenced by her husband.

With time the father became a little more tolerant of the situation and talked with John about almost any topic except John's sexual orientation. Although his mother was usually kind and caring, at times even she would remind John that, "This is upsetting to your father, who only wants you to be like other men." The parents nevertheless worked hard and sent John to college. Two years ago John graduated from college with an engineering degree. For the past 2 years his career has been going great. In fact, he had never been happier until he received the diagnosis of AIDS.

Sequentially, then, upon learning that John has AIDS, his father and mother couldn't believe they were hearing correctly. First, they had to live with John being a homosexual, and now AIDS. Initially John's parents were very upset with him, and in the beginning they said some hurtful things to him. In fact, John returned to Chicago thinking he never wanted to see them again. After several phone calls from his mother, John decided to visit his parents. Although the visit was strained, his parents made an attempt to be friendly. At one point his mother said, "We love you no matter what." John thought about the statement and realized its intent was to convey that no matter how difficult his being gay, and now AIDS, has been, they love and accept him as their son.

Stages of Loss Related to Counseling Interventions

Counselors should understand how family members react to the news that a member has AIDS, for the reaction will determine the counseling interventions. Table 3 presents a means to conceptualize what is likely to occur within the family system. The first column names the stage, the second contains an explanation of it, and the third provides an example of the family's reaction at a specific stage. The stages of grief may or may not be experienced sequentially. Some families do not reach the fifth stage (acceptance). Almost all experience stages 1 and 2 (denial, anger), and most experience stage 3 or 4 (bargaining, depression). A recent article substantiates evidence for the passage of stages (Barret, 1989). It mainly discusses stages 1 and 2 and then adds a stage between stages 2 and 3, which might be labeled stage 2A, guilt. The counselor should realize that although reaching stage 5 is desirable, this doesn't always happen.

In the case of John's family, initially both parents experienced denial, and then John's father expressed a great deal of resentment. When families are experiencing stage 1 and 2 reactions, they often will not accept family counseling. Sometimes one of the family members (often the mother) will seek individual counseling. Usually at stage 1, however, the family wants concrete information and seems to benefit from a concrete educational approach in which questions are answered.

At stage 2 individual counseling should be encouraged as an avenue for family member(s) to express feelings (often anger) in a safe environment rather than venting it on the PWA. Because many hurtful expressions can emerge at stage 2, the PWA often needs to seek the help of counselors and significant friends. In the example of John, the counselor should help him express his feelings toward his family's anger. By stage 5, a family intervention approach is likely to be beneficial.

Table 3
Family Reaction to AIDS and Loss

Stage	Explanation	Example
1. Denial	Most families respond with shock and disbelief when they are told that a member has AIDS. A typical response is, "Surely this isnt true."	Mr. and Mrs. Jones had just celebrated their 25th wedding anniversary. About a week after the celebration, they were told their oldest child has AIDS. Their response was, "I can't believe it...not my child."
2. Anger	After realizing that the AIDS diagnosis is true, many families become hostile and angry toward the member who has AIDS. The anger is directed not only toward the afflicted person, but it is often displaced toward others as well. They often look in envy at other families experiencing harmony.	Mr. and Mrs. Fine, a 45-year-old couple, had been model parents to their only son, John—at least they thought they were. Their response to John's diagnosis of AIDS was an outburst of anger with unpleasant name-calling. In discussing their plight, a constant theme emerged: "How dare he bring this on us. We've devoted our lives to him, and now look.... Why us?"
3. Bargaining	The family members realize the person with AIDS is getting worse by the day. The AIDS diagnosis is indeed true. They pray, "If you'll just give John another chance, we'll be better people."	Mr. and Mrs. Smith realize their child is going to die unless a cure is found for AIDS very soon. They ask the doctor, "Can't you do something to let him live just a little longer?" They also pray, "Just let my child live long enough to graduate from college; then we'll let him go."

Table 3 (continued)
Family Reaction to AIDS and Loss

Stage	Explanation	Example
4. Depression	The family realizes the fight to save the AIDS member is lost. At this stage there is often a desire to spend a lot of time alone thinking. The days become so long and depressing that they dread getting out of bed each day. They're embarrassed and afraid friends and neighbors will learn of the AIDS. They need emotional release. The mother cries alone, while the father refuses to give in to emotions. As they reach the depths of despair, emotional release comes. After the release, the deep depression begins to lift.	Mr. Ruiz, 50, and his wife Martha, 48, realize their child's life is almost over—a child who just turned 21 last week. Mr. and Mrs. Ruiz realize there is nothing they can do to save him. They would give their last dollar to cure him. As they think back over their lives, they remember their child's birth, first step, first days at school. The pain becomes depressing, and they find themselves alone thinking about their child and AIDS. Finally they acknowledge their grief and cry their hearts out. The deep depression begins to lift.
5. Acceptance	The family at this stage doesn't like what has happened but nevertheless begins to accept the inevitable.	Mr. and Mrs. Smith, age 39, know they must accept the inevitable. Although it is not what they want, they realize that AIDS is winning. So with courage and dignity they conclude, "Time is almost up. We'll continue to help our child and do the best we can."

Not all (actually many) families respond the way that John's family responded. Some respond by almost total rejection. Often the family does not know that the PWA is homosexual or bisexual, and the revelation may be a "double whammy." In other instances one family member may know about the AIDS diagnosis but hadn't told other family members—a situation that may cause friction and distrust within the family (Deuchar, 1984; Donlou, Wolcott, Gottlieb, & Landsverk, 1985; Faltz & Mandover, 1987; Flaskerud, 1987). In still other instances a family member (usually parent) may have known about the PWA's sexual orientation, and the diagnosis of AIDS just confirmed his or her worst fears. Robinson, Skeen, and Walters (1987) reported that 71% of the parents of gay men worried that their child might contract AIDS.

AIDS and Family Stress

To say that AIDS is a stressor in the lives of the parents and the AIDS victim is an understatement for, indeed, AIDS is a major stressor. In some families AIDS is the only stressor, but in most families additional stressors exist. Because stressors can accumulate and in turn influence family members' reactions toward the PWA, the counselor might check to see if other stressors are present.

One means for assessing life stressors is the Social Readjustment Rating Scale (Holmes & Rahe, 1967). This scale lists 43 major stressors, such as divorce, death, fired at work, and places a mean value on the stressor. As examples, death is given a value of 100, divorce a value of 73, fired at a job a 47, and sleeping habit change a 16. The values of each stressor are added. A total stressor value of over 300 indicates a high amount of stress. In contrast, a score under 100 indicates a lack of major stress in the individual's life.

The scale and its interpretive guide contain specific means for interpreting the score. The basic point is that counselors should realize that too much stress in a family member's life can indeed influence his or her acceptance or rejection of the AIDS diagnosis. Additionally, these circumstances can take their toll on one's patience and health.

Spouses and Lovers of Homosexual and Bisexual Men

Spouses and lovers of persons with AIDS have some of the same reactions as parents of PWAs but often experience many different reactions as well. For example, they may fear for their own health and become hyper-vigilant about illness, especially AIDS. They also may feel guilty because they are not ill and their spouse (lover) is terminally ill with AIDS. Further, they may have escalating anticipatory grief as the PWA's death becomes more imminent. They may devote themselves to being the total caregiver of the PWA and often experience all of the stresses that are characteristic of those who provide care for terminally ill patients.

Sometimes the stresses become so great that the spouse (lover) may become immobilized to the point of avoiding the issue. If this occurs, the counselor might help the client remember critical decisions from the past. The accompanying exercise, entitled "A Critical Decision," contains 10 questions that help clients remember a past decision and how that decision was handled. The ninth question asks the client, "Do you see any similarities between the way you handled the past decision and the way you are handling your current decision (decision produced by the diagnosis of AIDS)?" The tenth question asks, "What is your greatest fear about your current decision?" This exercise can be very helpful for the counselor to assist the client in looking at the past as a lever for understanding and improving the present.

In the case of the PWA, problems may arise regarding decision making during the illness. These include important decisions such as which physician to select and who will make the decision(s). It is best if the PWA makes those decisions. But some PWAs either neglect to make decisions or do not want to make them. In the absence of either verbal or written decisions by the PWA, parents and lovers may experience conflict in the decision-making process, especially if the parents did not know or did not accept the lover prior to the illness (Faltz & Mandover,. 1987; Flaskerud, 1987; Wolcott et al, 1985).

In deciding who has the legal right to make decisions for the PWA when he or she becomes incapable of doing so, the legal right usually is awarded to the parents unless the PWA has given, via legal document, power of attorney to the lover. If legal power of attorney has not been provided, parents can make decisions for the PWA prior to death. After death, unless a legal will has been made, the parents can inherit all property, bank accounts, and the like that belonged to the PWA. This can be devastating to the lover, psychologically as well as financially. The counselor must be cognizant of the need to discuss these issues with the PWA, recognizing that some clients have attended to the legal issues via formal documents and others have not.

In the case of the bisexual PWA, the spouse may be shocked to learn of this sexual orientation. It is not uncommon for a wife to have assumed that her marriage has been monogamous for the past 10 years and then to learn, following the diagnosis of AIDS, that her husband is bisexual. The spouse, therefore, may experience denial, fear, and a high level of anger.

Further, the care and reactions of children may be a compounding issue in the family of the PWA. The counselor should try to explore three

A Critical Decision

Directions to Client: Take a few minutes to think about a past situation that involved a major change in your life—a change that was unwanted. (After the client has identified the situation, proceed with the following 10 questions.)

1. What was the decision?
2. What major change did the decision involve?
3. What were your feelings at the time you were aware of your need to make the decision?
4. Did your feelings remain the same, or did they change during the decision process?
5. How did you proceed in making the decision? (Be specific as possible about the stages.)
6. What was the outcome of the decision?
7. How did you feel about yourself after you made the decision?
8. If you were to have the opportunity to remake the decision, would you make any changes? (Be as specific as possible.)
9. Do you see any similarities between the way you handled the past decision and the way you are handling your current decision about your spouse (lover) and the AIDS diagnosis?
10. What is your greatest fear about your current decision? (Be as specific as possible.)

broad issues with the spouse (and with the children, if they are old enough to be cognizant of the issues): (a) survival issues, (b) personal issues, and (c) work/family issues.

In terms of survival issues, the counselor may need to help the spouse explore some of the following issues: Can she and the children survive financially? What is the medical prognosis for her husband? With regard to personal issues, the counselor might help the spouse explore her feelings upon learning that her husband is bisexual. How will the bisexual relationship impact their marriage? In terms of family issues, the counselor should explore what effect the bisexual relationship is having on the family as a system and on individual family members. What impact has the relationship had or will the relationship have on the family's interaction with acquaintances (friends, neighbors, co-workers)?

Friends of Homosexual Men, Bisexual Men, and IV Drug Users

Friends of homosexual men, bisexual men, and IV drug users may fear contagion because they identify with the PWA's lifestyle and activities. This in turn can force them to evaluate their own lifestyles. Further, they may over-identify with the PWA, resulting in worry-related anxiety states (Wolcott et al, 1985). Some individuals may over-identify so much that they may exhibit AIDS symptoms without being HIV-positive. Glaser (1987) related the feelings of this group to those experienced by the survivors of the bombing of Hiroshima; survivors may have the feeling that the whole world is dying around them.

Biological Families and Spouses/Lovers of IV Drug Users

The percentage of AIDS cases related to IV drug use has been increasing steadily in the past few years. This is now a primary source of heterosexual and prenatal transmission of the HIV virus, from the sharing of needles and from having sexual contact with infected partners. In the United States, 25% of AIDS cases have IV drug use as a risk factor, including 8% who also have male homosexual activity as a risk factor (Des Jarlais & Friedman, 1988). AIDS can have a devastating effect on the family of the IV drug user. Family dynamics may include conflicts over illegal activities, estrangement, co-dependency, and child care.

In some instances in which the IV drug user is estranged from the family because of the drug use, the AIDS diagnosis may cause the family to evaluate its present situation and possibly reconcile. In other cases the AIDS diagnosis may lead to further alienation among members. For some families the AIDS diagnosis may lead to revelation of drug use or drug use/homosexual activity—a situation that may shock family members (Greif & Porembski, 1987).

In all of these situations, the family may be asked to be the primary caregiver for the PWA. The personal financial resources of many families may be too limited to allow proper care for the PWA. Children also may present a problem for this group, especially if the PWA is their primary caregiver. For these children for whom other resources are unavailable, the counselor might refer them to social service agencies. Finally, bereavement issues should be addressed to help the children deal with the loss of a parent.

Case Illustration: Sylvia

Sylvia is a bright 35-year-old woman. Upon graduation she moved to San Antonio, where she accepted a job with an accounting firm. She met a man at work, and together they began to smoke pot. One thing led to another, and they were into IV drug use. Sylvia experienced some symptoms similar to those of a cold or the flu. Despite medication, the symptoms would not go away. Sylvia's doctor said she was just "run-down," and with the new medication she would be well soon. The symptoms continued off and on for 6 months and Sylvia often felt even worse, so she visited her doctor again. After much testing, the doctor informed Sylvia by phone that she has AIDS and asked that Sylvia not return to his office but to seek medical help elsewhere (some physicians do not want to see AIDS patients: in addition to the fear of AIDS is the fear of losing other patient business).

About a year after the AIDS diagnosis, Sylvia decided to tell her parents. She recalls, "This was the most difficult decision of my life. I went home for the weekend and tried to tell my parents that I have AIDS. I just couldn't. I returned to San Antonio. A month later I visited my parents again. I told them together. My mother cried and cried. My dad did as I knew he would—he yelled and yelled at me. I hate to think what he said. His final statement was 'Get out! You are no child of mine.

I don't ever want to hear or see you again...ever!' That was a year ago. I haven't heard from them."

In reviewing Table 3, Sylvia's father clearly is at stage 2, Anger. Stage 2 can be a long one for many parents. For other parents, it is never lost, although parents who remain in stage 2 have a lot of parental guilt. Usually the guilt is reflected in a parental response, "Where did we go wrong?" Some parents, however, mask the guilt with overt anger directed at the PWA. Until the parents are ready to deal with their issues, they often reject the help a counselor can offer. In fact, during the early part of stage 2, many families do not consider counseling as an option.

If family therapy isn't feasible, the counselor might help the PWA locate other support. Often it is possible to increase the support from others such as friends, co-workers, other PWAs, and siblings. It should be noted that siblings sometimes substitute for their parent's rejection, and other times siblings follow their parent's path of rejection.

Although Sylvia's parents experienced a lot of anger, denial was likely their initial reaction. Sometimes counselors miss the importance of denial because it is camouflaged by the intense anger. The counselor should try to determine if denial occurred over a long period of time, and also why it occurred.

In the case of Sylvia's family, the intense anger could be the result of a fear of stigma. In many instances parents of PWAs are afraid to tell friends, co-workers, and other family members about their child having AIDS because they are afraid of their friends' reactions, the stigma it will produce, and the change in their community interactions. The display of anger can indeed mean, "Look what you've caused for us among our family and neighbors." Counseling can be very beneficial for these parents, in many instances, because the counselor might be the only person to whom they dare say, "My child has AIDS." Even though counseling often begins on an individual basis, family support groups have been very beneficial in encouraging parents to talk with others about issues evolving from their child's diagnosis of AIDS (Flaskerud, 1987; Graham & Cates, 1987).

Families of Hemophiliacs

In the United States 92% of individuals with severe hemophilia A, the most common form of hemophilia, have been exposed to the HIV virus; in 1988, one in every 26 of these persons has acquired AIDS (Mason et al., 1988). Because hemophilia is a hereditary blood coagulation disease, entire families may be affected by the HIV virus.

Case Illustrations: Parrish and Teer Families

Mrs. Aguilar, a school counselor, has two children in her school with AIDS. Both acquired HIV infections through contaminated blood products. She has been helping teachers, parents, and other children to provide the best learning experience for these children with AIDS. John Parrish is a 10-year-old fourth-grader whose mother is a hemophiliac carrier. Mr. and Mrs. Parrish talked with Mrs. Aguilar about arranging for a visiting teacher to visit John at the hospital to prevent him from getting behind in his school work.

John has been hospitalized with *esophageal candidiasis*. When Mrs. Parrish came to talk to Mrs. Aguilar, she berated herself about her son's illness, saying, "I'm to blame for my son's illness! I should have never had children." Mr. Parrish also blames himself for his son's illness and expresses this through statements such as, "I knew that there were risks involved because of my wife's family history, and now our child is suffering. It's all our fault."

The Teer family also visits Mrs. Aguilar. When they talk about their son George's illness, they express more anger toward outside sources than anger toward themselves. George has been ill now for many months, and they do not think he will live to be released from the hospital. Mrs. Aguilar has been a source of support for the family since the beginning of George's illness a year ago.

In these two cases, attributions play a large role in the family's adjustment and acceptance of their child's illness. Figure 1 shows how attributions influence the family's coping style. As Figure 1 illustrates, counselors need to be cognizant of how a family views the cause of the AIDS infection. Often this is expressed by internalizing or externalizing blame. Counselors should encourage families to stop assigning blame for AIDS. Instead families should be encouraged to seek the best workable solution to the problem. Often this means that the counselor will need to help family members express their feelings about their child's illness without self-guilt being imposed.

Internal Attributions

Parental Statements

"Maybe I should not have had a child since I knew that hemophilia ran in my family."
"Where did I go wrong?"
"Could I have done something different?"

↓

lead to self-deprecation, guilt, self-grief, depression

External Attributions

Parental Statements

"They should have checked the blood supply more closely!"
"People who donate blood should be sure they aren't HIV-positive!"

↓

lead to anger at society and outside persons

Neutral Attributions

Parental Statements

"I'm upset that our child is ill, but I must do something now to provide her with the best quality of life possible."
"My child has died, and now I want to do something to see that other children will not get ill. I'm going to volunteer time working on the city's AIDS hotline."

↓

lead to acceptance and action

Figure 1

Conclusions

AIDS is spreading in epidemic proportions. It is apparent from its incidence that AIDS is not a respecter of persons. It can be acquired by men, women, or children of any age. Further, AIDS is indiscriminate of membership in any social group or of socioeconomic level. It is typically spread by risky sexual practices, IV drug abuse, and contaminated blood or blood products.

AIDS has impacted, and will continue to impact, the American family system. At times the family affected by AIDS is the family of origin, especially the biological parents. In other instances the family is the *chosen family*, often the lover and close friends. In still other instances, family includes both the *biological* and *chosen family.*

Unlike other diseases, AIDS elicits strong, negative reactions, which often are accompanied by guilt. Counselors must be aware of the needs of the family of the PWA. These families often experience severe emotional, social, and financial trauma. Despite this, the family's needs have been largely under-recognized and unmet by society. Counselors can help fill these unmet needs by understanding the stages of loss and grief and the issues unique to members of these families.

References

Baer, J., Hall, J., Holm, K., & Lewitter-Koehler, S. (1987). Challenges in developing an inpatient psychiatric program for patients with AIDS and ARC. *Hospital & Community Psychiatry, 38*, 1299–1303.

Baltimore, D., & Wolff, S. (1986). *Confronting AIDS: Directions for public health, healthcare and research.* Washington, DC: National Academy Press.

Barret, R. L. (1989). Counseling gay men with AIDS: Human dimensions. *Journal of Counseling & Development, 67*, 573–576.

Bohm, E. (1987). AIDS: Effects on psychotherapy in New York City. *Journal of Psychosocial Nursing & Mental Health Services, 25*, 26–31.

Bor, R., Miller, R., & Perry, L. (1988). Systematic counseling for patients with AIDS/HIV infections. *Family Systems Medicine, 6*, 31–39.

Bruttn, J. G. (1989). Counseling persons with a fear of AIDS. *Journal of Counseling & Development, 67*, 455–458.

Center for Disease Control. (1984). Antibodies to a retro-virus etiologically associated with AIDS in populations with increased incidence of the syndrome. *Morbidity & Mortality Weekly Reports, 33,* 377–379.

Coats, T., Temoshak, L., & Mandel, J. (1984). Psychosocial research is essential to understanding and treating AIDS. *American Psychologist, 39,* 1309–1314.

Cooper, T. (1988). *Confronting AIDS: Update 1988.* Washington, DC: National Academy Press.

Craig, E. (1989). *Human development.* Englewood Cliffs, NJ: Prentice-Hall.

Des Jarlais, D., & Friedman, S. (1988). The psychology of preventing AIDS among intravenous drug users. *American Psychologist, 43,* 865–870.

Destounis, N. (1987). AIDS: A medical disaster. *European Journal of Psychiatry, 1,* 44–49.

Deuchar, N. (1984). AIDS in New York City with particular reference to the psycho-social aspects. *British Journal of Psychiatry, 145,* 612–619.

Donlou, J., Wolcott, D., Gottlieb, M., & Landsverk, J. (1985). Psychosocial aspects of AIDS and AIDS-related complex: A pilot study. *Journal of Psychosocial Oncology, 3,* 39–55.

Erikson, E., & Erikson, J. (1981). On generativity and identity: From a conversation with Erik and Joan Erikson. *Harvard Educational Review, 51,* 249–269.

Essex, M., & Kanki, P. (1988). The origins of the AIDS virus. *Scientific American, 259,* 64–72.

Faltz, B., & Mandover, S. (1987). Treatment of substance abuse in patients with HIV infections. *Advances in Alcohol & Substance Abuse, 7,* 143–257.

Flaskerud, J. (1987). AIDS: Psychosocial aspects. *Journal of Psychosocial Nursing & Mental Health Services, 25,* 8–16.

Galea, R., Lewis, B., & Baker, L. (1988). Voluntary testing for HIV antibodies among clients in long-term substance abuse treatment. *Social Work, 33,* 265–268.

Gallo, R. C. (1987). The AIDS virus. *Scientific American, 256,* 47–56.

Gallo, R. C., & Montagnier, L. (1988). AIDS in 1988. *Scientific American, 259,* 40–52.

Ginzberg, H. (1984). Intravenous drug users and AIDS. *Pharm-Chem Newsletter, 13,* 1–9.

Glaser, C. (1987, September). AIDS and A-bomb disease. *Christianity & Crisis,* 311–314.

Gold, M., Seymour, N., & Sahl, J. (1986). Counseling HIV seropositives. In L. McKusick (Ed.), *What to do about AIDS.* Berkeley: University of California Press.

Graham, L., & Cates, J. (1987). AIDS: Developing a primary health care task force. *Journal of Psychosocial Nursing & Mental Health Services, 25,* 21–25.

Grant, D., & Anns, M. (1988). Counseling AIDS antibody-positive clients: Reactions and treatment. *American Psychologist, 43,* 72–74.

Greif, G., & Porembski, E. (1987). Significant others of IV drug abusers with AIDS: New challenges for drug treatment programs. *Journal of Substance Abuse, 4,* 151–155.

Heyward, W., & Curran, J. (1988). The epidemiology of AIDS in the U.S. *Scientific American, 259,* 72–82.

Holmes, T. H., & Rahe, R. (1967). The social readjustment rating scale. *Journal of Psychosomatic Research, 11,* 213–218.

Jaffe, L., & Wortman, R. (1988). Guidelines to the counseling and HTLV-III antibody screening of adolescents. *Journal of Adolescent Health Care, 9,* 84–86.

Koop, C. (1986). From the Surgeon General. U.S. Public Health Services. *Journal of the American Medical Association, 256,* 2783.

Krieger, I. (1988). An approach to coping with anxiety about AIDS. *Social Work, 33,* 263–264.

Kubler-Ross, E. (1969). *On death and dying.* New York: Macmillan.

Kubler-Ross, E. (1987). *AIDS: The ultimate challenge.* New York: Macmillan.

Lomax, G., & Sandler, J. (1988). Psychotherapy and consultation with persons with AIDS. *Psychiatric Annals, 18,* 253–259.

Mason, J. (1985). Public health service plan for the prevention and control of acquired immuno-deficiency syndrome. *Public Health Reports, 100,* 453–455.

Mason, P., Olson, R., & Parish, K. (1988). AIDS, hemophilia, and prevention efforts within a comprehensive care plan. *American Psychologist, 43,* 971–976.

Mejta, C. L. (1987). Acquired immunodeficiency syndrome (AIDS): Implications for counseling and education. *Counseling & Human Development, 20,* 1–12.

Mills, S. (1986). Attitudes and trends: Public perception of AIDS. *Focus: A review of AIDS Research, 2,* 1–3.

Morin, S., Charles, R., & Malyon, A. (1984). The psychological impact of AIDS on gay men. *American Psychologist, 39, 1288–1293.*

National Center of Health Statistics. (1988). AIDS knowledge and attitudes for September 1987: Provisional data from the National Health Interview Survey. *Advance Data from Vital and Health Statistics, No. 148.* (Ditas Pub. No [PHS] 88-1250). Hyattsville, MD: Public Health Service.

Nichols, S. (1985). Psychosocial reactions of persons with the acquired immunodeficiency syndrome. *Internal Medicine, 103*, 765–767.

Posey, E. C. (1988). Confidentiality in an AIDS support group. *Journal of Counseling & Development, 66*, 226–227.

Robinson, B., Skeen, P., & Walters, L. (1987). The AIDS epidemic hits home. *Psychology Today, 21*, 48–52.

Skeen, P., & Robinson, B. (1985). Gay fathers' and gay nonfathers' relationship with their parents. *Journal of Sex Research, 21*, 86–89.

Stevens, L., & Muskin, P. (1987). Techniques for reversing the failure of empathy towards AIDS patients. *Journal of the American Academy of Psychoanalysis, 15*, 539–551.

Stulberg, I., & Smith, M. (1988). Psychosocial impact of the AIDS epidemic on the lives of gay men. *Social Work, 33*, 277–281.

Widen, H. (1987). The risk of AIDS and the defense of disavowal: Dilemmas for the college psychotherapist. *Journal of American College Health, 35*, 268–273.

Witt, M. (Ed.). (1986). *AIDS and patient management: Legal, ethical and social issues*. Owings Mills, MD: Rynd Communications.

Wolcott, D., Fawzy, F., & Pasnau, R. (1985). Acquired immune deficiency syndrome (AIDS) and consultation-liaison psychiatry. *General Hospital Psychiatry, 7*, 280–292.

This article was originally published in *Counseling and Human Development,* Vol. 22, 1989, pp. 1–12. Reprint permission granted by Love Publishing.

Chapter 6

The Future—Images and Projections

The future of marriage and family counseling and therapy in the areas of training, accreditation, licensure, and so forth, is difficult to predict due to political and ideological forces operating around these areas. Perhaps other aspects of marriage and family counseling/therapy can be more accurately predicted based on current thinking and trends in the field. These topics include: an emphasis on managed health care, advocacy for brief therapy models, integrating individual and systemic approaches, broadening the definition of systems, revisiting standards for accreditation, and a need for accountability. The authors writing in this chapter examine each of these areas in an attempt to more clearly determine their effects on practicing marriage and family counselors/therapists, and on those individuals now involved in training.

Locke and Canfield in a closing article speak of the need for professionals to focus on what is really important in marriage and family counseling/therapy. By alluding to how individuals, states, licensure boards and organizations often become sidetracked, the authors help bring to the forefront that which we should be about—working effectively with problems encountered by couple and family systems.

Future Projections for Marriage and Family Counseling and Therapy

Robert L. Smith
Patricia Stevens-Smith

All indicators point to an increase in concern about the family itself and the marital subsystem that serves as the foundation for the family. Societal changes and individual stressors have radically affected our definition of "family," its structure, members' roles, and general functioning. The focus on the family has spawned an interest in and increased the development of methods used in family therapy: diagnosing family systems, and examining family therapy as related to other therapeutic approaches. In addition, there is an increased concern about the efficacy of methods historically advocated to alleviate family problems.

Future projections related to marriage and family counseling and therapy need to be considered in light of larger systems that influence and affect this arena. Managed health care is one area that will determine how family therapy is defined as well as the amount of time devoted to working with family systems. Family therapy and its interaction with other therapeutic approaches, particularly individual psychotherapy, also provide an interesting phenomenon. As a result of this interaction there is broadening of how systems are defined. A greater understanding and acceptance of individual, society, career, and larger systems and their interplay with the family exists. As these systems have integrated together, different therapeutic models have gained recognition and increased utilization as viable approaches to working with family problems.

The area of marriage and family counseling and therapy has matured over the past several years. The arguments of linearity versus circularity are not as relevant as they were in the 70s and 80s. Professionals are less likely to label other practitioners as linear thinkers or as intrapsychically oriented in order to establish one's own identity as a "systems therapist." We see marriage and family counseling and therapy changing within its ranks as well as being changed by forces from the outside. Changing family systems, managed health care, research and family therapy, gender role changes, and training specifics are issues and topics briefly addressed that will significantly affect the future of this field.

Changing Family Systems: Practices Appropriate for Multiple Systems

High divorce rates, remarriage, dual career families, single-parent households, blended families, same-sex families, and so forth, antiquate research that has used the traditional family as its mode. Today's families with different relationship structures present diverse problems for therapists. Therapeutic methods appropriate for varied family systems will be the focus of the future. New practices will need to be implemented and researched as they relate to varied family models. Treatment modalities for "healthy" single-parent families, "healthy" stepfamilies, and "healthy" dual-career families will be closely examined and discussed. Therapeutic techniques will need to be flexible and responsive to the diverse family systems and more creative depending on different family arrangements.

Managed Health Care

Marriage and family therapists face major changes in the manner in which their services are delivered. In order to survive, marriage and family therapists will need to meet demands being made by managed mental health care (MMHC). Innovative, efficient, but definitely result-oriented delivery systems are being required by health management organizations.

In order for today's practitioners to meet the demands of MMHC, certain activities require immediate attention. First and foremost is a need to provide quality services. The authors believe that therapeutic agencies providing quality result-oriented services will survive. Included within this is the utilization of existing training standards for marriage and family counselors and therapists. Graduates of accredited programs, CACREP or AAMFT, will be in the best position to have their credentials recognized.

MMHC organizations require standardized expertise for members. These efforts, along with national certification through our professional organizations will provide the standard accepted by MMHC systems.

It is projected that marriage and family counselors and therapists will be providing services utilizing a wide variety of theoretical principles and approaches. Practitioners, although not calling themselves eclectic, will more likely be practicing from an eclectic model. The application of therapy itself will transcend traditional methods previously utilized. Brief approaches with clear concise goals and treatment methods will be demanded. MMHC (Foos, Otten, & Hill, 1991) will transform the field of marriage and family counseling and therapy with greater emphasis on efficiency, costs, diagnosis, and accountability of a profession. It is therefore necessary that we strive in our training programs and in our licensure efforts to standardize our requirements for practice. Only then will we be recognized for "third party payment" that is essential for survival in private practice. Time lines for working with presenting problems are the norm. MMHC systems will influence marriage and family counseling and therapy to move toward a scientific results-oriented model. Creativity, spontaneity and diversity must take place within the boundaries stressed by MMHC systems.

Efficacy and Family Therapy

Betty Carter (1986) stated that some rather elementary questions surrounding family therapy need to be answered. Some of the questions asked by Carter are:

1. What is the purpose of family therapy?
2. What is the role of the therapist?
3. How does change come about?

These are questions that will be wrestled with by family counselors and therapists in this decade.

The literature is abundant with theory and position papers regarding marriage and family counseling and therapy. Many theories have been included in the basic texts dealing with marriage and families. Standards for training (CACREP, AAMFT) and licensure in marriage and family counseling and therapy have been promulgated. The 1990s bring with them questions surrounding the effectiveness of family therapy. Questions begging to be addressed go beyond the acquiescent acceptance that family therapy is the treatment of choice for marriage and family problems. These blanket statements are comforting but need to be carefully examined in efforts to clarify treatment for specific family arrangements and presenting problems. There is a need for research that examines the family system and therapeutic procedures used with specific presenting problems. Research examining the overall efficacy of family therapy is needed.

Carter (1986) and others have also stated there is little evidence that any of the schools of family therapy are better or worse than the others. Furthermore, it is stated that beyond the serious need to give claims to validity there exists a need to train practitioners to research and report their findings. This will continue, leaving training programs and recognized family clinics to serve as the research centers for marriage and family therapy.

Gender Role Changes and the Future of Family Therapy

We no longer deny the powerful effect of gender as a determinate of how individuals view and organize the world. Gender is not just a set of behaviors and expectations but rather is a principal of social organization that structures relations, especially the power relations, between men and women (Crawford & Maracek, 1989). Combine gender role changes with the dramatic shifts in family structure over the past decade, and there is reason to wonder how family therapy will look in the 21st century.

Changes and awareness created by the feminist movement in society on the whole will remain. However, there is now a conservative backlash that tempers some of these advances for women. The current debate over abortion and the possible overturning of Roe v. Wade is a public display of that conservatism. Yet, in many more subtle ways these advances are also being curtailed. For example, the majority of women in the workplace are still responsible for the child rearing and the housekeeping. The government's recent emphasis on "family values" may be viewed as a way of maintaining traditional roles and restricting both men and women in their desire for change (Scher & Good, 1990).

Nancy Chodorow (1978) stated that one of the tragedies of this system is its repetitiveness. Feminist family therapists are still fighting many of the battles that began in the 1970s. In 1992, much of the same cycle of masculinity and femininity still exists. Males who did not experience fathers who were involved and expressive became fathers who behaved in the same manner. In the future, both men and women must continue to question the rigid stereotypical roles that society has imposed on them.

A related concern is that family therapy has been slow to recognize the need for incorporating gender role expectations in practice. Many authors are now writing in the area of feminist family therapy. This writing is creating an awareness of the necessity of continued change. The true test of influence is how these techniques are being used in the therapy sessions and supervision sessions across the country (Carter, 1992). As of now, there is little research that examines this effect.

Although women continue to be more disadvantaged by society, in the future it may be productive to look at "gender-sensitive" therapy as opposed to feminist family therapy (Carter, 1985). The term feminist does align the therapist with one gender when the true goal is to facilitate growth, change and healthy functioning for both genders (Zucal, 1992). Also, as feminist family therapists and the women's movement have matured, a celebration of gender differences and complementarity has developed.

Gender-sensitive awareness will continue to have an effect on marriage and family therapy. The extent of this effect will depend on the direction taken by the larger systems to which we belong. The truth of systems theory is that we are affected by and responsible to the systems in which we live. The effort that we expend to change the larger systems (political, educational, professional, and familial) will determine how successful we are in our future awareness of diversity.

Implications for Future Training

Most behavioral science programs train students well in the basics of intervention. Theory and techniques of individual, group, and family counseling are often taught in separate courses and then punctuated by repetition in other courses such as human services, career development, substance abuse, multicultural education, human development, and professional seminars. Students leave an entry-level training program comfortable in their knowledge of traditional theories and "tried and true" techniques for change in working with couples and families.

The problem comes when the student begins to work. Students, now therapists, see clients and their families who are out of work, homeless, HIV positive; whose children or who themselves belong to violent gangs and claim these gangs as "family"; clients faced by the overwhelming use of drugs of all kinds, sometimes by children as young as 5 or 6 years of age. Divorce, remarriage, stepchildren, complicated extended families; gay and lesbian relationships and families; increased domestic violence, rape, incest; and so many more issues that are common in today's society face the neophyte therapist.

The theories that were developed in the 1940s, 1950s and 1960s were developed to solve the problems faced by therapists working in that time frame. Although important as a foundation, those theories must be revised or new theories developed to assist in solving the problems of today's families. No longer is the rigid hierarchical structure of Minuchen or Bowen's masculine-biased *Differentiation of Self Scale* effective for facilitating change in family structures.

Training programs have tended to ignore issues that are controversial and difficult to teach. In the future, if we are to continue to serve our clients effectively, students must be trained in techniques that give clients the skills needed to function in this rapidly changing society.

Training programs must do more than pay lip service to the issues that face counselors/therapists and clients today. The changing American family structure, gender role expectation shifts, the impact of ethnicity on families and individuals, and the impact of AIDS must be addressed in practical and useful ways within the curriculum.

One method of training students is through individual courses that are specific to each topic or to a related group of these topics. Although one course may only introduce a student to the particular problem, such as substance abuse, it would give them a foundation on which to build. Obviously the problem of number of semester hours needed to digest all of this information becomes apparent immediately.

Ideally, these issues would be incorporated within each of the courses that are taught in programs. In the same way that these issues affect our day-to-day functioning in all aspects, so these issues would be intertwined throughout the coursework, whether the primary emphasis of the course was theory, technique, careers, human development, or professionalism. This would require a revamping of many training programs as well as a cooperative effort by faculty to compliment content within various courses.

The problems facing individuals today and in the future are too serious, too overwhelming to be only mentioned in training. They are problems that will most likely, touch us personally as well as professionally at some time in our lives. Divorce, substance abuse, remarriage, stepchildren, teen pregnancies and AIDS, all are far too common to be left for "others" to learn how to handle.

Professions that work with couples and families, as well as the American family structure, will continue to evolve in the 21st century. Training programs must begin to honestly and openly address these issues in order to be of service to our clients in the future.

Closing Comments—*The Future*

It is recognized that the family system in today's society is in a state of transition. Therefore, treatment and research approaches will need to change. The focus will be on working with healthy single-parent families, healthy stepfamilies, healthy culturally diverse families, and other new family systems. Societal changes, high divorce rates, remarriages, dual career families, and so forth, provide the therapist with a new set of problems involving unique relationship arrangements. New family systems and arrangements require additional study so they can be more clearly defined and dealt with appropriately. Other issues involving gender awareness, training, and managed health care are beginning to be addressed (Steven, 1991; Foos, Otten, & Hill, 1991).

A final note for the future of family therapy involves its interface with other systems. The study of the family within the context of society, schools, career, culture and other interacting forces needs immediate attention. The idea of changing the family system without consideration of broader and more far-reaching systems is no longer acceptable. Family systems interact with outside forces in the same manner that other systems do. Future marriage and family counselors and therapists will be expected to work with macrosystems. Therapists of tomorrow will need to expand their skills, learn new information, and develop better intervention strategies. By working with larger systems, marriage and family counseling/therapy will continue to grow and impact society.

References

Carter, B. (1986). Success in family therapy. *Family Therapy Networker, 10*, 16–22.

Carter, B. (1992). Stonewalling feminism. *The Family Therapy Networker*, 64–69.

Chodorow, N. (1978). *The reproduction of mothering, psychoanalysis, and the sociology of gender.* Los Angeles: University of California Press.

Crawford, M., & Maracek, J. (1989). Psychology reconstructs the female. *Psychology of Women Quarterly, 13*, 147–165.

Davis, F. (1991). *Moving the mountains: The women's movement in America since 1960*. New York: Simon & Schuster.

Foos, J. A., Ottens, A. J., & Hill, L. K. (1991). Managed mental health: A primer for counselors. *Journal of Counseling & Development, 69*(4), 332–336.

Scher, M., & Good, G. E. (1990). Gender and counseling in the twenty-first century: What does the future hold? *Journal of Counseling and Development, 68*, 388–391.

Smith, R., & Stevens-Smith, P. (1992). A critique of healthy family functioning. *Topics in Family Psychology and Counseling, 1*(1), 6–14.

Stevens-Smith, P. (1992). Gender issues in training. *Awareness: The Journal of the Colorado Association for Counseling and Development, 20*, 12–20.

Zucal, B. (1992). Gender issues in couples therapy. In Joan D. Atwood (Ed.), *Family therapy: A systemic behavioral approach* (pp. 59–69). Chicago: Nelson-Hall Publishers.

Professional Identity and Family Therapy

Brian S. Canfield
Don W. Locke

What is the role and function of marriage and family practitioners in the mental health field? Is there an identity problem? Are clinicians who work with relationship issues adequately trained to provide competent services? Such questions arise as the field of marriage and family therapy continues to evolve.

Rather than a singular professional identity, marriage and family practitioners are affiliated with an array of professional organizations. The International Association for Marriage and Family Counseling (IAMFC) has been one of the fastest growing divisions of the American Counseling Association (ACA). The American Association for Marriage and Family Therapy (AAMFT), and the American Psychological Association (APA) Division 43-Family Psychology continue to have large affiliation from the ranks of mental health professionals. However, despite such growth, the field of marriage and family therapy is struggling with its identity. Who is a "family therapist" and what constitutes "real" family therapy is hotly debated.

Many people view "marriage and family therapy" as an autonomous and independent mental health profession on a parity with psychology or social work. This is the view held by the membership of the American Association for Marriage and Family Therapy (AAMFT). Other groups view family therapy as a "therapeutic approach" or "treatment modality." This is the view generally held by members of the American Psychological Association (APA) and the American Mental Health Counselors Association (AMHCA). However, while professionally factionalized and theoretically varied, family therapy professionals generally support the view that "family therapy" involves the utilization of a "systemic" perspective in addressing client concerns.

In order to gain a perspective on this intense debate, it is helpful to develop an understanding about the history and development of "professions" in general. Law, medicine, and theology, formed the core disciplines around which universities were created and developed.

Professions initially found their identity through the structure of the university and its academic traditions. In practice, a profession attempts to maintain a balance between applied skills and abstract intellectual training. It is this duality of purpose that originally distinguished a profession from an occupation or trade. Professions, as they exist today, are also heir to the trade guilds which developed during the late Middle Ages. These groups formed largely to protect the welfare and economic self interest of their members.

Understanding the unique status of a true profession is important to the larger society, since it is the professional who serves an identified critical need of the society. A profession is more than an identifiable occupation. The status of a professional and the nature of his or her work requires a degree of personal autonomy independent of any particular work setting. A traditional point of view holds that professionals function neither as capitalists or workers, nor are they typically government administrators or bureaucrats. This view underscores the relatively high degree of autonomy necessary in a truly professional role. Because a professional makes available a set of services which are of vital need to society, the professional is conveyed a special status. This status insures economic compensation for services, but prohibits exploitation of the society. Professionals have historically been prohibited from soliciting business while at the same time holding an obligation to make their services readily available to the public.

The need for exclusive status is recognized as necessary in many instances in order to provide quality services and ethical standards of practice. The public has a right to be protected from under qualified or unscrupulous individuals who would exploit a particular vital need of the society. In exchange for providing critical services without exploitation, professions are typically entrusted with singular control over certain resources.

The strength or power of a profession is directly related to its ability to control and exploit those resources which are essential to the needs of society. Typically, the more crucial the social concern, the more powerful the profession. Conversely, if the services of the group are not generally viewed by the society as essential, then it does not merit true professional status.

A profession, in the true sense of the term, can only exist when it is legitimized by the larger society. The profession is granted an "exclusive position" in society in order to meet vital needs. This exclusive position requires that members of a profession maintain a certain degree of functional autonomy independent of whatever work setting in which they may be employed. As such, a profession is more than an identifiable occupation. Although the primary rationale for granting professional status to a group is to protect the interests of society, efforts toward enfranchising professional status are almost universally instigated by members of the group, rather than the general public. The economic security of the group may be more than a concomitant consideration in many instances.

In contemporary society, it is relatively easy to identify established professions such as law and medicine. However, this identification becomes more difficult when attempting to ascertain the professional status of emerging, less powerful, or arguably less essential groups. True professional status requires more than self identification as a "professional." Society, through its various representatives and agencies must grant some type of legal recognition to the group. The group must also have some type of exclusive position with regard to performance of certain functions and roles. A profession, in the true sense of the word, occupies a singularly identifiable position in society. Thus, professions are by necessity exclusionary.

Is marriage and family therapy a "profession," or is it merely a "sub specialty" of a parent profession (such as counseling, psychiatry, or psychology)? The answer in the 1990s is neither, and possibly both.

By viewing the emergence of marriage and family therapy in historical context, we may better understand what the future holds. One hundred years ago there existed only one generally recognized "mental health" profession which provided primary direct client care: psychiatry, which itself existed only as a specialty of the profession of medicine. However, with the political and disciplinary emergence of psychology and more recently social work, counseling, marriage and family therapy, and other mental health groups, psychiatry has lost its once exclusive position in treating mental health concerns. Despite the loss of exclusivity, psychiatry (or more properly medicine) continues to exert enormous political and economic influence and control over much of the mental health service system.

The lack of a singular "profession" in the mental health field is increasingly problematic for both mental health practitioners and consumers of mental health services. Rather than enjoying the societal benefits of professional status, mental health practitioners are largely polarized into competing groups and factions. For the most part, these groups display extensive overlap with regard to the types of services provided. Many individuals from markedly different backgrounds are doing essentially the same type of work. The field can be largely characterized as one of "task competition" instead of "exclusive position." This trend toward factionalism creates an atmosphere of professional and economic competition among various groups. Each group attempts to retain or establish their "exclusive" position in the field, while often resisting the efforts of other groups to do the same.

Brayfield (1968) noted, with regard to the relationship between psychology and other mental health professions, that when the contributions of a psychologist are supplementary and distinctive, they are usually welcomed, but when they overlap with the contributions of other professions, misunderstandings arise. Remley (1991) in discussing counseling as an "emerging profession" stated that counseling stands on shaky ground because "we are constantly challenged to explain how we are different from similar mental health professions." The same would appear to hold true for family therapy.

The proliferation of mental health provider groups in the past several decades has raised important questions as to who are the most qualified and appropriate providers of particular services. Finding answers to these questions is confounded by the inherent political and economic self interests of various groups. Task competition, combined with an inconsistent patchwork of often contradictory and restrictive regulatory laws, has created a most confusing situation with regard to mental health practice in many areas.

Factionalism creates an atmosphere of territorial and economic competition among various groups. To varying degrees, each group within the mental health field attempts to retain or establish an "exclusive" position in the larger society, while often opposing (sometimes vehemently) the efforts of other groups to do the same. This burgeoning factionalism shows no signs of abating and sustains a growing level of competition and adversity. Such factionalism requires on-going expenditure of vital resources on the part of competing groups.

The National Institute of Mental Health and its allied governmental agencies currently recognize five "core mental health disciplines," each of which ostensibly occupies a separate and distinct niche in the provision of mental health services. These five core disciplines are psychiatry, psychology, psychiatric nursing, social work, and marriage and family therapy. At the level of individual state regulation there exists a variety of licensure and certification laws which are inconsistent and often contradictory. Such regulatory statutes often emphasize who may have exclusive use of certain "titles" and "descriptive terms." For example, in most jurisdictions the term "psychological" or "psychologist" remain exclusive to licensed psychologists. However, in many states which lack adequate regulation the terms "counseling," "psychotherapy," "family therapy," "therapy," and so forth, have no legal meaning. Consequently, in many settings anyone may be free to employ such terms regardless of their level of preparation.

Exclusive title use is often the initial focus of newly enacted regulatory laws. While protection from misleading "titles" may on the surface appear appropriate, it often gives the consumer public a false sense of security by creating the impression that regulated "titles" are synonymous with "professional competency." Such laws, when accompanied by weak practice regulation, create a curious situation in which the public may be protected from the indiscriminate use of terminology, but unprotected from inappropriate treatment.

Unfortunately, form rather than function continues to be a primary emphasis of regulation in the mental health field. The quality of mental health services available to the consumer public over the next several decades will in all likelihood not be decided by theoretical or clinical advances, but by the political lobbying efforts and legislative leverage exerted by various interest groups. Appropriateness of treatment modality has to a large extent become secondary to economics and the issue of "professional territoriality."

Approaching this phenomena systematically, it is important to view the needs and aspirations of various groups in the mental health field as they relate to each other and the needs of the larger society. Cooperation and an understanding of the strengths and weaknesses of the various service provider groups will be required in order for each group to establish and retain a professional niche. Such strengths and weaknesses are fundamentally centered in differing educational and training standards. However, the debate as to who should legitimately occupy a given professional niche is largely colored by political and economic considerations. As professionals it is necessary to approach all efforts concerning professional status and recognition based on the central need of the larger society to receive competent mental health services.

In order to remain abreast of the needs of society, professional development of the mental health field will require an increased recognition of the interrelated concepts of "competency" and "identity." Society, through its various legislative and regulatory agencies, will fail to legitimize any "would be" profession which cannot demonstrate competency in addressing the tasks to which it has been entrusted. Conversely, competency on the part of individual practitioners without some unifying professional identity among such individuals will perpetuate a state of confusion among both trainees in the general public.

Albert Einstein is said to have remarked that the formulation of a problem is often more essential than its solution. What is the problem faced in the field of marriage and family therapy? Professional identity? Exclusive position? Assurance of competent services? Professional status, while critically important, should always be secondary to provision of the highest quality of services possible to clients.

Marriage and family therapists recognize that their job, first and foremost, is to help people. Consistently high quality services can only be ensured through adequate education and training. Professionals and training programs alike are in a position to advocate and support development of consistent and appropriate educational and training standards, regardless of the semantic preference one may have for the "discipline," "specialty," "field," and/or "profession" of marriage and family "therapy" or "counseling." The future will provide marriage and family therapy professionals with the opportunity to concentrate, not on exclusivity of professional identity, but on the competency of the individuals providing services, and how the public can identify such individuals.

References

Brayfield, A. (1968). Psychology as a profession. *American Psychologist, 23*(3), 195–200.

Canfield, B. S., & Locke, D. W. (Fall, 1991). Are we asking the right questions? *Newsletter, International Association for Marriage and Family Counseling.*

Remley, T. P. (May 30, 1991). Perspectives—competition within. *Guidepost.*

ERIC/CAPS

Educational Resources Information Center—ERIC

ERIC is a decentralized nationwide information system founded in 1966 and currently sponsored by the Office of Educational Research and Improvement within the U.S. Department of Education. It is the largest education related database in the world. ERIC is designed to collect educational documents and journal articles and to make them readily available through a number of products and services: the ERIC database, abstract journals, microfiche collections, online and CD-ROM computer searches, document reproductions, and information analysis publications. The ERIC audience is equally wide-ranging and includes teachers, counselors, administrators, supervisors, policy makers, librarians, media specialists, researchers, students, parents, and other educators and interested persons.

Counseling and Personnel Services Clearinghouse—CAPS

CAPS is one of the 16 subject-oriented clearinghouses of the ERIC system. CAPS' exceptionally broad coverage includes K–12 counseling and guidance, post-secondary and adult counseling services, and human resource development in business, industry and government. Topics addressed by CAPS are many and varied and include: preparation, practice and supervision of counseling professionals; career planning and development; marriage and family counseling; and services to special populations (substance abusers, students at-risk).

Other Resources from CAPS

Student Self-Esteem
A Vital Element of School Success
Garry R. Walz and Jeanne C. Bleuer

A comprehensive and useful resource on K–12 student self-esteem and staff development for teachers and counselors. Seventeen chapters provide 58 articles written by outstanding authorities on self-esteem, offering practical and field-validated program and practice ideas. Each chapter begins with a breakout of the key ideas and describes many useful approaches. Includes a special chapter on renewing your information about self-esteem. 510 pages. *Jointly published by ERIC/CAPS and ASCA.*

Item No. EC193 **$29.95**

CounselorQuest
Compiled by Garry R. Walz

CounselorQuest is unique among publications in the amount of practical and reliable information it offers counselors on a wide variety of topics of critical importance to them. Over 165 succinct and highly readable digests and three indexes (title, topic, and educational level). An indispensable counseling tool. Reproducible for classroom use, too! 350 pages.

Item No. EC133 **$19.95**

Crème de la Crème Series

The "Best of the Best"—Reserved for Publications of High Substance and Uncommon Utility

Empowering Young Black Males

Courtland C. Lee

This monograph focuses on the empowerment model Dr. Lee has developed for assisting young Black males in acquiring attitudes and skills which will enable them to cope more effectively. Of particular importance are four training modules designed to be used by counselors and other educators. 95 pages.

Item No. EC189 **$14.95**
Item No. EC149—Compelling 60-minute videotape featuring Courtland C. Lee **$19.95**

Learning Styles Counseling

Shirley A. Griggs

New and expanded edition of a CAPS bestseller. Prepares counselors K–12 to diagnose and infuse learning style approaches into their counseling. Useful in consulting with teachers on accommodating learning styles in the classroom. 161 pages.

Item No. EC137 **$16.95**

Comprehensive Guidance Programs That Work

Norman C. Gysbers

Successful comprehensive guidance programs in eight school settings in six states are described. Includes practical suggestions and advice for how to bring about change in K–12 school guidance programs and make them truly comprehensive. 171 pages.

Item No. EC106 **$18.95**

The Teacher Advisor Program
An Innovative Approach to School Guidance
Robert D. Myrick and Linda S. Myrick

Describes six teacher advisor programs that creatively meet the developmental needs of middle and high school students by providing them with a friendly adult in the school who knows and cares about them in a personal way. Many practical ideas and approaches. 125 pages.

Item No. EC129 **$16.95**

Invitational Learning for Counseling and Development
William W. Purkey and John J. Schmidt

Explains how integrating the principles of invitational learning and counseling into guidance programs was a positive force for change in seven different school settings. An excellent approach for responding to students at risk and minimizing dropouts. 138 pages.

Item No. EC123 **$16.95**

***Note:** All prices are subject to change without prior notice.*

For an update on prices, including special discounts, additional information on ordering or for a brochure on other publications available from ERIC/CAPS call or write:

ERIC/CAPS Publications
2108 School of Education
The University of Michigan
Ann Arbor, Michigan 48109-1259
(313) 764-9492
Fax (313) 747-2425